Teach Yourself®

Complete French

Thomas Chaurin, James Fowler
and Ana de Medeiros

First published by Teach Yourself in 2025
An imprint of John Murray Press

1

A CIP catalogue record for this title is available from the British Library

Trade Paperback ISBN 9781399818681
ebook ISBN 9781399818698

Typeset in FS Albert Pro light 10.5/12 by Integra Software Services Pvt. Ltd. Pondicherry, India.

Printed and bound by Oriental Press, Dubai.

John Murray Press policy is to use papers that are natural, renewable and recyclable products and made from wood grown in sustainable forests. The logging and manufacturing processes are expected to conform to the environmental regulations of the country of origin.

John Murray Press
Carmelite House
50 Victoria Embankment
London EC4Y 0DZ

Teach Yourself
123 S. Broad St., Ste 2750
Philadelphia, PA, 19109

www.teachyourself.com

The authorised representative in the EEA is Hachette Ireland, 8 Castlecourt Centre, Dublin 15, D15 XTP3, Ireland (email: info@hbgi.ie)

John Murray Press, part of Hodder & Stoughton Limited
An Hachette UK company

Contents

Resources available online at library.teachyourself.com

- Audio recordings
- My Takeaway study guide
- Assessments for A1, A2, and B2 levels
- CEFR and ACTFL can-do statements
- Grammar summary
- French–English Glossary
- English–French Glossary

Meet the authors

Thomas, James, and Ana have extensive experience teaching French as a foreign language.

Thomas says: "I am passionate about language learning and teaching. I speak French, Spanish, and English and I have taught French in various institutions in France, Slovakia, Zimbabwe, Kenya, Chile, Canada, the USA, and the UK. Since 2019, I have been the director of Languages for All at the University of Edinburgh, promoting and supporting languages for the local community as well as among staff and students. As part of my role, I am honored to teach a foundation French course for adult learners whose aim is to return to learning after a break, to gain the qualifications which will allow them to progress to degree studies."

James says: "I studied Modern Languages at Oxford University before writing a PhD on French Literature at King's College London. I have taught at a number of fantastic UK institutions including the Universities of Durham, Manchester, and Warwick. I also spent two wonderful years at the École normale supérieure, Paris. I feel very fortunate in all these respects. My core belief is that opportunities to study other languages and cultures should be available to all. I have always found a sense of fulfillment in teaching students in France about the English language and aspects of life in the UK, and students in the UK about the world of francophone literature, culture, and cinema."

Ana says: "Speaking other languages and experiencing different cultures is an integral part of who I am. The languages I speak on a daily basis (English, French, and Portuguese) are a part of my identity on both a personal and professional level. I have taught languages in the USA, France, Germany, and the UK over the last 30 years, and every day of teaching has been enjoyable. Since 2015, as the director of the King's College Language Centre, it has been my pleasure to work with lecturers and students from around the world. In this role, I strive to foster a truly hospitable environment where different cultures can flourish interdependently."

Acknowledgments

The authors of *Complete French* would like to say un grand merci (*a big thank you*) first and foremost to the incredible members of the commissioning and editorial team at John Murray Press who have allowed this volume to become a reality. In particular Sarah, Emma, Chloe, Eric and Ana have shown great skill, patience and good humor in guiding us from first notions to the final product.

We are also most grateful to friends and family who have answered queries, read drafts and given us moral support through the past two years. Their input helped to keep us focused on our goals as we developed the story of four young friends whose experiences reflect a world where the French language belongs to multiple cultures, and where values such as sustainability and inclusivity are reflected in movies, books and bandes dessinées (comic-strip albums) — not to mention buildings, transport and other aspects of le quotidien (daily life).

Finally we would like to say **vielen Dank**, **grazie mille** and **muchas gracias** (*thank you!*) to the authors of the *Complete German*, *Italian* and *Spanish* textbooks. These friends and colleagues share in our passion for all things language and culture, and have helped us with unfailing cheerfulness along the way.

We dedicate this volume to our feline friend Jade whose ronronnement (*purring*) was the musical score of our working sessions.

How to use this book

Congratulations on deciding to learn French, and thank you for choosing Teach Yourself. This book was designed specifically with the independent student in mind, so it is designed to provide as much motivation and support as possible. As you embark on your learning journey, you will get to know four characters quite well. Joséphine (Jo) and Charles are twins raised in the Île-de-France (Paris and the surrounding region). You meet them as Jo, while still a student, is embarking on a career as a photographer, and Charles, who has moved to Brussels, is training to be a master chocolatier. Jo mainly socializes with her co-student and close friend Assia. Charles, meanwhile, meets Eva, a Swiss national living and working in Brussels. Through travel, conversation, and study, the four friends learn more about francophone culture throughout the world, from cuisine and photography to music and cinema.

WARMING UP

This book begins with an introduction to the French alphabet in order to familiarize you with the basic sounds and rhythms of French and give you a chance to warm up and practice your pronunciation. As you practice, you'll get a few key expressions under your belt before you begin.

CORE UNITS

The core of the book comprises **20 units**, designed to help you communicate in practical, everyday situations and steadily build up your vocabulary and overall knowledge of French. Every unit is divided into two evenly balanced parts, structured as follows:

The **Culture point** introduces a theme and a context. Rather than presenting francophone culture as a one-way influence spreading from France to other nations, this section emphasizes the plurality of francophone *cultures* in the world: their vitality, their constant evolution, and their openness to new influences. Many Culture points also feature a QR code, which you can scan to learn more about the topic. This is a window onto authentic sources, allowing you to explore the French language and francophone culture(s) more broadly.

The **Vocabulary builder** introduces key words and phrases relevant to the unit, accompanied by an audio. After an initial read-through, it is a good idea to listen to the recording several times, repeating each word. Another technique you will find useful is to re-read the vocabulary list several times, alternately covering the French and the English terms to test your memory. **Vocabulary practice** immediately follows the Vocabulary builder and is always based on the words and phrases you have just encountered. Besides reinforcing these, the Vocabulary practice prepares you for the Conversation that follows.

The **Conversation** is a dialogue between two or more characters. It is through the Conversations that the story of Jo, Charles, Eva, and Assia unfolds. The Conversations are also recorded so that you can listen to them, practice your pronunciation, and engage in creative role play. On first listening, it is not necessary to catch every word; it is enough if you can follow the gist of the conversation, as that is a key language skill. Below the Conversation you will find questions and follow-up activities to guide you.

Two **Language builders** follow the Conversation. Each Language builder opens with a **Language discovery** activity, in which your attention will be drawn to something said by one or more of the characters in the Conversation. Based on this, you will be invited to think about a question or questions concerning how the French language works; this approach is known as the **Discovery method**. Immediately afterward, you will find our own explanation of the point(s) you have been thinking about, so you can cross-check your ideas there. Read more about the benefits of the **Discovery method** of learning below (see **How to be a successful language learner**). Throughout the units, you will find **Tips** with additional explanations, and cultural insights to enhance your learning.

Each **Language practice** offers a variety of exercises so that you can practice the points covered in the preceding Language discovery. The **Skill builder** section at the end of each unit provides additional practice, and you will have ample opportunity for **Speaking**, **Listening**, **Reading**, and **Writing practice**.

Test yourself puts together everything covered in the unit and helps you assess what you have learned. It is a good idea to do the tests without consulting the text and check your answers in the **Answer key**. If you are happy with your results, move ahead to the next unit. Otherwise, go back and review the unit before moving on. There are also three assessments available online, at A1, A2, and B1 CEFR levels (Intermediate Low, Mid-, and High ACTFL levels) to help you gauge your overall progress at key junctures.

Reference resources—in the back of the book, you'll find additional tools to support you and help you find the answers you need. The **Answer key** applies to all the exercises, tests and assessments in the book. You can look up the language topic you need in the **Index of grammatical topics** to find the relevant units where it's covered. Online, you will find additional resources. Look up any word in the course in the two-way **Glossary** and quickly access key grammar patterns in the **Grammar summary**.

A LITTLE GOES A LONG WAY!

Try to use the book little and often, rather than for long stretches at a time. You might well find that your ideal study time per session is between 15 and 30 minutes. This will help you to create a study habit, in much the same way you would practice a sport or musical instrument. Leave the book somewhere handy so that you can pick it up for just a few minutes to refresh your memory concerning your most recent session. The book is structured so that you can work through one half-unit (Culture Point, Vocabulary Builder, Conversation, Language Builder) per sitting, if that is what suits you best.

MAKE A PLAN, TRACK YOUR PROGRESS, AND REFLECT ON THE PROCESS!

Setting goals affects the programming of your brain, strengthening neural pathways and ultimately making it more likely that you will achieve those goals. Before you begin, think about how much time you want to devote to learning, and which skills or areas you want to focus on. Identify specific ideas you want to be able to communicate or activities you want to engage in. **In this unit you will learn** will help you identify what you should be able to do in French by the end of the unit and will help you set your personal goals for each unit. Each unit opens with a dashboard where you can note your personal goals.

Studies show that holding yourself accountable is another great way to stay motivated. Use the **Progress tracker** at the beginning of each unit to help you keep track of your progress and the work you do.

Personalize the tools. You can use the progress tracker to keep track of the date or day, or you can enter an increment of time (15 minutes, 30 minutes ...). Add columns for culture, vocabulary, grammar, or any other area you wish to focus on. Give yourself a star when you feel you've done particularly well. Make it your own! Review your tracker regularly and see which areas could use more practice.

At the end of each unit, you can review your progress and reflect on the learning experience. Use the **Self check** to assess your progress. You will need to go back to the unit opener page to do this and to review your progress against your goals and the unit objectives. A **My takeaway** template page is available online. Here you can jot down things you noted about your study habits in **My process**—What worked? What would you have done differently? Is there a new strategy you want to try? Note the highlights of the unit in **Best of ...** (favorite word or phrase, important language rule). Are there any questions you still need answered? Finally, make the language your own! Try to write a few personal sentences by responding to the prompts in **In my own words**, also available online. Don't worry about making mistakes. Use the language to talk about yourself and your life.

In this unit, you will learn how to:

Each unit begins with an overview of the language you will be learning and skills you will be acquiring.

My progress tracker

Use the progress tracker to keep a record of what you've accomplished. The first column tracks time, and the remaining 5 columns represent the skills you'll be working on: listening, pronunciation, reading, writing, and spoken interaction.

1

In this lesson you will learn how to:

» Greet people and introduce yourself
» Use personal pronouns
» Distinguish between formal and informal forms of address
» Exchange basic information using the present tense of regular verbs
» Describe someone using the verb **être** (*to be*)

Nouveaux amis

My study plan

I plan to work with Unit 1

○ Every day
○ Twice a week
○ Other ___________

I plan to study for

○ 5–15 minutes
○ 15–30 minutes
○ 30–45+ minutes

My progress tracker

Day / Date	Listening	Pronunciation	Reading	Writing	Spoken interaction
	○	○	○	○	○
	○	○	○	○	○
	○	○	○	○	○
	○	○	○	○	○
	○	○	○	○	○
	○	○	○	○	○
	○	○	○	○	○

My goals

Make a note of your goals. They can be general (*I want to be able to say three sentences about myself in French*) or specifically related to the topic at hand (*I want to be able to order breakfast at a café*). At the end of the unit, take a look at your goals and see whether you feel you've accomplished them.

My study plan

Use My study plan to plan how often and for how long you plan to study.

My goals

What do you want to be able to do or say in French when you complete this unit?

		Done
1	....	○
2	....	○
3	....	○

My review

SELF CHECK

	I can ...
●	... greet people and introduce myself.
●	... use personal pronouns.
●	... distinguish between formal and informal forms of addressing people I meet.
●	... exchange basic information about myself using the present tense of regular verbs.
●	... describe someone using the verb être (*to be*) + an adjective.

My review

Use this checklist at the end of each unit to review your progress and to reflect on what you can do, and what you need to look at again.

TRY TO PRACTICE EACH SKILL EVERY DAY

The icons in the progress tracker are used throughout the book to help you easily identify and locate the skills you want to practice:

 Listening skills

 Speaking—pronunciation skills

 Reading skills

 Writing skills

 Speaking—conversation skills

Remember: there are many ways to build your skills in addition to those provided in this book—use a language-learning app, listen to music or podcasts, watch TV shows or movies, go to a restaurant, follow social media accounts in French, read blogs, newspapers or magazines, switch the language settings in your apps to French, or sign up for a language exchange or a tutor. And remember to use the online resources to keep a record of the sources you've found.

Above all, talk to other French speakers or learners, if at all possible; failing that, talk to yourself, to inanimate objects, to the imaginary characters in this book (warn your family and friends!). If you can find someone else to learn along with you, that is a great bonus. Do all the exercises and do them more than once. Make maximum use of the audio: play it as background, even when half your mind is on something else, as well as using it when you are actually studying. The main thing is to create a continuous French "presence," so that what you are learning is always on your mind. Finally—enjoy yourself and celebrate your progress!

How to be a successful language learner

The Discovery method

There are lots of philosophies and approaches to language learning, some practical, some quite unconventional, and far too many to list here. Perhaps you know of a few, or even have some techniques of your own. In this book we have incorporated the Discovery method of learning, a sort of DIY approach to language learning. What this means is that you will be encouraged throughout the course to engage your mind and figure out the language for yourself, through identifying patterns, understanding grammar concepts, noticing words that are similar to English, and more.

Simply put, if you figure something out for yourself, you're more likely to understand it. And when you use what you've learned, you're more likely to remember it. And because many of the essential but (let's admit it!) dull details, such as grammar rules, are introduced through the Discovery method, you'll have more fun while learning. Soon, the language will start to make sense and you'll be relying on your own intuition to construct original sentences independently, not just listening and repeating.

Everyone can succeed in learning a language—the key is to know how to learn it.

Learn to learn

There are many strategies that can help you become a successful language learner. Different people have different learning styles and some of these approaches will be more effective for you than others. Use this list as a point of inspiration when you want to find the most effective ways to advance your skills and begin your journey to fluency.

VOCABULARY

Words are the building blocks of language. The more you use the words you're introduced to, the more quickly they'll lodge into your memory. These study tips will help you remember better:

- Say the words out loud as you read them. Listen to the audio several times.
- Write the words over and over again. Create flash cards, drawings, and mind maps.
- It helps to group new words in categories—e.g. food or furniture—or according to the situations in which they occur—e.g. restaurant, hotel, sightseeing—or their functions—e.g., greetings, thanks, apologizing.
- Cover up the English side of the vocabulary list and see whether you remember the meaning of the word. Then cover up the French side and see whether you can remember the word itself.

- Use mnemonic tricks for the words with similar-sounding words in English, for example think of people talking in a parlor to remember that parler means ***to talk***.
- Write words for objects around your house and stick them to objects.
- Pay attention to patterns in words, for example adding -ment to an adjective turns it into an adverb in much the same way that we add *-ly* in English: probable → probablement (*probable* → *probably*).

GRAMMAR

Grammar gives your language structure. It allows you to experiment with the vocabulary you learn because you'll understand how words work together to create meaning. That's to say, you'll begin to develop a feel for the language. Here are some tips to help you study more effectively:

- Write your own grammar glossary and add new information and examples as you go.
- Experiment with grammar rules. Use old vocabulary to practice new grammar structures.
- Try to find examples of grammar in conversations or other articles.
- When you learn a new verb form, review other verbs you know that follow the same pattern.
- Compare French structures with your own language or other languages you may already speak. Try to find out some rules on your own and be ready to spot the exceptions.

PRONUNCIATION

The best way to improve your pronunciation is simply to practice as much as possible. Study individual sounds first, then full words and sentences. Don't forget, it's not just about pronouncing letters and words correctly, but using the right intonation. So, when practicing words and sentences, mimic the rising and falling intonation of French speakers.

- Repeat all of the conversations, line by line. Listen to yourself and try to mimic what you hear.
- Record yourself and compare yourself to the recordings.
- Make a list of words that give you trouble and practice them.

LISTENING AND READING

The conversations in this book include questions to help guide you in your understanding. But you can go further by following some of these tips:

- Imagine the situation. Try to imagine where the scene is taking place and who the main characters are. Let your experience of the world help you guess the meaning of the conversation. For example: if a conversation takes place in a café, you can predict the kind of vocabulary that will be used.
- Concentrate on the main part. When watching a foreign film, you usually get the meaning of the whole story from a few individual shots. Understanding a foreign conversation or article is similar. Concentrate on the main message and don't worry about individual words.

- Learn to cope with uncertainty—don't overuse your dictionary! You don't have to look up every word you don't know—try to deduce the meaning from context. Concentrate on trying to get the gist of the passage and underline the words you don't understand. If after the third time there are still words which prevent you from getting the general meaning of the passage, look them up in the dictionary.

WRITING

You'll have plenty of writing practice using this book. Creating vocabulary lists are grammar summaries and taking good notes as you study are other great opportunities to practice writing.

If you're keeping your lists or notes on your smartphone, computer, or tablet are remember to switch the keyboard language to be able to include all accents and special characters.

Here are some other ways to practice writing:

- Write out the answers to all Practice and Test yourself questions.
- Create your own vocabulary lists and a grammar summary.
- Look up writing prompts for language learning or write a daily gratitude journal in French.
- Write out your to-do and shopping lists in French.
- Join online forums and discussion groups about or in French.

SPEAKING

The greatest obstacle to speaking a new language is the fear of making a mistake. Keep in mind that you make mistakes in your own language—it's simply part of the human condition. Accept it. Focus on the message. Most errors are not serious, and they will not affect the meaning—for example if you use the wrong article, wrong pronoun, or wrong adjective ending. So, concentrate on getting your message across and use the mistakes as learning opportunities.

Here are some useful tips to help you practice speaking French:

- When you're going about your day—e.g. buying groceries, ordering food and drink—do it in French in your mind! Look at objects around you and try to name them in French. Look at people around you and try to describe them.
- Answer all of the questions in the book out loud. Say the dialogues out loud, then try to replace sentences with ones that are true for you. Role-play different situations in the book.
- Keep talking. The best way to improve your fluency in a language is to talk every time you have the opportunity to do so: keep the conversations flowing and don't worry about the mistakes. If you get stuck for a particular word, don't let the conversation stop; simplify what you want to say; paraphrase or replace the unknown word with one you do know.

Learning a language takes work. But the work can be a lot of fun! So, let's begin!

Pronouncing French

When speaking French, remember that, quite often, not all the letters of a word are pronounced. You might already know how to say *I speak French*: je parle français. This serves as an example: you do not pronounce the -s at the end of français. Speaking more generally, a consonant at the end of a word is usually (but not always) silent. The audio recordings that accompany each Unit will guide you towards correct pronunciation. Some internet resources allow you to hear the pronunciation of any given word by clicking on an icon; here are two examples:

Dico en ligne Le Robert: 

Collins Robert:  and 

Pronouncing vowels in French

In written French, vowels are represented by five letters (a, e, i, o, u) plus œ. The pronunciation of these letters varies according to where in the word they appear, whether they are combined with another letter and/or whether they have an accent or mark (à, â, é, è, ê, ï, ô, ù, û, ü). If the last letter of a word is e and it does not have an accent, the e is silent. You will also notice that two or three vowels combined are often pronounced as one sound. For example, eau (*water*) is pronounced rather like **oh** in English.

If you listen to the recording of the alphabet (track 00.04), you will be able to hear how different vowels are pronounced in French.

Pronouncing consonants in French

You will find it useful to note a couple of rules concerning the pronunciation of consonants in French, in particular c, ç and g. Let's start with g. In English, we can pronounce *g* as hard (as in ***give***) or soft (as in ***general***). In French, the same applies, and fortunately the spelling of the word always contains an indication as to whether g is hard or soft.

00.01

See if you can tell whether g is pronounced as hard or soft from the spelling of each word. Then listen to the pronunciation and repeat in the pauses.

garage	*garage*	geôle	*jail*	gouvernement	*government*
gendarme	*gendarme*	gîte	*cottage, cabin*	guide	*guide*

Where g is followed by e or i, it is soft (see first column), and where it is followed by a, o, or u (see third column), it is hard.

00.02

Listen to the pronunciation of the following words and repeat in the pauses. Notice when the c is pronounced hard or soft.

Similar rules of pronunciation apply to the letter c. When it appears in a word it might be pronounced as hard (like *c* in *cat*) or soft (like *c* in *ceiling*). As with g, it is soft when followed by e or i, and hard when followed by a, o, or u, or by any consonant:

centime	catalogue	culture
cigarette	coucou	crème

In addition, when the letter c is followed by an a, o, or u you will sometimes see the letter c with a cedilla attached to it: Ç or ç. In these cases, it is always soft:

00.03

Listen and repeat in the pauses provided. Notice when the c is pronounced hard or soft.

façade	garçon	reçu

French word	Meaning	Hard or soft? Over to you ...
un cœur	*heart*	hard
une puce	*microchip*	
ici	*here*	
une ancre	*anchor*	
cela	*that*	
ça	*that (abbreviation of* cela*)*	
culbuter	*to tumble*	

Finally, when followed by h, c is normally pronounced like *sh* in the English word *shop: so a cat* is un chat, where ch sounds like *sh*.

Spelling your name using the French alphabet

00.04

Listen to the French alphabet and the French names that start with each letter.

In French, when you need to spell your name over the phone, it is usual to say each lettre (*letter*) followed by comme (*like*) and a name beginning with the letter. So if your name is Claude, you would spell it by saying: **c** comme Catherine, **l** comme Louis, **a** comme Alain, **u** comme Ursule, **d** comme Daniel, **e** comme Étienne. There is no single standard list of names used for this purpose, but below is a table with examples.

A	comme	Alain	N	comme	Noémie
B		Bernard	O		Oscar
C		Catherine	P		Patrick
D		Daniel	Q		Quentin
E		Émile	R		Robert
F		François	S		Sophie
G		Georges	T		Thérèse
H		Henri	U		Ursule
I		Isabelle	V		Valérie
J		Jean	W		Walter
K		Kléber	X		Xavier
L		Louis	Y		Yvonne
M		Michel	Z		Zoé

Now try spelling your name using the French alphabet.

Days of the week and months of the year

00.05

These are the days of the week in French. Listen and repeat during the pause:

lundi	*Monday*
mardi	*Tuesday*
mercredi	*Wednesday*
jeudi	*Thursday*
vendredi	*Friday*
samedi	*Saturday*
dimanche	*Sunday*

1 Match the days of the week, except for dimanche (*Sunday*), on the left to the deity or heavenly body they are named after on the right. Can you find out why dimanche is different?

a lundi	**1** Mercure/Mercury
b mardi	**2** Vénus/Venus
c mercredi	**3** Jupiter/Jupiter
d jeudi	**4** Mars/Mars
e samedi	**5** la lune/the moon
f vendredi	**6** Saturne/Saturn

00.06

Listen to the months of the year, and repeat each one during the pause. Then move on to question 2 below.

2 Match the months of the year in French, listed in alphabetical instead of chronological order, to the months in English on the right.

a août	**1** January
b avril	**2** February
c décembre	**3** March
d février	**4** April
e janvier	**5** May
f juin	**6** June
g juillet	**7** July
h mai	**8** August
i mars	**9** September
j novembre	**10** October
k octobre	**11** November
l septembre	**12** December

In English, days of the week and months of the year always begin with a capital letter, but not in French. For instance, in French we write lundi and mars for *Monday* and *March*.

Numbers

00.07

Listen to the recording of the French numbers from 1 to 20 and repeat each word in the pause.

un	*one*	six	*six*	onze	*eleven*	seize	*sixteen*
deux	*two*	sept	*seven*	douze	*twelve*	dix-sept	*seventeen*
trois	*three*	huit	*eight*	treize	*thirteen*	dix-huit	*eighteen*
quatre	*four*	neuf	*nine*	quatorze	*fourteen*	dix-neuf	*nineteen*
cinq	*five*	dix	*ten*	quinze	*fifteen*	vingt	*twenty*

00.08

Listen to the French numbers ending in 0 (zéro) up to 100 and repeat them.

dix	*ten*
vingt	*twenty*
trente	*thirty*
quarante	*forty*
cinquante	*fifty*
soixante	*sixty*
soixante-dix	*seventy*
quatre-vingts	*eighty*
quatre-vingt-dix	*ninety*
cent	*one hundred*

French speakers in France and Belgium use different words for 70 and 90. In France, 70 is soixante-dix and 90 is quatre-vingts-dix, while in Belgium those numbers are septante and nonante.

There are also numbers we use to put items in order, e.g. the floor you live on:

premier/première (*first*) ; deuxième (*second*) ; troisième (*third*) ; quatrième (*fourth*) ; cinquième (*fifth*) ; sixième (*sixth*) ; septième (*seventh*) ; huitième (*eighth*) ; neuvième (*ninth*) ; dixième (*tenth*).

Useful phrases

Listen to each short expression and repeat during the pauses provided.

If you are travelling in a French-speaking country, as well as knowing how the numbers and letters are pronounced, it is useful to learn the words and expressions below which you will often hear or see written down:

Pardon !	*Excuse me! Sorry!*
Merci !	*Thank you!*
S'il vous plaît	*Please*
Je vous en prie.	*You're welcome.*
Salut !	*Hi!/Goodbye!*
Bonjour !	*Hello!*
Bonsoir !	*Good evening!*
Au revoir !	*Goodbye!*
Je ne comprends pas.	*I don't understand.*
Vous pouvez répéter ?	*Can you repeat?*
un horaire	*a timetable*
un plan/une carte	*a map*
entrée	*entrance*
sortie	*exit*
sortie de secours	*fire escape*
quai	*platform*
arrivée	*arrival*
départ	*departure*

1

In this lesson you will learn how to:

» Greet people and introduce yourself
» Use personal pronouns
» Distinguish between formal and informal forms of address
» Exchange basic information using the present tense of regular verbs
» Describe someone using the verb **être** (*to be*)

Nouveaux amis

My study plan

I plan to work with Unit 1

○ Every day
○ Twice a week
○ Other ________

I plan to study for

○ 5–15 minutes
○ 15–30 minutes
○ 30–45+ minutes

My progress tracker

Day / Date	Listening	Speaking	Reading	Writing	Conversation
	○	○	○	○	○
	○	○	○	○	○
	○	○	○	○	○
	○	○	○	○	○
	○	○	○	○	○
	○	○	○	○	○
	○	○	○	○	○

My goals

What do you want to be able to do or say in French when you complete this unit?

		Done
1	....	○
2	....	○
3	....	○

My review

SELF CHECK

	I can ...
●	... greet people and introduce myself.
●	... use personal pronouns.
●	... distinguish between formal and informal forms of addressing people I meet.
●	... exchange basic information about myself using the present tense of regular verbs.
●	... describe someone using the verb être (*to be*) + an adjective.

CULTURE POINT 1

Bruxelles : Capitale du chocolat *Brussels: The chocolate capital*

Pralines are a gift that les Belges (*Belgians*) enjoy giving and receiving. These chocolats (*chocolates*) contribute greatly to the reputation of la Belgique (*Belgium*) as la capitale du chocolat (*the chocolate capital*). Each artisan chocolatier (*chocolate maker*) has developed their own recipe, so there is something for everyone. À Bruxelles (*In Brussels*) the scent of chocolate is everywhere, tempting chocolate lovers who come to Belgium from all over the world. The Sablon and the Mont des Arts, the Grand-Place and the Galeries Royales Saint-Hubert are ideal zones to visit if you wish to learn more about chocolate and/or sample its many varieties. For un apprenti chocolatier (*an apprentice chocolatier*) there is no place like Brussels! Beyond Chocolate, a Belgian initiative that works towards a sustainable chocolate industry and ensures that Belgian chocolate is good not only for consumers but also for those working to produce it. Beyond Chocolate aims to ensure that farmers in countries such as la Côte d'Ivoire (*Ivory Coast*), le Ghana (*Ghana*), l'Indonésie (*Indonesia*), and la République démocratique du Congo (*Democratic Republic of Congo*) will earn at least a living wage.

Learn more about Beyond Chocolate and its sustainability goals for the chocolate industry.

Find out how many companies are part of Beyond Chocolate. What percentage of the Belgian chocolate production market is that?

VOCABULARY BUILDER 1

Look at the words and phrases below. Find the missing English words. Then listen to the recording and imitate the pronunciation of the speaker.

Se présenter *Introductions*

LES SALUTATIONS	*GREETINGS*
Bonjour !	....
À bientôt !	*See you soon!*
Salut !	*Hi/Bye!*
Au revoir !	*Goodbye!*

LES PRESENTATIONS	*INTRODUCTIONS*
Je vous présente ...	*Let me introduce ...*
Tu t'appelles comment ?	*What is your name?* (informal)
Je m'appelle Charles.	....
Monsieur/M. Garcia	....
Madame/Mme Dubois	....
Enchanté !/Enchantée !	*Nice to meet you!* (masculine/feminine)
Bienvenue à Bruxelles !	*Welcome to Brussels!*
Pardon !	*Excuse me!*
Et toi ?	*And you?* (informal, singular)
Et vous ?	*And you?* (formal and/or plural)
Ça va ?	*How's it going?/How are things?* (informal)
Tu vas bien ?	*Are you well?* (informal)
Oui, très bien, et toi ?	*Yes, very well, and you?* (informal)
Vous allez bien ?	*Are you well?* (formal)
Oui, et vous ?	*Yes, and you?*
Très bien merci, et toi ?/et vous ?	*I'm fine, thank you, and you?* (informal/formal)
Je viens de (+ ville/pays)	*I am from (+ town/country)*

EXPRESSIONS	*EXPRESSIONS*
Jean et Marc habitent dans une ville.	*Jean and Marc live in a town/city.*
Marie habite dans un village.	*Marie lives in a village.*
Il habite au cinquième étage.	*He lives on the fifth floor.*
Je parle français, anglais et espagnol.	*I speak French, English, and Spanish.*
Nous parlons français tous les deux.	*We both speak French.*

In the Vocabulary builder, you can see that the French for ***a town/city*** is une ville, while ***a village*** is un village. So two slightly different words—un and une—both mean ***a***. This happens because words for things always have a gender (masculine or feminine) in French. When you see un before a word you know it is masculine, and when you see une before a word you know it is feminine.

Vocabulary practice 1

Match the brief dialogues below with the appropriate pictures.

a

b

c

d

1 Bonjour Madame Dubois !
Bonjour Monsieur Garcia ! Vous allez bien ?
Très bien, et vous ?

2 Salut Béatrice !
Salut, Louisa ! Ça va ?
Oui, très bien, et toi ?

3 Bonjour Madame !
Bonjour, un café s'il vous plaît.

4 À bientôt !
À bientôt !

If you are ordering food or drink in a café, to say *please* just add s'il vous plaît to your sentence. Note the accent on the î—it's called a *circumflex* accent.

Pronunciation practice 1

01.02

1 Listen to the pronunciation of these words and expressions, paying attention to the ending of each word, and note which final letters are pronounced.

Bonjour !
Bonjour Madame !
Bonjour Madame Dubois !

Bonsoir !
Bonsoir Monsieur !
Bonsoir Monsieur Garcia !

Salut !
Salut Jo !
Salut Charles !

In French, words are not stressed, but the last vowel of a group of words is slightly longer. In Bonsoir ! the last vowel is slightly longer. In Bonsoir Madame !, the accent moves to the second a of Madame. And in Bonsoir Madame Halimi ! the stressed vowel moves to the last i of Halimi.

2 Practice pronouncing the following words:

Bonjour Bonsoir Salut Madame Monsieur

CONVERSATION 1

Le nouveau voisin *The new neighbor*

01.03

1 Listen to the conversation a few times without looking at the text. Try to make out a few new words and phrases each time. Then listen again and read along.

Charles has just moved into his new apartment in Brussels where he has come to be an apprenti chocolatier. He quickly makes a new friend, his voisine (*neighbor*), Eva, who is from Switzerland, another country famous for its chocolats. Note how Charles and Eva speak to each other and address Madame Willems.

Eva	Bonjour ! Tu es le nouveau voisin ?
Charles	Oui, bonjour, je suis Charles, et toi ? Tu t'appelles comment ?
Eva	Je m'appelle Eva.
Charles	Enchanté !
Eva	Moi aussi, enchantée ! Bienvenue à Bruxelles !
Charles	Merci !
Eva	Tu viens de France ?
Charles	Oui ! Mes parents habitent à Paris.
Eva	Ohhhh Paris, j'adore ! Ma famille habite à Lausanne.
Charles	Ahhhh, tu parles italien ?
Eva	Oui, je parle italien, anglais et français. Et toi ?
Charles	Moi, je parle français, anglais et espagnol.

Another neighbour walks into the building.

Eva	Bonjour Madame Willems, vous allez bien ?
Mme Willems	Bonjour Eva, ça va bien merci ! Bonjour... euh...
Eva	Je vous présente Charles, le nouveau voisin, il habite au cinquième étage, ses parents habitent à Paris.
Mme Willems	Bonjour Charles ! Bienvenue !
Charles	Merci ! Enchanté !
Mme Willems	Au revoir !
Eva et Charles	Au revoir !

2 Answer the questions.

a Where does Eva's family live?
b Where does Charles come from?
c Which languages do Eva and Charles speak?
d Who is Madame Willems?
e What floor does Charles live on?

LANGUAGE BUILDER 1

Language discovery 1

1 Notice how people speak to each other in Conversation 1. In particular, what word for *you* do Eva and Charles use:

a when they speak to each other?
b when they speak to Madame Willems?

2 Complete the sentences from the conversation with either tu or vous.

a .... viens de France ?
b .... parles italien ?
c .... allez bien ?

3 What do you think is the difference between tu and vous?

How to say *you* in French

In English we address all people in all situations with *you*. However, when you speak to someone in French, you need to choose between tu (*you*, informal) or vous (*you*, formal). In general, use tu for speaking to a friend, family member, child, or close colleague; otherwise, use vous. If in doubt, it's best to say vous until you are addressed as tu.

Informal	Formal
Bonjour Émilia, tu vas bien ?	Bonjour Monsieur Alaoui, vous allez bien ?
Tu parles anglais ?	Vous parlez anglais, Madame Sabran ?
Tu habites à Lyon ?	Vous habitez à Lyon, Monsieur Didier ?

Vous is also used when talking to two or more people, in both formal and informal contexts.

Charles et Eva, vous habitez à Bruxelles ? — *Charles and Eva, do you live in Brussels?*

Monsieur et Madame Willems, vous habitez au cinquième étage ? — *Mr. and Mrs. Willems, do you live on the fifth floor?*

Language practice 1

01.04

1 Listen to the recorded sentences/questions and imagine the situations in which they occur. Indicate whether the sentences below are formal (F) or informal (INF).

a Bonjour Madame Takahashi, vous allez bien ? F INF
b Salut Maria Luisa, tu vas bien ? F INF
c Pierre, je te présente Mario. F INF
d Monsieur Meyer, je vous présente Madame Papadimitriou. F INF
e Tu t'appelles comment ? F INF
f Je m'appelle Geneviève, et vous ? F INF
g Bonjour Monsieur Kazem. F INF

2 Complete the sentences below with tu or vous.

a Bonjour Madame Hernandez, ... allez bien ?

b Salut Franz, ... vas bien ?

c .... allez bien, Helena ?

d Ça va bien, merci, et .... , ... allez bien ?

e .... vas bien, Fatima ?

LANGUAGE BUILDER 2

Language discovery 2

Listen to the conversation between Eva, Charles and Mme Willems one more time. Repeat each line in the pauses provided while imitating the intonation you hear.

Match the words in the left- and right-hand columns to recreate sentences you heard in the conversation. Then, look carefully at the French words for *live* and *lives*. What is the difference in spelling? Is there a difference in pronunciation?

1 Eva	**a** parle français, anglais et espagnol.
2 Charles et Eva	**b** habitent à Bruxelles.
3 La famille de Charles	**c** habite à Lausanne.
4 Charles	**d** parle italien, français et anglais.
5 La famille d'Eva	**e** habite à Paris.

Actions in the present

Verbs usually express actions (e.g., *jump*, *speak*, *go*). Verbs in English are fairly simple—they generally only change in the third person (*I speak* but *she speaks*). French verbs, however, change to reflect who is performing the action (e.g., je parle, tu parles, vous parlez). The good news is that a large group of verbs follows the same pattern. All you have to do is drop the -er ending from the infinitive (that's the form of the verb you'll find in a dictionary) and replace it with a personal ending. To see how it works with habiter, look at the table below. Using this information, can you complete the table for parler?

habiter (*to live*)		**parler (*to speak*)**	
j'habite (*I live*)	nous habitons (*we live*)	je parle (*I speak*)	nous **c** ....
tu habites (*you live*)	vous habitez (*you live*)	tu **a**	vous **d** ....
il/elle/iel habite (*he/she lives*)	ils/elles/iels habitent (*they live*)	il/elle/iel **b**	ils/elles/iels parlent (*they speak*)

Notice that all the singular forms and the ils/elles/iels form all sound the same (so don't worry about making a mistake when speaking—the odds are in your favor!): J'habite à Bruxelles. Il habite à Tokyo. Elles habitent à Santiago.

The pronoun iel (plural iels) first entered the *Robert Dico en ligne* (the *Robert Online Dictionary*) in the 2020s. This is a nonbinary or gender-neutral alternative to using il or elle. For instance, it is possible to write: Marie et Jean sont chez moi. Iels vont rester trois jours. (*Marie and Jean are at my place. They will stay for three days.*)

Language practice 2

1 Complete the sentences below using habiter or parler as appropriate. Say the conjugated verbs out loud.

a J'..................... à Louvain.

b Tu .... anglais.

c Nous .... à Alger.

d Je .... français.

e Tu .... à Londres.

f Nous .... arabe.

01.06

2 Listen to the conversation between Charles, Eva, and Mme Willems, and play the role of Charles. Practice asking formally and informally how people are.

CULTURE POINT 2

Paris, ville de la gastronomie *Paris, city of gastronomy*

Since the Middle Ages, the world has looked upon Paris as a culinary capital. If you visit, you can find traditional French cuisine (*cuisine*) as well as special plats (*dishes*) from all corners of the world. There is a range of hybrid restaurants (*restaurants*), with different neighborhoods specializing in food from specific national regions, or indeed fusion cuisine. The vitality and reach of France's gastronomy are reflected in its global reputation, and also in the many ways it is integrated in its own national culture through art, literature, and design. Various products have become symbolic of French cuisine, the most iconic being, probably, the humble baguette (*baguette*). An annual competition for the best baguette in Paris has been held since 1994. The winner of the Grand Prix de la Baguette de tradition française de la Ville de Paris (*Traditional French Baguette Competition, Paris*) receives national attention and takes over the role of official provider to the Élysée Palace, residence of the president of the French Republic.

Learn about the European Institute of the History and Culture of Food. You can follow the Villa Rabelais on Instagram if you wish. Can you find out when the François Rabelais award was first given out? If you do some research, you can guess why the Institute named its award after the French Renaissance author François Rabelais.

VOCABULARY BUILDER 2

Look at the list of restaurants and cuisines in the Vocabulary builder below and supply the missing English words and expressions. Then listen to the recording and try to imitate the pronunciation of the speakers. You will hear adjectives of nationality in the masculine and feminine forms. This is because, in French, adjectives have a *gender* (masculine or feminine) that matches the gender of the person or thing they describe.

LE SECTEUR DE LA RESTAURATION	*CATERING INDUSTRY*
un restaurant algérien/la cuisine algérienne	*Algerian restaurant/cuisine*
un restaurant marocain/la cuisine marocaine	*Moroccan restaurant/cuisine*
une restaurant mexicain/la cuisine mexicaine	.... *restaurant/cuisine*
un restaurant belge/la cuisine belge	*Belgian restaurant/cuisine*
un restaurant français/la cuisine française	*French restaurant/cuisine*
un restaurant japonais/la cuisine japonaise	.... *restaurant/cuisine*
un restaurant grec/la cuisine grecque	*Greek restaurant/cuisine*
un restaurant turc/la cuisine turque	.... *restaurant/cuisine*
un restaurant québécois/la cuisine québécoise	*Quebecois restaurant/cuisine*
un restaurant chinois/la cuisine chinoise	.... *restaurant/cuisine*
un restaurant espagnol/la cuisine espagnole	*Spanish restaurant/cuisine*
EXPRESSIONS	***EXPRESSIONS***
Il aime la cuisine chinoise.	*He likes Chinese cuisine.*
un chef cuisinier/une cheffe cuisinière	*male chef/female chef*
un restaurant 3 étoiles	*three-star restaurant*
un nouveau restaurant québécois	*new Quebecois restaurant*
une pizza	*pizza*
une spécialité	*specialty*

Vocabulary practice 2

1 Identify the adjectives of nationality in the sentences below. Then translate each sentence into English. The first one has been completed as an example.

a Rachel est <u>anglaise</u>. *Rachel is English.*

b Lian est chinois. ....

c Fatima est marocaine. ....

d Naomi est japonaise. ....

2 You may have noticed that masculine and feminine adjectives of nationality fall into one of three categories: a) those that look and sound the same; b) those that are spelled differently but sound the same; c) those that are spelled differently and sound different. Bearing this in mind, can you fill in the table below by marking a, b, or c, as appropriate?

Adjectifs de nationalité ***Adjectives of nationality***

Adjective	Same spelling and sound	Different spelling, same sound	Different spelling and sound
Il est chinois. Elle est chinoise.			
Il est belge. Elle est belge.			
Il est grec. Elle est grecque.			

Some adjectives are the same in the masculine and feminine, for example: belge (*Belgian*). Compare: Mme Willems est belge (*Mrs. Willems is Belgian*); M. Willems est belge (*Mr. Willems is Belgian*).

Pronunciation practice 2

1 Listen to the pronunciation of the following words and expressions, paying attention to the verbs aimer (*to like, to love*) and manger (*to eat*): notice these are verbs ending in -er.

J'aime la cuisine espagnole.
Ils aiment manger la cuisine chinoise.
Ce soir je mange au restaurant turc.
Nous mangeons au restaurant japonais.
Vous aimez la cuisine algérienne ?
Tu aimes la cuisine mexicaine ?

2 Practice the verbs aimer and manger out loud:

aimer (*to like, to love*)

j'aime	nous aimons
tu aimes	vous aimez
il aime	ils aiment

manger (*to eat*)

je mange	nous mangeons
tu manges	vous mangez
il mange	ils mangent

CONVERSATION 2

Les étoiles de la gastronomie *Stars of gastronomy*

01.09

1 Here are some expressions you will hear in the conversation.

les Champs-Élysées	*the Champs-Élysées (a famous avenue in Paris)*
Elle est malienne.	*She is Malian.*
créative, passionnée et ambitieuse	*creative, passionate and ambitious*
génial	*great*

01.10

2 Listen to the conversation without looking at the text. How much can you understand? Play it a few times and see whether you can make out a few new words and phrases each time. Then listen again and read along.

Joséphine (Jo for short) is Charles's twin sister and she lives in Paris with their parents. She is meeting her best friend, Assia, in *l'Atelier*, the restaurant which Jo's parents manage. They are going to work on their new website on Parisian restaurant chefs. Each of them has conducted an interview with a famous chef ...

Jo Salut Assia, ça va ?

Assia Salut Jo, ça va bien ! Et toi ?

Jo Super, merci !

Assia Je te présente Fatou Diallo, elle est cheffe cuisinière à la Grande Brasserie Française, le restaurant 3 étoiles des Champs-Élysées. Elle est malienne et française. Elle est créative, passionnée et ambitieuse !

Jo Génial ! Et moi, je te présente Tom Wang, il est chef cuisinier à la Taverne de Montréal, le nouveau restaurant québécois. Il est canadien et français, comme moi !

Assia Génial !

Jo Il est modeste et généreux !

Assia Parfait ! Deux experts pour notre blog de la gastronomie internationale ! Et deux restaurants fantastiques, c'est super !

Jo Oui ! Je suis contente.

3 Choose the best way to complete each of the sentences below.

a Fatou Diallo works in a restaurant / a pub.

b Fatou is French-Canadian / Malian and French.

c Tom Wang works in an Indian restaurant / a Canadian restaurant.

d Assia and Jo are working for a newspaper / writing a blog.

LANGUAGE BUILDER 3

Language discovery 3

01.11

Listen to the conversation again and focus on the pronunciation of the adjectives which describe Fatou Diallo and Tom Wang. Now read the adjectives in the table below. Can you notice at least one masculine adjective that is the same in the singular and in the plural?

Les adjectifs pluriels *Plural adjectives*

So far we have looked at adjectives that describe one person or thing at a time. So what if we wanted to describe two people at once, e.g. *Sophie and Christine are Canadian*? In many (but not all) cases, the solution is easy: just add an -s to the singular adjective: Sophie et Christine sont canadiennes. But now look at the table below. In which two cases do you *not* add an -s to make the adjective plural?

Remember not to worry too much if you are speaking, as there is no difference in pronunciation between singular and plural adjectives.

Singular pronoun + adj.	Plural pronoun + adj.
Il est canadien. Elle est canadienne.	Ils sont canadiens. Elles sont canadiennes.
Il est modeste. Elle est modeste.	Ils sont modestes. Elles sont modestes.
Il est chinois. Elle est chinoise.	Ils sont chinois. Elles sont chinoises.
Il est généreux. Elle est généreuse.	Ils sont généreux. Elles sont généreuses.

Can you formulate a rule to cover all cases by completing the following sentence:

If a singular adjective ends in an .... or an ...., you do not add an -s to make it plural. Check your idea in the Answer key.

Historically a plural adjective used to describe a mixed-gender group is masculine. For instance, while all French speakers would say Jo et Assia sont françaises, most French-speaking people would also say Jo, Assia et Charles sont français (without the -es). However, the use of the masculine generic is now being challenged, and more inclusive formulations are recommended, for example Assia et Jo sont françaises et Charles est français, or Assia, Jo et Charles sont de nationalité française (*Assia, Jo, and Charles are of French nationality*), nationalité being a feminine noun.

Language practice 3

1 Complete the second sentence, using the same adjective as in the first. Make sure the adjective agrees with the person or persons it describes. The first one has been completed as an example.

a Ils sont ambitieux. Elles sont *ambitieuses.*

b Ils sont chinois. Elles sont …………………… .

c Elles sont indiennes. Ils sont …………………… .

d Jean et Marc sont généreux. Sophie et Carole sont …………………… .

e Alice et Sally sont modestes. Bob et Jack sont …………………… .

2 Choose the correct plural adjective in each case.

a Elles sont maliens / maliennes.
b Ils sont canadiens / canadiennes.
c Tom et Richard sont généreux / généreuses.
d Sophie et Florence sont créatifs / créatives.

LANGUAGE BUILDER 4

Language discovery 4

01.12

Listen to the conversation again and repeat each line in the pauses provided. Try to imitate the phrasing and intonation you hear.

Look at the conversation again and find where Jo says je suis contente. Were you able to figure out what this means? Can you also figure out what the underlined words mean in the short dialogue below?

Tom	Jo et Assia, <u>vous êtes</u> contentes ?
Jo et Assia	Oui, <u>nous sommes</u> contentes.

Using the verb être

Être (*to be*) is, of course, one of the most important French verbs. It is irregular. Study the table, then try to translate the sentences below into English.

être (*to be*)

je suis	*I am*	nous sommes	*we are*
tu es	*you are*	vous êtes	*you are*
il/elle est	*he/she is*	ils/elles sont	*they are*

a Je m'appelle Jean et je suis chef.

b Marie, tu es cheffe ?

c Nous sommes italiennes.

d Vous êtes généreux.

Language practice 4

When French speakers use the verb être followed by a profession, generally there is no article, e.g. Marie est cheffe (*Marie is a chef*). See Unit 2 for more examples.

1 Complete the sentences using the verb être. Say the complete sentences out loud. Then write two short sentences about yourself giving your name, your nationality and the language(s) you speak.

a Charles .... français et il .... apprenti chocolatier.

b Joséphine .... française et elle .... blogueuse (*a blogger*).

c Je m'appelle Fatou et je .... cheffe.

d Nous habitons à Bruxelles et nous .... belges.

e Vous .... japonais et vous parlez japonais et français.

f Tu .... canadienne ? Et tu parles anglais et français ?

g Jo et Charles .... français.

01.13

2 Now play the conversation again and play Assia's role. Speak in the pauses. Try not to refer to the text.

SKILL BUILDER

1 Use your imagination to describe one of the people you see in the image. What is their name, what languages do they speak, where do they live, and what is their nationality? Once you have decided what you want to say, try to write it down and say it out loud. Now choose a photo of your own and describe the people in it.

2 Frédérique is learning Spanish and is looking for someone to help her practice. She posts the description below onto a language tandem platform. Read her message and answer *true* (vrai) or *false* (faux) to the five statements beneath.

Frédérique

Bonjour ! Je m'appelle Frédérique. Je suis canadienne. Je parle français et anglais. Je suis journaliste, je travaille à Radio Canada International. J'habite à Montréal. J'aime le cinéma, le soccer, la salsa et la cuisine péruvienne. J'apprends l'espagnol et je cherche une personne pour pratiquer.

a	Frédérique habite à Toronto.	vrai	faux
b	Elle parle français et italien.	vrai	faux
c	Elle est péruvienne.	vrai	faux
d	Elle aime le tango.	vrai	faux
e	Elle travaille à Radio Canada.	vrai	faux

TEST YOURSELF

1 Choose the correct word or words to complete each sentence.

a Salut Eva .... vas bien ? (tu, vous)

b .... Charles, ça va ? (Bonjour, Au revoir)

c La famille d'Eva .... à Lugano. (habite, habitent)

d Les parents de Charles .... à Paris. (habite, habitent)

e Charles .... trois langues. Il parle français, anglais et espagnol (parle, parlons)

f Eva et Charles .... français ensemble. (parlez, parlent)

g Les cousins habitent au Canada, ils sont .... (canadiens, canadiennes)

h Elles habitent aux États-Unis, elles sont .... (américains, américaines)

i Je .... français, tu .... française ? (suis, sommes, es, êtes)

j Assia et Jo .... contentes. (sont, est)

2 Match the subjects to the verbs. You can use each verb once only.

a Nous
b Vous
c Il
d J'
e Iels
f Tu

1 aimez
2 parlons
3 habite
4 parle
5 es
6 parlent

3 Choose the correct words to complete the sentences below.

habite	parle	est	Bruxelles	anglais
français	espagnol	canadien	malienne	

a Jo .... française, elle .... à Paris.

b Charles est .... Il parle .... , ... et ....
Il habite à ....

c Fatou est ....et française.

d Tom .... chef cuisinier et il est .... et ....

e Eva .... à Bruxelles et elle .... italien, français et ....

Before you move on to the next unit, assess your progress using the **My review** section on the first page of the unit, and reflect on your learning experience with the **My takeaway** section available online.

2

In this lesson you will learn how to:

» Talk about your profession
» Talk about your family
» Indicate your age
» Talk about your possessions

Au travail et en famille

My study plan

I plan to work with Unit 2

○ Every day
○ Twice a week
○ Other ________

I plan to study for

○ 5–15 minutes
○ 15–30 minutes
○ 30–45+ minutes

My progress tracker

Day / Date	Listening	Speaking	Reading	Writing	Conversation
	○	○	○	○	○
	○	○	○	○	○
	○	○	○	○	○
	○	○	○	○	○
	○	○	○	○	○
	○	○	○	○	○
	○	○	○	○	○

My goals

What do you want to be able to do or say in French when you complete this unit?

		Done
1	....	○
2	....	○
3	....	○

My review

SELF CHECK

	I can ...
●	... introduce myself and exchange basic information.
●	... talk about relatives.
●	... speak about professions.
●	... ask questions.

CULTURE POINT 1

Bruxelles : la capitale de l'Union européenne *Brussels, the capital of the European Union*

Bruxelles (*Brussels*) is the de facto capitale (*capital*) of l'Union européenne (*the European Union*), and you will find many of the government immeubles (*buildings*) in un quartier (*a neighborhood*) known as le quartier européen (*the European Quarter*). In Bruxelles you will find most types of professions represented, with several thousand people working directly for l'Union européenne as juristes or avocats (*lawyers*), secrétaires (*secretaries*), administrateurs (*administrators*), professeurs et éducateurs (*teachers and educators*), représentants, députés (*representatives, members of parliament*), and in many other roles. Alongside the official buildings you can also find coworking spaces nestled in le quartier européen, should you wish to immerse yourself in the vibrant work atmosphere of Bruxelles. When you want a break, you can leave the cityscape behind in just a few steps and relax in the Parc Léopold, which provides a touch of nature right in the heart of the metropolis. As you walk through the city, especially if you visit the Quartier Marolles, you are bound to notice that various streets bear the names of professions, for instance the Rue des Orfèvres (*Goldsmiths Street*) or the Rue des Charpentiers (*Carpenters Street*). Although such names have survived, often the professions they evoke are no longer present in those areas. So the street signs that serve to guide us today also help bring to life the history that helped make Bruxelles une ville capitale.

The Parlamentarium is an ideal destination to learn more about how democracy works at the heart of Europe.

VOCABULARY BUILDER 1

Read the words and phrases below and supply the missing English words. Then listen to the recording and imitate the pronunciation of the speakers.

Parlons boulot *Let's talk shop*

LES PROFESSIONS (MASCULIN/FÉMININ)	*PROFESSIONS*
un architecte/une architecte	....
un avocat/une avocate	*lawyer*
un serveur/une serveuse	*server*
un médecin/une médecin	*doctor*
un infirmier/une infirmière	*nurse*
un informaticien/une informaticienne	*computer scientist*
un chocolatier/une chocolatière	*chocolate maker*
un chef/une cheffe	....
un cinéaste/une cinéaste	*filmmaker*
un journaliste/une journaliste	....
un blogueur/une blogueuse	*blogger*
un ingénieur/une ingénieure	*engineer*
un boulanger/une boulangère	*baker*
un professeur/une professeure	*teacher*
un photographe/une photographe	*photographer*
un président/une présidente	*managing director/president*
un vendeur/une vendeuse	*salesperson*

In French most names of professions are gendered as masculine or feminine. For instance, a male lawyer is un avocat, while a female lawyer is une avocate.

LE LIEU DE TRAVAIL	*THE WORKPLACE*
un bureau, un espace de coworking	*office, coworking space*
un stage	*internship*
une startup	....

EXPRESSIONS	*EXPRESSIONS*
Je travaille à l'hôpital.	*I work at the hospital.*
Tu fais quoi ?	*What do you do?*
Je fais un stage chez Michelin.	*I have an internship with Michelin.*
Quel est votre métier ?	*What is your job? (formal)*
Je suis serveur au restaurant du coin.	*I am a waiter at the local restaurant.*
Il est ingénieux et prometteur.	*He is ingenious and promising.*
Elle travaille dans une école.	*She works in a school.*

Chez is primarily used to mean *at the house of*, but it can also be used for a business or company: il travaille chez Lancôme (*he works at Lancôme*).

Vocabulary practice 1

1 Complete the following sentences.

a Je suis infirmière, je travaille à l' …………………… .

b Charles est chef. Il fait un stage dans un …………………… du coin.

c Fabienne est professeure. Elle travaille dans une …………………… .

As a general rule, French speakers do not use un or une when stating someone's profession. So, *Sandrine is a teacher* corresponds to: Sandrine est professeure.

2 Fill in the gaps in the following sentences with the same profession:

a Florence est avocate ; Richard aussi est ………………… .

b Jeanne est cinéaste ; Marc aussi est ………………… .

c Jean-Claude est professeur ; Marie-Laure aussi est ………………… .

Pronunciation practice 1

02.02

1 Listen to the different forms of travailler (*to work*) paying special attention to the sound of the double ll:

travailler (*to work*)

je travaille	nous travaillons
tu travailles	vous travaillez
il travaille	elles travaillent

In French, i + ll (e.g. in une fille) is generally pronounced like the letter *y* in *yes*.
Note: the common word une ville (*town*) is an exception to this rule of pronunciation.

CONVERSATION 1

Au co-working d'Eva *At Eva's coworking office*

02.03

1 Here are some words and phrases to help you understand the conversation. Note their meanings and pay attention to how questions are formed. In particular, note the use of quoi (*what*) or comment (*how*) at the end of a sentence.

Tu dessines quoi ?	*What are you drawing?*
Elle s'appelle comment ?	*What is her name?*
mon ami	*my friend*
ma voisine de bureau	*my neighbor at the office, "office neighbor"*
Les Danois comme les Belges...	*The Danish, like the Belgians ...*

02.04

2 Listen to the conversation without looking at the text below. Then listen again and follow along in the text.

Eva goes to her coworking office with Charles and introduces him to the colleagues she has already met there.

Eva	Bonjour Jeannette ! Je te présente mon ami Charles. Charles, voici Jeannette, ma voisine de bureau.
Jeannette	Bonjour Eva, bonjour Charles, enchantée !
Eva	Jeannette est architecte, elle est néerlandaise.
Charles	Tu es architecte ? Cool ! Tu dessines quoi ?
Jeannette	Un nouveau Musée de la musique.
Charles	Waouh ! Génial !
Eva	Là, c'est le bureau de [...]. Elle travaille chez elle aujourd'hui.
Charles	Elle s'appelle comment ?
Eva	Joana.
Charles	Quelle est sa profession ?
Eva	Elle est journaliste. Et voici Bjorn ! Bjorn, je te présente Charles ! Charles, je te présente Bjorn ! Bjorn est informaticien, il habite à Copenhague mais il travaille à Bruxelles.
Bjorn	Salut ! Et toi, Charles, tu fais quoi ?
Charles	Je suis apprenti chocolatier.
Eva	Oui ! Un apprenti chocolatier prometteur !
Bjorn	Tu fais des chocolats ! Super ! Les Danois comme les Belges adorent le chocolat !

3 Complete the table with the information from the conversation.

	Métier/Job	Nationalité/Nationality
Eva	photographe	
Charles		
Jeanette		
Bjorn		danoise

LANGUAGE BUILDER 1

 Language discovery 1

Look again at the part of the dialogue where Eva tells Charles that Jeanette is an architect. Note that she follows the general rule that we should not use un/ une before a profession. Then compare that with the last lines, where Eva compliments Charles on being a great chocolatier.

Does she still follow the general rule, or does she do something different, and if so, why?

Professions + adjectifs *Professions + adjectives*

As you know, generally French speakers do not use un or une when stating someone's profession: Eva est photographe. However, if they want to use an adjective (e.g. génial), they do then put in un or une: Eva est une photographe géniale.

1 Complete the table. Remember to think about whether you need to use un or une.

Eva est photographe.	Eva est une photographe géniale.
Charles est apprenti chocolatier.	Charles est **a** .... formidable.
Jeannette est **b**	Jeannette est une architecte créative.
Bjorn est informaticien.	Bjorn est **c** .... ingénieux.

Companies and institutions recommend the use of écriture inclusive to avoid gender bias in written French. This involves either using the point médian (un·e avocat·e) or using both the masculine and the feminine form. The desirability of this change is a subject of topical debate.

2 Which sentence uses inclusive writing?

a Jean-Claude et Laurence sont professeur·e·s.
b Jeanne et Marc sont ingénieurs.
c Florence et Richard sont avocats.

Language practice 1

02.05

Listen and choose the correct ending for each sentence. Then listen again and practice saying each sentence out loud. Finally, add a new sentence following the same format, but this time describe the profession of someone you know.

a Marie est infirmier / infirmière.

b Béatrice est avocat / avocate.

c Simon est vendeur / vendeuse.

d Paul est écrivain / écrivaine.

e Joseph est boulanger / boulangère.

LANGUAGE BUILDER 2

Language discovery 2

02.06

Listen to the conversation again and repeat each line in the pauses provided. Try to imitate the phrasing and intonation you hear.

Toward the end of the conversation Bjorn asks: Et toi, Charles, tu fais quoi ? Then, when he finds out that Charles is a chocolatier, Bjorn exclaims: Tu fais des chocolats ! Super ! How would you translate tu fais in each case?

The verb faire *(to do, to make)*

02.07

Listen and practice the verb faire (*to make, to do*). Focus on the first three forms. Can you hear any difference between fais, fais, and fait? How many ways is faire pronounced in total?

faire (*to make, to do*)

je fais	nous faisons
tu fais	vous faites
il/elle fait	ils/elles font

The verb faire generally means *to make* or *to do*. It is irregular, but the singular forms are all pronounced the same. It can also be used to talk about someone's job.

Je fais des gâteaux.	*I make cakes.*
Je fais mes devoirs de français.	*I am doing my French homework.*
Je fais du sport.	*I do/play sports.*
Tu fais quoi ?—Je suis infirmier.	*What do you do?—I am a nurse.*
Vous faites quoi ?—Je suis architecte.	*What do you do?—I am an architect.*

Language practice 2

1 Complete the questions and sentences, using faire. For each one, state whether *do* or *make* would be used in the English translation.

a Vous .... un gâteau ?

b Nous .... nos devoirs d'arabe.

c Elles .... leurs devoirs de chinois.

d Charles .... des chocolats délicieux.

e Tu .... tes devoirs d'allemand.

02.08

2 Now play the conversation again and play Charles's role. Speak in the pauses. Try not to refer to the text.

CULTURE POINT 2

L'univers de Goscinny *The Goscinny universe*

René Goscinny was born in Paris in 1926, six years after son frère (*his brother*) Claude. René grew up partly in Buenos Aires, where he and Claude attended schools based on the French school system. He went on to become France's best-selling author abroad, along with cocreator Albert Uderzo. Together they created *Astérix*, a bande dessinée (*comic strip*) about a small village in Gaul resisting their would-be Roman conquerors in 50 BCE. *Astérix* went on to become a worldwide phenomenon, translated into more than 100 languages and dialects and leading to 15 film adaptations. It is so well loved that France's first satellite launched into space was named Astérix. *Le Petit Nicolas* (*Little Nicholas*) is another of Goscinny's very popular creations: the focus of this collection of stories falls on a fils unique (*only child*) and his many adventures in an idealized 1950s famille française (*French family*). René married Gilberte Pollaro-Millo who was also a writer, and the couple collaborated on several projects. They were mariés (*married*) for 10 years and had une fille unique (*an only daughter*), Anne. Anne, too, has become une écrivaine (*a female author*). She explains that she struggled to understand her place in her famous father's life and his oeuvre. René Goscinny died in 1977 aged 51. His works have sold over 500 million copies and continue to be read by des enfants, des parents et des grands-parents (*children, parents, and grandparents*). Did you know that one in four books sold in France is a bande dessinée and 77% of infants read a comic at least once a week, but their parents aren't far behind—almost half of adults share the same hobby!

Visit a famous museum in Brussels dedicated to the art of bandes dessinées. It has a reading room housing a collection of over 700,000 albums in up to 40 languages.

VOCABULARY BUILDER 2

Read the list of family members below and supply the missing English equivalents. Then listen to the recording and imitate the pronunciation of the speakers.

La famille *The family*

les enfants	*children*
une mère, un père	*mother, father*
maman, papa	....
une fille, un fils	*daughter, son*
un frère, une sœur	*brother, sister*
une grand-mère, un grand-père	*grandmother, grandfather*
les parents	....
les grands-parents	....
les beaux-parents	*parents-in-law*
une belle-sœur/mère	*sister-/mother-in-law*
un beau-frère/père	*brother-/father-in-law*
une fille unique, un fils unique	*only daughter, only son*
un conjoint/une conjointe	*partner (male/female)*
une femme, un mari	*wife, husband*
une épouse/un époux	*spouse (female/male)*
un oncle, une tante	*uncle, aunt*
un cousin/une cousine	....
un neveu, une nièce	*nephew, niece*
un petit frère	*younger brother*
une grande sœur	*older sister*
un mariage, un divorce	*marriage, divorce*

In French, belle-sœur has two meanings: ***sister-in-law*** or ***stepsister***. Similarly, beau-frère can mean either ***brother-in-law*** or ***stepbrother***, and beaux-parents can mean ***parents-in-law*** or ***stepparents***. The meaning is inferred from the context.

EXPRESSIONS	*EXPRESSIONS*
une fête d'anniversaire	*birthday party*
une grande famille	*big family*
ici c'est, là c'est	*here is, there is*
Qui ?	*Who?*
donc	*therefore, so*
tout le monde	*everyone*
Ma mère a aussi deux sœurs.	*My mother also has two sisters.*
Il a six ans ; il est mignon !	*He is six years old; he's cute!*
Tu as combien de cousins ?	*How many cousins do you have?*
le lien de parenté	*family link*

Vocabulary practice 2

Deduce the family relationships between René, Claude, Gilberte, and Anne as described in the Culture point. Then complete the sentences below.

a René est le frère de Claude. Anne est la fille de René ; elle est donc la .... de Claude.

b Claude est l'.................... d'Anne.

c René est le .... de Gilberte. Ils sont tous les deux les .... d'Anne.

d Gilberte est la .... de Claude, et Claude est le.................... de Gilberte.

e René et Gilberte sont .... et ....

Pronunciation practice 2

Listen to the tongue twister below and then read it out loud as quickly as you can.

02.10 Ma sœur est mère, mon père est frère, ma mère est sœur, mon frère est masseur.

My sister is a mother, my father is a brother, my mother is a sister, my brother is a masseur.

CONVERSATION 2

La photo de famille *The family photo*

02.11

1 Listen to the conversation a few times without looking at the text below. Then listen again and follow along in the text.

Jo and Assia are looking at family photos. Jo finds a photo of her mother's family.

Jo Regarde ! C'est une photo de la fête d'anniversaire de ma grand-mère, pour ses 80 ans.

Assia C'est une grande famille !

Jo Oui, nous sommes plus de 60 personnes sur la photo. Ma mère a deux sœurs, mes tantes Catherine et Brigitte. Et elle a aussi deux frères, mes oncles Alain et Pascal.

Assia Tu as combien de cousins ?

Jo J'ai douze cousins et cousines. Ici, c'est ma cousine Annette, son mari Antonio et leurs deux enfants, Lola et Diego.

Assia Et là, c'est qui ?

Jo C'est mon neveu Yanis.

Assia Il est mignon ! Il a quel âge ?

Jo Il a six ans. Je l'adore !

Assia Quelle belle photo de famille !

2 Answer the questions.

a What birthday is being celebrated in the photo Jo is describing to Assia?
b How many people attended the birthday party?
c How are Catherine and Brigitte related to Jo?
d Who is the youngest person described in the photo, and how are they described?

3 If you like, draw a family tree in French with the information contained in the conversation.

LANGUAGE BUILDER 3

Language discovery 3

In Conversation 2, when talking about her family, Jo says: ma grand-mère, ma mère, ma cousine Annette, and mon neveu. What do the words before each family member mean? Can you figure out why she uses mon before neveu, though she uses ma before grand-mère, mère, and cousine?

Les possessifs *Possessives*

Possessives serve to indicate who or what something belongs to. In English, we can talk about *my brother*, *your sister*, and so on, where the words *my* and *your* indicate whose brother or sister we refer to. Possessive adjectives in French work in the same way. But it is important to remember that they agree with the nouns they are attached to. So *my brother* is mon frère (masc. sing.), *my sister* is ma sœur (fem. sing.), and *my parents* are mes parents (masc. plural). Here are all the possessives in French:

Before singular masc. noun	Before singular fem. noun	Before any plural noun
mon (*my*)	ma (*my*)	mes (*my*)
ton* (*your*)	ta* (*your*)	tes* (*your*)
son (*his, her*)	sa (*his, her*)	ses (*his, her*)

Before singular masc. noun	Before singular fem. noun	Before any plural noun
notre (*our*)	notre (*our*)	nos (*our*)
votre (*your*)	votre (*your*)	vos (*your*)
leur (*their*)	leur (*their*)	leurs (*their*)

* used to address one person only, and in an informal way

Mon frère est boulanger et ma sœur est avocate. — *My brother is a baker and my sister is a lawyer.*

Nous faisons nos devoirs. — *We're doing our homework.*

Ta copine est où ? — *Where is your friend* (fem.)*?*

When a feminine noun begins with a vowel, replace ma with mon: mon assiette (*my plate*). The same applies to ta and sa: we say ton assiette, son assiette.

Language practice 3

1 Look carefully at the table below and fill in the gaps. The first one has been completed.

mon beau-père ma belle-mère	*my father-in-law* *my mother-in-law*	notre grand-père **d** .... grand-mère	*our grandfather* *our grandmother*
ton oncle **a** .... tante	*your uncle* *your aunt*	**e** .... cousin votre cousine	*your (male) cousin* *your (female) cousin*
b .... frère **c** .... sœur	*her brother* *his sister*	leur beau-frère **f** .... belle-sœur	*their brother-in-law* *their sister-in-law*

2 Then listen to Conversation 2 again and write down a description of at least three different family members in French.

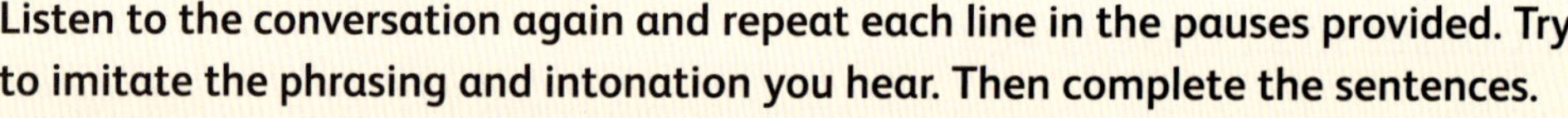

LANGUAGE BUILDER 4

Language discovery 4

02.12

Listen to the conversation again and repeat each line in the pauses provided. Try to imitate the phrasing and intonation you hear. Then complete the sentences.

Ma mère .... deux sœurs.

Tu .... combien de cousins ?

J'.............. douze cousins et cousines.

Can you figure out the meaning of the verb?

The verb **avoir** (*to have*)

The verb avoir (*to have*) is obviously very useful. It is used to indicate possession.

J'ai un frère. *I have a brother.* J'ai une maison. *I have a house.*

avoir (*to have*)

j'ai	*I have*	nous avons	*we have*
tu as	*you have*	vous avez	*you have*
il/elle a	*he/she has*	ils/elles ont	*they have*

In French, avoir is also used to express how old you are:

Mon frère a 25 ans. *My brother is 25 years old.*

In English we "are" our age (I am 25 years old) while in French we "own" the years of our life (j'ai 25 ans). The way we refer to age helps shape how we see ourselves and others. When we learn a new language, it is important to remember that our choice of words reflects our culture. This sometimes means that translation can become a challenging puzzle rather than a straightforward equivalence of *a* to *b*.

Language practice 4

1 Complete the sentences below using the verb avoir. Then circle all the possessives (see the table under the heading Les possesifs on the previous page).

a Vous .... deux filles ?

b Sa mère .... 40 ans et son père .... 38 ans.

c Ton frère .... un appartement à Bruxelles.

d Nous .... deux nièces et un neveu.

e J'.................... 25 ans et mon petit frère .... 23 ans.

f Ils .... une maison à Paris.

02.13

2 After Conversation 2 you answered four questions. Listen to them in French this time and answer them in French.

a Quel anniversaire est célébré sur la photo que Jo décrit à Assia ?
b Combien de personnes assistent à la fête d'anniversaire ?
c Quel est le lien de parenté entre Catherine, Brigitte et Jo ?
d Qui est la personne la plus jeune décrite sur la photo – comment est-elle décrite ?

02.14

3 Listen again to the conversation between Jo and Assia and this time play the role of Jo. Then practice indicating who the members of your family are.

SKILL BUILDER

1 Complete the following sentences.

a Charles habite à ....

b Yanis.................... six ans.

c Tom .... chef cuisinier et il .... 25 ans.

d Eva .... à Bruxelles et elle .... italien, français et anglais.

2 Match the subjects to the conjugated verbs. You can use each verb once only.

a Nous	d J'	1 aimez	4 parle
b Vous	e Ils	2 parlons	5 as
c Il	f Tu	3 habite	6 aiment

3 Match the questions to the potential responses.

a Tu as quel âge ?	1 Je m'appelle Anne.
b Vous habitez où ?	2 J'ai 22 ans.
c Tu t'appelles comment ?	3 Oui, j'ai des frères et sœurs.
d Ils aiment quoi ?	4 j'habite à Lyon.
e Tu as des frères et sœurs ?	5 Ils aiment les langues.
f Et là, c'est qui ?	6 Elle s'appelle Yasmine.
g Comment s'appelle ton amie ?	7 Là, c'est mon oncle.

4 Look at the photos of people learning French with this book and read the introductions. Present the three French students using the information in each introduction and then introduce yourself to them, following the same structure.

a

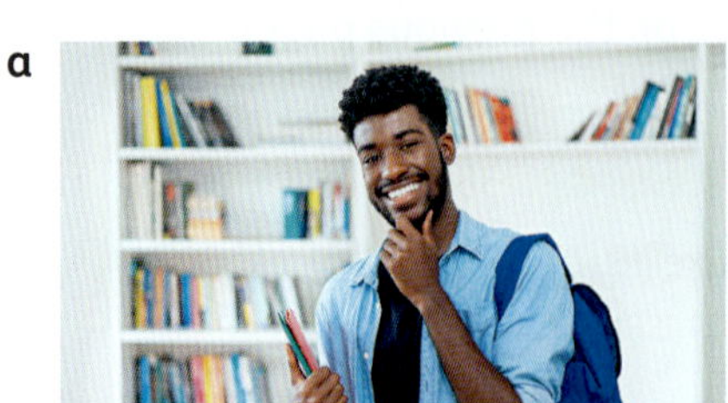

Bonjour, je m'appelle Agu. Je suis nigérien. J'ai 20 ans. Je suis étudiant en biologie à Abuja. Je parle igbo, yorouba et anglais. J'aime le cinéma et le jazz. J'ai un frère et une sœur.

b

Bonjour, je m'appelle Vitoria. Je suis ingénieure dans l'aéronautique. J'ai 36 ans. Je suis brésilienne et j'habite à São Paulo. Je parle portugais et anglais. J'ai deux enfants, João et Maria Luiza. J'aime les voyages et le football.

c

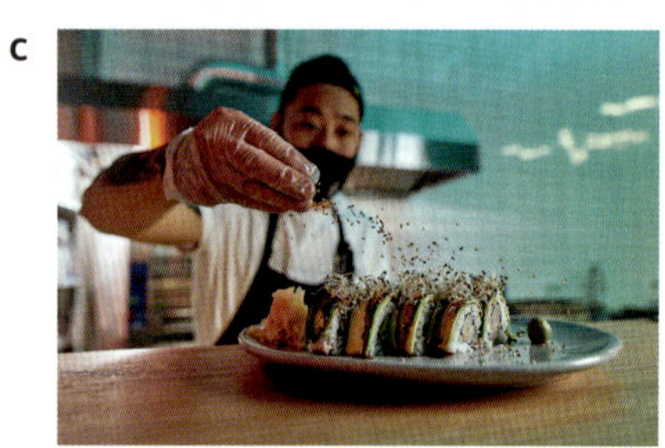

Bonjour, je m'appelle Aki. Je suis japonais. J'ai 45 ans. Je suis chef de cuisine et j'habite à Tokyo. J'ai un petit chien. Il s'appelle Yoshi. J'adore les chiens.

TEST YOURSELF

1 Complete the questions and responses.

a Que fais-tu le week-end ?
Le week-end je .... mes devoirs.

b As-tu beaucoup de devoirs ?
Oui, j'..................... beaucoup de devoirs.

c Tes parents font quoi ?
Ma mère .... un job à l'hôpital, et mon père .... un job dans un restaurant.

d Eva, ta famille aime faire du ski ?
Oui, ... famille aime faire du ski.

e Charles, tes parents aiment Paris ?
Oui, ... parents aiment beaucoup Paris.

f Nous aimons les films de Claire Denis. Toi aussi ?
Oui, c' est une grande ....

g Bjorn est ...., il travaille chez Apple. Et toi ?
Je suis .... Je travaille à l'hôpital et mon mari Marc est médecin aussi.

h La tante d'Eva travaille pour *Le Temps* à Genève ?
Oui, elle est ...., et son mari, l'..................... d'Eva, il est journaliste aussi.

Before you move on to the next unit, assess your progress using the **My review** section on the first page of the unit, and reflect on your learning experience with the **My takeaway** section available online.

3

In this lesson you will learn how to:

» Talk about your hobbies
» Say what you like and don't like doing
» Plan a day or an evening out

Les passe-temps

My study plan

I plan to work with Unit 3

○ Every day
○ Twice a week
○ Other ___________

I plan to study for

○ 5–15 minutes
○ 15–30 minutes
○ 30–45+ minutes

My progress tracker

Day / Date	Listening	Speaking	Reading	Writing	Conversation
	○	○	○	○	○
	○	○	○	○	○
	○	○	○	○	○
	○	○	○	○	○
	○	○	○	○	○
	○	○	○	○	○
	○	○	○	○	○

My goals

What do you want to be able to do or say in French when you complete this unit?

		Done
1	....	○
2	....	○
3	....	○

My review

SELF CHECK

	I can ...
●	... talk about sports.
●	... talk about music.
●	... ask questions.
●	... answer questions negatively as well as positively.

CULTURE POINT 1

Un esprit sain dans un corps sain *A healthy mind in a healthy body*

The 170-square-kilometer Forêt de Fontainebleau (*Forest of Fontainebleau*) is part of the Gâtinas regional nature park, which has a variety of geological formations and diverse wildlife. It's a wonderful stretch of wilderness to be found so near Paris. It is perfect for family outings, with areas to enjoy any of the following: l'équitation (*horse riding*), l'accrobranche (*tree climbing*), la varappe (*rock climbing*), la randonnée (*hiking*), les pique-niques (*picnics*), and more. Fontainebleau is also known for its amazing château (*castle/chateau*), which has been listed as a UNESCO World Heritage Site since 1981. The Château de Fontainebleau was used by all the French rulers from the twelfth to the nineteenth centuries. Napoleon was one of the great restorers of the Château, which now houses a museum dedicated to his reign. The castle and the Jardin royal (*Royal Garden*) are open to the public and serve as a perfect machine à remonter le temps (*time machine*), providing us with opportunities to glimpse French history in the making over 900 years. The Grand Parquet (*large stadium*) in Fontainebleau is another key attraction, as it hosts le Printemps des Sports Équestres (*the Spring of Equestrian Sports*), a great horse-riding festival to enjoy with family and friends. The local government fosters le développement durable (*sustainable development*) through its heritage attractions and its commitment to l'écotourisme (*ecotourism*), to ensure the preservation and continued development of this wonderful area.

Learn more about the Forêt de Fontainebleau. What activities can you do there?

VOCABULARY BUILDER 1

03.01

Read the words and phrases below and supply the missing English words. Then listen to the recording and imitate the pronunciation you hear.

Tu fais du sport ? *Do you play sports?*

l'alpinisme (masc.)	*mountain-climbing*
le basket	*basketball*
la pétanque	*pétanque*
le cricket	....
le cyclisme	*cycling*
les échecs	*chess*
le football	*football/soccer*
le golf	*golf*
la natation	*swimming*
la randonnée	*walking, hiking*
le ski	*skiing*
le tennis	....
le rugby	....
le volley	*volleyball*
une balle	*ball (for cricket, tennis)*
un club (de golf)	*(golf) club*
un volant	*shuttlecock*

EXPRESSIONS	***EXPRESSIONS***
L'équipe est sur le terrain.	*The team is on the field.*
Le joueur/La joueuse a le ballon.	*The player (male/female) has the ball.*
Elle fait du cheval/de l'équitation.	*She goes horseback riding.*
Elle fait de la varappe.	*She goes rock-climbing.*
Je n'aime pas trop la voile.	*I don't like sailing very much.*

> To say you practice a sport in French use je fais + du (or de la) + the name of the sport, as in je fais du tennis (*I play tennis*) or je fais de la voile (*I go sailing*). More on this to come later on.

Vocabulary practice 1

1 Match the sports on the left with the sporting equipment on the right.

a le rugby	**1** un club
b le badminton	**2** un ballon
c le tennis	**3** une balle
d le golf	**4** un volant

> French distinguishes between un ballon, an inflated ball, and une balle, a non-inflated ball. So while un ballon is used in le rugby or le football, une balle is used in le tennis or le cricket.

Pronunciation practice

03.02

Listen to the recording, and practice pronouncing the sentences. Look at the underlined words. Which final letters are a) pronounced? b) silent?

1 Vous <u>faites</u> du tennis.	*You play tennis.*
2 Nous sommes <u>joueuses</u> de football, et vous ?	*We are soccer players, and you?*
3 Mon tonton <u>fait</u> de la natation.	*My uncle goes swimming.*
4 Ils aiment le <u>tennis</u> de table.	*They like table tennis.*

CONVERSATION 1

Les activités du week-end *Weekend activities*

03.03

1 Here are some words and phrases to help you understand the conversation.

Qu'est-ce que tu as envie de faire ?	*What do you feel like doing?*	sportif, sportive	*sporty*
la musculation	*weight training*	plutôt	*rather*
l'escrime	*fencing*	de temps en temps	*from time to time*

03.04

2 Listen to the conversation a few times without looking at the text. Then listen to the conversation again and read the text.

It's Sunday, and Jo and Assia are making plans.

Assia	Salut Jo ! Qu'est-ce que tu as envie de faire ?
Jo	J'ai envie de faire du sport.
Assia	Oui, bonne idée. Quels sports est-ce que tu aimes ?
Jo	J'aime la pétanque, la musculation et j'adore l'escrime ! Et toi ?
Assia	Waouh, tu es très sportive ! Moi j'aime la voile.
Jo	Ah non, moi je n'aime pas la voile, je préfère faire du vélo.
Assia	Ah oui, j'aime bien le cyclisme ! Tu veux aller où ?
Jo	On va à la forêt de Fontainebleau ?
Assia	Génial ! On peut aussi faire de la varappe et de l'équitation à Fontainebleau.
Jo	Est-ce que tu fais du cheval ?
Assia	Oui, de temps en temps.
Jo	Moi aussi ! Alors, vélo et cheval ?
Assia	Oui, parfait, c'est un beau programme !

3 Answer the questions.

a What sports does Jo practice?
b Does Jo like sailing?
c Does Assia like cycling?
d Apart from cycling, what sports are available in Fontainebleau?
e What do Assia and Jo choose to do?

LANGUAGE BUILDER 1

Language discovery 1

In the Conversation above, Jo is curious to know whether Assia goes horse-riding. She could have asked: Tu fais du cheval ? (*Do you go horse-riding?*). But, instead, she uses a longer form: Est-ce que tu fais du cheval ? This form looks like the first question at the start of the conversation, where Assia asks Jo: Qu'est-ce que tu as envie de faire ?

Can you figure out what this opening question means?

Poser des questions *Asking questions*

As you learned in previous units, by using rising intonation you can transform a statement such as Charles est là (*Charles is there*) into a question Charles est là ? (*Is Charles there?*). An alternative way to ask a yes/no question is to use Est-ce que... ? (literally *Is it (the case) that ...?*). This phrase can be placed in front of any statement to form a question:

Est-ce que Charles est là ? *Is Charles there?*

To ask a question such as *What is Charles doing?* you can use Qu'est-ce que...? (literally *What is that ...?*): Qu'est-ce que Charles fait ? Here are some examples:

Qu'est-ce que tu fais ?	*What are you doing?*
—Je fais mes devoirs.	*—I am doing my homework.*
Est-ce que tu fais tes devoirs ?	*Are you doing your homework?*
Oui, je fais mes devoirs.	*—Yes, I am doing my homework.*
Est-ce que Jo et Assia font du cheval ?	*Are Jo and Assia riding?/Do Jo and Assia ride?*
—Oui, elles font du cheval.	*—Yes they ride/are riding.*

When followed by a word beginning with a vowel, est-ce que and qu'est-ce que lose the final e: Est-ce qu'il est à Paris ? Qu'est-ce qu'il fait ?

Language practice 1

1 Match the answers to the questions.

a Elles font du cyclisme.
b Oui, elle aime la voile, par exemple.
c Elle aime la voile.
d Non, elles font du cyclisme.

1 Qu'est-ce que Sophie aime ?
2 Est-ce qu'elles font du cheval ?
3 Est-ce que Sophie aime le sport ?
4 Qu'est-ce qu'elles font ?

2 Complete the questions using Est-ce que or Qu'est-ce qu'.

a .... Marine est là ?

b .... elle fait ?

c .... Pierre aime le football ?

d .... il fait ?

e .... il aime ? La voile ? Le tennis ?

3 Transform the sentences below into questions using Est-ce que or Est-ce qu'. The first one has been completed.

a Jean aime la voile. *Est-ce que Jean aime la voile ?*
b Béatrice et Marc aiment l'équitation.
c Vous aimez faire du ski.
d Ils aiment aller au restaurant le week-end.
e Leïla aime le golf.

LANGUAGE BUILDER 2

Language discovery 2

03.05

Listen to the conversation again and repeat each line in the pauses provided. Try to imitate the phrasing and intonation you hear. In the conversation you heard Jo say Je n'aime pas la voile, which means *I don't like sailing*.

How would you say *I like sailing* in French? Compare the positive and negative statements: what is the difference between them? Can you see how a positive sentence becomes negative?

La négation *Negative statements*

In English, we can form negative statements by using the word *not*: e.g. *Henriette is not* (= *isn't*) *there*. In written French, two words are necessary to express *not*: ne + pas. Ne usually comes before the verb and pas immediately follows it: Henriette n'est pas là. So, the order of words in this kind of sentence is: subject + ne + verb + pas. Note, too, that (as in this example) ne is contracted to n' if it precedes a vowel (or a non-aspirate h). Here are some more examples of negative sentences:

Je ne suis pas irlandaise.	*I am not Irish.*
Tu n'es pas étudiante ?	*You are not a student?*
Elle n'a pas 21 ans.	*She is not 21.*
Nous ne faisons pas nos devoirs.	*We are not doing our homework.*
Vous n'allez pas au restaurant.	*You are not going to the restaurant.*
Ils n'ont pas beaucoup de temps.	*They don't have much time.*

Language practice 2

1 Fill in the gaps to create negative sentences and questions, using ne and pas as necessary.

a Je n'aime .... le golf.
b Elle .... aime pas les chocolats.
c Vous .... allez .... au cinéma ce soir ?
d Ils .... travaillent .... le samedi.

2 Transform the negative sentences below into positive ones.

a Elle ne va pas au cinéma.
b Il ne mange pas au restaurant.
c Isabelle n'aime pas la voile.
d Béatrice et sa sœur n'aiment pas le football.

3 Transform the positive sentences into negative ones.

a Elle va au match de football.
b Ils mangent au restaurant.
c Milou travaille le week-end.
d Ismaël habite à Lyon.

4 Answer each of the following questions in the negative.

a Est-ce que tu aimes jouer au cricket ?
b Est-ce qu'Eva est française ?
c Est-ce que Charles habite à Marseille ?
d Est-ce qu'ils travaillent le week-end ?

03.06

5 Now play the conversation again and play Assia's role. Speak in the pauses. Try not to refer to the text.

CULTURE POINT 2

Les nocturnes des musées *Museums by night*

Belgium was home to some of the biggest names in Art Nouveau and their legacy is everywhere in the city. Look out for the trademark curves and flourishes in wood, metal, and stained glass, as well as ornate mosaics. Le musée Horta (*The Horta Museum*) is located in the private house and studio of Victor Horta (1861–1947), in Brussels. It was built between 1898 and 1901 at 23–25 rue Américaine in the Saint-Gilles district, and is typical of Art Nouveau at its height. For music lovers Le musée des Instruments de Musique known as MIM (*The Musical Instruments Museum*) has a prodigious collection of over 1,200 instruments Musicaux (*musical instruments*) including the oldest saxophone created by the Belgian Adolphe Sax who patented le saxophone in 1846. The MIM also offers wonderful lunchtime concerts in a Greek-style salle de concert (*concert hall*) which allows for an intimate performance and connection between le public et les artistes (*public and artists*). Every year for Museum Night Fever more than 30 museums in Brussels stay open past midnight and host special events. And, of course, there are the famous afterparties.

Explore the Nocturnes des musées bruxellois website. Can you find the museums mentioned above? Which museums would you like to visit if you go?

VOCABULARY BUILDER 2

Look at the words and phrases and provide the missing English words and expressions. Then listen and try to imitate the pronunciation of the speakers.

La musique *Music*

LES INSTRUMENTS À CORDES	***STRINGED INSTRUMENTS***
une guitare	*guitar*
un sitar	....
un violon	*violin*
LES INSTRUMENTS À VENT	***WIND INSTRUMENTS***
une clarinette	*clarinet*
une cornemuse	*bagpipes*
une flûte	....
un saxophone	....
une trompette	....
LES INSTRUMENTS À PERCUSSION	***PERCUSSION INSTRUMENTS***
des cymbales (fem.)	*cymbals*
un triangle	....
un xylophone	....
LES INSTRUMENTS À CLAVIER	***KEYBOARD INSTRUMENTS***
un accordéon	....
un piano	....
un orgue	*organ*
EXPRESSIONS	***EXPRESSIONS***
C'est original !	*That's unusual!*
J'aime les visites mystères.	*I like mystery tours.*
Nous aimons le jazz.	*We like jazz.*
C'est mon musée préféré !	*It's my favorite museum!*
Le musée est ouvert toute la nuit.	*The museum is open all night long.*
le Musée Mode et Dentelle	*the Museum of Fashion and Lace*

Vocabulary practice 2

Match the names of the following instruments with their definitions to form sentences:

1 La flûte est...
2 La guitare est...
3 Les cymbales sont...
4 Le piano est...

a un instrument à percussion.
b un instrument à vent.
c un instrument à clavier.
d un instrument à cordes.

CONVERSATION 2

On sort ce soir ? *Shall we go out tonight?*

03.08

1 Listen to the conversation without looking at the text. Then listen to the conversation again and read the text.

Charles and Eva are making plans for the famous Nuit des Musées in Brussels. Where do they decide to go?

Charles	Salut Eva, c'est La Nuit des Musées cette semaine, tu as envie d'aller au musée ?
Eva	Ben oui, pourquoi pas ! Quel est le programme ?
Charles	Il y a une visite mystère du Musée de la Bande Dessinée.
Eva	Super ! Et quoi d'autre ?
Charles	Un concert de musique contemporaine au Musée des Instruments de Musique.
Eva	Bof ! Tu aimes la musique classique, toi ?
Charles	Oui, je joue de la trompette et j'adore aller au concert. Et toi, tu joues d'un instrument de musique ?
Eva	Oui, je joue de la cornemuse et du piano.
Charles	C'est original ! Il y a aussi une performance au Musée Mode et Dentelle.
Eva	Ah oui ? C'est mon musée préféré ! Qu'est-ce que nous faisons alors ?
Charles	Nous visitons le musée de la mode et le musée de la BD ?
Eva	C'est possible ?
Charles	Oui, les musées sont ouverts toute la nuit !
Eva	Formidable !

2 Answer the questions.

- **a** What is la Nuit des Musées?
- **b** Which museums does Charles mention?
- **c** Which instruments do Charles and Eva play?
- **d** What is happening at the Musée de la Bande dessinée?
- **e** What do they decide?

LANGUAGE BUILDER 3

Language discovery 3

Here are a few extracts from Conversation 2. Can you fill in the missing word in each of the extracts?

When planning their evening Eva asks Charles Quel est **a** .... programme ? (*What's the plan?*) and whether he likes **b** .... musique classique (*classical music*). Charles answers that he does, and also expresses an interest in **c** .... bande dessinée (*the comic strip*). Finally, Charles confirms that **d** .... musées (*the museums*) are open all night.

Do you see a parallel between, on the one hand, le, la, and les, and, on the other hand, un, une, and des, which you have learned about in previous units? Do you think the difference between le and la might be the same as the difference between un and une?

The definite article: le, la, les

To say *I like the piano* in French, you would say j'aime le piano. You may have noticed that there are several ways to say *the* in French, depending on the noun that follows: le, la, and les. As you might have guessed, the article agrees in gender and number with the noun.

masculine singular	feminine singular	plural
le	la	les
le piano	la guitare	les cymbales

Notice that le or la is shortened to l' when used with a noun that begins with a vowel: j'aime l'accordéon.

The, along with its French equivalents le, la, and les, is known as *the definite article* because it's used to refer to something already known to the speaker or is a specific instance, i.e. something *definite* or *defined*. Compare the use of the indefinite and definite articles:

Il y a un concert ce soir. — *There's a concert tonight.*

Le concert est au musée. — *The concert is at the museum.*

Its usage is very similar to English, but sometimes the definite article is used in French where it would not be used in English, such as when referring to a general category:

J'aime la musique. — *I like music.*

J'aime les chocolats. — *I like chocolates.*

Language practice 3

1 Complete the sentences with the appropriate definite article : le, la, l', or les.

- **a** Sophie n'aime pas .... musique classique.
- **b** Est-ce que maman aime .... nougat ?
- **c** C'est bien ! .... joueuses et joueurs de football sont là.
- **d** Moi, j'aime .... alpinisme, et toi ?

2 Below you will find a passage in English followed by an incomplete French translation. Complete the sentences using un/une/des or le/la/les, as needed.

Jo likes classical music a lot. Assia prefers jazz. This evening, there is a concert in town. On the programme there are classical artists and jazz artists. The two friends are happy!

Jo aime beaucoup .... musique classique. Assia préfère .... jazz. Ce soir, il y a .... concert en ville. Au programme il y a .... artistes classiques et .... artistes jazz. .... deux amies sont contentes !

LANGUAGE BUILDER 4

Language discovery 4

03.09

Listen to the conversation again and repeat each line in the pauses provided. Try to imitate the phrasing and intonation you hear.

If you want to talk about playing a musical instrument in French, you need to use jouer (*to play*) + de + the name of the instrument. For example, in Conversation 2, Charles says je joue de la trompette (*I play the trumpet*). But when he asks Eva if she plays an instrument, she replies je joue de la cornemuse et du piano (*I play the bagpipes and the piano*).

Try to figure out where the word du comes from in Eva's answer by filling in the gaps to complete the rule:

in French, we never use **a** .... followed by le. Instead we use a single word: **b** ....

Jouer à ou jouer de ? *To play*

As in English, in French you can **jouer** (play) a sport or a musical instrument. However, the preposition changes. While you use jouer **de** to talk about playing a musical instrument, to talk about playing a competitive game you need to use jouer **à**.

Je joue à la pétanque.	*I play pétanque.*
Je joue au tennis.	*I play tennis.*
Elle joue du piano et elles jouent de la guitare.	*She plays the piano and they play the guitar.*

It is important to note that you should never use de followed by le. Instead, you should use the shorter form du. This explains why *I play the piano* is je joue du piano. Similarly, you should never use à followed by le, but use the shorter form au instead. For instance, *I go to the supermarket* is je vais au supermarché (where au replaces à + le). To remember this, you can learn the following rule by heart: à plus le becomes au, and de plus le becomes du. For examples, see the following table, which also shows the plural forms aux and des:

Preposition + definite article ...	... results in ...	Example
à + la	à la	Je vais à la fête de la musique.
à + le	au	Je vais au musée.
à + les	aux	Je joue aux échecs.
de + la	de la	Je joue de la guitare.
de + le	du	Je joue du piano.
de + les	des	Je joue des cymbales.

Language practice 4

1 Complete the sentences with the appropriate preposition.

a Nous jouons .... violon.

b Tu joues .... football.

c Elle joue .... clarinette.

d Elles jouent .... pétanque.

e Ils jouent .... air hockey.

f Je joue .... orgue.

g Vous jouez .... cymbales.

h Ils jouent .... échecs.

03.10

2 Now play the conversation again and play Eva's role. Speak in the pauses. Try not to refer to the text.

SKILL BUILDER

1 The announcement below is posted in the student union at a university. Read it and answer the questions that follow.

a What part of the university is being advertised?
b Which activities are listed?
c Sort the activities based on whether they take le, la, or l'.
d What do you need to do to obtain more information or register?

03.11

2 Listen to the recording of three sample conversations between two friends talking about sports. Imagine what questions you would ask a friend in order for them to give you the answers you hear after the three mini dialogues below.

Dialogue 1:	**Dialogue 2:**	**Dialogue 3:**
Est-ce que tu fais du sport ?	Est-ce que tu aimes le football ?	Tu aimes la natation ?
Oui, je fais du yoga, et toi ?	Oui, j'adore le football, et toi ?	Non, je n'aime pas l'eau.
Moi, je fais de la natation.	Moi, je préfère le basket.	Dommage, moi j'adore.

Q: .... ?

Oui, je fais du vélo à la Forêt de Fontainebleau.

Q: .... ?

Oui, c'est vrai, j'adore l'escalade.

Q: .... ?

Non, je n'aime pas la natation.

TEST YOURSELF

1 Complete the sentences on the left with words from the list on the right, then translate each sentence into English:

a Ils .... du piano.	**1** jouent
b Vous .... des chocolats.	**2** Qu'est-ce qu'
c Tu fais de l' .... ?	**3** équitation
d .... elles font ? Elles jouent de la guitare.	**4** varappe
e Je fais de la .... à Fontainebleau.	**5** faites
f .... ? Oui !	**6** cornemuse
g Eva joue de la	**7** Est-ce que tu fais tes devoirs
h Assia et Jo aiment le	**8** cyclisme

2 Complete the sentences using the translations provided to guide you.

a .... tu aimes faire le weekend ? J'aime .... football.
What do you like doing on the weekend? I like to play football.

b Avez-vous .... piano à la maison ? Oui, nous avons .... piano de notre grand-père.
Do you have a piano at home? Yes we have our grandfather's piano.

c .... tu veux jouer .... ce soir ? Oui, je veux jouer .... ce soir.
Do you want to play basketball tonight? Yes, I want to play basketball tonight.

d .... Jo et Assia font de l'équitation ? Oui, elles font .... cheval.
Do Jo and Assia go horseback riding? Yes, they go horseback rising.

e Je travaille .... hôpital, je .... infirmier et .... 30 ans. Je .... aime pas .... football et je .... joue .... du piano mais j'aime .... tennis et j'aime jouer .... guitare.
I work at the hospital, I am a nurse, and I am 30 years old. I don't like football and I don't play the piano. I do like tennis and I like to play the guitar.

Before you move on to the next unit, assess your progress using the **My review** section on the first page of the unit, and reflect on your learning experience with the **My takeaway** section available online.

4

In this lesson you will learn how to:

» Talk about your neighborhood
» Talk about your food shopping
» Give directions
» Give and understand commands

Chez soi en ville

My study plan

I plan to work with Unit 4

○ Every day
○ Twice a week
○ Other ______

I plan to study for

○ 5–15 minutes
○ 15–30 minutes
○ 30–45+ minutes

My progress tracker

Day / Date	Listening	Speaking	Reading	Writing	Conversation
	○	○	○	○	○
	○	○	○	○	○
	○	○	○	○	○
	○	○	○	○	○
	○	○	○	○	○
	○	○	○	○	○
	○	○	○	○	○

My goals

What do you want to be able to do or say in French when you complete this unit?

		Done
1	....	○
2	....	○
3	....	○

My review

SELF CHECK

	I can ...
●	... give directions.
●	... give a command.
●	... talk about what is in my city.
●	... talk about my food shopping.

CULTURE POINT 1

Bruxelles : capitale de la bande dessinée (BD) *Brussels: comic strip capital*

Belgium has a rich tradition of albums BD (*comic strip albums*), nourished by teams of writers and illustrators working mainly in French or Flemish. In Brussels this tradition is celebrated both by the existence of a magnificent Musée de la BD (*Comic Strip Museum*) and by the Parcours BD (*Comic Strip Route*) through the city. Among the most famous créateurs de BD (*comic-strip creators*) is Georges Rémi, who used his inverted initials to form his penname Hergé (pronounced like the French letters **r** + **g**). The Parcours BD includes a huge fresco of Hergé's most famous characters, Tintin, le capitaine Haddock, and Milou (*Snowy* in English editions), an intrepid little fox terrier. Hergé's characters make an appearance in different parts of the city; in the Parcours you can find them at rue de l'Étuve 37. Brussels Airlines has created a painted fleet of Airbuses depicting iconic images related to the city's history of BDs. Their first was named *Rackham* after *Red Rackham's Treasure*. Many other artistes (*artists*) have adapted the ligne claire (*clear outline*) style associated with Hergé; others have become established using different styles which continue to evolve. While Hergé is symbolic of the traditional, male-dominated world of BDs, 2015 saw the foundation of Le Collectif des créatrices de bande dessinée contre le sexisme (*Collective of Female Comic Strip Creators Opposed to Sexism*). Aurélie Neyret is an illustratrice (*female illustrator*) whose series of albums Les Carnets de Cerise (*Cici's Journal*) has received critical acclaim. Her work is represented in the Parcours at the rue des Trois Pertuis 4.

Watch the following video and search for the French names of the famous comic characters.

VOCABULARY BUILDER 1

Read the words and phrases below and supply the missing English words and expressions. Then listen to the recording and repeat each word/expression.

Naviguer la ville *Getting around town*

PAYSAGE URBAIN	*CITYSCAPE*
un arrêt de bus	*bus stop*
une banque	....
une bibliothèque	*library*
une boucherie	*butcher's*
une boulangerie (bio)	*(organic) bakery*
une charcuterie	*delicatessen*
une épicerie	*grocery store/shop*
une fromagerie	*cheesemonger's, cheese shop*
une librairie	*bookshop*
un magasin de fleurs	*florist's*
un parc	....
la poste	....
une poissonnerie	*fishmonger's*
un salon de coiffure	*hair salon*
un supermarché	....

PRODUITS	*PRODUCTS*
le lait	*milk*
le pain	*bread*

EXPRESSIONS	*EXPRESSIONS*
Il y a beaucoup de produits.	*There are many products.*
y compris	*including*
Quand on a besoin d'argent/de fromage/ de viande...	*When one needs money/cheese/meat ...*
Quand on cherche un livre/un bouquet...	*When one is looking for a book/a bouquet ...*
Quand on veut une baguette...	*When one wants a baguette ...*
C'est vrai !	*That's right (lit. true)!*
Tu as raison.	*You are right.*
Qu'est-ce qu'il manque ?	*What is missing?*
C'est ça.	*That's it.*

The personal pronoun on (*one*) takes the same endings as il or elle: for instance, *she speaks* is elle parle, and *one speaks* is on parle. However, unlike the English *one*, on is used widely in French as an alternative to other pronouns such as *we*, provided that the context makes it clear who you are talking about. So, *Are we going to the supermarket?* might become On va au supermarché ?

Vocabulary practice 1

Complete the sentences below. The first one has been completed for you.

a Quand on a besoin d'argent, on va à la *banque*.

b Quand on cherche un ...., on va à la bibliothèque.

c Quand on a besoin de viande, on va dans une ....

d Quand on a besoin de ...., on va dans une fromagerie.

e Quand on veut une baguette on va dans une ....

f Quand on cherche un ...., on va dans un magasin de fleurs.

Pronunciation practice 1

Listen to the recording of the passage below. Then read out the passage, imitating the pronunciation of the speaker. Do you notice a difference in the pronunciation of the masculine and feminine words for professions?

Mme Lebrun est fromagère, et son mari est fromager. Dans une fromagerie, il y a beaucoup de fromage.

Monsieur Lamadon est épicier, et sa femme est épicière. Il y a beaucoup de produits dans une épicerie, y compris des épices.

Practice saying the following words you just heard:

le fromage	*cheese*
la fromagerie	*cheesemonger's*
le fromager	*cheesemonger* (male)
la fromagère	*cheesemonger* (female)
l'épice	*spice*
l'épicerie	*grocery store/shop*
l'épicier	*grocer* (male)
l'épicière	*grocer* (female)

CONVERSATION 1

Dans ma rue, il y a... *In my street, there is ...*

04.03

1 Here are a few words and expressions to understand the conversation.

alors	*well, so*	même	*even*	derrière	*behind*
à côté de	*next to*	après	*after*	par contre	*however*
déjà	*already*				

04.04

2 Listen to the conversation without looking at the text. Then listen to the conversation again and read the text.

The Mairie de Paris (*City of Paris*) is asking the inhabitants of Jo's street what service or shop they would like to see on the ground floor of the new city housing building which is being planned. Assia and Jo are listing the existing shops to find out what is missing before answering the consultation survey.

Jo Alors, euh.... à côté de chez moi, il y a déjà une boulangerie.

Assia Oui, il y a au moins deux ou trois boulangeries, et même une boulangerie bio.

Jo C'est vrai, tu as raison. Il y a aussi un bureau de poste.

Assia Et à côté de la poste, il y a une banque.

Jo Et aussi, une charcuterie, une poissonnerie et une fromagerie. J'ai faim chaque fois que je passe devant.

Assia Et un salon de coiffure.

Jo Un café et des restaurants.

Assia Qu'est-ce qu'il manque ? Est-ce qu'il y a un magasin de fleurs ?

Jo Oui, après le restaurant indien.

Assia Ah oui, c'est vrai ! Et une épicerie ?

Jo Oui, derrière l'arrêt de bus.

Assia Mais oui !!! Euhhhh... un parc ?

Jo Oui, avant le cinéma Alice Guy. Par contre, il manque une librairie.

Assia C'est ça ! Il manque une librairie !

3 Answer the questions.

a Is there a bakery in Jo's street?
b List all the other food stores in Jo's street.
c Is there a florist in Jo's street?
d What can you find behind the bus stop?
e What can you find before you get to the cinema/movie theater?
f What's missing in Jo's street?

Alice Guy is known as the first female filmmaker. Follow the link to find out more about this amazing pioneer.

LANGUAGE BUILDER 1

Language discovery 1

1 In the conversation, how many times do Jo and Assia use the expression il y a?

2 What does il y a mean?

Il y a *There is, there are …*

In the Conversation you heard the expression il y a being used several times, for example: il y a une boulangerie and il y a au moins deux ou trois boulangeries. If we wanted to say the same thing in English, we would say *there is a bakery/there are at least two or three bakeries*. So we need only one expression in French where in English we need two! You will often see il y a followed by un/une/des. Using this information, complete the translation of each sentence below and see if you can explain why we need to use un, une, or des.

a Il y a .... à côté de chez moi. *There is a bakery next to my house.*

b Il y a .... derrière le supermarché ? *There are banks behind the supermarket?*

c Il y a .... après le cinéma. *There is a park after the cinema.*

d Il y a .... avant l'arrêt de bus. *There are hair salons before the bus stop.*

Language practice 1

1 Complete each sentence below by inserting one of the words on the right.

a J'ai envie de lire un roman. Est-ce qu'il y a une .... ?

b Dans ma rue il y a un ....

c À Lyon, il y a plusieurs ....

d Dans le centre ville, ... deux magasins de ....

1 parcs

2 il y a

3 fleurs

4 supermarché

5 bibliothèque

Many words in English and French are very similar to one another, for example cinéma and *cinema*. Others look similar but have different meanings—for example, a librairie is a *bookshop* and a bibliothèque is a *library*. We refer to these words as faux amis (*false friends*).

2 Translate the questions below.

a Est-ce qu'il y a une boulangerie ?

b Est-ce qu'il y a deux boulangeries ?

c Est-ce qu'il y a un bureau de poste ?

d Est-ce qu'il y a deux bureaux de poste ?

LANGUAGE BUILDER 2

Language discovery 2

04.05

Listen to the conversation again and repeat each line in the pauses provided. Try to imitate the phrasing and intonation you hear.

1 **Jo states that there is a grocery store derrière (*behind*) the bus stop. Can you find out other words in the conversation that help to explain where one thing is in relation to another?**

2 **From the context of the conversation can you provide the English for these words:** **a** après **b** avant **c** à côté de

Donner des directions *Giving directions*

Prepositions of place are used to indicate the position of things or people in relation to something or someone.

Ma sœur est à côté de mon frère et ils sont devant la librairie. — *My sister is next to my brother and they are in front of the bookshop.*

Some prepositions of place are followed by de which means that you may need to modify de and make it into du (de + le) or des (de + les). For example:

Les enfants sont près des jets d'eau de la fontaine. — *The children are near the jets of water of the fountain.*

Here are some other common prepositions of place:

sur ta gauche	*on your left*	sur ta droite	*on your right*
tout droit	*straight ahead*	loin de	*far from*
près de	*near to*	devant	*in front of*
derrière	*behind*	sur	*on top of*

Indicate which of the four sentences below could not describe any of the images.

a Les deux enfants sont près de la fontaine.
b Un enfant est sur la fontaine et l'autre enfant est devant la fontaine.
c Un enfant est loin de la fontaine et l'autre enfant est près de la fontaine.
d Les deux enfants sont devant la fontaine.

Language practice 2

1 Complete the sentences by inserting a preposition of place based on the Conversation.

a L'épicerie est .... l'arrêt de bus.

b La banque est .... la poste.

c Le magasin de fleurs est .... le restaurant indien.

d Le parc est .... le cinéma Alice Guy.

04.06

2 Listen to Charles explain where various stores are located in and around his quartier (*neighborhood*), and then respond to questions 3 and 4.

Charles	Alors, on va faire un petit tour du centre-ville ?
Jo	Oui, volontiers.
Charles	J'ai besoin de faire quelques courses. Je voudrais acheter du pain, du vin et des fleurs.
Jo	Et moi, je voudrais aller à la librairie.
Charles	Très bien.
Jo	Et tes courses ?
Charles	C'est facile. La librairie est à côté du supermarché.
Jo	Et... Il est où, le parc ?
Charles	Il est tout près, pas loin du supermarché.
Jo	Génial ! Et on rentre chez toi en bus ?
Charles	Oui, l'arrêt de bus est près de la librairie.
Jo	Super ! On y va ?
Charles	Oui, allons-y !

3 Indicate which of the following statements are true and which are false.

a The bookshop is quite close to the bus stop.	vrai	faux
b The bookshop is next to the supermarket.	vrai	faux
c The supermarket is a long way from the park.	vrai	faux

4 Complete these sentences based on what you heard.

a La librairie est .... supermarché.

b Le parc n'est pas .... supermarché.

c L'arrêt de bus est .... librairie.

04.07

5 Now play Conversation 1 again and play Jo's role. Speak in the pauses. Try not to refer to the text.

CULTURE POINT 2

L'Escargot parisien *The Parisian Snail*

Paris is variously referred to as the capital de la mode (*of fashion*), de la cuisine (*of cuisine*), or des lumières (*of light*). Each arrondissement (*city district*) has its micro-culture, each avenue its claim to fame, each street and each coin de rue (*street corner*) its fans. Paris is often spoken of as though it were divided into two main areas by la Seine (*the river Seine*). La Rive gauche (*the Left Bank*), to the south, is the more bohemian, fostering art and creation. It boasts la tour Eiffel (*the Eiffel Tower*) and le Quartier latin (*the Latin Quarter*). La Rive droite (*the Right Bank*) is traditionally seen as being quite elegant and formal, with the Champs-Elysées being its most famous avenue. The cathedral of Notre-Dame de Paris is situated on l'Île de la Cité, a small island on the Seine. The city is divided into 20 numbered arrondissements. Each of these can be referred to by its official number (1–20), or by a name associated with the district. For example, the 9th arrondissement is called le quartier de l'Opéra (*the Opera Quarter*), after the Opéra Garnier that stands at its center. Les arrondissements are arranged and numbered in a spiral pattern, affectionately known as l'Escargot (*the Snail*). Street signs include a reference to the arrondissement as well as the name of the rue (*street*). This is not the only time that the humble mollusk has lent its form to physical structures in the Hexagon. Lyon, the third-largest city in France and the former capitale des Gaules (*capital of the Gauls*), is famous for its escaliers en colimaçon (*spiral staircases*).

Visit Maps-Paris. What monuments can you see in the 7th arrondissement?

VOCABULARY BUILDER 2

Read the words and phrases below and supply the missing English words and expressions. Then listen to the recording and imitate the pronunciation you hear.

Ma ville *My city*

ESPACES URBAINS	*CITY SPACES*
un carrefour	*intersection/crossroads*
une fontaine	*fountain*
une gare	*train station*
un jardin public	*public garden*
un parking	*parking lot/car park*
un passage piétons	*crosswalk/pedestrian crossing*
une piscine	*swimming pool*
une place	*square*
un quartier	*district*
une rue	*street*
un square	....
une église	*church*
une mosquée	....
une synagogue	....

EXPRESSIONS	*EXPRESSIONS*
Quand j'ai envie de nager...	*When I feel like swimming ...*
utiliser un passage piétons	*to use a pedestrian crossing*
Il y a beaucoup de verdure.	*There is a lot of greenery.*
par exemple	*for example/for instance*
près d'ici	*near here/nearby*
Je note.	*I'm taking notes./I'm writing it down.*
Comment ça s'écrit ?	*How is it spelled?*
C'est bon.	*All good./It's fine.*
Tu plaisantes ?	*You're joking?*
Devine mon âge !	*Guess my age!*

Vocabulary practice 2

Complete the sentences with words and phrases from the Vocabulary builder.

a Quand j'ai envie de nager, je cherche une ....

b Quand je traverse la rue, je préfère utiliser un ....

c Pardon, Monsieur ! Il y a un .... de bus près d'ici, s'il vous plaît ?

Pronunciation practice 2

04.09

In the Vocabulary builder there are several words and phrases which are easy to translate because they are similar to English words and phrases. These include une banque, un cinéma, un parking. To practice saying these words as French speakers do, listen to the recording and imitate the pronunciation you hear.

Il y a une banque   il y a un cinéma   il y a un parking

CONVERSATION 2

Les directions *Directions*

04.10

1 Here are some expressions you will hear in the conversation.

Pour venir chez moi...	*To come to my place ...*	la première rue	*the first street*
jusqu'à la fin	*until the end*	à votre gauche	*on your left*
au bout de	*at the end of*	péchés mignons	*guilty pleasures*
environ	*approximately*		

04.11

2 Listen to the conversation without looking at the text. Then listen to the conversation again and read the text.

Jo and Assia are visiting Brussels. Having arrived at the Gare du Midi, Jo calls her brother to find out how she and Assia can walk from the train station to his apartment.

Charles Pour venir chez moi à pied, sortez de la Gare du Midi et demandez la rue d'Angleterre. Prenez la rue d'Angleterre jusqu'à la fin.

Jo Je note : à la sortie de la gare, rue d'Angleterre.

Charles Oui, c'est ça. Au bout de la rue d'Angleterre, vous prenez la rue Blaes.

Jo Comment ça s'écrit ?

Charles B, L, A, E, S.

Jo Ok.

Charles Continuez tout droit. Après un kilomètre environ, tournez à droite dans la rue Notre Seigneur.

Jo Notre Seigneur.

Charles C'est ça. Au bout de la rue Notre Seigneur, tournez à gauche, dans la rue Haute. Puis vous prenez la rue des Chandeliers, c'est la première rue à droite.

Jo Rue Haute et rue des Chandeliers.

Charles Puis vous tournez à gauche dans la rue de la Samaritaine, et le numéro 25 est à votre gauche. C'est bon ?

Jo Oui, c'est bon ... Et bien sûr, j'ai des cadeaux de la part de maman !

Charles	C'est quoi ?
Jo	Devine !
Charles	Du nougat et de la guimauve ?
Jo	Oui, bien sûr. Tes péchés mignons !

3 Answer the questions.

a What is the first street which Charles tells Jo and Assia to take?

b Once they have reached the end of rue Notre Seigneur, what street should they take?

c What treats is Jo bringing for Charles?

LANGUAGE BUILDER 3

Language discovery 3

1 Look at Conversation 2 again and find examples of how Charles directs Jo and Assia on how to reach his apartment.

a What form of the verb does he use?

b Which word that typically accompanies a verb is missing?

2 In the following examples, indicate which two sound like an order or instruction:

a Vous parlez français ?   b Parlez !   c Tournez à gauche.   d Vous tournez à gauche.

Donner des instructions et des ordres *Giving instructions and commands*

The *indicative form* is how we refer to verbs used in a sentence such as Je chante (*I sing*), Nous sommes là (*We're there*), or Vous jouez à la pétanque ? (*Do you play pétanque?*). In both languages there is another form of the verb, the *imperative*, which can be used to invite or order someone to do something. (The word *imperative* literally means *giving a command.*) In the case of -er verbs, the imperative typically takes one of three forms, corresponding to tu, vous, and nous.

Look at the table and decide which two imperative forms are identical to the simple statements? And which form is different? (See the answer beneath the table.)

Statement		Imperative	
Tu regardes.	*You look/are looking.*	Regarde !	*Look!*
Vous regardez.	*You look/are looking.*	Regardez !	*Look!*
Nous regardons.	*We look/are looking.*	Regardons.	*Let's look.*

In the imperative, the nous and the vous form are unchanged but the tu form drops the -s.

Language practice 3

1 Complete the table.

	Imperative: **tu form**	*Imperative:* **vous form**	*Imperative:* **nous form**
écouter (*to listen*)	écoute	**a**	écoutons
arrêter (*to stop*)	arrête	arrêtez	**b** ....
rester (*to remain*)	**c**	restez	**d** ....

2 Indicate which examples are in the imperative.

a Arrêtons de travailler.
b Est-ce que vous restez ?
c Tu habites au Québec ?
d Nous allons à la banque.
e Parle en français, s'il te plaît.
f Parlez en français, s'il vous plaît.
g Vous parlez français.
h Arrête de jouer tout de suite !
i Tu es marrante.

LANGUAGE BUILDER 4

Language discovery 4

04.12

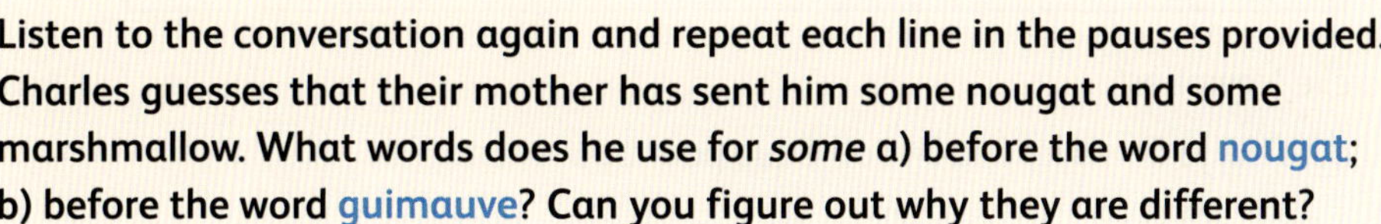

Listen to the conversation again and repeat each line in the pauses provided. Charles guesses that their mother has sent him some nougat and some marshmallow. What words does he use for *some* a) before the word nougat; b) before the word guimauve? Can you figure out why they are different?

L'article partitif *The partitive article*

In French and in English, words that refer to things that can be counted are called *countable nouns* and can be preceded by a number, e.g., baguette and orange (we can buy deux baguettes or six oranges). There are also *uncountable nouns*. Often these are preceded by the word *some* in English. For instance, we can buy *some bread*, *some flour*, or *some water*. In French, *some* is expressed using a partitive article. Study the table below.

	Before a consonant	Before a vowel
Masculine	du pain (*bread*)	de l'argent (*money*)
Feminine	de la farine (*flour*)	de l'eau (*water*)

In negative statements and with the phrases avoir besoin de (*to need*), avoir envie de (*to want*), and avoir beaucoup de (*to have a lot of*), the following forms are generally used:

Je n'ai pas d'argent. — *I don't have any money.*
J'ai besoin de fromage. — *I need some cheese.*

J'ai beaucoup de beurre. — *I have a lot of butter.*

Language practice 4

1 Complete each sentence below with the words in the box.

chocolats	farine	eau	lait

a Les plantes ont besoin d'.................... .

b Mon chat Mistipouf veut du ....

c Charles fait des .... ?

d Je fais un gâteau pour maman ; est-ce que tu as de la .... ?

04.13

2 Now play the conversation again and play Charles's role. Speak in the pauses. Try not to refer to the text.

SKILL BUILDER

1 Complete the sentences with words from the box then translate each sentence into English.

livre	illustratrice	épicier	loin	vingt	du
café	beurre	écoutons	voulons	banque	

a Aurélie Neyret est ....

b Aujourd'hui je dois aller à la bibliothèque pour trouver un ....

c J'ai besoin d'argent – tu veux aller à la .... avec moi ?

d Nous faisons nos courses chez l'.................... .

e Nous .... acheter du pain avant le dîner.

f Est-ce que la librairie est .... de ta maison ?

g Il y a .... arrondissements à Paris.

h .... de la musique ce soir.

i Au petit déjeuner je prends .... pain avec du .... et un ....

2 Using a map of your hometown, give directions on how to go from the post office to the police station and then to the bus station.

3 Imagine you are creating a virtual town as part of an online game. Describe the town. What types of shops and services do you want to have on a central street? You may want to listen to the Conversations in this unit and the Vocabulary builders again to refresh your memory.

TEST YOURSELF

Complete the sentences using the translations to guide you.

a Dans une ville il y a normalement ....
In a city there are usually banks, bookstores, cinemas, parks, and supermarkets.

b Oui, dans mon quartier .... aussi une grande .... et une belle ....
Yes, in my neighborhood there is also a large bookstore and a beautiful bakery.

c Et il y a aussi un grand parc ....
And there is also a large park next to the library.

d Est-ce que vous .... le week-end ?
Do you go to the movies on the weekend?

e Oui, surtout parce que le cinéma .... de notre ....
Yes, especially because the movie theater/cinema is close to our house.

f .... et allons au cinéma maintenant.
Let's stop working and let's go to the movie theater/cinema now.

g Quelle bonne idée ! Et j'ai même .... chocolats et .... eau !
What a great idea! And I even have some chocolates and water.

Before you move on to the next unit, assess your progress using the **My review** section on the first page of the unit, and reflect on your learning experience with the **My takeaway** section available online.

In this lesson you will learn how to:

- Talk about everyday actions
- Make short-term plans
- Plan short-distance travel
- Indicate preferences between near and distant objects

Les projets du week-end

My study plan

I plan to work with Unit 5

- ○ Every day
- ○ Twice a week
- ○ Other ___________

I plan to study for

- ○ 5–15 minutes
- ○ 15–30 minutes
- ○ 30–45+ minutes

My progress tracker

Day / Date	Listening	Speaking	Reading	Writing	Conversation
	○	○	○	○	○
	○	○	○	○	○
	○	○	○	○	○
	○	○	○	○	○
	○	○	○	○	○
	○	○	○	○	○
	○	○	○	○	○

My goals

What do you want to be able to do or say in French when you complete this unit?

		Done
1	....	○
2	....	○
3	....	○

My review

SELF CHECK

	I can ...
●	... give information about my personal routine.
●	... describe my journey to work/school.
●	... talk about immediate plans.
●	... indicate objects which are near/far.

CULTURE POINT 1

Le week-end *The weekend*

Le week-end is generally a time with its own, special rhythm of activities. Des familles (*families*) may se lever plus tard (*get up later*) and take the opportunity to déjeuner en famille (*eat lunch as a family*). Also, of course, there is more time for leisure! One pursuit that is especially popular in Brussels is cinema, known for historical reasons as le septième art (*the seventh art*). There are numerous offers to attract the public—such as the Cinéville (*ticket card*). For over 40 years the Brussels Independent Film Festival has shone a light on emerging filmmakers and their world. In the summer Brussels hosts the Brussels International Film Festival, and then in early fall Belgium celebrates la Fête du cinéma and all tickets are heavily reduced. Cinemas also traditionally offer discounted tickets for students, seniors, and club members. There are often reductions for daytime séances (*screenings*) or even nocturnes (*evening shows*) on less busy nights such as Mondays. You will also notice that foreign films tend to be available en version originale (*subtitled*) or doublés (*dubbed*). Les ballets, la danse et des concerts (*ballets, dance, and concerts*) are, of course, accessible to speakers of any language, as are les expositions d'art (*art exhibitions*) or expositions photographiques (*photography exhibitions*). If you happen to be in Brussels on June 21, you can enjoy the traditional Fête de la musique. The free annual musical celebration dates back to 1982 when the French Minister of Culture, Jack Lang, created it. This joyful event spread beyond Paris and is now celebrated in more than 1,000 cities in 120 countries.

What can you do in Brussels over the coming weekend? Visit the website Visit Brussels and find out!

VOCABULARY BUILDER 1

Read the words and phrases below and supply the missing English words and expressions. Then listen to the recording and repeat what you hear.

Le quotidien *The everyday*

LES OBJETS DU QUOTIDIEN	*EVERYDAY OBJECTS*
un bain, une douche	*bath, shower*
une brosse à cheveux/à dents	*hairbrush, toothbrush*
un peigne	*comb*
un pyjama	....
la salle de bains, les toilettes	*bathroom,* ....
le savon, une serviette	*soap, towel*
le shampooing	....
un tube de dentifrice	*a tube of toothpaste*
un vêtement, mes vêtements	*piece of clothing, my clothes*

EXPRESSIONS	*EXPRESSIONS*
Tu te couches tard/tôt.	*You go to bed late/early.*
Je m'endors dans le train.	*I fall asleep in the train.*
Ils se réveillent tôt.	*They wake up early.*
Nous nous douchons tous les jours.	*We shower every day.*
La petite s'habille toute seule.	*The little one gets dressed all by herself.*
Je me brosse les dents trois fois par jour.	*I brush my teeth three times a day.*
Elles se maquillent pour sortir.	*They put on makeup to go out.*
Je me lave les mains encore une fois.	*I am washing my hands again.*
Nous prenons le petit déjeuner ensemble.	*We have breakfast together.*
Vous déjeunez au restaurant ?	*You are having lunch at the restaurant?*
Le week-end je fais la grasse matinée.	*On the weekend I sleep in.*
On fait le ménage tous les jours.	*We do housework/cleaning every day.*
Je me repose le week-end.	*I rest on the weekend.*
Je ne suis pas du matin.	*I am not a morning person.*

Vocabulary practice 1

Match the action with the object. Use each option once only.

1 Je me réveille tôt et m'habille vite.
2 Je me lave les mains.
3 Je me douche le matin.
4 Je me couche tard.
5 Je me brosse les dents après le petit déjeuner.

a le savon
b le dentifrice
c les vêtements
d le shampooing
e le pyjama

Pronunciation practice 1

05.02

Below you will see the pattern of endings for s'appeler (*to be called*) and se lever (*to get up*). Listen to the recording, where the speaker reads out the table. Pay attention to how the underlined letters are pronounced. Can you see a connection between how those letters are pronounced and how the verb is spelled?

je m'appelle je me lève	*I am called* *I get up*	nous nous appelons nous nous levons	*we are called* *we get up*
tu t'appelles tu te lèves	*you are called* *you get up*	vous vous appelez vous vous levez	*you are called* *you get up*
il/elle s'appelle il/elle se lève	*he/she is called* *he/she gets up*	ils/elles s'appellent ils/elles se lèvent	*they are called* *they get up*

CONVERSATION 1

Qu'est-ce que tu fais ce week-end ? *What are your plans for the weekend?*

05.03

1 Listen to the conversation without looking at the text. Then listen to the conversation again and read the text.

Charles and Eva have had a busy week. Here they are talking about what they usually do at the weekend and making plans to fit in a relaxed Sunday brunch together and get to know each other better.

Charles Qu'est-ce que tu fais ce week-end ?

Eva Je me repose ! Je vais faire le ménage, lire, dormir, appeler mes parents...

Charles OK ! On va bruncher dimanche ?

Eva Oui, bonne idée ! Mais pas trop tôt ! Le dimanche, j'aime faire la grasse matinée ! Je me réveille vers 10 heures, je reste au lit pour lire le journal, je me lève vers 11 heures, je me douche, je m'habille, je me maquille... Je prends mon temps...

Charles C'est drôle, moi je me réveille tôt, même le week-end, je me lève tout de suite et je vais faire du sport !

Eva Oh là là ! Moi je ne suis vraiment pas du matin.... Mais toi, tu te couches tôt, non ?

Charles C'est vrai, je me couche vers 22 h 30 et je m'endors immédiatement ! Bon, on dit midi pour le brunch ?

Eva Parfait !

2 Answer the questions.

a How are Charles's and Eva's daily routines different?

b What does Charles enjoy doing on the weekend after he wakes up?

c What does Eva like to do in bed on Sunday before getting up?

d Who is more likely to say that they enjoy getting up early—Charles or Eva?

e What does Eva intend to do during the weekend?

LANGUAGE BUILDER 1

Language discovery 1

In the conversation, Eva and Charles use a number of expressions with the word me or m' inserted between je and the verb. For instance, Eva says: je me réveille and je me lève.

a How many are there in total?

b When do the speakers use m' and when do they use me?

c Can you figure out what all the verbs in question have in common, or why the word me or m' is used with them all?

Verbes réfléchis *Reflexive verbs*

Compare these two sentences in English: *I wash myself*; *I wash the cups*. In the first sentence, I am doing something to myself, and in the second I am doing the same thing to something else. Verbs which describe doing something to oneself are known as *reflexive verbs*. In French, they work just like other verbs, but they always take a reflexive pronoun: me, te, se, nous, vous, se. Notice that the word for *myself*, *yourself*, *him/herself* etc. comes *before* the verb in French, while in English it comes *after* the verb. Let's see how it works with se laver (*to wash oneself*). Can you complete the table for se réveiller (*to wake up*)?

se laver (*to wash oneself*)

je me lave	I wash myself	nous nous lavons	we wash ourselves
tu te laves	you wash yourself	vous vous lavez	you wash yourselves/yourself
il/elle se lave	he/she washes him/herself	ils/elles se lavent	they wash themselves

se réveiller (*to wake (oneself) up*)

je me réveille	nous nous réveillons
tu …………………	vous vous réveillez
il/elle se réveille	ils/elles …………………

Note that many verbs which are reflexive in French are not so in English: se coucher (*to go to bed*), s'endormir (*to fall asleep*), se réveiller (*to wake up*). These are often translated with *get* or *take* in English: se doucher (*to take a shower*), se baigner (*to take a bath*), s'habiller (*to get dressed*), se laver (*to get washed*), se lever (*to get up*).

Language practice 1

1 Complete each of the sentences by matching it with the correct verb.

a Tu te	**1** réveille.
b Elle se	**2** lavons.
c Nous nous	**3** réveilles.
d Ils se	**4** lavez.
e Vous vous	**5** réveillent.

LANGUAGE BUILDER 2

Language discovery 2

05.04

Listen to the conversation again and repeat each line in the pauses provided. Try to imitate the phrasing and intonation you hear.

In the conversation, Eva says Je vais faire le ménage. Does this refer to something she is doing now? How would you translate it into English?

Aller faire quelque chose *To be going to do something*

When we talk about events happening now, we are using the present tense, but we have to use *future tenses* to talk about events that have not yet happened. One way to do this is to use the verb aller in the present tense, followed by a second verb. This is called the near-future tense.

Nous allons voir un film.	*We're going to see a movie.*
Nous allons foir un film.	*We're going to see a movie.*
Je vais appeler mes parents.	*I'm going to call my parents.*

Notice the structure: *subject* (je/nous) + *the verb* aller *in the present tense* + *a second verb in the infinitive* (voir). The verb aller (*to go*) is irregular in the present tense.

aller (*to go*)

je vais	I go	nous allons	we go
tu vas	you go	vous allez	you go
il/elle va	he/she goes	ils/elles vont	they (m/f) go

Remember that, as in English, you can also use the present tense to express actions in the immediate future:

Je t'appelle plus tard.	I'll call you later.
Je pars à 11 heures.	I'm leaving at 11 o'clock.

Language practice 2

1 Here is a table setting out the verb manger (*to eat*) in the near-future tense. Some gaps have been left—can you fill them in?

je <u>vais</u> manger	nous **a** .... manger
tu vas **b**	vous **c** .... manger
il/elle **d** .... manger	ils/elles vont **e** ....

2 Complete these sentences using the verbs in parentheses to indicate something will happen in the near future. The first one has been completed.

a Le film *va commencer* (*commencer*) à neuf heures.

b Le train .... (*partir*) à 17 h 30.

c Nous .... (*prendre*) le train de 17 h 30.

d Ils .... (*manger*) au restaurant ce soir.

e Est-ce que vous .... (*faire*) des courses en ville ?

f Elle .... (*se laver*) après son petit-déjeuner.

g Je .... (*aller*) au cinéma.

05.05

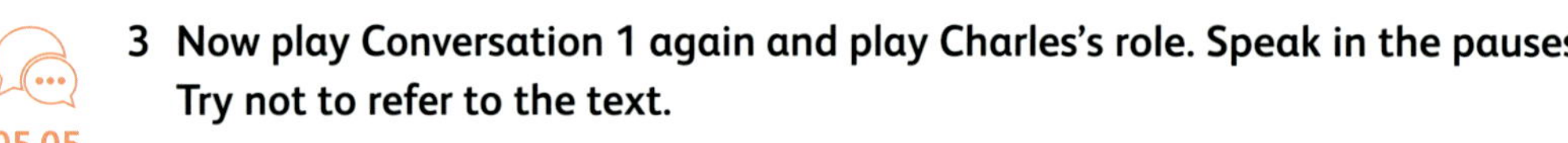

3 Now play Conversation 1 again and play Charles's role. Speak in the pauses. Try not to refer to the text.

CULTURE POINT 2

Le métro *The subway*

Paris has an extensive, efficient réseau (***network***) of public transportation, comprising subway, bus, and tram. Another means of transportation available in Paris is Vélib', a system allowing the public to rent and return des vélos à assistance électrique (*electric bicycles*) using a bank card. The subway system is made up of two interconnecting réseaux (*networks*): le Métro (*the Metro*) and le Réseau express régional/RER (*Regional Express Network/RER*). For instance, if you are at the Champs-Elysées and want to go to Montmartre, you could go down into the Charles de Gaulle metro station near the top of the famous avenue and take ligne 2 (*Line 2*) in the direction of Nation and get off at Pigalle just 10 minutes later. Ligne 2 is so numbered because it was the second line to open; it has been in operation since 1900. At Pigalle, you could then catch the Montmartre Funicular, which will take you to Sacré-Cœur in 90 seconds or, if you prefer, you can walk up 220 steps... It is also useful to know that you can buy a travel pass depending on how long you will be in Paris.

Underground Paris is not just home to an extensive metro system. In the 18th century, les Catacombes de Paris (Paris Catacombs) were created to house the contents of many Parisian cemeteries, and over a period of 30 years the remains of several million people were transferred there. It is now the world's largest ossuary and has been open to the public since the 19th century. You can also visit a World War II bunker which was used to plan the Liberation of Paris. The famous jazz club le Caveau de la Huchette also has its main rooms underground which you can reach from the main door at 5 rue de la Huchette (just a five-minute walk from Notre-Dame).

Have a look at the map of the Métro: Follow Line 6 and identify metro stations which sound familiar to you.

VOCABULARY BUILDER 2

05.06

Read the words and phrases below and supply the missing English words and expressions. Then listen to the recording and repeat what you hear.

Un voyage *A trip*

LES TRANSPORTS	*MEANS OF TRANSPORTATION*
une voiture	*car*
un avion	*airplane*
un bateau, des bateaux	*boat, boats*
un car	*coach*
un fauteuil roulant électrique	*electric wheelchair*
une mobylette, un scooter	*moped,* ....
une moto	....
une navette	*shuttle*
un tramway	....
les transports en commun	*public transportation*
une trottinette	*step scooter*

In informal settings, French speakers typically use contracted forms of certain nouns and expressions. Examples include: sympa for sympathique (*nice*); le tram *for* le tramway; la fac for la faculté (*university*); à plus for à plus tard (*see you later*).

EXPRESSIONS	*EXPRESSIONS*
Je me déplace en train/à bicyclette.	*I get around by train/by bicycle.*
Ils sont en route mais ils sont à pied.	*They are on their way, but they are on foot.*
Je m'oriente bien en ville.	*I know how to get around in the city.*
J'utilise mon passe Navigo dans le Métro.	*I use my Navigo card in the metro.*
On prend la ligne 12.	*We take line 12.*
Je descends à la station Montparnasse.	*I get off at Montparnasse.*
La circulation à Paris est un problème.	*Traffic in Paris is a problem.*
J'aime prendre le tramway/tram	*I like taking the tram.*
J'ai un rendez-vous à la Gare du Nord.	*I have a meeting at the Gare du Nord.*
Nous sommes libres ce dimanche.	*We are free this Sunday.*

Vocabulary practice 2

Complete the following sentences using items from the Vocabulary builder.

a À Paris, on peut se .... en métro, en bus ou à pied.

b J'habite en banlieue, et je prends le .... pour aller au travail.

c Pour m'.................... dans le métro, j'utilise le plan de métro.

d J'utilise toujours les .... en commun.

e Vous .... voyager en bateau?

Pronunciation practice 2

05.07

Listen to the recording and imitate the speaker.

Some vowels in French, known as nasal vowels, are pronounced by passing air through the nose at the same time as the mouth. Some vowels in English are slightly nasalized: when we say *thing* or *ring*, we use our nasal passages a little for the *i* sound, which we don't when we say *fig* or *stick*. There are three nasalized vowel sounds you need to learn. Here is an example of all three in one sentence: Je cherche du bon vin blanc (*I am looking for some good white wine*). Dictionaries use the symbols [õ], [ɛ̃], [ɑ̃] respectively for these sounds.

You might find it difficult at first to hear the difference between the nasal vowels used in the French words en (*in*) and on (*one*). It helps to remember that the difference is produced by rounding the lips more for on than for en.

lin, lent, long	*linen, slow, long*
main, ment, mont	*hand, tells lies, mount*
pain, paon, pont	*bread, peacock, bridge*
thym, tant, ton	*thyme, so much, your*
vin, vent, vont	*wine, wind, go*

CONVERSATION 2

Les moyens de transport *Means of transportation*

05.08

1 Here are few expressions to help you understand the conversation.

Ça te dit ?	*Are you interested?*	sympa	*nice, pleasant (informal)*
Ça te va ?	*Is that good for you?*	À demain !	*See you tomorrow!*

05.09

2 Listen to the conversation without looking at the text. Then listen to the conversation again and read the text.

Jo and Assia are making plans for the weekend. Eva's work is being included in a photography exhibition for new talent at the Salon de la Photo. The two friends can't wait to see Eva's work, especially her photos of Marie Nimier at the Salon du Livre (*Book Fair*).

Assia	Salut Jo. Ce week-end, je vais au Salon de la Photo. Samedi, ça te dit ?
Jo	Oui, quelle bonne idée. C'est où ?
Assia	À la Porte de Versailles...
Jo	Parfait, je suis libre après le déjeuner ; 15 h 00 ça te va ?
Assia	Très bien ! On y va en métro ou en bus ?
Jo	Il y a beaucoup de circulation le samedi après-midi, prenons le métro.

Assia	D'accord. On peut prendre la Ligne 10 à Jussieu, direction Boulogne, on descend à Sèvres-Babylone et on prend la Ligne 12, direction Mairie d'Issy jusqu'à Porte de Versailles. J'adore cette Ligne de métro.
Jo	Ou alors, on peut prendre la Ligne 7 à Censier jusqu'à Porte d'Italie et ensuite prendre le tramway jusqu'à Porte de Versailles.
Assia	C'est la Ligne 3a, direction Pont du Garigliano ? Bonne idée, le tram c'est plus sympa, prenons cet itinéraire !
Jo	Rendez-vous à 15 h 00 à la station de métro Censier, rue Monge ?
Assia	Super, à demain !

3 Answer the questions.

a Where is Assia planning to go on Saturday?
b How does Jo suggest they get there?
c Why is the metro better than the bus at this time?
d Why do they choose Jo's route instead of the one indicated by Assia?

LANGUAGE BUILDER 3

Language discovery 3

1 **In Conversation 2, Jo says prenons le métro, and Assia suggests on peut prendre la ligne 10 ... et on prend la ligne 12. Which of these verbs (prenons, prendre, prend) is an infinitive, i.e. the form you would find in a dictionary? What do you notice about this infinitive compared with parler (*to speak*) or manger (*to eat*)?**

2 **There is one other verb in Conversation 2 that has the same ending as on prend; can you spot it?**

Regular verbs ending in -re

Descendre (*to get off*) and prendre (*to take*) are known as -re verbs because their infinitive ends in -re. These verbs follow a different pattern from -er verbs (such as parler or manger), but the process is the same: drop the -re ending and replace it with the appropriate personal ending. Let's see how it works with descendre (*to go down, to get off*).

descendre (*to get off, to go down*)

je descends	nous descendons
tu descends	vous descendez
il/elle descend	ils/elles descendent

Descendre can mean *to come/go downstairs*, e.g. Je descends immédiatement (*I'm coming downstairs immediately*), or it can mean to get off a train, bus, or other means of transportation.

If you look at descendre, you will see that the endings are: -s, -s, (no extra ending), -ons, -ez, -ent. Other verbs that follow this pattern are: vendre (*to sell*), attendre (*to wait/to wait for*) and dépendre (*to depend*):

Ils descendent à Porte de Versailles. *They get off at Porte de Versailles.*

Prendre departs slightly from the standard pattern for the endings of -re verbs (illustrated by descendre): there is no d in the nous and vous forms.

prendre (*to take*)

je prends	nous prenons
tu prends	vous prenez
il/elle prend	ils/elles prennent

Language practice 3

1 Complete the sentences by choosing the appropriate verb.

a Pour visiter la ville, vous .... l'autobus ?

b Est-ce qu'il .... l'autobus ou le métro aujourd'hui ?

c Tu .... à pied ?

d Nous .... à Saint-Michel pour aller au cinéma.

1 prend

2 descends

3 descendons

4 prenez

LANGUAGE BUILDER 4

Language discovery 4

05.10

Listen to the conversation again and repeat each line in the pauses provided. Try to imitate the phrasing and intonation you hear.

When talking about traveling on tram line 3a, Jo says le tram c'est plus sympa, prenons cet itinéraire ! Focus on the word cet as it is used here. Notice that it simply means *that*. Earlier in the dialogue Assia said J'adore cette ligne (*I adore that line*).

1 Can you figure out why French speakers may need different ways of saying *that*?

2 Can you guess how to translate ce as used in the sentence below into English? Do you think it serves a similar purpose to cet and cette?

Salut Jo. Ce week-end, je vais au Salon de la Photo.

Ce, cet, cette, ces *This, that, and those*

In English, we use *that/those* to focus on objects at a distance, and *this/these* to focus on objects close to the speaker. However, in French the same word is used for both meanings, so that ce train can mean *this train* or *that train*, and you will have to get the meaning from context. Like all adjectives, ce agrees with the noun in gender and number. As a result, it has three words for *this/that* (ce, cet, cette) and one word for *these/those* (ces).

Before a masc. sing. noun that begins with a consonant, use **ce**.	Before a masc. sing. noun that begins with a vowel, use **cet**.	Before any fem. sing. noun, use **cette**.	Before any plural noun, use **ces**.
ce train	**cet avion**	**cette voiture**	**ces bateaux**

Ces trains sont des trains directs. Les autres trains sont moins rapides et ils s'arrêtent souvent.

These/Those trains are direct trains other trains are slower and they stop often.

Cette voiture est très belle et elle roule vite aussi.

This/That car is very beautiful and it drives fast too.

Cet avion est en panne—notre vol ne peut plus partir aujourd'hui.

This/That plane has broken down—our flight can no longer depart today.

Ces bateaux à voile font partie de la semaine à voile de l'Île de Ré.

These/Those sailing boats are part of the Île de Ré sailing week.

Language practice 4

1 Match the words on the left with those on the right:

a Ce...	**1** voitures
b Cet...	**2** navette
c Cette...	**3** avion
d Ces...	**4** scooter

05.11

2 Now play the conversation again and play Assia's role. Speak in the pauses. Try not to refer to the text.

SKILL BUILDER

1 Place the following activities in chronological order, starting at bedtime:

se coucher	se lever	se réveiller	s'habiller	se doucher	s'endormir

....

....

2 Sort the following activities in the table below.

faire la grasse matinée   se lever   bruncher   prendre le petit-déjeuner
se coucher   déjeuner   dîner   s'habiller

le matin	vers midi	le soir

3 Look at the map of the Montreal Metro and write out itineraries for the trips below.

Example: place des Arts ⟶ Jean-Talon : *Prendre la ligne 1 à place des Arts, direction Honoré-Beaugrand, descendre à Berri-UQAM, prendre la ligne 2, direction Montmorency, descendre à Jean-Talon.*

a Gare centrale ⟶ Université de Montréal

b Mont-Royal ⟶ McGill

....

....

....

....

4 Tell one of your friends the best way to get from your home to your favorite restaurant by using public transportation. You might want to get started with:

Je prends le bus numéro.... et je descends à.....

TEST YOURSELF

1 Complete the sentences that describe a typical daily routine using the verb indicated.

a Je .... tôt le matin. (se réveiller)

b Je .... dans la salle de bain. (se laver)

c Je .... (s'habiller)

d Je .... les dents et les cheveux. (se brosser)

e Je .... mon petit déjeuner. (prendre)

f Je .... le métro pour aller à mon université. (aller attendre)

g Je .... à la station Saint-Michel. (descendre)

h Je .... mon travail avec mes collègues. (aller faire)

i Je .... mon déjeuner dans un petit restaurant du coin. (prendre)

j Le soir je .... à 23 h 00. (se coucher)

2 Complete the sentences using the verb in parentheses.

a Bonjour, Monsieur. Vous .... du pain bio ? (**vendre**)

b Tu fais quoi ? — J'..................... mon amie Laurence. (**attendre**)

c Vous allez voir ce film ? — Ça .... ; il est long ? (**dépendre**)

d Nous .... la ligne 7 pour venir chez vous. (**prendre**)

3 Complete the sentences using ce, cet, cette, or ces as appropriate. The first one has been completed.

a Je préfère *ces* TGV (Trains à Grande Vitesse/*high-speed trains*).

b Vous prenez .... tramway ?

c .... mobylette est italienne.

d Tu prends .... avion ce soir ?

e J'adore .... bateaux ; ils sont magnifiques.

Remember to use **My review** and **My takeaway** to assess your progress and reflect on your learning experience.

6

In this lesson you will learn how to:

» Describe and discuss clothing
» Indicate preferences
» Voice possibilities and wishes
» Compare and contrast objects

La mode et les préférences

My study plan

I plan to work with Unit 6

○ Every day
○ Twice a week
○ Other ________

I plan to study for

○ 5–15 minutes
○ 15–30 minutes
○ 30–45+ minutes

My progress tracker

Day / Date					
	○	○	○	○	○
	○	○	○	○	○
	○	○	○	○	○
	○	○	○	○	○
	○	○	○	○	○
	○	○	○	○	○
	○	○	○	○	○

My goals

What do you want to be able to do or say in French when you complete this unit?

		Done
1	....	○
2	....	○
3	....	○

My review

SELF CHECK

	I can ...
●	... describe items of clothing.
●	... ask questions to differentiate between similar objects.
●	... express what I want.
●	... express what I can do.

CULTURE POINT 1

Nous sommes ce que nous portons *We are what we wear*

There are many reasons why people shop for vintage clothes in les magasins solidaires (*charity shops*), les vide-greniers (*garage sales, car boot sales*), les brocantes (*second-hand markets*), les marchés aux puces (*flea markets*), or online. As well as helping to preserve l'environnement (*the environment*), these sources allow you to discover unique items and to support les bonnes causes (*good causes*). Seeking out vintage or simply secondhand items is also a fun way to spend a day out—but remember to expect the unexpected! In recent years, circular fashion has become a buzzword in the industry, as more people recycle leurs vêtements (*their clothes*) and more marques (*brands*) offer the option of buying items new or d'occasion (*secondhand*). Although the term circular fashion is relatively new, the concept has been with us for many years. In the 19th century, Paris was already known as le centre (*the center/hub*) of the secondhand clothing trade.

Have a look at the calendar of brocantes and foires (fairs) which provides details of events in France by region (at the top) and in la Suisse, la Belgique et le Luxembourg (at the bottom). Which one would you like to visit?

VOCABULARY BUILDER 1

Read the words and phrases below and supply the missing English words and expressions. Then listen to the recording and imitate the pronunciation you hear.

Les vêtements et les couleurs *Clothes and colors*

LES VÊTEMENTS	***CLOTHES***
un anorak, un manteau	....
des chaussettes (fem.)	*socks*
des chaussures (fem.), des mocassins (masc.)	*shoes, loafers*
des tennis (fem.), des sandales (fem.)	*sneakers,* ....
une chemise, un chemisier	*shirt, blouse*
des gants (masc.)	*gloves*
un pantalon, un short	*pants, shorts*
un jupe, une robe	*skirt, dress*
un pullover/pull	....
un tee-shirt	....
une veste	*jacket*

LES COULEURS	***COLORS***
Ma couleur préférée est le...	*My favorite color is ...*
bleu	*blue*
vert	*green*
jaune	*yellow*
orange	*orange*
rouge	*red*
rose	*pink*
noir	*black*
blanc	*white*
gris	*gray*
marron	*brown*
clair, foncé	*light, dark*

EXPRESSIONS	***EXPRESSIONS***
Le costume gris clair coûte combien ?	*How much does the light-gray suit cost?*
J'essaye une écharpe en laine blanche.	*I am trying on a white woolen scarf.*
Quelle taille tu fais ? Je fais du 42.	*What size are you? I am a size 42.*
Tu as de la chance, la cabine est libre !	*You are in luck; the changing room is free!*
Est-ce que je peux vous aider ?	*May I help you?*
Je cherche...	*I am looking for ...*
Ça coûte combien ?	*How much does it cost?*
Je peux l'essayer ?	*May I try it on?*

Vocabulary practice 1

1 Label the images with the correct words from the box.

un tee-shirt	des tennis	des chaussures	des chaussettes	un pull	un manteau

Pronunciation practice 1

The letter r is generally pronounced in French, the main exception being infinitives of -er verbs such as aimer (where the final r is silent). In French, r is a guttural sound. It's pronounced in the throat, close to where you pronounce *g* as in *game*, but it's a continuous sound. It's a bit like the *ch* in *loch* in Scottish but voiced. If you can't get the r right away, don't worry, just keep practicing!

06.02

Bearing this in mind, listen to the recording; then, using the list below, read out the phrases you have just heard. Make sure to pronounce every r:

un costume noir   un pantalon vert   un magasin solidaire   un short bleu
une écharpe rouge

CONVERSATION 1

Vous faites quelle taille ? *What size are you?*

06.03

1 Here are a few words and expressions to understand the conversation. Notice two new items of vocabulary, used for asking what (Quelle… ?) and which (Lequel… ?).

un modèle	*style*	Vous préférez lequel ?	*Which one do you prefer?*
plus cher	*more expensive*	puisque je suis là	*since I'm here*
uni	*plain*	Quelle trouvaille !	*What a find!*

06.04

2 Listen to the conversation without looking at the text. Then listen to the conversation again and read the text.

Eva is going to be doing a photo shoot for an article on the benefits of circular fashion. To research this, she is visiting a thrift store, and while she is there she does some shopping. Charles agrees to keep her company. They are speaking with une vendeuse (*a salesperson*).

Vendeuse	Bonjour Madame, bonjour Monsieur. Je peux vous aider ?
Eva	Bonjour. C'est pour moi ; je cherche un pantalon de costume.
Vendeuse	Oui, les vêtements pour femme sont ici. Vous faites quelle taille ?
Eva	Je fais du 38.
Vendeuse	Vous cherchez quelle couleur ?
Eva	Je préfère le gris.
Vendeuse	Vous avez de la chance. Voici deux modèles, un pantalon rayé gris clair, en laine, et un pantalon gris foncé, uni, en velours.
Eva	Merci ! Ils coûtent combien ?
Vendeuse	Le pantalon en laine coûte 78 € et l'autre, en velours, est plus cher. Il coûte 119 €.
Eva	Ils sont très élégants. Je peux essayer ?
Vendeuse	Bien sûr, la cabine est là, à gauche [...] Alors ? C'est la bonne taille ?
Eva	Oui, c'est parfait !
Charles	Oui, ils te vont bien. Oui, ils te vont très bien.
Vendeuse	Vous préférez lequel ?
Eva	J'aime les deux, mais je préfère le pantalon en laine, la coupe est plus cintrée (*the cut is more slim-fitting*).
Charles	Et moi, je vais peut-être acheter des gants chauds pour l'hiver, puisque je suis là.
Vendeuse	Nous avons ces gants rouges, en laine.
Charles	Super ! Quelle trouvaille !

3 Answer the questions.

- **a** What is Eva looking for in the thrift store?
- **b** What color or colors does she prefer?
- **c** What two items does the salesperson offer her, and which one is more expensive?
- **d** Does Charles express a preference?
- **e** What does Charles decide to buy for himself?

LANGUAGE BUILDER 1

Language discovery 1

Imagine that the discussion continues, and the salesperson offers Eva a choice between un pantalon rayé gris and une chemise bleue décontractée et légère. How many adjectives do you see here? Where are the adjectives placed? Can you find similar sentences in the conversation where several adjectives are used to describe one item?

Adjectives (continued)

Adjectives are words we use to describe a person or an object. In Unit 1, you learned some adjectives to describe someone's personality (e.g. généreux, ambititieux, créatif, passionné, modeste) and some adjectives of nationality or origin (la cuisine française, des chocolats belges). You also know that adjectives agree in *number* and *gender* with the nouns they describe. In French, adjectives are mostly placed *after* the noun. (Later in this book, we will look at some exceptions.)

Je porte une jupe blanche	*I am wearing a white skirt*
Elle porte un pantalon gris clair	*She is wearing light-gray pants*

Adjectives of color generally follow the same rules of agreement as adjectives in general. Bearing this in mind, fill in the five gaps in the table below. It will also help if you compare the color adjectives in the table with each other, to spot patterns or tendencies.

un pantalon	une jupe	des tee-shirts (m)	des vestes (f)
blanc	blanche	blancs	blanches
gris	grise	gris	grises
vert	verte	verts	**c** ....
bleu	bleue	**a**	**d** ....
rouge	rouge	**b**	**e** ....

Adjectives are often combined with très (*very*) and trop (*too*), as well as plus (*more*) and moins (*less*) for emphasis: un costume très cher, une jupe très élégante; cette robe est trop chère, ce pantalon est trop court; cette chemise est plus belle; ce pantalon est moins cher. Plus and moins obviously always imply a comparison: if I say ce pantalon est moins cher (*this pair of trousers is less expensive*), I must be comparing it with some other, more expensive pair of trousers.

Language practice 1

1 Based on the table complete the following statements by circling the correct answer.

a When a masc. adjective ends with an e (see rouge), the fem. form is *different / the same*.

b When a masc. adjective ends in a letter other than e, the fem. form is *different / the same*.

c When a sing. masc. adjective ends in an s (see gris), the plural version is *different / the same*.

2 Complete the following statement in your own words.

The word for *white* is different from the others in the grid in that ....

3 Below are singular and plural nouns, paired with adjectives of color. Fill in the missing adjectives (the first one has been completed).

a un anorak bleu / des anoraks *bleus*

b une chemise blanche / des chemises ....

c un costume .... / des costumes gris

d une tennis .... / des tennis rouges

e un pantalon noir / des pantalons ....

LANGUAGE BUILDER 2

Language discovery 2

Listen to the conversation again and repeat each line in the pauses provided. Try to imitate the phrasing and intonation you hear.

Towards the end of Conversation 1, referring to two pairs of gray trousers, the salesperson asks Vous préférez lequel ? (*Which one do you prefer?*). Imagine once again that Eva inquires about other types of clothing: un anorak, une jupe, des gants, and des chaussures. Here's how the salesperson could respond. Can you figure out why he uses different forms of lequel?

Eva cherche...	Le vendeur demande...
un anorak	Vous préférez lequel ?
une jupe	Vous préférez laquelle ?
des gants	Vous préférez lesquels ?
des chaussures	Vous préférez lesquelles ?

Offering a choice: *which (one)*?

When talking about one option among several, use quel (*which*, also often translated as *what*). Like any adjective, quel agrees with the noun it describes. The forms are:

	singular	plural
masculine	quel	quels
feminine	quelle	quelles

Quel désastre ! — *What a disaster!*

Vous cherchez quelle couleur ? — *Which color are you looking for?*

Tu préfères quelles chaussures ? — *Which shoes do you prefer?*

When referring to something that was previously mentioned, use the pronoun lequel. It also agrees in gender and number with the noun it refers to.

	singular	plural
masculine	lequel	lesquels
feminine	laquelle	lesquelles

Vous préférez lequel ? — *Which one do you prefer?* (*one* = le pantalon)

Voici deux jupes. Vous essayez laquelle ? — *Here are two skirts. Which one will you try on?*

> If you remove the first two letters from lequel and laquelle, you have the words quel or quelle, both of which can also mean *Which…?* The difference is that these shorter forms are used before a noun, as follows: Tu préfères quel costume/quelle écharpe/quels gants/quelles chaussures ?

Language practice 2

1 Complete the following sentences using quel, quelle, quels, and quelles as appropriate.

a .... anorak est-ce que tu veux ?

b .... jupes est-ce que tu aimes ?

c .... robe est en laine ?

d .... chemisiers sont d'occasion ?

2 Complete the following sentences using lequel, laquelle, lesquels, or lesquelles as appropriate.

a Voici deux jupes. Tu préfères .... ?

b Voici deux pantalons noirs. Vous préférez .... ?

c .... est-ce que nous allons choisir : les chaussures rouges ou les blanches ?

d Nous avons des gants noirs et des gants marron. Vous préférez .... ?

06.06

Listen to Conversation 1 again and play the role of the salesperson. Speak in the pauses provided. Are there extra questions the salesperson could have asked?

CULTURE POINT 2

La slow fashion est à la mode *Slow fashion is in vogue*

La fast fashion (*fast fashion*) is a phenomenon that took off in the 1990s. Sa popularité (*its popularity*) is due to its promise of affordability together with des gammes (*ranges*) that change every season. More recently, however, la slow fashion (*slow fashion*) has been growing in significance. Ce mouvement (*this movement*) encourages les gens (*people*) to consommer moins mais mieux (*to consume less, but better*). Not only should clothes be durable, but they should be produced in ethical conditions and without unnecessary harm to the environment. Supporters of slow fashion argue that it is also a way to faire des économies (*make savings*), since des vêtements de meilleure qualité (*better-quality clothes*) last longer. Slow fashion also involves producing clothes that are aimed at a local market, rather than being transported long distances par avion (*by air*) or par mer (*by sea*). Increasingly, des labels Made in... (*'Made in' labels*) are used to emphasize cette tendance (*this tendency*). The label *Made in Portugal* is becoming especially popular, as le Portugal (*Portugal*) produces des vêtements éco-responsables (*sustainable clothes*) that are bought across the Union européenne (*European Union*).

The website WEDRESSFAIR proposes nine criteria to help les consommateurs et les consommatrices (*consumers*) to distinguish true slow fashion from le greenwashing (*greenwashing*), also known as l'écoblanchiment. Do you agree with each of the nine criteria?

VOCABULARY BUILDER 2

Read the words and phrases below and supply the missing English words and expressions. Then listen to the recording and imitate the pronunciation you hear.

Faire des descriptions *Describing*

LES MÉTIERS	*PROFESSIONS*
un artiste, une artiste	*artist (male), artist (female)*
un présentateur, une présentatrice	....
un styliste, une styliste	*designer (male), designer (female)*
ADJECTIFS	***ADJECTIVES***
agréable	*nice/pleasant*
beau/belle	*handsome, beautiful*
bon/bonne	*good*
mauvais	*bad*
chic	*chic/smart*
décontracté	*relaxed*
éco-responsable	....
élégant	....
léger/légère	*light (not heavy)*
long/longue, court	*long, short*
magnifique	*magnificent*
original	*original*
petit, grand	*small, big*
pratique	....
superbe	*superb/great*
talentueux/talentueuse	*talented*
unisexe	....
vif/vive	*lively*
EXPRESSIONS	***EXPRESSIONS***
J'adore sortir avec mes amis.	*I love going out with my friends.*
Nous allons regarder la télé ce soir.	*We are going to watch TV tonight.*
Tu commentes souvent les nouveaux jeux.	*You often comment on new games.*
Jean-Pierre fête son anniversaire aujourd'hui.	*Jean-Pierre is celebrating his birthday today.*
Je porte mes vêtements préférés.	*I am wearing my favorite clothes.*
Nous sortons le weekend.	*We go out at the weekend.*
Je vous souhaite la bienvenue.	*I welcome you.*
Bonsoir à toutes et à tous !	*Good evening to all!*
Cette année je vais rester en France.	*This year I am going to stay in France.*

Vocabulary practice 2

Complete the sentences using the words in the box.

adore	fête	rester	regarder	sortir

a Ce soir, je vais .... la télé.

b Aujourd'hui, maman .... son anniversaire.

c Tu vas .... ce soir, ou .... chez toi ?

d J'............................ ce café : il est chic et décontracté.

Pronunciation practice 2

In French, certain consonants (b, p, and t) sound softer than in English. Listen to the recording and repeat the phrases below, while concentrating on softening your pronunciation of b, p, and t. The last sentence is a well-known French tongue-twister which you might enjoy learning!

C'est beau.

C'est pratique.

Ce vêtement est superbe.

Bienvenue à toutes et à tous !

Pauline porte une cravate verte.

Si mon tonton tond ton tonton, ton tonton sera tondu.
(*If my uncle shaves your uncle, your uncle will be shaved.*)

There are some words in French that are used mainly by children, or by adults when speaking to children. One such word is tonton (*uncle*), based on the vowel sound in oncle.

CONVERSATION 2

Le défilé de mode *The fashion show*

06.09

1 Here are a few words and expressions to help you understand the conversation.

un boubou	*boubou*	un thème	*theme*
une création	*creation*	la créativité	*creativity*

06.10

2 Listen to the conversation a few times without looking at the text. Then listen to the conversation again and read the text.

Assia and Jo are watching a fashion show on TV. They are quite excited as it's taking place in Dakar, a city which Assia hopes to visit with a group of young photographers.

Une présentatrice	Bonsoir à toutes et à tous, et bienvenue à la vingtième édition du défilé de la Dakar Fashion Week.
Un présentateur	Cette année, le thème est la mode éco-responsable avec des créations originales et des artistes et des stylistes talentueuses et talentueux.
Jo	Assia, tu veux venir ? Le défilé commence... Ohhh ! Je veux cette robe rouge, elle est magnifique !
Assia	Oui, elle est très belle ! Tu peux porter une robe de cette coupe pour le travail ou pour sortir ! C'est pratique !
Jo	Et ce costume gris, il est très élégant !
Assia	Oui, il est très beau ! Et j'adore le gris.
Jo	Je n'aime pas ce pull-là en jaune, il est trop clair.
Assia	Et ce pull-ci, à droite, en vert foncé ?
Jo	Ah oui ! Je préfère les couleurs foncées.
Assia	J'adore ces chaussures noires, elles sont superbes !
Jo	Je peux voir ? Ahhh voilà les boubous, c'est unisexe, c'est élégant et très agréable à porter.
Présentatrice	Le défilé continue, avec des créations très décontractées, des vêtements légers, des robes longues, et des couleurs vives : rouge, bleu, jaune, vert.

3 Answer the questions.

a Why is the red dress practical, according to Assia?
b Which pullover does Jo prefer?
c What type of colors does Jo prefer?
d Based on Assia's last comment, describe a boubou.
e Which colors are characteristic of the fashion show, according to the female presenter?

LANGUAGE BUILDER 3

Language discovery 3

1 Find the missing words.

Speaking of an item in the fashion show, Jo exclaims Je .... cette robe rouge ! (*I want that red dress!*) and Assia comments: Tu .... porter une robe de cette coupe pour le travail ou pour sortir (*You can wear a dress with that cut for work or for going out*).

What do you notice about the verb endings you just wrote down and that makes them different from any verbs you have come across so far?

2 Can you think of how you might explain how vouloir and pouvoir work with other verbs in this conversation (venir, porter, voir)?

Expressing desire and ability: vouloir and pouvoir

Vouloir (*to want*) and pouvoir (*to be able to*) are two verbs that are very similar to one another and a little bit different from all the verbs you have learned so far. They are irregular, but you will hear and use them frequently, which will help you remember them.

It is good to learn pouvoir and vouloir by heart. It is helpful to know that you will find exactly the same pattern of vowels in both verbs.

Complete the two tables below, reading up and down as well as across to figure out how to fill the empty boxes.

pouvoir (*to be able to*)	
je peux	nous ....
tu	vous pouvez
il/elle peut	ils/elles peuvent

vouloir (*to want*)	
je	nous voulons
tu veux	vous voulez
il/elle	ills/elles ....

Note that pouvoir and vouloir are often followed by another verb in the infinitive:

Je veux faire les courses.	*I want to do the shopping.*
Vous pouvez préparer le dîner ce soir.	*You can make dinner tonight.*

As in English, vouloir can also be used with a noun:

Je veux un café.	*I want a coffee.*

Language practice 3

Complete the sentences using the correct form of vouloir or pouvoir, then translate the sentences into English.

a Tu .... acheter des chaussettes pour moi ? (*pouvoir*)

b Vous .... acheter quelle chemise ? (*vouloir*)

c Elle .... venir ce soir. (*pouvoir*)

d Ils .... aller au musée. (*vouloir*)

e Je ne .... pas nager aujourd'hui. (*vouloir*)

f Nous .... déjeuner très vite. (*pouvoir*)

g Vous .... participer à la séance photo ? (*vouloir*)

h Qu'est-ce qu'on .... faire pour aider ? (*pouvoir*)

i Tu .... préparer le petit déjeuner ? (*pouvoir*)

j Nous .... attendre jusqu'à 10 heures. (*pouvoir*)

LANGUAGE BUILDER 4

Language discovery 4

06.11

Listen to the conversation again and repeat each line in the pauses. Try to copy the phrasing and intonation you hear.

Complete the phrases Assia and Jo use to discuss which pullover Jo prefers.

Je n'aime pas ce pull ...., en jaune.

Et ce pull ...., à droite, en vert foncé ?

What do you think the missing words mean? What is useful about them?

Here and *there*: -ci and -là

In English, *this* is typically used to indicate an object near the speaker, while *that* is used for one farther away. As you know, the French demonstratives (ce, cet, cette, ces) do not have such a precise meaning: ce pull can mean *this pullover* or *that pullover*. To mark the difference between *this one* and *that one*, simply add -ci (*here/this*) or -là (*there/that*) to the end of the noun. For example, ce pull-ci means *this pullover* (i.e. the one near me), while ce pull-là means *that pullover* (i.e. the one that is farther away).

When referring to something that has previously been mentioned, you can use the pronoun celui (*this one*) with -ci and -là. For example, instead of asking Tu aimes ce pull-ci ? (*Do you like this pullover?*), you can ask Tu aimes celui-ci ? (*Do you like this one?*). Note that, like all pronouns, celui agrees in gender and number with the noun it represents.

	This one/These ones ...	That one/Those ones ...
Quel pull ? (masc. sing.)	Celui-ci.	Celui-là.
Quelle robe ? (fem. sing.)	Celle-ci.	Celle-là.
Quels gants ? (masc. pl.)	Ceux-ci.	Ceux-là.
Quelles chaussures ? (fem. pl.)	Celles-ci.	Celles-là.

Language practice 4

1 Match the French phrases with their English equivalents.

a cette jupe-ci
b cet anorak-là
c ces chaussettes-là
d cette jupe-là
e ces chaussettes-ci
f cet anorak-ci

1 these socks
2 those socks
3 this skirt
4 that skirt
5 this anorak
6 that anorak

2 Complete with one of the following: celui-ci/là, celle-ci/là, celles-ci/là, or ceux-ci/là. The first one has been completed as an example.

a J'aime ce pull-ci. Mais Marie aime *celui-là*.

b Je descends à cette gare-ci. Toi, tu descends à ....

c Tu prends ces chaussettes-ci. Je prends ....

d Robert préfère ce pantalon-ci. Je préfère ....

e Nous aimons beaucoup ces chemisiers-ci. Vous aimez ....

06.12

Listen to Conversation 2 again and play the role of Jo. Speak in the pauses provided. Are there some clothes you would like to buy this weekend? Imagine asking the salesperson if they have the items you are planning to purchase.

SKILL BUILDER

1 Read the message below, where Jo explains to Assia that her little cousin Diego is celebrating his sixth birthday and has chosen to dress in his favorite blue clothes. How many ways is the French word bleu spelled? Why does the spelling change?

Salut Assia ! Je suis chez ma cousine Annette. Aujourd'hui c'est l'anniversaire de son fils Diego. Il porte une chemise bleue, un pantalon bleu, des chaussettes bleues, et des mocassins bleus. Devine quelle couleur il préfère !

2 Write your wish list for next year, using the verb vouloir. Then write a list of all possible options for your next holiday, using the verb pouvoir. Don't forget to add what you don't want to do or cannot do.

3 Complete the questions and then imagine asking a friend each of the questions and what their answers would be. The first one has been completed. You could then imagine your friend asking you the questions, and it is up to you to answer them and indicate your preferences.

Quelle est ta couleur préférée ? Ma couleur préférée, c'est *le bleu*.

.... est ton sport préféré ? Mon sport préféré, c'est ....

.... sont tes livres préférés ? Mes livres préférés, ce sont ....

.... est ton repas préféré ? Mon repas préféré, c'est ....

TEST YOURSELF

Below are incomplete short dialogues, each starting with a statement. Ask a question to receive information about the object mentioned in each statement. Then, to complete each mini dialogue, imagine a possible answer to your question.

a J'aime le pullover marron. *Lequel est-ce que tu aimes ?—J'aime celui-ci.*

b Je porte un chemisier aujourd'hui. ....

c Nous voulons des chaussures. ....

d J'aime les robes. ....

e Elle veut acheter une jupe. ....

f Nous aimons les chemises. ....

g Ils cherchent un tee-shirt. ....

h Elles aiment le défilé de mode. ....

i Vous voulez acheter un costume ? ....

j Tu aimes les pulls ? ....

Remember to use **My review** and **My takeaway** to assess your progress and reflect on your learning experience.

7

In this lesson you will learn how to:

» Make plans to go out
» Discuss options and make choices
» Indicate where you are going

La culture quotidienne

My study plan

I plan to work with Unit 7

○ Every day
○ Twice a week
○ Other ____________

I plan to study for

○ 5–15 minutes
○ 15–30 minutes
○ 30–45+ minutes

My progress tracker

Day / Date	Listening	Speaking	Reading	Writing	Conversation
	○	○	○	○	○
	○	○	○	○	○
	○	○	○	○	○
	○	○	○	○	○
	○	○	○	○	○
	○	○	○	○	○
	○	○	○	○	○

My goals

What do you want to be able to do or say in French when you complete this unit?

		Done
1	....	○
2	....	○
3	....	○

My review

SELF CHECK

	I can ...
●	... plan a cultural outing.
●	... speak about daily actions.
●	... confirm plans.

CULTURE POINT 1

Moteur, ça tourne, action ! *Lights, camera, action!*

Les frères Lumière (*the Lumière brothers*), who invented moving picture technology, were born in Besançon in the early 1860s. France is therefore proud of its status as the birthplace of cinema, celebrated annually at le Festival de Cannes (*the Cannes Film Festival*), famous the world over. French cinematography is particularly well known for la Nouvelle Vague (*the New Wave*) of the 1950s and 1960s, a movement that brought une renommée internationale (*international fame*) to des acteurs (*actors*) including Jean Seberg, Jeanne Moreau, and Jean-Paul Belmondo, and also to cinéastes (*filmmakers*) such as François Truffaut, Jean-Luc Godard or Agnès Varda. Women have always been active in French cinema, derrière la caméra (*behind the camera*) as well as sur l'écran (*on screen*). But since the 1990s, a 'new wave' of réalisatrices (*female directors*) such as Claire Denis has made its influence felt. Meanwhile, le cinéma francophone (*francophone cinema*) has flourished in many nations and regions. This has led to a truly international film industry, enriched by cultural exchange. Among the many works that have emerged from cette évolution (*this development*) is the award-winning *Monsieur Lazhar*. This film, adapted from une pièce de théâtre (*a play*) written by the Canadian actor-writer Évelyne de la Chenelière, tells the story of an Algerian refugee in Montreal who becomes a teacher. The rich culture of different film movements is often celebrated through les rétrospectives (*retrospectives*). As the name suggests, these screenings allow the audience to catch up on the movies of yesterday that influence today's writers, artists, and directors.

Visit the Cannes Film Festival website. What is the profession of the members of the jury?

VOCABULARY BUILDER 1

Read the words and phrases below and supply the missing English words and expressions. Then listen to the recording and imitate the pronunciation you hear.

Le monde du cinéma *The world of cinema*

LA MISE EN SCÈNE	***PRODUCTION AND DIRECTION***
un acteur/une actrice	*actor*
un comédien/une comédienne	*actor*
un comique/une comique	*comedian*
un écran	*screen*
un film, tourner un film	*movie/film, to shoot a movie*
un réalisateur/une réalisatrice	*director*
LES GENRES	***GENRES***
un biopic	....
une comédie	....
un dessin animé	*cartoon/animation*
un film d'action	*action movie*
un film d'horreur	*horror movie*
un film noir	*a film noir*
ALLER AU CINÉMA	***GOING TO THE MOVIES***
un billet, un billet plein tarif, un carnet de billets	*ticket, full-price ticket, booklet of tickets*
une billetterie, une billetterie en ligne	*ticket office, online ticket office*
une place/un siège	*seat*
un sous-titre, un film sous-titré/doublé	*subtitle, subtitled/dubbed movie*
le générique	*credits (at the end of the movie)*
en v.o./en version originale	*in the original language*
Elles proposent d'aller voir un film ensemble.	*They suggest going to see a film together.*
Qu'est-ce qu'il y a à l'affiche ?	*What's showing?/What's on?*
La séance commence à 19 h 30.	*The program starts at 7:30.*
On se retrouve devant le cinéma.	*We are meeting up in front of the movie theater.*
Tout me va !	*I'm happy with anything!*

If you intend to visit the cinema in a francophone country and you see en version originale (en v.o.) after an English-language movie title, it means that the soundtrack is in English (*in its original form*) and the movie most probably has French-language subtitles. Reading these as you watch is a great way to learn new words! Also, many streaming platforms let you choose which language you want subtitles in, and this can offer the same kind of learning opportunity wherever you happen to be. Finally, watching a French-language movie is a great way to develop listening skills.

Vocabulary practice 1

1 When going to see a movie, you might use some or all of the phrases below. Translate each of the underlined words or phrases into French.

Example: Consult the program and choose a movie. *le programme — un film*

a Check if the movie is subtitled or dubbed. ....

b Locate the ticket office. ....

c Buy a ticket and choose a seat. ....

d Read the credits. ....

2 Using words from the Vocabulary builder, translate the following into French:

a When we go to the movies en famille, we watch a cartoon.

b She likes the seats in this movie theater.

c I prefer to watch the movie in the original language.

Pronunciation practice 1

In most cases where you see the sequence of letters -ill-, as in billet (*ticket*), the double l sounds rather like *y* in the English word *yes*. In a few cases, however, the double l is pronounced as in the English word *vanilla*.

07.02

Read the sentences below out loud, then check your pronunciation of the underlined words against the recording.

Chaque semaine, les Français achètent des millions de billets de cinéma.
Every week, the French buy several million cinema tickets.

La ville où j'habite avec ma famille est tranquille.
The city where I live with my family is quiet.

CONVERSATION 1

Une soirée au cinéma *A night at the movies*

07.03

1 Here are a few words and expressions to understand the conversation.

un cycle	*cycle*	pas mal	*not bad/great*
la Palme d'or	*Golden Palm (award for the best film at Cannes)*	drôle	*funny, amusing*

07.04

2 Listen to the conversation without looking at the text. Then listen to the conversation again and read the text.

Eva and Charles make plans to go to the movies with friends. Luckily for them Brussels prides itself on hosting a number of film festivals, as well as focussing on rising talent from all over the francophone world. So they have plenty to choose from!

Eva Tu as envie de sortir samedi ? Nathalie et Morna proposent d'aller voir un film ensemble.

Charles Oui, super, bonne idée ! Qu'est-ce qu'il y a à l'affiche ?

Eva Plusieurs films sortent cette semaine. Attends, je regarde le programme.

Charles Pas la peine, j'ai le programme sur mon téléphone. Il y a un cycle de films de réalisatrices : *Anatomie d'une chute*, de Justine Triet, Palme d'or à Cannes et *Dalida*, un biopic de Lisa Azuelos...

Eva Il y a aussi *Cœurs vaillants*, de Mona Achache, avec Camille Cottin...

Charles ... Et *Atlantique*, de Mati Diop, meilleur premier film du Festival du film de Londres, une rétrospective Agnès Varda et *Chien et Chat*, la nouvelle comédie de Reem Kherici.

Eva J'aimerais bien revoir *Dalida*, j'adore ses chansons ! Et toi ?

Charles Moi, *Anatomie d'une chute*, les critiques sont excellentes. Et Nathalie et Mona, qu'est-ce qu'elles aiment ?

Eva Je crois qu'elles préfèrent les comédies.

Charles Une comédie, c'est bien aussi ! Les films de Reem Kherici sont très drôles ! La séance est à quelle heure ?

Eva La séance est à 19 h 30 mais il y a des publicités, et le film commence vers 19 h 45. Il y a aussi une séance à 21 h 30, mais le film finit vers 23 h 30, c'est tard, non ? Je préfère la première séance.... On se retrouve devant le cinéma à 19 heures ?

Charles Parfait ! Tout me va !

3 Answer the questions.

a On what day do Eva's friends want to go to the movies?

b What do all the films on the program have in common?

c What is Charles's first preference?

d Does Eva have a preference? Do Nathalie and Morna?

e When and where will the friends meet?

LANGUAGE BUILDER 1

Language discovery 1

Find the following sentences in Conversation 1 and fill in the missing verbs. What do you notice about these verbs compared to the forms you already know?

a Tu as envie de .... samedi ?

b Plusieurs films .... cette semaine.

c Le film .... vers onze heures et demie.

Verbs ending in -ir

So far you have mainly learned to use verbs ending in -er or -re. Another group of verbs ends in -ir. As with -er and -re verbs, simply drop the -ir ending and replace with the appropriate personal ending: -is ; -is ; -it ; -issons ; -issez ; -issent. Notice that the endings used with nous, vous and ils/elles are similar to ones you have seen before...

finir (*to finish*)

je fin<u>is</u>	I finish	nous fin<u>issons</u>	we finish
tu fin<u>is</u>	you finish	vous fin<u>issez</u>	you finish
il/elle fin<u>it</u>	he/she finishes	ils/elles fin<u>issent</u>	they finish

Other -ir verbs that follow this exact pattern are: choisir (*to choose*) and réfléchir (*to think*).

Je choisis un film drôle. *I choose a funny film.*

Nous réfléchissons avant de choisir. *We are thinking about it before making a choice.*

However, a number of -ir verbs have their own, separate pattern. You will learn these gradually, as you come across each one. Here are a few common ones:

dormir (*to sleep*)	je dors	tu dors	il/elle dort	nous dormons	vous dormez	ils/elles dorment
partir (*to leave*)	je pars	tu pars	il/elle part	nous partons	vous partez	ils/elles partent
sortir (*to go out/come out*)	je sors	tu sors	il/elle sort	nous sortons	vous sortez	ils/elles sortent
venir (*to come*)	je viens	tu viens	il/elle vient	nous venons	vous venez	ils/elles viennent

Ils partent demain. *They're leaving tomorrow.*

Tu sors avec nous ? *Are you coming out with us?*

Language practice 1

Complete the sentences using the verb indicated.

a Est-ce que tu .... ce soir ? (*sortir*)
b Quel genre de film est-ce qu'ils .... normalement ? (*choisir*)
c Nous .... toujours mieux chez nous. (*dormir*)
d Le travail .... à cinq heures aujourd'hui. (*finir*)

LANGUAGE BUILDER 2

Language discovery 2

07.05

Listen to Conversation 1 again and repeat each line in the pauses provided. Try to imitate the phrasing and intonation you hear.

Towards the end of Conversation 1, Eva suggests: **On se retrouve devant le cinéma à 19 heures ?**

Can you figure out a way of translating this question that sounds natural in English?

Using the pronoun on

In French, the personal pronoun on (*one*) is used in two different ways. First, it can be used to make statements about people in general. For instance, if you say on ne sait jamais (*one never knows*), you are not referring to any particular person/group of people but to people in general. Second, on can be used, somewhat informally, as an alternative to nous. For instance, imagine a situation where you and your friends have arranged to go on a trip and you suggest leaving at two o'clock. Instead of saying Nous partons à deux heures, you could say On part à deux heures. Both sentences mean *We're leaving at two o'clock*.

Language practice 2

1 Rewrite the sentences below, replacing on with nous and vice versa. Change the verbs to match. The first one has been done for you.

a Nous allons sortir ce weekend. — *On va* sortir ce weekend.
b Nous aimons les comédies. — .... les comédies.
c On va faire des courses en ville. — .... faire des courses en ville.
d Nous préférons les dessins animés. — .... les dessins animés.
e On va voir un film d'action. — .... voir un film d'action.

07.06

2 Listen to Conversation 1 again and play the role of Eva. Speak in the pauses provided. What movie would you choose to see?

CULTURE POINT 2

J'aime la papeterie *I love stationery*

In Belgium and in France les communications manuscrites (*handwritten communications*) are important for one's social life. Visitors to France are often surprised to experience the discreet charm of une papeterie (*a stationery store*). In such stores, they will typically find a selection of products that is carefully curated and beautifully presented. Customers can find cards for all kinds of occasion: les anniversaires (*birthdays*), of course, but also les naissances (*births*) or les mariages (*marriages*), not forgetting the typically French carte de vœux (*New Year's card*). Part of the store might be set aside for du papier à lettres de haute qualité (*high-quality letter-writing paper*) in attractive colors. For school or university, un cahier (*a notebook*) typically contains du papier à carreaux (*squared paper*), which helps students to practice their écriture (*handwriting*). Producers of stationery increasingly emphasize their use of papier recyclé (*recycled paper*), or papeterie Made in France et éco-responsable. Clairefontaine and Rhodia are two brands that most children begin to use in school and continue to seek out as adults when they need writing supplies. Clairefontaine manages several hundred hectares of fir and spruce trees in the Vosges, and still relies on its own, original paper mill. In brief, traditional papeteries continue to thrive in the new era of digital communication.

Nous vous present
nos meilleurs souh
de l'an et vous
souhaitons bonne
continuation.

Check this website. What kind of product is papier d'Arménie?

VOCABULARY BUILDER 2

Read the words and phrases below and supply the missing English words and expressions. Then listen to the recording and imitate the pronunciation you hear.

ÉCRIRE, CORRESPONDRE	*TO WRITE AND CORRESPOND*
une carte d'anniversaire	*birthday card*
une carte de vœux	*greetings card*
une carte de félicitations	*congratulations card*
un faire-part de naissance/de mariage	*a birth/wedding announcement*
une feuille, une feuille de papier	*leaf, sheet of paper*
une invitation	....
un stylo, un stylo (à) bille	*pen, ball-point pen*

PROFESSIONS	*PROFESSIONS*
une cantatrice	*lead opera singer (a woman)*
un chanteur/une chanteuse	*singer*
un conservateur/une conservatrice	*curator*
un disc-jockey	....
un musicien/une musicienne	....
un/une pianiste	....

EXPRESSIONS	*EXPRESSIONS*
Je t'accompagne.	*I'll accompany you.*
Je te rejoins au musée.	*I'll meet you at the museum.*
On se réunit tous les mois.	*We meet/get together every month.*
Paul est occupé.	*Paul is busy.*
Tant mieux !	*Good!/So much the better!*
Je n'ai rien à me mettre.	*I have nothing to wear.*
Ils ont un code vestimentaire.	*They have a dress code.*
On peut y aller en tenue de tous les jours ?	*Can we go wearing everyday clothing?*
On sort en boîte de nuit.	*We are going out to a night club.*

Vocabulary practice 2

Match the professions to the cultural venues.

a un disc-jockey
b une cantatrice
c un conservateur
d un/une pianiste

1 un musée
2 un club de jazz
3 une boîte de nuit
4 un opéra

CONVERSATION 2

Une invitation *An invitation*

07.08

1 Listen to the conversation without looking at the text. Then listen to the conversation again and read the text.

Assia continues to grow in expertise and to develop her network in the field of photography. One morning Jo brings the mail up, including an envelope addressed to Assia ...

Jo	Tiens, regarde, une lettre pour toi de la Maison européenne de la Photographie.
Assia	Ouvre s'il te plaît, je suis occupée.
Jo	C'est une invitation au vernissage de l'expo des jeunes photographes, pour deux personnes.
Assia	Ah, génial ! C'est quand ?
Jo	Le jeudi 24 octobre, à 19 h 00.
Assia	Cool ! Tu es libre ? On y va ensemble ?
Jo	Euh, je n'ai pas très envie d'y aller...
Assia	Allez ! Accompagne-moi ! On va s'amuser, les soirées à la MEP sont toujours très amusantes !
Jo	Oui, mais je n'ai rien à me mettre.
Assia	Ah ! C'est ça ! Alors, je te rassure, il n'y pas de code vestimentaire, les gens y vont en tenue de tous les jours.
Jo	Ben non, c'est pas drôle, moi, j'aime être bien habillée pour un vernissage !
Assia	Tu as raison, on va à la boutique solidaire ?
Jo	Ouiiiii !
Assia	Allons-y !

2 Answer the questions.

a Why does Jo open Assia's letter?
b What kind of invitation does she find inside the envelope?
c How many people are invited?
d Is Jo pleased to find out there is no dress code?
e What do the friends decide to do before they attend the event?

LANGUAGE BUILDER 3

Language discovery 3

Assia invites Jo to the opening of a photography exhibition by saying:

On .... va ensemble ? ***(Shall we go to it together?)***

Jo, who is not keen at first, replies:

Euh, je n'ai pas très envie d'.................... aller. ***(Er, I don't feel very much like going there/to it.)***

The same word is missing from each sentence—can you find it? What do you think the missing word means?

The pronoun y

Imagine a context where you are speaking English and talking about someone you know named Louise who goes to the swimming pool every week. If you say *Louise goes every week*, these words count as a complete sentence. However, if you were to say Louise va chaque semaine, a French speaker would be waiting for you to tell them *where* Louise is going. In other words, your sentence would be incomplete. So, you would need to say one of the following: Louise va à la piscine or Louise y va. The word y replaces the phrase à la piscine, so à + a noun can be replaced by y. Below are some more examples, where the phrases replaced by y are underlined.

Mo va <u>à la fête</u> samedi. → Mo y va samedi.

Tu vas <u>au marché aux puces</u> ? → Tu y vas ?

Jeanne ne travaille pas <u>aux Halles</u>. → Jeanne n'y travaille pas.

Do you notice all the underlined phrases begin with the preposition à (remember: à + le = au, à + les = aux)? Note, too, that y goes just before the verb. Even in the negative, y remains directly before the verb:

Louise y va. →	*Louse goes there/to it.* →
Louise n'y va pas.	*Louise does not go there/to it.*

When y is used in structures that involve two verbs (e.g., on veut aller), it goes before the second verb: on veut y aller. This also applies in the negative: on ne veut pas y aller.

Language practice 3

1 Rewrite the sentences below, replacing the underlined phrase with y. Pay attention to the word order.

Example: Elles vont au café avant le cinéma. *Elles y vont avant le cinéma.*

a Nous allons au concert vers dix-huit heures.

b Est-ce que vous allez au festival de la musique cette année ?

c Jean-Pierre ne va pas à l'école aujourd'hui.

d Je ne reste jamais au travail après six heures du soir.

2 Rewrite the sentences below to create longer versions, replacing y by à + the noun indicated.

Example: Nous y allons toutes les semaines. (*le cinéma*)
Nous allons au cinéma toutes les semaines.

a Jean-Jacques veut y aller demain. (*la piscine*)

b Louise n'aime pas y aller. (*les Catacombes*)

c Fatou préfère y aller à pied. (*l'école*)

d Marie-Laure ne veut pas y assister. (*le match de rugby*)

LANGUAGE BUILDER 4

Language discovery 4

Listen to the conversation again and repeat each line in the pauses provided. Try to imitate the phrasing and intonation you hear.

1 In Language discovery 3 we looked at Jo's remark Je n'ai pas très envie d'y aller. If we remove très, we have a simple statement: Je n'ai pas envie d'y aller. This can be translated as *I don't feel like going to it*. Can you work out how to say:

a I feel like going to it.

b I feel like drinking a coffee?

2 Can you figure out how to say *I feel like a coffee* (instead of the longer version *I feel like drinking a coffee*)?

Avoir envie de (faire) *To feel like (doing)*

To talk about things you (don't) feel like doing, use the expression avoir envie de with another verb

J'ai envie d'aller au restaurant.	*I feel like going to the restaurant.*
J'ai envie de rester chez moi ce soir.	*I feel like staying home tonight.*

Avoir envie de can also be used with a noun:

J'ai envie d'un café.	*I feel like a coffee.*
J'ai envie d'une glace.	*I feel like an ice-cream.*

Incidentally, in a situation where people are suggesting an activity or something to eat or drink, they might typically ask: Tu en as envie ? or Vous en avez envie ? (*Do you feel like it?*) Notice how the word en is used here; you will learn more about this in Unit 8.

Language practice 4

1 Translate the following into French, using avoir envie de.

- **a** Florence and Mo, do you feel like going to the movies?
- **b** And Paul, do you feel like coming with us?
- **c** He does not feel like seeing a horror movie.
- **d** Marie and Djamel feel like eating at the restaurant.

2 Turn each of these sentences/questions into shorter ones following the example.

Example: J'ai envie de boire un café. *J'ai envie d'un café.*

- **a** Est-ce que vous avez envie de prendre un thé ?
- **b** Nous n'avons pas envie de boire un café.
- **c** Tu as envie de manger un croissant ?

07.10

3 Listen to Conversation 2 again and play the role of Assia. Speak in the pauses provides. What exhibitions would you like to see?

SKILL BUILDER

Add the missing words to the dialogue between Jo and Assia as they plan their outings over the weekend. You can use the translation as a guide.

After another week of work, Eva and Charles make plans to go to the movies with friends.

Jo	Tu as envie de .... ce weekend ?
Assia	Oui ! .... ce soir. J'..................... aller au restaurant et au cinéma.
Jo	Parfait. Je .... de préparer ce gâteau aux framboises et au chocolat et ensuite je .... chez toi. C'est une nouvelle recette de Charles.
Assia	Miam, miam. .... se retrouve plutôt chez toi...
Jo	Super ! Et je texte Pierre et Thomas au cas où ils voudraient nous retrouver au cinéma.
Assia	Oui, dis-leur que nous allons voir une rétrospective de Varda à l'UGC Rotonde.
Jo	Chouette ! Pierre dit qu'ils nous .... retrouvent.
Assia	Et après le film .... va prendre un verre à Montparnasse ?
Jo	Ou .... va aller jusqu'à St-Michel au Caveau de la Huchette ?
Assia	Et où est-ce qu'on va manger ?
Jo	Une bonne crêperie rue du Montparnasse.... ?
Assia	Super ! On .... va à pied ou en métro ?
Jo	Comme tu préfères ! Je .... que le week-end commence tout de suite !
Assia	Moi aussi. Je t'embrasse, à tout à l'heure !

Jo: Do you want to go out this weekend? **Assia**: Yes! Let's go out tonight. I feel like going to a restaurant and to the movies. **Jo**: Perfect. I am finishing this raspberry and chocolate cake and then I'll come to your place. This is a new recipe from Charles. **Assia**: Yum, yum. We'll meet up at your place instead... **Jo**: Great! And I'll text Pierre and Thomas in case they want to meet us at the cinema. **Assia**: Yes, tell them that we are going to see a retrospective of Varda at the UGC Rotonde. **Jo**: Great! Pierre says that they will meet us there. **Assia**: And after the film we'll have a drink at Montparnasse? **Jo**: Or we'll go to St-Michel to the Caveau de la Huchette? **Assia**: And where are we going to eat? **Jo**: A good creperie on rue du Montparnasse...? **Assia**: Perfect! Are we getting there on foot or by metro? **Jo**: As you prefer. I want the weekend to start right away! **Assia**: Me too. Kisses, see you later!

TEST YOURSELF

1 Give the infinitif (*infinitive form*) of the verbs underlined below. The first one has been done for you.

a Ils sortent ce soir, mais ils ne partent pas avant dix heures. *sortir ; partir*
b Elles viennent avec nous. ....
c Tous les films à l'affiche finissent avant minuit. ....
d Le cinéma ouvre à huit heures du soir. ....

2 Fill in the gaps, using the verbs indicated in brackets.

a Nous .... toujours des places près de l'écran si possible. (*choisir*)
b Tu .... ce soir ? Vers quelle heure ? (*sortir*)
c Jean-Marc, ... ! Tes amis sont là ! (*venir*)
d Vous .... où ce soir : à l'hôtel ou chez votre cousine ? (*dormir*)

3 Complete the passage below using the verbs indicated. Then translate the passage and compare your version with the translation provided.

En été, nous .... (*sortir*) souvent, surtout pour aller au cinéma. Au mois de juin, nous .... (*partir*) en vacances. Nous .... (*réfléchir*) toujours longtemps avant de décider, mais nous .... (*finir*) le plus souvent par choisir la Corse.

During the summer we often go out, especially to go to the movies. In June we go on holiday. We always think for a long time before reaching a decision but more often than not we end up choosing Corsica.

Remember to use **My review** and **My takeaway** to assess your progress and reflect on your learning experience.

Congratulations on completing the first level of your studies! Now it's time to put your skills to the test—take the A1 Assessment online at library.teachyourself.com and see how much you've learned.

8

In this lesson you will learn how to:

» Talk about specific measures
» Talk about quantities in general
» Order a meal at a restaurant
» Go shopping in a market

L'art de vivre

My study plan

I plan to work with Unit 8

○ Every day
○ Twice a week
○ Other ____________

I plan to study for

○ 5–15 minutes
○ 15–30 minutes
○ 30–45+ minutes

My progress tracker

Day / Date	Listen	Speak	Read	Write	Converse
	○	○	○	○	○
	○	○	○	○	○
	○	○	○	○	○
	○	○	○	○	○
	○	○	○	○	○
	○	○	○	○	○
	○	○	○	○	○

My goals

What do you want to be able to do or say in French when you complete this unit?

		Done
1	....	○
2	....	○
3	....	○

My review

SELF CHECK

	I can ...
●	... order a meal in a restaurant.
●	... buy ingredients in a market.
●	... speak about specific quantities.
●	... indicate general measurements.

CULTURE POINT 1

La cuisine belge *Belgian cuisine*

Belgium's cuisine draws on two mutually enriching traditions. One of these is historically associated with the region of Belgium known as la Flandre (*Flanders*), the other with Belgium's neighbor France. These traditions continue to develop and have been complemented by influences from many other nations, so that now the country offers une corne d'abondance (*a cornucopia*) of culinary delights. As far as la cuisine de rue (*street food*) goes, les frites avec mayonnaise (*fries with mayonnaise*) and les gaufres (*waffles*) have achieved un statut d'icône (*iconic status*). Other dishes seen as typically Belgian are moules frites (*mussels with fries*), carbonades flamandes (*meat simmered in a beer sauce*), and chicons au gratin (*endives with béchamel sauce, wrapped in ham*). Tempting options for vegetarians and vegans are becoming more widespread in Belgium, as they are in many other European countries. If you are in central Brussels and you want to treat yourself without blowing the budget, you are likely to find several restaurants offering des menus fixes (*set menus*) in the rue des Bouchers. If you visit Belgium, you will probably find that the locals are all the more welcoming if you display cultural sensitivity when you speak to people in restaurants and shops: remember that there are three official languages in Belgium.

Check this website and decide which food you would most like to try in Belgium.

VOCABULARY BUILDER 1

Read the words and phrases below and supply the missing English words and expressions. Then listen to the recording and imitate the pronunciation you hear.

Allons au restaurant *Let's go to the restaurant*

LES RESTAURANTS, LES MENUS	*RESTAURANTS AND MENUS*
une brasserie	....
une carte	*menu*
une crêperie	*crêperie, pancake house*
un menu fixe/à la carte	*set/à la carte menu*
une pizzeria	....
Les consommations – Bon appétit !	*Food and drinks—Enjoy!*
un apéro/apéritif	....
une bouillabaisse	*bouillabaisse, fish soup*
un dessert	....
une entrée	*starter*
une glace	*ice cream*
une boule/deux boules	*one scoop/two scoops*
un plat sans gluten/végétarien/végan	*gluten-free/vegetarian/vegan dish*
le plat principal/le plat du jour	*main course/dish of the day*
un steak-frites	*steak and fries*
le sucre	*sugar*
un tiramisu	....

EXPRESSIONS	*EXPRESSIONS*
Nous voudrions commander à boire.	*We would like to order something to drink.*
Ne grignote pas avant les repas !	*Don't snack before meals!*
Installez-vous !	*Take a seat.*
Je vous laisse regarder le menu/la carte.	*I'll let you look at the menu.*
Je te/vous recommande...	*I recommend ...*
un bol d'olives	*bowl of olives*
On partage une salade niçoise ?	*Shall we share a niçoise salad?*
L'addition, s'il vous plaît !	*The bill, please!*
Je reviens dans quelques minutes.	*I'm coming back in a few minutes.*
Les enfants prennent leur goûter à quatre heures.	*The children have their afternoon snack at four.*

Vocabulary practice 1

Match the following statements with who is most likely to have said them (the server or the customer).

a Installez-vous. *server* *customer*
b Nous voulons commander trois cafés. *server* *customer*
c Aujourd'hui le plat principal est la bouillabaisse. *server* *customer*
d Est-ce qu'il y un menu fixe ? *server* *customer*

Pronunciation practice 1

In French, the letter s sometimes sounds like *s* in English, and sometimes like *z*. It is pronounced as *z* in two cases:

(a) when it appears alone (-s-, not -ss-) between two vowels, as in un visage (*face*);

(b) when it forms a liaison, as in mes_amis, where the s of mes is pronounced as *z*.

1 Bearing this in mind, in which (two) of the following phrases is s pronounced as *z*?

a une salle **b** un poisson **c** mes amis **d** un visage

08.02

2 Practice saying the words in pauses in recording. Then listen to the two virelangues (*tongue twisters*) and practice saying them quickly:

Poisson sans boisson c'est poison — *fish without drink is poison*

Zazie causait avec sa cousine en cousant — *Zazie was chatting with her cousin while sewing*

> The measure un demi de bière refers to different volumes of beer depending on the country you are in. In Belgium it might be half a liter, while in France it is commonly a quarter of a liter.

CONVERSATION 1

Au restaurant *At the restaurant*

08.03

1 Here are few expressions to help you understand the conversation.

prendre une commande — *take down an order*
des moules-frites — *mussels with fries*
un chicon — *chicory, endive*
une croquette — *croquette*
se régaler — *to have a feast*
un demi de bière pression — *half a draft beer*

08.04

2 Listen to the conversation without looking at the text. Then listen to the conversation again and read the text.

Charles and Eva enjoy going out on the weekend to sample the local cuisine, and in Brussels there is never a shortage of interesting dishes to enjoy.

La serveuse	Bonjour ! C'est pour déjeuner ?
Eva	Bonjour ! Oui, pour deux personnes.
La serveuse	Parfait ! Installez-vous. Je vous laisse regarder la carte. Je reviens dans quelques minutes pour prendre votre commande.
Eva	Alors, je te recommande bien sûr les moules-frites ou la carbonade.
Charles	J'adore les moules-frites.
Eva	Moi aussi ! Et en entrée, la salade de chicons ou les croquettes.
Charles	Qu'est-ce que tu vas prendre, toi ?
Eva	Moi, je vais prendre la salade, il y a assez de calories dans les frites !
Charles	OK, moi je prends les croquettes. Et pour le dessert ?
Eva	Le tiramisu au spéculoos ou la gaufre au chocolat.
Charles	Hmmmm ! C'est tentant... On partage ?
La serveuse	Alors, vous désirez ?
Eva	Oui, en entrée une salade de chicons et des croquettes, et pour le plat principal deux moules-frites.
La serveuse	Des desserts ?
Eva	Oui, une gaufre au chocolat.
La serveuse	Très bien. Vous voulez boire quelque chose ? De la bière, du vin, de l'eau minérale ?
Eva	Pour moi, un verre de vin blanc. Et un peu d'eau, s'il vous plaît.
Charles	Moi, je prends un demi de bière pression.
La serveuse	C'est parfait, merci, bon appétit !

In Belgium chicon means *endive/chicory*; in parts of France, the same word refers to a type of lettuce. (French nationals use une endive for *endive*.) For historical reasons, terms for herbs and spices often differ among francophone cultures.

3 Answer the questions.

a What meal are Eva and Charles going to have at the restaurant: lunch or dinner?
b What does Eva recommend as a main course?
c What two starters do Eva and Charles decide to order?
d Do they plan to share the starter, the dessert or both?
e Are they likely to share the main course? Why/Why not?

LANGUAGE BUILDER 1

Language discovery 1

1 Towards the end of Conversation 1, the waiter offers a choice of drinks: De la bière, du vin, de l'eau minérale. Why does the waiter use different words (first de la, then du, then de l') to say *some* (*beer/wine/water*)?

2 Eva asks for un verre de vin blanc and de l'eau, and Charles orders un demi de bière. Which one of these three forms does not specify a quantity?

a un verre de vin **b** un demi de bière **c** de l'eau minérale

Precise quantities

In Unit 4, you learned that the partitive article (du, de l', de la) is used to talk about a non-specific amount of something.

Tu as du lait ? *Do you have any milk?*

Du, de l', de la should never be used when speaking about specific amounts (i.e. how much or how many) of anything. In fact, when precise amounts are mentioned, French and English work in a similar way. English speakers might ask for *a bottle of water*, *two glasses of wine*, or *500 g of cheese*. The equivalent phrases in French are une bouteille d'eau, deux verres de vin, or 500 g de fromage. All these phrases mentioning specific amounts follow a similar pattern, as shown by the tables below.

Quantité *Amount*	**+ de** *+ of*	**+ nom** *+ noun*
une bouteille *a/one bottle*	**d'*** *of*	**eau** *water*
deux verres *two glasses*	**de** *of*	**vin** *wine*
500 grammes *500 grams*	**de** *of*	**fromage** *cheese*
un kilo *a/one kilo*	**de** *of*	**pommes** *apples*

* de is shortened to d' before a noun that begins with a vowel (such as eau).

Language practice 1

Complete the sentences by translating the phrases in parentheses into French. The first one has been completed as an example.

a On va commander *de l'eau.* (*some water*)

b On va commander .... (*a bottle of water*)

c Je voudrais .... (*some wine*)

d Je voudrais boire .... (*a glass of wine*)

e S'il vous plaît, je voudrais commander .... (*some ice cream*)

f On voudrait .... s'il vous plaît. (*two scoops of ice cream*)

g Nous voudrions .... s'il vous plaît. (*some olives*)

h Tu vas commander .... ? (*a bowl of olives*)

i J'ai envie d'une .... (*an ice cream*)

j J'ai envie de .... (*three scoops of ice cream*)

If you are ordering in a café or restaurant, it is rather impolite to say je veux... (*I want...*). So to order a coffee you should say Je voudrais un café, s'il vous plaît (*I would like a coffee, please*). On the other hand, Un café s'il vous plaît (with no verb at all) is sufficiently polite.

LANGUAGE BUILDER 2

Language discovery 2

Listen to the conversation again and repeat each line in the pauses provided. Try to imitate the phrasing and intonation you hear.

With healthy eating in mind, Eva says that she will order salad as a starter because il y a assez de calories (*enough calories*) dans les frites. And to drink, she orders un verre de vin (*a glass of wine*) and un peu d'eau (*a little water*).

What do all these expressions of quantity have in common?

Assez, beaucoup, trop... *Enough, a lot, too much ...*

Earlier you learned how to talk about precise quantities in French by using the following pattern: quantity + de + noun, e.g., un kilo de farine. The same pattern is used after *approximate* expressions of quantity such as un peu de (*a little*), assez de (*enough*), beaucoup de (*a lot*), and trop de (*too much*).

Je mange un peu de sucre	*I eat a bit of sugar*
Elle ne mange pas assez de sucre	*She does not eat enough sugar*
Nous mangeons beaucoup de sucre	*We eat a lot of sugar*
Ils mangent trop de sucre	*They eat too much sugar*

The same rule applies to both countable and non-countable nouns. Compare:

trop de pommes	*too many apples*
trop de pain/de farine/d'eau	*too much bread/flour/water*

To ask a question about quantities, use combien + de.

Tu as combien de farine ?	*How much flour do you have?*
Tu as combien de pommes ?	*How many apples do you have?*

Language practice 2

1 Complete the table.

Tu as du beurre.	*You have some butter.*
a	*You have too much butter.*
Tu as combien de beurre ?	*How much butter do you have?*
Karine a du lait.	*Karine has some milk.*
b	*Karine has enough milk.*
c	*Karine has a lot of milk.*
Nous avons de l'eau.	*We have some water.*
d	*We have a bit of water.*
Nous avons combien d'eau ?	*How much water do we have?*
Tu as des pommes ?	*Do you have any apples?*
Mo a trop de pommes.	*Mo has too many apples.*
e	*How many apples does Mo have?*

08.06

2 Now play the conversation again and play the role of le serveur. Speak in the pauses. Try not to refer to the text.

CULTURE POINT 2

Les marchés *Markets*

Les marchés alimentaires (*food markets*) are a feature of life in many French-speaking cultures. They bring fresh foodstuffs, often locally sourced, to the center of villages and towns, large and small. Paris abrite (*is home to*) numerous markets of this kind. The oldest of all is situated in the area of Paris known as le Marais (*the Marsh*). Here, in 1615, a petit marché du marais (*small market of the marsh*) was constructed on the orders of King Louis XIII. It has been known since the 18th century as le Marché des Enfants Rouges, on account of an orphanage that used to exist near the site: you can guess what color uniform the children are supposed to have worn! The market was threatened with demolition in the mid-1990s, but instead it was refurbished and reopened in 2000 to general acclaim. Now it offers tastes of world cuisine including ingredients for les plats libanais, marocains et corses (*Lebanese, Moroccan, and Corsican dishes*), not forgetting traditional French farm produce. Another Parisian food market with an even greater claim to internationalism is found not far from the famous church Sacré-Cœur (*Sacred Heart*), in the 18th arrondissement. Le Marché de Château Rouge is known for its large éventail (*broad range*) of products reflecting African and Caribbean traditions, though other world regions such as China and the Indian subcontinent are also represented there. It has become a magnet for enthusiasts of world cuisine from Paris and beyond.

Check this list of markets. Which one(s) would you like to visit?

VOCABULARY BUILDER 2

Read the words and phrases below and supply the missing English words and expressions. Then listen to the recording and imitate the pronunciation you hear.

Allons au marché *Let's go to the market*

LES PLATS-REPAS	***SINGLE-DISH MEALS***
un cassoulet	*cassoulet (dish of white beans with meat)*
un couscous	*couscous*
un tajine	*tagine*
LES LÉGUMES ET AUTRES INGRÉDIENTS	***VEGETABLES AND OTHER INGREDIENTS***
une banane, une banane plantain	*banana, plantain*
une carotte	....
la coriandre	*cilantro/coriander*
le curcuma	*turmeric*
le gombo	*okra*
une patate douce	*sweet potato*
le manioc	*manioc/cassava*
un oignon	....
le persil	*parsley*
le piment	*chili pepper*
un pois chiche/des pois chiches	*chickpea/chickpeas*
une tomate	....
LES FRUITS DU MARCHÉ	***FRUITS***
un ananas	*pineapple*
une mangue	*mango*
une papaye	....
une pastèque	*watermelon*
EXPRESSIONS	***EXPRESSIONS***
Ce ne sont pas mes oignons.	*It's not my business (literally: those are not my onions).*
Il cuisine comme un chef.	*He cooks like a chef.*
voilà.../Voilà !	*here is .../Here it is!*
J'ai besoin d'un litre de lait.	*I need a liter of milk.*
Il mange une tranche de pain.	*He is eating a slice of bread.*
Est-ce que tu veux un morceau de sucre ?	*Would you like a lump of sugar?*
J'ai envie d'une barquette de fraises.	*I would like a punnet of strawberries.*
Ce pot de confiture est pour ma mère.	*This jar of jam is for my mother.*

Vocabulary practice 2

Although different regions of the world have their own versions of couscous, they generally use the following ingredients: onions, tomatoes, carrots, turmeric, and cilantro (coriander). Imagine you are preparing a couscous to serve for lunch followed by a fruit salad—continue writing a shopping list of ingredients you will need to have for those two dishes.

Pour le couscous, j'ai besoin de... ....

....

Pour la salade de fruits, j'ai besoin de... ....

....

Pronunciation practice 2

When French words end in an -s, that letter is generally not pronounced. However, there are exceptions. Here are some examples related to eating and drinking (they are all masculine): ananas (*pineapple*); cassis (*blackberry, blackberry liqueur*); couscous (*couscous*); maïs (*corn*). Other such words (once again, they are all masculine) include bus (*bus*); cactus (*cactus*); campus (*campus*); ours (*bear*); virus (*virus*).

08.08

Listen to the recording, then read the sentences below out loud. Make sure to pronounce the -s at the end of each underlined noun. Then listen again and imitate the pronunciation of the speaker.

Je voudrais un ananas, des cassis et du maïs.
I would like a pineapple, some blackberries, and some corn.

Elle ne va pas au campus à pied. Elle prend plutôt le bus.
She doesn't walk to the campus. She takes the bus instead.

Sur cette photo, on voit un ours, allongé près d'un cactus.
In this photo, we see a bear, stretched out near a cactus plant.

CONVERSATION 2

Au marché *At the market*

08.09

1 Here are a few words and expressions to help you understand the conversation.

Je voudrais un bouquet de coriandre.	*I would like a bunch of coriander.*
Ce sera tout ?	*Will that be all?*
Vous voulez autre chose ?	*Do you want anything else?*
Je vous dois combien ?	*How much do I owe you?*
Huit euros quatre-vingts, s'il vous plaît.	*Eight euros eighty (cents), please.*
Faire suer les oignons	*Sweat the onions (fry the onions until soft)*

08.10

2 Listen to the conversation without looking at the text. Then listen to the conversation again and read the text.

Jo et Assia are visiting le Marché de Château-Rouge together as they want to prepare a Caribbean meal. Assia's friend Maryse has advised her that this is the go-to market for the ingredients she is looking for.

La vendeuse	Bonjour Mesdames ! Qu'est-ce que je vous sers ?
Assia	Alors, je voudrais de la coriandre et du curcuma s'il vous plaît.
La vendeuse	Oui, vous voulez combien de coriandre ?
Assia	Un bouquet s'il vous plaît.
La vendeuse	Et le curcuma ? Vous en voulez combien ?
Assia	Un petit sachet s'il vous plaît. Et un kilo de gombos.
La vendeuse	Vous voulez autre chose ?
Assia	Non, merci. Combien je vous dois ?
La vendeuse	Huit euros quatre-vingts s'il vous plaît.
Le vendeur	Et vous, Madame ?
Jo	Je voudrais des courgettes. Cinq s'il vous plaît. Vous avez du manioc ?
Le vendeur	Oui, bien sûr. Vous en voulez combien ?
Jo	Deux kilos s'il vous plaît.
Le vendeur	Voilà, Madame. Avec ceci ?
Jo	Ce sera tout, c'est combien ?
Le vendeur	Six euros trente.
Jo	Voilà, Monsieur.
Le vendeur	Merci. Au revoir, Mesdames.

Later, at home, the friends are preparing their couscous.

Jo	Bon, nous avons préparé tous les légumes : oignons, courgettes, carottes, etc. Alors, selon la recette, on fait quoi maintenant ?
Assia	Attends, je lis : "Faire suer les oignons dans de l'huile d'olive pendant 10 minutes. Ajouter les carottes, les courgettes et un peu d'eau..."
Jo	D'accord. Tu peux me passer l'huile d'olive s'il te plaît ?

3 Answer the questions.

- **a** What ingredients does Assia buy?
- **b** How much does Assia spend at the market?
- **c** What vegetable does Jo want five of?
- **d** Who spends less money at the market—Jo or Assia?
- **e** If they wanted to prepare a couscous following this recipe, what other ingredients would they need?

LANGUAGE BUILDER 3

Language discovery 3

When Assia asks for de la coriandre (*some cilantro*) and du curcuma (*some turmeric*), the stallholder asks (a) Vous voulez combien de coriandre ? (b) Et le curcuma, vous en voulez combien ? So in question (b), the stallholder uses en instead of using de + curcuma.

1 Can you figure out how the questions below could be shortened using en? The first one has been done for you.

- **a** Vous voulez combien de carottes ? Vous en voulez combien ?
- **b** Vous voulez combien de croissants ?
- **c** Tu veux combien de sucre ?

2 Complete this rule of thumb: In French, en replaces .... + a noun.

Vous en voulez combien? *How much do you want?*

To ask *How much cilantro do you want?* a French speaker would say: Vous voulez combien de coriandre ? A briefer version of the same question would be: Vous en voulez combien ? (*How much of it do you want?*). Here, two words in the longer version (de + coriandre) have been replaced by the single word en. You should also notice that en is (and must be) placed directly before the verb.

En can be used in the same way with plurals:

Tu veux combien de piments ? or Tu en veux combien ?	*How many chilli peppers do you want?* or *How many of them do you want?*
Jules achète combien de pommes ? Il en achète trois.	*How many apples is Jules buying?* *He is buying three.*

Language practice 3

1 In the following questions, replace de + noun with en.

- **a** Djamel et Marie ont combien d'enfants ?
- **b** Vous allez acheter combien de curcuma ?
- **c** Il y a combien de restaurants dans le quartier ?

2 Rewrite each sentence below using en.

- **a** Il boit beaucoup de café. Il ....
- **b** J'ai un peu de pain chez moi. J'..................... .
- **c** Nous avons trop de fromage. Nous ....
- **d** Vous avez assez de pommes. Vous ....

If an expression includes y and en together, then y is placed before en. For instance, to say *there are three of them* you would say il y en a trois.

LANGUAGE BUILDER 4

Language discovery 4

08.11 **Listen to the conversation again and repeat each line in the pauses provided. Try to imitate the phrasing and intonation you hear.**

In the conversation, Assia reads from her recipe for couscous, which begins as follows:

Faire suer les oignons dans de l'huile d'olive. Ajouter les carottes, le courgettes et un peu d'eau.

What do you notice about the form of the verb in the recipe?

Les recettes, les consignes *Recipes, instructions*

In English-language recipes, the imperative form is typically used to give instructions: *mix, add, leave to rest* (etc.) Similarly, the vous-form imperative is often used in French-language recipes: mélangez, ajoutez. But you should note that in French (unlike English) the infinitive can be used as an alternative to the imperative: mélanger, ajouter. And writers of recipes aimed specifically at children generally favor the tu-form imperative: mélange, ajoute.

Language practice 4

1 Imagine you are writing a recipe book for children. Below is a recipe for making œufs brouillés (*scrambled eggs*), followed by a translation into English. Complete the recipe, using tu-form imperatives (the first one has been done for you):

Dans une casserole, casse trois œufs puis (ajouter) **a** .... deux cuillères à soupe de lait, du sel et du poivre, et 10 g de beurre. (Laisser) **b** .... cuire à feu doux, sans cesser de fouetter. Hors du feu, (ajouter) **c** .... encore une noix de beurre. (Fouetter) **d** .... encore. Et voilà, c'est prêt...

Break the eggs into a pan then add two tablespoons of milk, some salt and pepper, and 10 g of butter. Allow to cook at a low heat, beating all the time. Off the stove, add another knob of butter. Beat again. And there you are...

08.12 **2 Now play the conversation again and play Jo's role. Speak in the pauses. Try not to refer to the text. Would you order different vegetables?**

SKILL BUILDER

1 Complete each sentence with what you would usually buy in each type of shop.

a À la boulangerie, j'achète ....
b À la poissonnerie, elle achète ....
c À la fromagerie, nous achetons ....
d À la boucherie, tu achètes....................
e À la pâtisserie, elles achètent....................

2 Complete each answer with en and then provide a translation of each.

a Tu veux combien de baguettes ? J'.................... veux trois.
b Elle mange trois bananes tous les jours ? Oui, elle .... mange beaucoup.
c Vous avez assez d'argent ? Oui, nous .... avons assez.
d J'ai trop de travail en ce moment. Et toi ? Oui, moi aussi j '.................... ai trop.

3 Match the measures/quantities on the left with the product on the right.

a un litre de
b un carré de
c une barquette de
d un pot de
e une tranche de
f un morceau de

1 sucre
2 lait
3 confiture
4 chocolat
5 pain
6 fraises

4 Put the events in order to describe what normally happens when you eat at a restaurant.

a demander l'addition
b manger le plat principal
c commander
d manger l'entrée
e prendre l'apéritif
f regarder la carte
g manger le dessert
h payer l'addition

5 Match the foods and drinks listed below to the typical meal when one might eat or drink them.

croissants céréales soupe de légumes café yaourt bœuf bourguignon
jus d'orange salade niçoise tartines charcuterie thé brioche
crème caramel fruits quiche lorraine

petit déjeuner	déjeuner	goûter	dîner

TEST YOURSELF

Complete the dialogue below using the translation as a guide.

Jo Je vais aller au marché, tu veux venir avec moi ?

Assia Oui je veux bien. J'ai envie d'acheter des pommes et **a** .... Nous **b** .... de lait et d' **c** ...., aussi.

Jo Est-ce qu' **d** .... est assez ou c'est **e** .... ?

Assia Un kilo c'est parfait. Comme ça **f** .... pour préparer une tarte et pour faire une salade.

Jo Et **g** .... est-ce qu'il te faut ?

Assia h .... ou peut-être deux—J'adore les fraises.

Jo Tu bois beaucoup de lait ?

Assia Pas tellement, mais on **i** .... pour le petit déjeuner.

Jo Fais attention et **j** .... un bon camembert bien affiné.

Assia Oui peut-être on peut demander au fromager de choisir.

Translation

Jo: I'm going to go to the market, do you want to go with me?

Assia: Yes, I do. I want to buy apples and strawberries. And we need milk and a little cheese, too.

Jo: Is a kilo of apples enough or too much?

Assia: A kilo is perfect. That way I have enough to prepare a pie and to put in a salad.

Jo: And how many strawberries do you need?

Assia: A punnet or maybe two—I love strawberries

Jo: Do you drink a lot of milk?

Assia: Not so much, but we need it for breakfast.

Jo: Make sure you choose a good, well-matured Camembert.

Assia: Yes, maybe we can ask the cheesemaker to choose.

Remember to use **My review** and **My takeaway** to assess your progress and reflect on your learning experience.

9

In this lesson you will learn how to:

» Talk about your health
» Talk about your body
» Describe people
» Express requirements and obligations

Le corps et l'image

My study plan

I plan to work with Unit 9

○ Every day
○ Twice a week
○ Other ____________

I plan to study for

○ 5–15 minutes
○ 15–30 minutes
○ 30–45+ minutes

My progress tracker

Day / Date	Listening	Speaking	Reading	Writing	Conversation
	○	○	○	○	○
	○	○	○	○	○
	○	○	○	○	○
	○	○	○	○	○
	○	○	○	○	○
	○	○	○	○	○
	○	○	○	○	○

My goals

What do you want to be able to do or say in French when you complete this unit?

		Done
1	....	○
2	....	○
3	....	○

My review

SELF CHECK

	I can ...
●	... describe basic symptoms to a doctor.
●	... call for urgent medical help.
●	... indicate what must be done.
●	... describe people.

CULTURE POINT 1

La santé *Health*

A number of initiatives that aim to promote des services de santé (*healthcare*) for all have their origins in francophone culture. Perhaps the best known of these is the ONG (*NGO*) Médecins sans frontières (*Doctors without Borders*). This ONG was set up in 1971 by French doctors and journalists who wanted to maximize access to medical care in all parts of the world, without regard to politics or religion. It has become a truly global movement, with headquarters in the Ivory Coast and an international office in Geneva. France itself has a highly developed healthcare system. If you are traveling in l'Hexagone (*France*) or other francophone regions of the world, you should know what to do if you are souffrant/souffrante (*unwell*). Minimally, you should know the phrases je me sens mal (I *feel unwell*) and j'ai mal (*I have a pain*). Apart from la douleur (*pain*), your symptômes (*symptoms*) might include une toux (*a cough*), une fièvre (*fever*), or une migraine (*headache*). In many countries, a pharmacy is indicated by une croix verte (*a green cross*). Telephone numbers for les urgences médicales (*medical emergencies*) vary. In France, the number is 112, while in Belgium it is either 112 or 100.

Look at this website from the French government. What are the emergency numbers in France?

VOCABULARY BUILDER 1

Read the words and phrases below and supply the missing English words and expressions. Then listen to the recording and imitate the pronunciation you hear.

LES PROFESSIONS DE LA SANTÉ	*HEALTH PROFESSIONS*
un dentiste/une dentiste	....
un médecin/une médecin	*doctor*
un pharmacien/une pharmacienne	*pharmacist*
se soigner	*to take care of oneself*
s'alimenter	*to feed oneself*
s'échauffer	*to warm (oneself) up*
s'hydrater	*to stay hydrated*
au cas où	*just in case*
une ambulance	....
un cabinet médical	*doctor's office*
un hôpital	....
une pharmacie	....
un médicament	*medicine/treatment*
la médecine	*the field of medicine*
des comprimés/un comprimé	*tablets/a tablet*
le sirop (pour la toux)	*(cough) syrup*
une trousse de premiers secours	*first-aid kit*

EXPRESSIONS	*EXPRESSIONS*
j'ai mal aux dents	*I have a toothache*
ça fait mal	*it hurts*
je me sens bien/mal	*I feel well/poorly*
tousser, j'ai de la toux	*to cough, I have a cough*
respirer, la respiration	*to breathe, breathing*
J'ai de la fièvre	*I have a fever*
il ne faut pas forcer	*one mustn't overdo it*
Tout le monde a peur d'être malade.	*Everyone is afraid of being sick.*

To hurt is faire mal. The expression ça fait mal means *it hurts*. You can add me, te, lui, nous, vous, or leur as appropriate, for example, ça leur fait mal (*it's hurting them*). To say *these shoes are hurting him/her* you would say ces chaussures lui font mal. Similarly, *this belt is hurting me* becomes cette ceinture me fait mal.

Vocabulary practice 1

1 Complete the following sentences, using words from the Vocabulary builder above:

a Madame Dutour travaille dans une pharmacie. Elle est ....

b Madame Richard a un cabinet médical. Elle est ....

c Quand j'ai une migraine, je prends des ....

d Je prends du sirop quand j'ai de la ....

e Quand on a ...., on doit aller chez le dentiste.

Pronunciation practice 1

09.02

In French, accents such as an acute (´), a circumflex (^), or a grave (`) can be attached to vowels, affecting their sound and pronunciation. In the case of the letter e, there is generally no difference in pronunciation between e + grave (è) and e + circumflex (ê). On the other hand, e + acute (é) sounds different from the other two (è/ê).

Listen to the recorded phrases. Then listen again while reading along and focusing on the underlined words. Can you hear and reproduce the difference between: è/ê and é? It might take more than one go...

Je vais prendre une tasse de café.
J'ai mal à la tête.
Je me lève tard le week-end.
Cet été, je vais peut-être aller chez mes parents.
J'ai lavé des vêtements pour demain.
Il se réveille très tôt.

CONVERSATION 1

Le marathon *The marathon*

09.03

1 Here are a few words and expressions to help you understand the conversation.

un entraînement	*training session*	sucré	*sugary, sweet*
un étirement	*stretch; stretching exercise*	un rythme	*rhythm*
		par contre	*on the other hand*
salé	*salty, savory*	des conseils	*advice*

09.04

2 Listen to the conversation without looking at the text. Then listen to the conversation again and read the text.

Eva and Charles are talking about the Beer Lovers' Marathon.

Eva Alors, cet entraînement pour le marathon, ça se passe bien ?

Charles Oui, ça va ! Je commence... Pour l'instant, je cours 10 km deux fois par semaine.

Eva Bravo, c'est bien ! Tu n'as pas mal aux pieds ?

Charles Non, j'ai des chaussures de qualité.

Eva C'est important. Tu n'as pas mal aux jambes ?

Charles Non, je fais des étirements après chaque entraînement.

Eva C'est bien. Il faut aussi s'hydrater souvent.

Charles Oui, je sais, et il faut aussi bien s'alimenter !

Eva C'est ça ! Il ne faut pas manger d'aliments trop gras, trop salés ou trop sucrés. Et la respiration, ça va ?

Charles	Oui, ça va, j'ai un bon rythme. Par contre, j'ai peur d'avoir mal à la tête.
Eva	Emporte de l'aspirine. Tu dois aussi t'échauffer avant de courir, et quand tu cours, il ne faut pas forcer ! Si tu veux, on peut courir ensemble le week-end prochain.
Charles	Super ! Oui, avec plaisir ! Merci pour tes conseils !

3 Answer the questions.

- **a** To train for his marathon run, how often does Charles run, and how far?
- **b** What does Eva ask about his feet and legs?
- **c** What advice does she have for him as far as food is concerned?
- **d** What does she advise him to do just before running and during each run?
- **e** When do Charles and Eva plan to run together?

LANGUAGE BUILDER 1

Language discovery 1

In Conversation 1, Eva asks Charles Tu n'a pas mal aux pieds ? (*Don't you have sore feet?*) and Tu n'as pas mal aux jambes ? (*Don't you have sore legs?*). Charles reassures her, but he admits: j'ai peur d'avoir mal à la tête (*I'm afraid of getting a headache*).

Look carefully at how Eva and Charles use avoir + mal + à + part of the body here. Then see if you can figure out how Eva would have asked: *Don't you have a sore arm?* Remember that the word for arm is un bras.

J'ai mal à la tête *My head hurts*

Many cultures use one-word exclamations to express certain feelings. You probably say *Ouch!* if something hurts. The French equivalent is Aïe ! If a French speaker wants to express pain using more than one word, they will probably say j'ai mal, which literally means *I have pain/a pain*. And if they want to say where this pain is, they simply add à followed by the body part, for example j'ai mal à la jambe. This phrase literally means *I have a pain in the leg* but could be translated in various ways, including *I have a sore leg* and *my leg hurts*. Now imagine you have been running and both your legs are hurting. You could say Aïe ! J'ai mal aux jambes ! (*Ouch! my legs hurt!*). You would use aux because à plus le becomes au and à plus les becomes aux. Here are four examples. Note that in English we tend to use the possessive to indicate pain, *my arm hurts*, while in French it is simply j'ai mal au bras—the expression j'ai mal means that we don't then use a possessive when indicating the part of the body that hurts.

J'ai mal au bras.	*My arm hurts.*
Il a mal au ventre.	*He has a stomach ache.*
Elle a mal à la tête.	*She has a headache.*
Ils ont mal aux dents.	*They have a toothache.*

Language practice 1

1 Match the sentence halves.

a J'ai mal aux ...	**1** ... jambe.
b J'ai mal à l'...	**2** ... pieds.
c J'ai mal à la ...	**3** ... bras.
d J'ai mal au ...	**4** ... estomac.

2 Match the sentences with the correct translations.

a J'ai mal aux dents.	**1** She has a headache.
b Vous avez mal ?	**2** Her arm is sore.
c Elle a mal à la tête.	**3** I have a toothache.
d Ça fait mal ?	**4** Does it hurt?
e Elle a mal au bras.	**5** Are you in pain?

LANGUAGE BUILDER 2

Language discovery 2

09.05

Listen to the conversation again and repeat each line in the pauses provided. Try to imitate the phrasing and intonation you hear.

1 Look for the four instances where Eva or Charles says il faut/il ne faut pas. Can you figure out what il faut means?

2 Eva's advice to Charles if he wants to avoid a headache is: Tu dois t'échauffer avant de courir, et quand tu cours, il ne faut pas forcer ! From the context, can you figure out what tu dois means?

Devoir et il faut: *Two ways of saying must*

One way to express obligation in French is using the verb devoir (*must, to have to*) followed by another verb. So, for instance, if you and a friend need to leave to catch a train, you might say: nous devons partir (*we have to leave*).

The verb devoir is irregular, but its pattern might remind you of boire. Compare devoir with boire in the tables below. What do the two verbs have in common when it comes to the nous and vous forms? Check your thoughts against the Answer key.

devoir (*to have to*)		**boire (*to drink*)**	
je dois	nous devons	je bois	nous buvons
tu dois	vous devez	tu bois	vous buvez
il/elle doit	ils/elles doivent	il/elle boit	ils/elles boivent

Another way to express obligation is with il faut (*it's necessary*):

Il faut partir. *We have to go.*

Il faut is usually interchangeable with devoir, but French speaker might prefer it just because it is shorter.

Language practice 2

1 Complete the sentences using devoir instead of il faut. The first one has been completed.

a Il faut éviter de boire trop de café. On *doit éviter de boire trop de café.*

b Il faut arriver chez Marie avant neuf heures. Nous ....

c Il faut travailler dur (*work hard*) ce soir pour finir la présentation. Vous ....

d Il faut se réveiller plus tôt. Tout le monde ....

2 Translate the sentences into French twice, using devoir then il faut. The first one has been completed.

a We must leave. *Nous devons partir/Il faut partir.*

b Marie and Luc, you must work this evening. ....

c You must go to school! (*said to a child*). ....

d One must work hard. ....

09.06

3 Now play the conversation again and play Eva's role. Speak in the pauses. Try not to refer to the text.

CULTURE POINT 2

L'invention de la photographie *The invention of photography*

The invention of photography is associated above all with France. In the 1830s, Louis Daguerre, a set designer, used a pinhole camera (or camera obscura) to fixer une image (*fix an image*) on a copper plate coated in silver emulsion. Named un daguerréotype (*a daguerreotype*) after its creator, this sowed the seeds of modern photographic techniques. In 1839, the French state bought the patent for Daguerre's technique and placed it in the public domain.

Other countries rapidly took to photography. In our own time, the northern European country of Luxembourg devotes special attention to this art. EMoPLux, sometimes shortened to EMoP, stands for the le Mois européen de la Photo à Luxembourg (*European Month of the Photograph at Luxembourg*). Le Festival EMoP (*EMoP Festival*) organizes exhibitions designed to refléter la diversité de la photographie d'aujourd'hui (*reflect the diversity of today's photography*). EMoP also facilitates meetings between les photographes en devenir (*emerging photographers*) and les conservateurs de musées et directeurs de festival (*museum curators and festival organizers*). Every two years, an EMoP Arendt Prize is awarded to a young artist. Founded in 1984 by Café-Crème asbl, a nonprofit photography association, EMop now views photographic art as including la vidéo et l'installation (*video and installations*). Since 2016, Brussels has proudly hosted the annual PhotoBrussels Festival located in a series of different venues in the capital city.

Check this website and list all the cities involved in le Mois européen de la Photographie.

VOCABULARY BUILDER 2

09.07

Read the words and phrases below and supply the missing English words and expressions. Then listen to the recording and imitate the pronunciation you hear.

LA PHOTOGRAPHIE	*PHOTOGRAPHY*
un appareil photo	*camera*
une photo (brillante/mate)	*(glossy/matt) photo*
noir-et-blanc	*black-and-white*
un paysage	*landscape*
un photograph, une photographe	*photographer*
un portrait	....
un selfie	....
un sujet	....
un téléphone portable	....

LES EXPRESSIONS	*EXPRESSIONS*
je photographie, photographier	*I photograph, to photograph*
je photoshope, photoshoper	....
Lina adore envoyer des photos par SMS.	*Lina adores sending photos via SMS.*
Alie fait un selfie devant le Louvre.	*Alie takes a selfie in front of the Louvre.*
Il a les yeux verts.	*He has green eyes.*
J'ai le nez court.	*I have a short nose.*

Vocabulary practice 2

Complete the text below using words and phrases from the vocabulary builder.

Jean a dix ans. Il adore la photographie. Il a un **a** .... de très bonne qualité. Il aime surtout faire des portraits ; ses **b** .... préférés sont ses amis d'école. Il n'aime pas les photos mates ; il préfère les photos **c** .... Sa sœur aînée, Florence, est **d** .... professionnelle. Elle voyage beaucoup parce qu'elle **e** .... souvent les paysages d'Afrique et d'Asie.

Pronunciation practice 2

An interesting challenge for English-speaking students of French is to learn the pronunciation of two vowels: (a) the letters o + u, as in vous, où, or pour, and (b) the letter u, as in tu, sur, or dessus. The ou sound is comparable but not identical to the *ooh*-sound in *you*, *food*, or *kangaroo*. By contrast, the u sound has no close equivalent in English.

09.08

Try saying i, but with rounded lips! Listen again and imitate the speaker.

Le curry est plus délicieux que le couscous.	*Curry is more delicious than couscous.*
Plus je pousse, moins ça bouge.	*The more I push, the less it moves.*

CONVERSATION 2

Une série de portraits *A set of portraits*

09.09

1 Here are a few words and expressions to help you understand the conversation.

Ça y est !	*Done it!*	avoir l'air heureux	*to seem happy*
prêt, prête	*ready*	un concours	*competition*
fin, fine	*fine, delicate*	difficile	*difficult*

09.10

2 Listen to the conversation without looking at the text. Then listen to the conversation again and read the text.

Assia has continued to develop her photography skills—and is now focusing on portraits so as to be able to enter a photography exhibition. She explains her work to Jo.

Jo Alors, ces portraits, je peux les voir ?

Assia Oui, ça y est, ils sont prêts, regarde !

Jo Ohhhh ! Quel magnifique portrait de groupe. C'est qui, là ?

Assia Lequel ?

Jo Celui-là. Tu vois ? Il a les yeux verts et les cheveux courts.

Assia Ah ! c'est Abou. C'est un bel homme ! Et là c'est Natalia. Elle a aussi un très beau visage.

Jo Oui, elle a de beaux cheveux châtains, et un très beau sourire.

Assia Et voilà la photo du couple, le jour du mariage.

Jo Ils ont l'air très heureux.

Assia Oui, je les adore, ils vont bien ensemble.

Assia and Jo continue looking at the photos.

Jo C'est une magnifique série de portraits, bravo !

Assia Oui, je suis contente. Maintenant, je dois en choisir deux pour le concours. Ça va être difficile. Tu peux m'aider ?

Jo Je les aime tous, mais oui, essayons d'en choisir deux.

3 Answer the questions.

a Has Assia finished her photos for the competition?

b What is the name of the person in the first photographic portrait which Jo admires?

c What is the name of the bride depicted in one of the portraits?

d Who has lovely chestnut-brown hair, according to Assia?

e What does Jo agree to help Assia with?

> Les cheveux (*hair*) is almost always plural in French. For instance, ***he has gray hair*** is il a les cheveux gris. The singular form cheveu is only used to talk about one individual hair, for example Regarde ! J'ai un cheveu gris ! (*Look! I have a gray hair!*).

LANGUAGE BUILDER 3

 **Language discovery 3**

1 **When Jo describes Abou's appearance, she says il a les yeux .... et les cheveux .... Can you find the missing words in the dialogue? This could be translated as: *he has green eyes and short hair*. What difference do you notice between the French sentence and the English translation?**

2 **See if you can supply the missing word for this rule of thumb: In French, you need to put the definite article (le, la, or les) before a part of the body when it is followed by an ...., for example brun or court.**

La description physique *Physical description*

If you want to translate *he has green eyes* into French, you should say il a les yeux verts. Notice the use of the definite article les, where the original sentence in English has no article. Similarly, *I have a short nose* would become j'ai le nez court, and *she has brown hair* would be elle a les cheveux bruns. You can see that these descriptions are made up of five elements: subject + avoir + definite article + body part + adjective.

Sometimes we might speak about color in a nuanced way, for instance by talking about *dark-brown hair* or *blue-grey eyes*. When we do this, we simply place two adjectives side by side. In French this kind of adjective is invariable. So *he has dark-brown hair* is il a les cheveux brun foncé; notice that there is no -s on brun. Similarly, *I have blue-green eyes* is j'ai les yeux bleu-vert — again, there is no -s on bleu-vert, though les yeux is masc. plural.

Generally speaking, adjectives agree in gender and number with the noun they refer to, but adjectives of color based on nouns (e.g. orange) are invariable. Other invariable adjectives are crème (*cream*), kaki (*khaki*), and noisette (*hazel*).

Language practice 3

1 **Complete the sentences using the colors indicated in parentheses; make any appropriate agreements.**

a J'ai les yeux .... (*bleu-gris*)

b Est-ce Jean a les cheveux blonds ou .... ? (*brun*)

c Je n'aime pas beaucoup ces chaussettes .... (*crème*)

d Marie a les cheveux .... (*châtain*)

LANGUAGE BUILDER 4

Language discovery 4

Listen to Conversation 2 again and repeat each line in the pauses provided. Try to imitate the phrasing and intonation you hear.

1 Identify all five adjectives in the following extracts from Conversation 2.

Quel magnifique portrait, c'est qui ?
Et là c'est Natalia, sa copine. Elle a aussi un très beau visage.
Elle a de beaux cheveux, et un très beau sourire.
C'est une magnifique série de portraits.

2 What do you notice about the placing or position of the adjectives?

Placement of adjectives

In French, the majority of adjectives come after the noun they describe. Sometimes, however, adjectives are placed *before* the noun. This can be because the adjective is used to express a strong value judgment and/or a strong reaction. The adjective magnifique, for instance, can be placed before a noun to emphasize the speaker's admiration (quel magnifique pont !). Positive-sounding adjectives of this type include gentil (*nice*), excellent (*excellent*), and merveilleux (*marvelous*). Negative adjectives of this type include affreux (*terrible*), malheureux (*unfortunate, miserable*), and méchant (*bad, wicked*).

Additionally there are a few adjectives that are generally placed before the noun as a matter of course. For instance, to speak about *a large dog*, French speakers would use un grand chien: notice that grand is placed before chien. Besides bon, adjectives of this type include jeune, petit, grand, and joli. Here is a table with examples:

adjective	masculine singular	feminine singular
bon/bonne	un bon médecin	une bonne médecin
jeune	un jeune homme	une jeune femme
petit/petite	un petit chien	une petite chienne
grand/grande	un grand chien	une grande chienne
joli/jolie	un joli chien	une jolie chienne

Some adjectives that generally precede the noun (beau/belle ; nouveau/nouvelle ; vieux/vieille) have an extra form: bel/nouvel/vieil. This is used for reasons of pronunciation before masculine singular nouns beginning with a vowel (or sometimes an h). Here are three examples: un bel avenir (*a fine future*); un nouvel anorak (*a new anorak*); un vieil homme (*an old man*).

Language practice 4

1 Translate the following phrases into French.

a A beautiful sea; a calm sea. (*sea* = une mer)
b A small puzzle; a difficult puzzle (*puzzle* = un puzzle)
c An expensive bouquet; a pretty bouquet. (*bouquet* = un bouquet)
d A young child; a robust child. (*robust* = robuste)
e An angry man; an old man. (*angry* = fâché)

2 Choose the correct adjective for each sentence. The first two have been done for you.

a J'ai un grand chien. (fort / grand).
b Vous avez une maison spacieuse. (belle / spacieuse)
c Elle a besoin d'un .... anorak. (jaune / nouvel)
d Je voudrais un vélo .... (électrique / nouveau)
e Nous avons acheté une .... boîte. (verte / vieille)
f C'est un .... garçon. (anglais / jeune)

09.12

3 Now play the conversation again and play Assia's role. Speak in the pauses. Try not to refer to the text.

SKILL BUILDER

1 Match the symptom with what you might do to relieve it.

a J'ai mal au dents.
b J'ai de la fièvre.
c Je tousse.
d J'ai mal à la tête.
e Je suis fatiguée.
f Je suis très malade.

1 Je bois un peu de sirop.
2 Je me repose.
3 Je vais chez le dentiste.
4 Je vais chez le médecin.
5 Je prends un comprimé.
6 Je compose le numéro 112.

2 Read the following sentences, then translate them. Note the different ways of expressing obligation.

Je dois bien m'alimenter, et nous devons tous les deux faire attention à ce que nous buvons si nous voulons être en forme pour le match ce week-end. Il faut surtout bien dormir pour ne pas être fatigués.

3 Choose a photo in your phone or one of the photos of people in this book and describe the people you see in it.

TEST YOURSELF

Complete the conversation using the English as a guide.

Eva	Est-ce que tu **a** .... ? (*Are you in pain?*)
Charles	Après le **b** .... j'**c** .... pieds et aux **d** .... (*After the marathon, my feet and my legs hurt.*)
Eva	Il **e** .... écouter ton corps. (*You must listen to your body.*)
	Tu **f** .... te reposer. (*You must rest.*)
Charles	Oui, tu as raison, je **g** .... faire attention. (*Yes, you are right, I must be careful.*)
Eva	Oui, je vois que tu as même un gros bleu au **h** .... droit. (*Yes, I can see you have a big bruise on your right arm.*)
Charles	Aïe ! Ça **i** .... quand je touche l'ecchymose. (*Ouch! It hurts when I touch the bruise.*)
Eva	Alors n'y touche pas. Tu peux mettre ton **j** .... pull
	k .... et personne ne va voir le **l** .... bleu. (*So don't touch it. You can put on your beautiful brown sweater and nobody will see the large bruise.*)

Remember to use **My review** and **My takeaway** to assess your progress and reflect on your learning experience.

10

In this lesson you will learn how to:

- » Talk about travel plans
- » Talk about future plans
- » Speak about time
- » Indicate where items are placed in relation to other objects

Genève et la Champagne

My study plan

I plan to work with Unit 10

- ○ Every day
- ○ Twice a week
- ○ Other ___________

I plan to study for

- ○ 5–15 minutes
- ○ 15–30 minutes
- ○ 30–45+ minutes

My progress tracker

Day / Date	Listening	Speaking	Reading	Writing	Conversation
	○	○	○	○	○
	○	○	○	○	○
	○	○	○	○	○
	○	○	○	○	○
	○	○	○	○	○
	○	○	○	○	○
	○	○	○	○	○

My goals

What do you want to be able to do or say in French when you complete this unit?

		Done
1	....	○
2	....	○
3	....	○

My review

SELF CHECK

	I can ...
●	... make travel plans.
●	... talk about future plans.
●	... explain where things are situated.
●	... speak of people or things without naming them.

CULTURE POINT 1

Genève *Geneva*

The city of Genève in Switzerland is a membre du Programme Cités interculturelles (*member of the Intercultural Cities Programme*) of the Council of Europe (*CoE*). This status reflects the cultural diversity of its inhabitants. According to the most recent CoE data, plus de 40 % (*more than 40%*) of the working-age population within the canton of Genève were nonnationals, and more than 20% were of Portuguese, French, Italian, or Spanish ethnicity. Moreover, Genève has a proud history of nurturing movements that promote international cooperation. For instance, it is home to the international office of Médecins sans frontières and the headquarters of la Croix rouge (*the Red Cross*). In fact, la Croix rouge, which helps populations in parts of the world threatened by war and other crises, owes its existence to several Genevois (*Genevans*). Foremost among these was Henry Durant. In 1862, Durant published Un Souvenir de Solférino (*A Memory of Solferino*), a book in which he recalls the battlefield where, in 1859, he had observed the fate of wounded and dying soldiers. This book inspired the beginnings of the Croix rouge movement. The city also hosts the Organisation mondiale de la Santé (*World Health Organization*) and is the site of one of the regional offices of Les Nations unies (*United Nations*). Finally, Genève is the location of CERN/Conseil européen pour la recherche nucléaire (*the European Council for Nuclear Research*). Apart from the mountains and the river Rhône, the canton doit sa beauté au Lac Léman (*owes its beauty to Lake Geneva*). The Rhône continues its journey from there through southeastern France, before flowing out into the Mediterranean Sea.

Check the Geneva tourism website here. What cruises would you like to go on?

VOCABULARY BUILDER 1

Read the words and phrases below and supply the missing English words and expressions. Then listen to the recording and imitate the pronunciation you hear.

VOYAGER	*TO TRAVEL*
un avion	*plane*
un bateau	*boat*
un train en provenance de	*train arriving from*
un train à destination de	*train leaving for*
un TGV/train à grande vitesse	*high-speed train*
un aéroport	....
une croisière	*cruise*
un itinéraire, une route	........................, *route*
un passeport	....
un vol	*flight*

EXPRESSIONS	*EXPRESSIONS*
une nouvelle, une grande nouvelle	*a piece of news, big news*
Nous espérons y passer le mois de novembre.	*We're going to spend November there.*
rendre visite à	*to visit a person*
visiter	*to visit a place*
On va aller jusqu'à Paris.	*We're going to/as far as Paris.*
normalement	*normally*
durant notre séjour	*during our stay*
J'ai hâte !	*I can't wait!*

Vocabulary practice 1

1 Match the type of travel on the left with the means of transportation on the right.

a un vol	**1** un bateau
b une croisière	**2** un train
c l'Orient-Express	**3** un avion

2 Complete the passage, using the words and phrases in the box.

espérons	itinéraire	jusqu'à
rendre visite	visiter	vol

Bonjour maman et papa ! Une grande nouvelle : nous allons passer le mois de novembre au Sénégal, pour **a** .... aux cousins de Mohammed ! Voici notre **b** .... : on va aller **c** .... Paris en TGV, puis prendre le RER jusqu'à l'aéroport. Normalement, le **d** .... dure quatre heures et demie (il est direct). Comme vous savez, les cousins de Mo habitent à Dakar. Durant notre séjour, on va **e** .... les villes de Gorée et de Touba, le lac rose, le désert de Lampoul. Avant notre départ, nous **f** .... passer quelques jours chez vous, si vous voulez bien... Bisous, Caroline et Mo.

Pronunciation practice 1

You may have noticed that the letter o can be pronounced in more than one way in French: compare un homme and une rose. We can express this difference by saying that the o in homme is open, while the o in rose is closed. A useful tip is that wherever you see an o with a circumflex (ô), as in le contrôleur you should pronounce it as a closed o.

Listen to the recording and repeat the words:

1 Open *o*

un passeport
une pomme
un téléphone

2 Closed *o*

un mot
une rose
un contrôleur
le Rhône

The closed o sound is generally also used to pronounce the letter combinations a-u and e-a-u. Words you have come across with these combinations include au, aux, eau, bureau, faux, and manteau.

CONVERSATION 1

À la découverte de la Suisse *Discovering Switzerland*

10.03

1 Here are a few words and expressions to help you understand the conversation.

connaître	*to know (a person or a place)*	avoir envie de faire quelque chose	*to feel like doing something*
un plaisir	*pleasure*	un accélérateur	*accelerator*
s'occuper de	*to take care of*	une particule	*particle*

10.04

2 Listen to the conversation a few times without looking at the text. Then listen to the conversation again and read the text.

Eva invites Charles to travel to Switzerland with her to visit her family. They will also make some pit stops at some carefully chosen chocolatiers.

Eva	Je vais voir mes parents le mois prochain. Tu as envie de venir avec moi ?
Charles	Oui, avec plaisir, je ne connais pas la Suisse !
Eva	Parfait, je m'occupe de tout ! Nous prendrons le train pour Genève, via Paris.
Charles	J'adore les voyages en train !
Eva	À Genève, nous rendrons visite à ma grand-mère, elle habite dans la vieille ville, près de la cathédrale. On fera une croisière en bateau sur le Lac Léman. Tu verras, c'est très beau ! Après, nous visiterons le CERN.
Charles	On va voir l'accélérateur de particules ?
Eva	Oui c'est ça !
Charles	Ah super ! ... Et on goûtera le fameux chocolat suisse ?
Eva	Mais oui bien sûr ! Ensuite, nous irons à Lausanne en train. On passera deux ou trois jours chez mes parents, ils vont t'adorer !
Charles	Tu es sûre ?
Eva	Mais oui, fais-moi confiance, tu verras.
Charles	C'est génial, j'ai hâte !

3 Answer the questions.

a Who is Eva planning to visit next month?
b Has Charles been to Switzerland before?
c How will they get to Geneva?
d What two outings in Geneva does Eva plan?
e Where will they go after Geneva, and by what means of transportation?

LANGUAGE BUILDER 1

Language discovery 1

Eva shares her plans for the visit to Switzerland using the following verbs: je vais voir ; nous prendrons ; nous rendrons visite à ; on fera ; tu verras ; nous visiterons ; on va voir ; on goûtera ; nous irons ; on passera ; ils vont t'adorer ; tu verras on finira.

1 Which ones are in the near-future tense (aller + infinitive)? What do you notice about the remaining verbs, which are all in le futur (*the future tense*)?

2 Focus particularly on visiter, goûter, and passer. Then see if you can complete the following rule of thumb:

The future tense of -er verbs is formed by adding the correct ending to the .... form of the verb.

Based on the verb finir, what do you think the rule for verbs that end in -ir is?

Le futur simple *The simple future*

So far, you have learned to talk about actions happening soon, using the near-future tense. But not all future events are just about to happen. To speak of future events more generally, you will need the simple future tense, which is mostly referred to as the future tense for short. To form the simple future, take the infinitive of the verb and add the future endings: -ai, -as, -a, -ons, -ez, -ent, -ont. The endings are the same for -er, -ir, and -re verbs.

aimer (*to love*)

j'aimer**ai**	I will love	nous aimer**ons**	we will love
tu aimer**as**	you will love	vous aimer**ez**	you will love
il/elle aimer**a**	he/she will love	ils/elles aimer**ont**	they will love

partir (*to leave*)

je partir**ai**	I will leave	nous partir**ons**	we will leave
tu partir**as**	you will leave	vous partir**ez**	you will leave
il/elle partir**a**	he/she will leave	ils/elles partir**ont**	they will leave

To make the future tense of -re verbs, remove the final -e from the infinitive before adding the appropriate ending.

prendre (*to take*)

je prendr**ai**	I will take	nous prendr**ons**	we will take
tu prendr**as**	you will take	vous prendr**ez**	you will take
il/elle prendr**a**	he/she will take	ils/elles prendr**ont**	they will take

Language practice 1

1 Replace all near-future tenses with the future tense in the sentences below. The first one has been done for you.

a Nous allons visiter la cathédrale. *Nous visiterons la cathédrale.*

b Nous allons passer chez vous la semaine prochaine. Nous ....

c Elles vont partir en vacances dans deux jours. Elles ....

d Karine et Luc vont arriver avant les autres. Karine et Luc ....

e Nous allons prendre le métro à Jussieu. Nous ....

2 Complete the sentences below with a future-tense verb. The first one has been done for you.

a À mon avis, vous *aimerez* le dernier film d'Audrey Dana. (*aimer*)

b Vous .... notre numéro de téléphone à Jean ? (*donner*)

c Est-ce que Christophe .... de travailler avant onze heures ? (*finir*)

d Je ne .... pas du théâtre avant la fin de la pièce. (*sortir*)

e Tu .... TGV pour aller en France ? (*prendre*)

LANGUAGE BUILDER 2

Language discovery 2

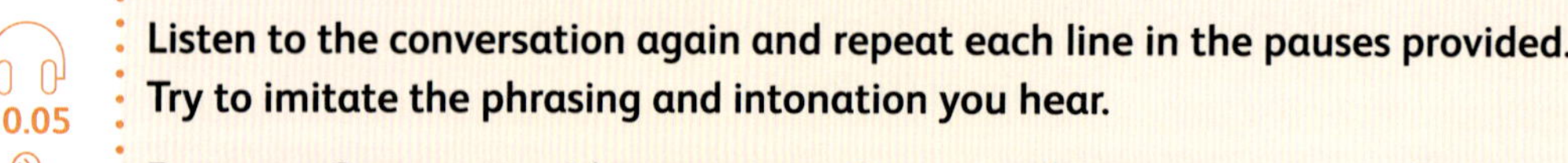

Listen to the conversation again and repeat each line in the pauses provided. Try to imitate the phrasing and intonation you hear.

Eva opens Conversation 1 by announcing Je pense aller voir mes parents le mois prochain (*I'm thinking of going to see my parents next month*).

Based on this, can you figure out how to say *next week*, *next weekend*, *next year*, and *next century*?

Here is some new vocabulary you will need: une semaine (*week*); un an (*year*); un siècle (*century*). Check your ideas in the Answer key.

Parler du temps *Talking about time*

To be able to talk about the order in which events take place, you'll need to use signposting words. Here are some of the essential signposting words.

Indicating the order of events	
d'abord	*at first*
puis	*then*
ensuite	*next*
avant	*before*
après	*after*
récemment	*recently*
finalement	*finally*
Indicating a moment in time	
aujourd'hui	*today*
demain	*tomorrow*
après-demain	*the day after tomorrow.*
la semaine/l'année prochaine	*next week/next year*
le mois prochain	*next month*

Note the difference between French and English in how we count days. To say ***a week from now*** French speakers can choose between dans une semaine or dans huit jours (*in eight days*, not seven). Similarly, *two weeks/a fortnight* translated into French is quinze jours, and une quinzaine is *about two weeks*.

Language practice 2

1 Arrange the following sentences in the correct order to form a narrative.

a Ensuite, nous prendrons un vol direct jusqu'à Madrid.
b L'année prochaine, nous visiterons l'Italie.
c Après une heure de vol, nous arriverons à notre destination.
d Le mois prochain, nous passerons deux semaines de vacances en Espagne. J'ai hâte !
e D'abord, nous prendrons le taxi jusqu'à l'aéroport.

10.06

2 Now play the conversation again and play Charles's role. Speak in the pauses. Try not to refer to the text.

CULTURE POINT 2

Champagne : le vin et la région *Champagne: the wine and the region*

The feminine noun la Champagne refers to the Champagne region of France; the masculine noun le champagne (or le vin de Champagne) is the name of the sparkling wine produced there. This wine began to be seen as a superior wine in the late 1670s, once the invention of les bouchons (*corks*) had made it possible to store the product in des bouteilles en verre (*glass bottles*). Deux siècles plus tard (*A couple of centuries later*), in 1919, the French government created a law declaring that the names of some types of wine and spirits, including champagne, could be used for only for products that come from those specific regions—so anytime you see the label Champagne on a bottle, it's clear that it comes from la Champagne. Certain hillsides, houses, and cellars of Champagne are now a UNESCO World Heritage Site. Besides vineyards, the area around Champagne known as le Grand Est (*the Great East*) is home to approximately trente mille fermes (*thirty thousand farms*). Many of these breed du cheptel (*livestock*), including des vaches (*cows*), des porcs (*pigs*), and des chèvres (*goats*). La Foire de Châlons (*the Châlons Fair*) includes extensive stalls where des animaux de ferme (*farm animals*) are displayed. The festival is working to optimize the conditions in which these animals are kept; for instance, they have reviewed the hours during which le cheptel can be viewed by the public, afin de maintenir (*in order to maintain*) the daily rhythms the animals normally live by.

Follow the link to discover la Route touristique du Champagne. How long is the itinerary? Which of the six tours would you choose?

VOCABULARY BUILDER 2

Read the words and phrases below and supply the missing English words and expressions. Then listen to the recording and imitate the pronunciation you hear.

ANIMAUX DE FERME	*FARM ANIMALS*
un animal, des animaux	....
un âne	*donkey*
un canard	*duck*
une chèvre	*goat*
un cochon/un porc	*pig*
un coq	*rooster*
une dinde	*turkey*
un mouton	*sheep*
une poule	*hen*
une vache	*cow*

LES CRIS DES ANIMAUX	*ANIMAL SOUNDS*
Cocorico !	*Cock-a-doodle-doo!*
Coin, coin !	*Quack, quack!*
Miaou !	....
Ouaf ouaf !	*Woof woof!*

EXPRESSIONS	*EXPRESSIONS*
Je fais ma valise.	*I'm packing my suitcase.*
Nous organisons une dégustation.	*We're organizing a tasting session.*
C'est un champagne bio/biologique.	*It's an organic champagne.*
On préfère les produits locaux.	*We prefer local products.*
Voir les animaux, ça amuse les petits.	*Seeing animals amuses young children.*
Vous connaissez/reconnaissez Paul ?	*Do you know/recognize Paul?*
Suzanne taquine son petit frère	*Suzanne is teasing her little brother.*

Vocabulary practice 2

Match the animals to the sounds they make.

a un coq	**1** Coin, coin !
b un chien	**2** Miaou !
c un canard	**3** Cocorico !
d un chat	**4** Ouaf ouaf !

CONVERSATION 2

Un week-end en Champagne *A weekend in the Champagne region*

10.08

1 Here are a few words and expressions to help you understand the conversation.

un produit fermier	*farm product*	Ça te va ?	*Do you like it?*
hébergement	*accommodation*	Impeccable !	*Great!*
un déjeuner gastronomique	*gourmet lunch*	Vas-y, réserve !	*Go ahead, reserve it!*

10.09

2 Listen to the conversation without looking at the text. Then listen to the conversation again and read the text.

Jo and Assia are planning a weekend away in the Champagne region where the champagne trails are a great way to enjoy the region and its famous bubbly product. The results of their trip will help inform the choice of which champagne will be served at the family's restaurant.

Jo	Salut, Assia. L'association des champagnes biologiques organise un week-end dégustation. On y va ?
Assia	Ouiii !!! C'est quand ?
Jo	Dans trois semaines, les 26 et 27 octobre.
Assia	Parfait, je suis libre. Quel est le programme ?
Jo	Le point de rendez-vous est à Reims à 15 h 00, aux Halles du Boulingrin, pour une dégustation de champagne et de produits fermiers locaux. Ensuite, visite d'une jeune maison de champagne bio dans la montagne de Reims.
Assia	Cool ! Et pour l'hébergement ?
Jo	Dîner et nuit à la ferme !
Assia	Parfait ! J'aime le chant du coq au réveil !
Jo	Oui ! Et le dimanche matin, visite de Reims, déjeuner gastronomique en ville et retour à Paris. Ça te va ?
Assia	Impeccable ! Vas-y, réserve !
Jo	Aie zut ! Je ne trouve pas mon portefeuille, tu sais où il est ?
Assia	Il est sur ton bureau, je le vois d'ici.
Jo	Où ? Je ne le vois pas ! Quel désordre !
Assia	Au-dessus ! Là !
Jo	Ah oui, merci !

3 Answer the questions.

- **a** How soon is the trip supposed to happen?
- **b** Where and when will the activities begin?
- **c** Where will participants spend Saturday night?
- **d** What will they do on Sunday?
- **e** Where is Assia's wallet?

LANGUAGE BUILDER 3

Language discovery 3

Towards the end of the conversation Assia cannot find her wallet, and Jo tells her: Il est sur ton bureau, je le vois d'ici. She never uses the word ***wallet*** here, but we know she is talking about it.

Which two words are used instead of le portefeuille in Jo's reply to Assia? (They can both be translated as *it*.)

Les pronoms compléments d'objet direct *Direct object pronouns*

You've already encountered French subject pronouns (je, tu, il/elle, nous, vous, or ils/elles) which are used to identify the subject of a sentence (the person or thing performing an action). Much like English, French also uses direct object pronouns, which indicate the person or thing that an action is being done to (the object).

Je vois la rue. Je la vois. — *I see the street. I see it.*

Marc voit la plage. Marc la voit. — *Mark sees the beach. He sees it.*

Notice that the object pronouns (me, te, le/la, nous, vous, or les) are placed directly before the verb.

Object pronouns in French	
Marc me voit.	Marc nous voit.
Marc te voit.	Marc vous voit.
Marc le voit.	Marc les voit.
Marc la voit.	

Language practice 3

1 Identify the object pronoun in each sentence. The first one has been done for you.

- **a** Je vois Julie et Julie me voit.
- **b** Tu regardes Mireille et Mireille te regarde.
- **c** Il reconnaît Jean et Jean le reconnaît.
- **d** Elle taquine Sophie et Sophie la taquine.
- **e** Nous aimons Franck et Franck nous aime.
- **f** Vous écoutez Djamel et Djamel vous écoute.
- **g** Ils adorent Mo et Mo les adore.
- **h** Elles amusent Karine et Karine les amuse.

> Note the object pronouns which end in a vowel: me, te, le, la are shorten to m', t', l', l' whenever they precede a word that begins with a vowel.
> Tu aimes le champagne bio ?
> — Oui, je l'aime beaucoup.

2 In the sentences below, replace each underlined noun with a direct object pronoun. The first one has been done for you.

- **a** Je regarde souvent la télé./Je *la* regarde souvent.
- **b** Nous voyons souvent nos voisins./Nous .... voyons souvent.
- **c** J'adore la Suisse./Je .... adore.
- **d** J'adore le Portugal. /Je .... adore.
- **e** Tu aimes les films italiens ?/Tu .... aimes ?

Pronunciation practice 2

The final letter of many French words is silent. But when these words come before a word that begins with a vowel (or, often, an h), those endings are generally pronounced.

When this happens, it is said that there is une liaison (*a link*) because the two words are run together to sound like one, longer word.

10.10

Listen to the word combinations in the recording, while reading along below. Is there a liaison between the pairs of words in each example?

a	un homme ; des hommes ; les hommes	liaison	no liaison
b	un canard ; des canards ; les canards	liaison	no liaison
c	un mouton ; des moutons ; les moutons	liaison	no liaison
d	un animal ; des animaux ; les animaux	liaison	no liaison

LANGUAGE BUILDER 4

Language discovery 4

Listen to the conversation again and repeat each line in the pauses provided. Try to imitate the phrasing and intonation you hear.

When Assia cannot find her wallet, Jo points out where it is by saying: Il est sur ton bureau, je le vois d'ici. *(It is on your desk, I can see it from here.)* When Assia still doesn't find it, Jo exclaims: Au-dessus! Là ! *(On top of it! There!)*

Bearing this in mind, see if you can complete the following rule of thumb: dessus **replaces .... + a noun. Choose from:**

a sous **b** sur **c** dans

Dedans, dessous, dessus

You already know the words dans (*in*), sous (*under*), and sur (*on*). These words (called **prepositions**) tell us where one thing is in relation to another. They are generally placed before a noun, for example dans cette boîte (*in this box*), sous la table (*under the table*), or sur la cheminée (*on the mantelpiece*).

Three related words are dedans (*inside* [*it*]), dessous (*underneath* [*it*]), and dessus (*on top* [of *it*]). These words (called **adverbs**), while similar in meaning, are not followed by a noun. Compare ton livre est dans cette boîte (*your book is in that box*) with ton livre est dedans (*your book is inside* [*it*]).

Tu vois ce livre ? Ta lettre est dessous. *You see that book? Your letter is underneath* [*it*].

Tu vois cette table ? Ton sac est dessus. *You see that table? Your handbag is on top* [of *it*].

Language practice 4

1 Complete sentences a–c below by choosing the most suitable word (1–3).

a Ton livre n'est pas sur le lit ? Alors, regarde .... ! **1** dedans
b Tu vois cette table ? Tu peux mettre les fleurs .... ? **2** dessous
c Prends cette boîte, et mets les bonbons .... ! **3** dessus

2 Now play the conversation again and play Assia's role. Speak in the pauses. Try not to refer to the text.

SKILL BUILDER

1 Read the passage below then write a dialogue where you tell your friend you are going to visit relatives and they ask you questions about your plans. Use the information in the passage to structure your dialogue.

Nous allons rendre visite à nos grands-parents le mois prochain. Ils n'habitent pas loin de chez nous. On va y aller en voiture ; on fera le trajet en deux heures et demie. On a fait la même route l'année dernière. Même avec les embouteillages, nous sommes arrivés en moins de trois heures. Nous avons hâte de les revoir ; on va fêter l'anniversaire de notre grand-mère pendant notre séjour. Pour le voyage de retour, nous nous mettrons en route vers dix heures du matin, pour éviter les heures de pointe.

2 Rewrite each sentence, using a pronoun to replace the underlined words.

Example: Vous aimez les films de François Truffaut ? → *Vous les aimez ?*

a Isabelle écoute <u>cette émission de Radio France.</u>

b Jean-Marc adore <u>Florence</u>.

c David, ne taquine pas <u>Francine</u> s'il te plaît !

d J'aime beaucoup <u>la campagne</u>.

e J'aime moins les <u>grandes villes</u>.

3 Read and complete the passage below by placing the relevant verbs in the future.

Ce week-end, nous allons acheter des vêtements d'été car le mois prochain, nous **a** .... (*commencer*) nos vacances dans le sud. Nous **b** .... (*prendre*) l'avion pour Toulon, nous y **c** .... (*passer*) une semaine, puis on **d** .... (*prendre*) le train pour Marseille pour rendre visite à des amis. La semaine d'après nous **e** .... (*se rendre*) à Aix-en-Provence, qui nous **f** .... (*servir*) de base pour visiter la Provence. À la fin de nos vacances, nous **g** .... (*retourner*) à Paris via Avignon où nous prévoyons de nous arrêter pour voir au moins une des pièces de théâtre du festival.

4 In Exercise 3, besides the verbs, which words give an indication of time and sequence of events? Identify them.

TEST YOURSELF

1 Complete the passage using either the future or the present tense, as indicated.

Jacques et Aimée **a** .... (**planifier**/*present*) leur retraite. Parce qu'ils **b** .... (**aimer**/*present*) la campagne, ils **c** .... (**acheter**/*future*) une maison ou peut-être une petite ferme dans un petit village, pas loin de Besançon. Aimée **d** .... (**cultiver**/*future*) des légumes. Jacques **e** .... (**élever**/*future*) des poules. Et ils **f** .... (**vendre**/*future*) leurs produits au village.

2 Complete the sentences with direct object pronouns.

a Je connais bien Laurent./Je .... connais bien.

b Est-ce que vous connaissez Madame Labori ?/Est-ce que vous .... connaissez ?

c Ils voient souvent Marie./Ils .... voient souvent.

d Nous aimons beaucoup Christophe./Nous .... aimons beaucoup.

3 Complete the sentences by choosing the correct option.

a Je vais mettre cette vase sur / dessus la table.

b Je viens de faire ce lit. Ne mets pas ta valise sur / dessus !

c Voici une valise vide. Tu peux mettre tes vêtements dans / dedans.

d S'il te plaît, mets ton vélo dans / dedans le jardin !

e Tu n'as pas ton téléphone ? Regarde sous / dessous la table.

f Tu vois le sapin de Noël (*Christmas tree*)? Les cadeaux (*presents*) sont déjà sous / dessous.

4 Complete the sentences using après-demain, l'année prochaine, demain, or la semaine prochaine.

a Aujourd'hui il pleut, j'espère qu'il fera beau ....

b Cette année, je vais en vacances en Corse, ... je visiterai la Sicile.

c Cette semaine j'ai beaucoup de travail. Heureusement, ... je serai en vacances.

d Tu arrives quand ? Demain ou .... ?

Remember to use **My review** and **My takeaway** to assess your progress and reflect on your learning experience.

In this lesson you will learn how to:

» Talk about your last weekend
» Indicate specific moments in the past
» Tell a story in the past

Récits de voyages

My study plan

I plan to work with Unit 11

○ Every day
○ Twice a week
○ Other ___________

I plan to study for

○ 5–15 minutes
○ 15–30 minutes
○ 30–45+ minutes

My progress tracker

Day / Date	Listening	Speaking	Reading	Writing	Conversation
	○	○	○	○	○
	○	○	○	○	○
	○	○	○	○	○
	○	○	○	○	○
	○	○	○	○	○
	○	○	○	○	○
	○	○	○	○	○

My goals

What do you want to be able to do or say in French when you complete this unit?

		Done
1	....	○
2	....	○
3	....	○

My review

SELF CHECK	
	I can ...
●	... describe events that have already taken place.
●	... talk about specific times in the past.
●	... speak about my past activities.

CULTURE POINT 1

Du grand tour au tourisme de masse *From the Grand Tour to Mass Tourism*

Once, exploring Europe for pleasure or education was le domaine réservé des ultraprivilégiés (*the preserve of the ultra-privileged*). L'aristocratie britannique (*the British aristocracy*) a longtemps favorisé (*long favored*) le Grand Tour (*the Grand Tour*), which was especially in vogue during the 1700s and 1800s. Au cours des dix-neuvième et vingtième siècles (*in the 19th and 20th centuries*), especially after the development of les réseaux ferroviaires (*railroad networks*), travel for leisure became increasingly available to les bourgeois et les bourgeoises (*middle-class people*). But it was during le vingtième siècle (*the 20th century*) that les voyages et l'hébergement à prix modéré (*budget travel and accommodation*) gradually made such travel possible for people in general. During this long development several années charnières (*pivotal years*) stand out. In 1930, a French politician, Marc Sangnier, a créé (*created*) La Ligue française pour les auberges de jeunesse (*the French League of Youth Hostels*), having just opened the first of these in his own town, Bierville. Another tournant (*turning point*) was the advent of the Communauté économique européenne (*European Economic Community*) in 1957. Shortly afterward, on a pu acheter pour la première fois (*one was able to buy for the first time*) a Pass Eurail (*Eurail Pass*), allowing unlimited rail travel across 13 countries. The Pass Interrail followed in 1972. Today, Interrail and Eurail provide access to more than 250,000 km of railroad across 33 different countries. In 2020, Eurail launched an all-in-one pass numérique (*digital pass*).

Visit the Interrail website. What are the different passes available? Which one would you choose?

VOCABULARY BUILDER 1

Look at the words and phrases and complete the missing English words and expressions. Then listen and try to imitate the pronunciation of the speakers.

LES VOYAGES	*TRIPS*
un aléa	*hazard, chance event*
une aventure, une mésaventure	....
une correspondance	*connection, connecting flight/train*
un hic	*hitch, snag*
les heures d'ouverture/de fermeture	*opening/closing times*
planifier un voyage	*plan a trip*
faire/annuler une réservation	....
attraper/rater le train	*to catch/miss the train*
une panne, tomber en panne	*a breakdown, to break down*
se retrouver	*to meet up (with someone)*
des points de repère	*points of reference*
hier	*yesterday*
avant-hier	*the day before yesterday*
la semaine dernière	....
le mois dernier	*last month*
l'année dernière	*last year*
la veille	*the day before*
il y a trois jours/un mois/deux ans	*three days/one month/two years ago*

EXPRESSIONS	*EXPRESSIONS*
Nous n'avons rien oublié ?	*We didn't forget anything?*
Nous avons fait la connaissance de ton cousin.	*We met your cousin.*
Zut ! J'ai raté le train !	*Oh heck! I've missed the train!*
Raconte !/Racontez !	*Tell me all about it! (informal/formal)*
Ils/elles sont adorables.	....
Marie fait le tour de l'Europe	*Marie's doing a tour of Europe.*
Nous avons visité la région	*We visited the region.*
quand même	*all the same*
minutieusement	*very carefully/in great detail*

Vocabulary practice 1

Complete the sentences using words and phrases in Vocabulary builder 1.

a Nous achetons nos billets et nous faisons une .... pour le train de 15 heures.
b Nous avons peur de .... notre correspondance car notre train a 45 minutes de retard.
c Fatou planifie son voyage .... afin d'éviter le ....
d Sophie et Charles vont se .... à la gare de Lyon avant de partir ensemble.

Pronunciation practice 1

In French, an h can be aspirated or unaspirated: an aspirated h is the kind that is like a consonant, and an unaspirated h is the kind that is like a vowel. Dictionaries generally indicate each aspirated h by a special mark. In the Glossary, have used an asterisk for this purpose (e.g. *hangar).

The liaison rule you learned in Unit 8 also applies to any noun that begins with an unaspirated h. The case of feminine nouns beginning with aspirated h is more subtle: speakers pause very briefly between une and the noun, separating the words instead of running them together.

11.02

Now read the list of words while listening to the recording. Then indicate all the nouns that start with an aspirated h.

un homme (*a man*)
un hic (*a snag*)
une haie (*a hedge*)
une heure (*an hour*)
une hirondelle (*a swallow*)
une halle (*a hall*)
des hamacs (*hammocks*)
des hôtels (*hotels*)
des hangars (*sheds/hangars*)

CONVERSATION 1

Tu a passé un bon week-end ? *How was your weekend?*

11.03

1 Here are a few words and expressions to help you to understand the conversation.

un frangin ; une frangine	*brother; sister (informal)*
Qu'est-ce que vous avez fait d'autre ?	*What else did you do?*
C'est romantique !	*That's romantic!*
parfumer	*to flavor*
à la fleur de sureau	*elderflower-flavored*
au miel d'acacia	*acacia honey-flavored*

11.04

2 Listen to the conversation a few times without looking at the text. Then listen again and read along.

Jo is eager to find out all about Charles and Eva's trip to Switzerland. She would also like to visit it one day and is especially curious about Geneva.

Jo	Bonjour frangin ! Ça va ? Et ce week-end en Suisse... raconte !
Charles	Salut frangine ! Nous avons passé un super week-end, les parents d'Eva sont adorables et la région est superbe !
Jo	Qu'est-ce que vous avez fait ?
Charles	Nous avons d'abord exploré la vieille ville de Genève, puis nous avons fait une croisière sur le Lac Léman...
Jo	Ah, ah ! Une croisière, c'est romantique !
Charles	Arrête avec ça, tu veux bien ! Il n'y a rien entre Eva et moi.
Jo	Je ne te crois pas, mais continue ! Qu'est-ce que vous avez fait d'autre ?
Charles	J'ai fait la connaissance de la grand-mère d'Eva. Et puis nous avons visité le CERN, c'est super intéressant ! Ensuite, nous avons fait une randonnée en montagne avec les parents d'Eva.
Jo	Et tu as goûté du chocolat, peut-être ?
Charles	Oui, bien sûr ! J'ai trouvé une chocolaterie tout à fait originale. L'artisan chocolatier utilise des plantes et des fleurs des montagnes pour parfumer son produit. J'ai mangé du chocolat à la fleur de sureau et au miel d'acacia, c'est délicieux !
Jo	Ahhh, intéressant...
Charles	Et toi, ton week-end à Reims ?
Jo	Justement, je viens d'écrire un blog dessus. Mais je te raconte quand même...

3 Answer the questions.

a Charles mentions a cruise on Lake Geneva—by what French name does he refer to this lake?

b What flavor chocolate did Charles try in Switzerland?

c Having finished telling Jo his news, what change of subject does Charles suggest?

LANGUAGE BUILDER 1

Language discovery 1

Look at how Charles talks about what he and Eva did on their trip to Switzerland: nous avons passé ; nous avons exploré ; nous avons fait (une croisière) ; j'ai fait (la connaissance de) ; nous avons visité ; nous avons fait (une randonnée) ; j'ai trouvé ; j'ai mangé.

Based on Charle's statements, choose the correct alternative (*each* or *none*).

a **Each / none** of the events mentioned by Charles happened more than once.
b **Each / none** of the verbs listed above is made up of two words.
c **Each / none** of the verbs listed above contains avoir in some form.

The passé composé of -er and -ir verbs

Look carefully at this short sentence: J'ai exploré la ville (*I explored/have explored the town*). The verb that is used here is in le passé composé, which is used to talk about the past. Here is the pattern for explorer in that tense:

explorer (*to explore*)

j'ai exploré	I (*have*) explored	nous avons exploré	we (*have*) explored
tu as exploré	you (*have*) explored	vous avez exploré	you (*have*) explored
il/elle a exploré	he/she (*has*) explored	ils/elles ont exploré	they (*have*) explored

As you can see, le passé composé is made up of two parts. The first is usually a form of avoir, which changes according to the subject (j'ai, tu as, il/elle a, etc.). The second verb (exploré) is in the *past participle* form. To form the past participle of -er verbs:

(a) remove the -er ending of the infinitive (with explorer, this leaves explor-);

(b) add -é: exploré.

And the past participle of -ir verbs such as finir is formed in a similar way:

(a) remove the last two letters from the infinitive (this leaves fin-);

(b) add -i (so you get fini).

J'ai fini mon repas. *I (have) finished my meal.*

In negative statements in the passé composé, ne...pas goes on either side of avoir.

Je **n'**ai **pas** fini mon repas. *I haven't finished my meal.*

Language practice 1

1 Complete the tables with the correct verb forms.

voyager (to travel)		**finir (to finish)**	
j'ai voyagé	nous avons voyagé	j'ai fini	nous avons fini
a tu as	**c** vous .... voyagé	**e** tu as	**g** vous .... fini
b il/elle a	**d** ils/elles .... voyagé	**f** il/elle a	**h** ils/elles .... fini

2 Give the past participle of the verbs.

a aimer (*to love*): ....

b agir (*to act*): ....

c prévenir (*to warn*): ....

d dormir (*to sleep*): ....

You will need to learn some past participles individually, as they follow an irregular pattern: fait (from faire, *to do, to make*), eu (from avoir, *to have*), été (from être, *to be*), ouvert (from ouvrir, *to open*), découvert (from découvrir, *to discover*) vu (from voir, *to see*).

3 Read the tip box above, then reformulate the questions using the passé composé.

Example: Tu finis de manger ? *Tu as fini de manger?*

a Elle ouvre la porte ? ....

b Tu passes trois semaines en Italie ? ....

c Elles visitent le musée d'art moderne ? ....

d Ils font le tour de la ville ? ....

e Vous aimez ce film ? ....

4 Answer the questions in exercise 3 with a negative reply using the passé composé.

LANGUAGE BUILDER 2

Language discovery 2

Listen to the conversation again and repeat each line in the pauses provided.

In English, when talking about past events we often use words and phrases such as *yesterday*, *the day before yesterday*, *three days ago*, or *last week* to explain how long ago the events in question happened. We can also use certain words to signpost the order in which they happened: words like *then* or *next*, or (in a list) *first*, *second*, *third*, etc.

In Conversation 1, Charles uses four words/phrases to indicate the order in which things happened during his trip to Switzerland. The first of these is d'abord. Can you find and translate the other three?

Temporal signposts

In French, you can use signposting words and phrases to situate events in time or in a series of events, for example:

d'abord (*first of all*)

alors/ensuite/puis (*then*)

enfin/finalement (*finally*)

hier (*yesterday*)

avant-hier (*the day before yesterday*)

To say *that morning*, *that afternoon*, or *that year*, use ce/cet/cette-là : ce matin-là (*that morning*); cet après-midi-là (*that afternoon*); cette année-là (*that year*).

To say *ago*, use il y a before the amount of time, il y a trois mois (*three months ago*).

> To talk about something that has happened very recently, in English we use *just*, for example they've just arrived. French speakers use the form venir + de + infinitive: Ils viennent d'arriver (*They've just arrived*). Here are some other examples: Je viens d'acheter mon billet (*I have just bought my ticket*); Nous venons de voir un film génial (*We've just seen a great movie*). This is known as using the *recent past*.

Language practice 2

1 Complete the following sentences by translating the words supplied in parentheses into French. The first one has been done as an example:

a Ils ont visité les Alpes *il y a quatre mois.* (*four months ago*)

b .... Florence a eu son permis de conduire. (*two weeks ago*)

c .... ils ont visité Lausanne. (*last month*)

d Sophie a envoyé une carte postale .... (*last week*)

e Karim a acheté une plante magnifique .... (*the day before yesterday*)

2 Put the sentences in chronological order.

a Maintenant, deux ans plus tard, je suis chauffeur d'autobus.

b Puis j'ai passé l'examen de conduite — j'ai obtenu mon permis du premier coup.

c Ensuite, j'ai pris six mois de cours.

d D'abord j'ai trouvé une école de conduite près de chez moi.

e Il y a deux ans, j'ai décidé de passer mon permis de conduire.

11.06

3 Now play the conversation again and play Jo's role. Speak in the pauses. Try not to refer to the text.

CULTURE POINT 2

La littérature de voyage *Travel writing*

Des écrivains (*authors*) writing in French have made a strong contribution to literature about fictional and real-life travel. In 1766, with the permission of the king of France, Louis-Antoine de Bougainville became the first French national to circumnavigate le monde (*the world*). His account was published as *Voyage autour du monde* (*Journey Around the World*) in 1771. The bougainvillea flower is named after the intrepid naval admiral and explorer. Such real-life adventures doubtless inspired Jules Verne when he began to write his wonderful stories about travel around the world, under the sea, and even to the moon. The most famous of these is *Le Tour du monde en quatre-vingt jours* (*Around the World in Eighty Days*), published in 1872. In the (1956) Hollywood movie of the book, Verne's hero, Phileas Fogg, crosses the Alps in a hot-air balloon. In our own time, the inhabitants of the French town of Thise in the Franche-Comté region might have felt that life was imitating art. On August 23 2023, they witnessed two ULMs, or ultra-légers motorisés (*microlights*), touch down in a field, having flown over the Alps followed by more than 30 young ibis chauves (*bald ibis*). It turned out that the female pilotes (*pilots*) of the aircraft were teaching the ibis how to migrate!

Alongside travel literature, and often intermingling with it, for the past 200 years travel guides have been written to encourage people to venture into the world. In the 19th century, the *Baedeker* series was de rigueur (prescribed by fashion) for every traveler. More recently, the *Lonely Planet Guidebooks* can be found everywhere, including in Alex Garland's 1996 *The Beach*, set in Thailand, alluding to the power of the guidebook and how its users can reshape the areas they visit in large numbers. France has a long tradition of creating travel guides. In 1841, the journalist Adolphe Joanne created la première collection de guides de voyages (*the first collection of travel guides*), published by Louis Hachette. These will become the famous Guides Bleus in 1919. Later on, the famous Guides Michelin arrived, and in 1973 le Guide du Routard was also published by Hachette.

Read the histoire rocambolesque (*incredible story*) as it was covered by France-Info, with accompanying pictures. What is the final destination of the trip?

VOCABULARY BUILDER 2

Look at the words and phrases and provide the missing English words and expressions. Then listen and try to imitate the pronunciation of the speakers.

LORSQU'ON DÉGUSTE…	*WHEN YOU'RE DOING A TASTING…*
une dégustation	*tasting, tasting session*
une spécialité de la région	....
un vignoble	*vineyard*
une vigne	....
un vigneron	*(male) winegrower*
une vigneronne	....
un vignoble avoisinant	*a neighboring vineyard*
des raisins	*grapes*
des raisins secs	*raisins*

EXPRESSIONS	*EXPRESSIONS*
Alors, on dresse la tente ?	*So, shall we put up the tent?*
Nous sommes de retour, heureusement.	*We're back, fortunately.*
Il a trouvé une auberge sympa/sympathique.	*They found a nice hostel.*
Peut-être que vous viendrez.	*Perhaps you will come.*
Vive les vacances !	*Hooray for the holidays!*
C'est à moins de 50 km d'ici.	*It's less than 50 km from here.*
… est mis en bouteille à la propriété.	*… bottled at the producer's vineyard.*

Vocabulary practice 2

Complete the sentences below with words and expressions from the Vocabulary builder.

a Le champagne est .... de la région.

b Il est mis .... à la propriété.

c Elles font du camping ce week-end et vont dresser une ....

d Nous avons visité les .... autour de Reims et nous avons fait plusieurs .... de produits locaux. C'est ce que j'appelle un week-end plein de délices.

CONVERSATION 2

J'ai perdu mon téléphone *I've lost my phone*

11.08

1 Here are a few words and expressions to understand the conversation.

à un tarif spécial	*at a special price*	C'est rapide.	*That's quick.*
animé, animée	*lively*	partout	*everywhere*
annuler	*cancel*	à l'heure prévue	*as scheduled*

11.09

2 Listen to the conversation without looking at the text. Then listen to the conversation again and read the text.

Charles and Jo discuss Jo and Assia's recent trip to Reims, in the Champagne region.

Charles Et toi, ton week-end à Reims, c'était bien ?

Jo C'était super ! J'ai adoré la ville de Reims, c'est une ville très animée !

Charles Vous avez bu du champagne ?

Jo Ben oui, c'est la spécialité de la région ! Nous sommes parties le samedi à 10 h 00 et nous sommes arrivées juste avant 11 h 00...

Charles C'est rapide.

Jo Oui moins d'une heure. Nous avons commencé par une dégustation de produits locaux. Ensuite nous sommes allées visiter une maison de champagne à quelques kilomètres, près de Reims. C'était très intéressant !

Et le soir, nous avons dîné et dormi à la ferme.

Charles Super ! Et le dimanche ?

Jo Ah, le dimanche, il y a eu un petit problème : j'ai perdu mon téléphone.

Charles Aïe !

Jo Oui, je ne te raconte pas le stress ! Nous l'avons cherché partout, à la cathédrale, au café, dans le bus, tout autour de l'arrêt d'autobus ! Finalement, nous l'avons retrouvé... dans ma chambre, à la ferme !

Charles Ouf !

Jo Oui, quelle chance ! Nous avons dû annuler le déjeuner gastronomique, mais nous avons trouvé un petit restaurant très sympa, et nous sommes rentrées à Paris à l'heure prévue...

3 Answer the questions

a How long did Jo and Assia's train journey to Rheims take?
b Where was the champagne producer they visited based?
c What went wrong on Sunday?
d How was the problem resolved?
e How did this incident affect their eating arrangements?

LANGUAGE BUILDER 3

Language discovery 3

In Conversation 2, Jo explains she lost her phone: j'ai perdu mon téléphone. **Using j'ai perdu as an example, see whether you can complete the following verb pattern for perdre in le passé composé:**

perdre (*to lose*)	
j'ai perdu	nous avons perdu
a tu	**c** vous ....
b il/elle	**d** ils/elles ....

Le passé composé of -re verbs

Most -re verbs form their past participle in a similar way to **-er** and **-ir** verbs:

(a) remove the letters -re from the infinitive;

(b) add -u.

vendre (*to sell*)

j'ai vendu	*I (have) sold*	nous avons vendu	*we (have) sold*
tu as vendu	*you (have) sold*	vous avez vendu	*you (have) sold*
il/elle as vendu	*he/she (has) sold*	ils/elles ont vendu	*they (have) sold*

Il m'a rendu le livre. *He returned the book to me.*

Elle a tendu la main. *She held out her hand.*

Ils ont vendu leur maison. *They sold their home.*

Some past participles of -re verbs are irregular and so must be learned separately.

Infinitive	Past Participle	Meaning
apprendre	appris	*to learn/learned*
conduire	conduit	*to drive/driven*
mettre	mis	*to put/put*
omettre	omis	*to omit/omitted*
prendre	pris	*to take/taken*
suivre	suivi	*to follow/followed*

Example: (Il m'a rendu le levre.. etc)

Ils ont conduit toute la nuit. *They drove all night.*

Est-que tu as pris tes clés ? *Did you take your keys?*

Nous avons suivi le guide. *We followed the guide.*

Language practice 3

1 Replace the present-tense verbs with verbs in le passé composé.

Example: Il conduit sa nouvelle voiture aujourd'hui ?
Il a conduit sa nouvelle voiture hier ?

a Vous vendez votre appartement ?
Vous .... votre appartement ?

b Elles rendent les clés de la maison aujourd'hui.
Elles .... les clés de la maison hier.

c Marie tend la main pour aider Jean.
Hier, Marie .... la main pour aider Jean.

d J'omets le sel quand je prépare ce plat.
Hier, j' .... le sel quand j'ai préparé ce plat.

e Anne conduit une Citroën.
Pendant cinq ans, Anne .... une Citroën.

f Normalement, Ahmed met des fleurs sur la table.
Hier, Ahmed .... des fleurs sur la table.

g Tu prends du sucre avec ton café ?
Avant-hier, tu .... du sucre avec ton café ?

h Nous suivons des cours de voile.
Pendant deux ans, nous .... des cours de voile.

2 Complete the sentences with le passé composé of the verbs indicated.

Example: Elle *a réservé* les billets. (*réserver*)

a Est-ce que vous .... la réservation ? (*faire*)

b Oui, mais ensuite j' .... (*annuler*)

c Vous .... la nouvelle ville ? (*explorer*)

d Nous .... la connaissance de Jean et Marie. (*faire*)

e Elles .... le musée principal. (*visiter*)

LANGUAGE BUILDER 4

Language discovery 4

Listen to the conversation again and repeat each line in the pauses provided.

Here, in order, are the passé composé verbs which Jo uses to describe what she and Assia did together: sommes parties ; sommes arrivées ; avons commencé ; sommes allées ; avons dîné ; avons dormi ; avons cherché ; avons retrouvé ; avons dû ; avons trouvé ; sommes rentrées.

1 Which of the following statements is true?

a All of these verbs are made up of avoir plus a past participle.
b Some of these verbs are made up of être plus a past participle.

2 Choose the correct ending to the statement.

Some of the past participles in the verbs listed above end in -es. These participles are...

a the ones that follow avoir.
b the ones that follow être.
c a mixture of a and b.

Le passé composé with être

You have already learned that le passé composé is generally formed using avoir + past participle. You should also note that sometimes it is formed using être + past participle. This generally applies to verbs expressing motion, such as aller or arriver, and all reflexive verbs.

singular	plural
je suis arrivé (masc.) je suis arrivée (fem.)	nous sommes arrivés (masc.) nous sommes arrivées (fem.)
tu es arrivé (masc.)/vous êtes arrivé (masc.)* tu es arrivée (fem.)/vous êtes arrivée (fem.)*	vous êtes arrivés (masc.)* vous êtes arrivées (fem.)*
il est arrivé (masc.) elle est arrivée (fem.)	ils sont arrivés (masc.) elles sont arrivées (fem.)

* Vous can also be singular (when the speaker addresses one male or one female person only). This gives two further possible spellings: vous êtes arrivé (masc. sing.) and vous êtes arrivée (fem. sing.).

Did you notice that when a verb takes être, the past participle agrees with the subject in gender and number? Other verbs that take être include descendre (*to go downstairs*), monter (*to go upstairs*), entrer (*to enter*), rentrer (*to go back in/go home*), rester (*to remain*), partir (*to leave*), sortir (*to go out*), and tomber (*to fall*).

Nous sommes arrivés trop tard.	*We arrived too late.*
Elle est partie?	*She left?*
Les filles se sont endormies.	*The girls fell asleep.*

Language practice 4

1 Match the sentence halves.

a Bonsoir Jean et Marie :	**1** quand est-ce que vous êtes arrivées ?
b Bonsoir Marie et Suzanne :	**2** quand est-ce que vous êtes arrivés ?
c Florence...	**3** sont arrivés assez tard.
d Paul...	**4** sont arrivées trop tard.
e Mo et Paul...	**5** est arrivé à l'heure.
f Claire et Florence...	**6** est arrivée assez tôt.

2 Complete each sentence using the given verbs. Then translate into English. The first one has been done.

a Il est entré dans la maison. (*entrer*) *He entered/has entered the house.*
b Elle est .... au premier étage. (*monter*)
c Coucou ! C'est Julie et Florence. Nous sommes .... ! (*arriver*)
d Jean et son frère sont .... pour ouvrir la porte. (*descendre*)
e Marine, tu es .... ? (*tomber*)

11.11

3 Now play the conversation again and play Charles's role. Speak in the pauses. Try not to refer to the text.

SKILL BUILDER

1 Read the postcard. Then complete the text with le passé composé of the verbs indicated. Use avoir or être as appropriate. When using être, make sure the past participle agrees with the subject.

Salut les amis !

Comme vous savez, Mireille, Patrick et moi avons décidé (décider) d'explorer l'Italie. Nous **a** .... (réserver) des chambres dans des auberges de jeunesse. Ensuite, on **b** .... (acheter) des billets interrail. Je **c** .... (partir) un peu avant les autres. Mireille et Patrick **d** .... (partir) deux jours plus tard à cause de leur travail. Mais nous nous **e** .... (se retrouver) à Rome. Après, on **f** .... (rester) ensemble pour le reste du trajet. Après Rome, nous **g** .... (visiter) Florence et Sienne, puis, dans le Sud, Pompéi et l'île de Capri. C'était super bien !

Bisous, Julie

2 Record a phone message for your parents telling them what you did on your first day of your vacation using the terms below to structure your story into three parts (morning, afternoon and evening).

Le matin... et ensuite l'après-midi... et finalement le soir...

TEST YOURSELF

1 Complete the following passage by adding the relevant verb in the past tense. Pay attention to endings in case of agreements.

Assia et Jo **a** .... (*faire*) une escapade le week-end dernier. Elles **b** .... (*aller*) à Reims visiter des vignobles de la région. Elles **c** .... (*prendre*) le train de Paris le matin et **d** .... (*arriver*) avant le déjeuner. Le dimanche soir elles **e** .... (*rentrer*) en fin de journée. Leur train **f** .... (*partir*) à 22 h 15 de Reims et il **g** .... (*arriver*) à Paris à 23 h 01. Elles **h** .... (*passer*) un très bon week-end.

2 Complete the following passage about what Charles did yesterday.

Hier je **a** .... (*se réveiller*) tard. Ensuite je **b** .... (*se laver*) et je **c** .... (*s'habiller*) rapidement. J' **d** .... (*prendre*) un brunch à 11 heures. Après, je **e** .... (*aller*) chercher Eva et nous **f** .... (*se promener*) au Parc du Cinquantenaire avant d'aller voir une exposition au Musée Art et Histoire.

Remember to use **My review** and **My takeaway** to assess your progress and reflect on your learning experience.

12

In this lesson you will learn how to:

» Talk about things that frequently happened in the past
» Use different verbs when describing past events
» Use pronouns instead of nouns to avoid repetition
» Compare things in relation to one another

Des souvenirs

My study plan

I plan to work with Unit 12

○ Every day
○ Twice a week
○ Other ________

I plan to study for

○ 5–15 minutes
○ 15–30 minutes
○ 30–45+ minutes

My progress tracker

Day / Date	Listening	Speaking	Reading	Writing	Conversation
	○	○	○	○	○
	○	○	○	○	○
	○	○	○	○	○
	○	○	○	○	○
	○	○	○	○	○
	○	○	○	○	○
	○	○	○	○	○

My goals

What do you want to be able to do or say in French when you complete this unit?

		Done
1	....	○
2	....	○
3	....	○

My review

SELF CHECK

	I can ...
●	... describe different things that happened in the past.
●	... use various pronouns instead of nouns.
●	... compare various things and people to one another.

CULTURE POINT 1

Les Alpes *The Alps*

When we hear any mention of les Alpes (*the Alps*), we might think of Switzerland at first. But the famous chaîne de montagnes (*mountain range*) stretches 1,200 km across eight countries including France, Italy, Germany, l'Autriche (*Austria*), and la Slovénie (*Slovenia*). Le Mont Blanc, la montagne la plus haute de l'Europe de l'ouest (*Mont Blanc, the highest mountain in western Europe*), extends on either side of la frontière France–Italie (*the French–Italian border*). The French Alps offer a wide variety of activities; not only plusieurs sports d'hiver (*several winter sports*), but durant les mois d'été (*during the summer months*), le vélo tout terrain/VTT (*mountain biking*), la via ferrata*, or even le parapente (*paragliding*). There is also the gentler option of strolling through the gorgeous scenery, where each year sheep broutent (*graze*) on slopes that will be under snow some months later. The beauty of the French Alps no doubt explains why millions of people visit the region every year. Face à ce tourisme de masse (*faced with this mass tourism*), some ski areas are working to achieve sustainability in the longer term. Look out for le Flocon vert (*the Green Flake*) label to find out more about which resorts are sustainable. Cependant (*meanwhile/however*), in November 2023, France put in a late bid, approved by the International Olympic Committee, to host the 2030 Winter Olympics. President Emmanuel Macron expressed confidence that des jeux innovants, durables et inclusifs (*innovative, durable, and inclusive games*) would faire rayonner la France et sa montagne (*make France and its mountains shine*).

*A kind of rock climbing supported by ropes, ladders, handrails etc. The term is based on the Italian for une voie ferrée (*iron pathway*).

Visit the Flocon vert website. What 20 criteria are evaluated?

VOCABULARY BUILDER 1

12.01

Look at the words and phrases and complete the missing English words and expressions. Then listen and try to imitate the pronunciation of the speakers.

LES DESTINATIONS DU GLOBE-TROTTEUR	*DESTINATIONS FOR THE GLOBE-TROTTER*
un globe-trotteur/une globe-trotteuse	*globetrotter (male/female)*
la mer	*sea*
la montagne	....
faire du camping	*to go camping*
la randonnée	*walking, walk*
la carte postale	....
le timbre	*stamp*
partir en vacances	....

EXPRESSIONS	*EXPRESSIONS*
Les Alpes sont tout aussi belles en été.	*The Alps are just as beautiful in summer.*
Des vaches broutent sur les pentes.	*Cows graze on the slopes.*
On voit cette chaîne depuis l'espace.	*You can see this range from space.*
Tu dois profiter de tes vacances.	*You must make the most of your vacation.*

Vocabulary practice 1

Complete the text with vocabulary from the Culture point and Vocabulary builder.

Finalement je suis arrivé/arrivée dans les Alpes ! Je vais faire du **a** .... (*mountain biking*) et peut-être du **b** .... (*paragliding*). J'espère aussi voir des chèvres et des vaches ; apparemment elles **c** .... (*graze*) sur les **d** .... (*slopes*) de la montagne. S'asseoir pour regarder, c'est aussi **e** .... (*making the most of*) la montagne !

Pronunciation practice

There is a mark known in French as un tréma that is composed of two dots, over a vowel. When a word contains a double vowel and they are pronounced separately, un tréma is placed over the second vowel. For instance, compare mais (*but*) and le maïs (*corn*). The same applies when un tréma is placed above the letter e, as in le Noël (*Christmas*).

12.02

Listen to the recording while reading the list. Then listen again and note each word that has un tréma. Finally listen and repeat the pronunciation.

Le maïs, c'est délicieux, mais je préfère les carottes. *Corn is delicious, but I prefer carrots.*
À Noël, nous allons chez nos parents. *At Christmas, we go to my parents' house.*
Est-ce que tu aimes la cuisine des Caraïbes ? *Do you like Caribbean cuisine?*

CONVERSATION 1

La carte postale *The postcard*

12.03

1 Here are a few words and expressions to understand the conversation.

emmener	*to take (a person)*
un endroit	*place*
recevoir	*to receive*
une sorte de rituel	*a sort of ritual*

12.04

2 Listen to the conversation a few times without looking at the text. Then listen again and read the text.

Charles and Eva discover that they share a love of postcards because of their childhood experiences and happy memories linked to sending and receiving postcards.

Charles	Tiens, une carte postale de Reims ! C'est sympa !
Eva	Oh, j'adore les cartes postales. Quand j'étais petite, j'aimais en envoyer et surtout en recevoir !
Charles	Oui, moi aussi !
Eva	Chaque été, ma sœur et moi nous partions en vacances avec nos grands-parents. Ils nous emmenaient à la mer, ou à la montagne.
Charles	Génial !
Eva	Oui, c'était super, on faisait du camping, de la randonnée en montagne, de la voile. On visitait la Suisse, on allait en Italie, en France, en Autriche... chaque année dans un endroit différent !
Charles	Et vous envoyiez des cartes postales à vos parents ?
Eva	C'est ça, c'était une sorte de rituel. On leur envoyait une carte postale, ou plutôt deux cartes, depuis chaque endroit. On achetait toujours un joli timbre, pour notre collection...
Charles	Ma sœur et moi, on adorait recevoir les cartes de mon oncle Paul, il écrivait des guides de voyage et voyageait tout le temps : les États-Unis, le Japon, la Thaïlande, la Tanzanie, le Pérou, Madagascar, les Philippines, Cuba, l'Indonésie, l'Égypte...
Eva	Un vrai globe-trotteur, quelle chance !

3 Answer the questions.

- **a** Charles received a postcard—where did it come from? Do you remember who recently visited the Champagne region and might have sent him a postcard?
- **b** Who often took Eva on vacation when she was a young child and where did they take her?
- **c** How did Eva and her sister benefit from the postcards that they sent their parents? What did they collect?
- **d** Did Charles receive postcards from his uncle Paul when Paul was traveling for pleasure, or when he traveled for work?

LANGUAGE BUILDER 1

Language discovery 1

1 In Conversation 1, Charles and Eva talk about past events but they are not using le passé composé. Instead, they use a tense known as l'imparfait. Here is a list of some of the verbs they use, with gaps. Can you complete the list by finding the missing imparfaits in the conversation? What do you notice about the form of verbs in imparfait?

J' .... (*from* être) ; j' .... (aimer) ; tu .... (écrire) ; nous partions (partir) ; on faisait (faire) ; on .... (visiter) ; on allait (aller) ; vous envoyiez (envoyer) ; on .... (acheter) ; on .... (adorer) ; il écrivait (écrire).

L'imparfait *The imperfect*

In French, besides le passé composé, there is another past tense: l'imparfait (*the imperfect*).

The imparfait is very regular, and all three verb groups work the same way:

- **a** take the (present tense) nous-form of the verb (e.g. for visiter → nous visitons);
- **b** remove ons to find the stem (e.g. visitons → visit-);
- **c** Add these endings: -ais, -ais, -ait, -ions, -iez, -aient. Here are the full patterns for visiter, finir, écrire, and être.

visiter (*to visit*)

je visitais	nous visitions
tu visitais	vous visitiez
il/elle/on visitait	ils/elles visitaient

faire (*to do*)

je faisais	nous faisions
tu faisais	vous faisiez
il/elle/on faisait	ils/elles faisaient

finir (*to finish*)

je finissais	nous finissions
tu finissais	vous finissiez
il/elle/on finissait	ils/elles finissaient

Note the double -ss- throughout the pattern for finir (based on nous finiss-ons)

écrire (*to write*)

j'écrivais	nous écrivions
tu écrivais	vous écriviez
il/elle/on écrivait	ils/elles écrivaient

être (*to be*)

j'étais	nous étions
tu étais	vous étiez
il/elle/on était	ils/elles étaient

The imparfait is typically used for:

1 events that occurred more than once, but where we don't know precisely over how long a period, or how many times they happened:

À une époque, nous allions au cinéma régulièrement.

At one time, used to go to the cinema regularly.

2 events that were interrupted by other events:

Il parlait à Jean-Luc quand Laure est arrivée.

He was speaking to Jean-Luc when Laure arrived.

Above, Laure est arrivée is in le passé composé and it is this single past action that interrupted the ongoing past action (Il parlait à Jean-Luc), which is in l'imparfait.

3 descriptions of people/things in the past:

L'inconnu avait les cheveux bruns. Dehors, le soleil brillait et le vent soufflait.

The stranger had brown hair. Outside, the sun was shining and the wind was blowing.

The imparfait might be translated into English in various ways. For instance, depending on the context, nous allions might be translated as *we went*, *we used to go*, *we would go*, or *we were going*.

Language practice 1

1 Transform the following present-tense sentences into past-tense sentences beginning with à une époque (*at one time*). The first one has been done for you.

a J'adore les films de Truffaut. — À une époque, *j'adorais les films de Truffaut.*

b Je parle allemand couramment (*fluently*). — À une époque, ...

c Elle habite en Italie. — À une époque, ...

d Ils arrivent toujours en retard (*late*). — À une époque, ...

2 Complete the sentences with the verbs given, using either le passé composé or l'imparfait as appropriate.

a À une époque, je .... régulièrement du piano. (*jouer*)
b Pendant que Jean ...., son téléphone a sonné. (*s'habiller*)
c Pendant que Paul parlait avec sa copine, Luc .... (*arriver*)
d Elle .... ce film trois fois, car elle l'aime beaucoup. (*voir*)
e Hier matin, elle .... assez tard. C' .... samedi, après tout ! (*se réveiller, être*)

LANGUAGE BUILDER 2

Language discovery 2

12.05

Listen to the conversation again and repeat each line in the pauses.

Just over halfway through Conversation 1, Charles asks Eva: Et vous envoyiez des cartes postales à vos parents ? to which Eva replies: On leur envoyait une carte postale...

Which three words in Charles's question does leur replace/refer back to?

Les compléments d'objet indirect *Indirect object pronouns*

You have learned that in a sentence such as je la vois (*I see her*), there is a subject pronoun (je) and an object pronoun (la). The subject performs the action (*I see*), the object is at the receiving end of the action (*it is seen*).

There is more than one way of being at the receiving end of an action. Look at the following sentence: Lucie donne une carte à Jean (*Lucie gives a card to Jean*). Here, Lucie is clearly doing the giving, so she is the subject. But there are two objects at the receiving end: the card and Jean. The postcard is the ***direct object*** and Jean is the ***indirect object***. In French, the indirect object generally follows the preposition à. So Lucie might give a card à Jean, or perhaps au frère de Jean, à l'ami de Jean or aux parents de Jean. Like subjects and direct objects, indirect objects can be replaced by a pronoun. Compare these with the direct object pronouns you have already learned.

Indirect object pronouns				Direct object pronouns			
me	*to me*	**nous**	*to us*	**me**	*me*	**nous**	*us*
te	*to you*	**vous**	*to you*	**te**	*you*	**vous**	*you*
lui	*to him/to her*	**leur**	*to them*	**le/la**	*him/her*	**les**	*them*

Assia offre un livre à Jo. — *Assia offers a book to Jo.*

→ Assia lui offre un livre. — *→ Assia offers her a book.*

Notice that the direct and indirect object pronouns are the same for all but the third person il/elle and ils/elles forms.

In Unit 10 you learned that direct object pronouns precede the verb. For example, *I see him* is je le vois and *I saw him* is je l'ai vu. The same applies to indirect object pronouns: *I'm giving her a present* is je lui donne un cadeau, and *I gave her a present* is je lui ai donné un cadeau.

Language practice 2

1 Replace the underlined words with an indirect object pronoun to form a shorter sentence.

Example: J'écris une lettre <u>à Francine et Lucille</u>. *Je leur écris une lettre.*

a Tu as envoyé un cadeau <u>à ta mère</u>. ....

b Tu vas envoyer un cadeau <u>à ton père</u>. ....

c Marie-Laure a déjà parlé <u>à ses sœurs</u>. ....

d Marc va écrire une lettre <u>à ses cousins</u>. ....

2 Complete the sentences using the following indirect object pronouns: me, te, lui, nous, vous, leur. Use each pronoun once.

a Tes parents .... rendent visite tous les mois ?

b Vos cousins .... rendent visite actuellement ?

c Voici Sophie. On doit .... parler pour organiser la fête d'anniversaire de sa mère.

d Je connais bien Tim. Il .... rend souvent visite quand il est en ville.

e Notre voisin est sympathique. Il .... prête des livres.

f Mo aime beaucoup ses jeunes cousins. Il .... écrit souvent.

12.06

Listen to Conversation 1 again and then take on the role of Eva and practice speaking with Charles.

CULTURE POINT 2

La Normandie *Normandy*

La Normandie (*Normandy*) is an area of northern France with a rich cultural history. Famous Normans of the Middle Ages include Guillaume le conquérant (*William the Conqueror*), Jeanne d'Arc (*Joan of Arc*), and Richard Cœur de Lion (*Richard the Lionheart*). Part of Normandy's medieval legacy is Mont Saint-Michel (*Saint Michael's Mount*). This hill, topped by an ancient abbey, is in fact a tidal island, linked to the mainland by un pont passerelle (*footbridge*). The 19th-century author Guy de Maupassant called it ce gigantesque bijou de granit, aussi léger qu'une dentelle (*this gigantic jewel made of granite, as light as a piece of lace*). At different times in history, the original abbey was repurposed as a fortress and a prison; now it is mainly known as a UNESCO World Heritage Site. If you visit it, it is also the place to try une omelette de la Mère Poulard (*Mother Poulard's omelette*), a specialty of the island depuis les années 1800 (*since the 1800s*). Another of Normandy's bijoux (*jewels*), but of more recent date, is the artist Claude Monet's garden at Giverny (a train journey from Paris to Vernon-Giverny takes 1.5 hours on average). Monet acquired this property with money he earned by painting, and he lived there until his death (1926). He created his famous Nymphéas (*paintings of water lilies*) in his Japanese garden at Giverny. To mark the end of World War I, Monet donated two huge water-lily paintings (each measuring roughly 2 × 4.25 m) to the French nation; he subsequently produced six further paintings to form a series. Since 1927, these Nymphéas have been displayed in two oval rooms designed for that purpose within the Musée de l'Orangerie, Paris. Each year, on June 6, commemorations of le Débarquement (*the D-Day Landings*), take place across Normandy.

Check this itinerary on the Normandy tourism office website. What are the four legs of the trip? What are the main points of interest on the way?

VOCABULARY BUILDER 2

Look at the words and phrases and complete the missing English words and expressions. Then listen and try to imitate the pronunciation of the speakers.

LA VILLE ET LA CAMPAGNE	*TOWN AND COUNTRY*
un cadre, un cadre de vie	*frame, environment/lifestyle*
cultiver des légumes	*grow vegetables*
élever des poules	*breed chickens*
vivre à la campagne/en ville	....
une vie idéale	....
calme	....
sain, saine	*healthy*
séparément	*separately*
un terroir	*soil (of a specific region)*
un espace vert	*green space*
pollué/polluée	*polluted*
un bruit	*noise*
bruyant, bruyante	*noisy*

EXPRESSIONS	*EXPRESSIONS*
Elle répond à une enquête.	*She is responding to an inquiry.*
Je n'ai rien reçu.	*I didn't get anything.*
poser une question	*to ask a question*
Il y a beaucoup d'animation.	*There is a lot going on.*
Quelle est ta préférence ?	*What is your preference?*
C'est mieux peut-être.	*Perhaps that's better.*
Il y a de la place.	*There's enough room.*
Je ne me vois pas habiter à la campagne.	*I don't see myself living in the countryside.*

Vocabulary practice 2

Complete the text with the correct words from Vocabulary builder 2.

Selon vous, quels sont les avantages de la vie à la campagne ?

Selon moi, la vie y est plus **a** .... (*calm*). Les enfants ont **b** .... (*lots of room*), et l'air est moins **c** .... (*polluted*). On peut **d** .... (*grow*) des légumes... C'est un **e** .... (*way of life*) plus **f** .... (*healthy*) ; la vie **g** .... (*the ideal life*), ou presque !

CONVERSATION 2

L'enquête *The survey*

12.08

1 Here are a few words and expressions to understand the conversation.

un institut de sondage	*polling company*	un commerce	*shop/business*
un sondage	*poll*	les gens	*people*
ses propres légumes	*your own/one's own vegetables*	une âme	*soul*

12.09

2 Listen to the conversation without looking at the text. Then listen to the conversation again and read the text.

Assia and Jo discuss the pros and cons of living in the countryside versus living in the city as they have received a survey on this topic. They have different points of view for a variety of reasons.

Jo Tu as reçu l'enquête de l'institut de sondage sur les préférences des Françaises et des Français ? On répond ?

Assia Non, je n'ai rien reçu. Quelle est la question posée ?

Jo Vous préférez vivre en ville ou à la campagne ?

Assia Moi, je préfère vivre en ville, je ne me vois pas habiter à la campagne.

Jo Moi, je préfère habiter à la campagne, dans un village. C'est plus calme, moins pollué, les gens sont moins stressés, il y a de la place, et on peut avoir un jardin et cultiver ses propres légumes.

Assia Oui, c'est vrai, c'est un cadre de vie plus sain que la vie en ville. Mais en même temps, il n'y a pas de transports en commun, et on est loin de tout : le cinéma, les musées, les restaurants.

Jo Oui, l'idéal, ce serait un village avec un marché et des commerces, quelques restaurants, un cinéma.

Assia Oui, c'est mieux ! Mais moi, j'aime l'animation de la ville, j'aime observer les gens dans le métro.

Jo Ben oui, je te comprends, c'est ton âme de photographe qui parle !

Assia Et moi aussi je te comprends, tu aimes les bons produits du terroir, les bonnes tables, le temps de vivre.

Jo Ben oui ! Je crois que, après tout, nous n'allons pas répondre à cette enquête !

Assia Ou on va y répondre séparément.

Jo Tu as raison, c'est la solution la plus logique !

3 Answer the questions.

- **a** Which institute prepared the survey that Jo received?
- **b** Why does Jo prefer to live in the countryside?
- **c** What does Assia think is missing in the countryside?
- **d** What would be ideal from Jo's point of view?
- **e** Why does Assia prefer to live in the city?
- **f** Why does Jo think that Assia prefers the city?
- **g** Why does Assia think that Jo prefers the countryside?
- **h** Will they reply to the survey together or individually?

LANGUAGE BUILDER 3

Language discovery 3

In English, to compare one thing with another we have two possibilities: (a) we put *more* or *less* in front of an adjective, e.g. *Natasha is more careful than Richard*, or *Tim is less fussy than Frank*. (b) we add -er to an adjective, for example *my dog is calmer than yours*, or *her company is bigger than his*.

Using examples found in Conversation 2, can you say how comparisons are made in French? Complete the rule:

To make comparisons in French, you can place .... or .... before an ....

Making comparisons

Here are some ways to make comparisons between people or things in French:

1 Using moins (*more*), aussi (*as*) and plus (*more*). Note that in this kind of expression the adjective agrees with the person or thing described; for instance: Jean est aussi grand que Marc ; Sophie est moins grand**e** que sa sœur ; Marc et Jean sont plus grand**s** que leur père.

In these sentences you can also see how que is being used as part of the comparison and can be can be translated by *as* or *than: Jean is as tall as Marc; Sophie is shorter than her sister; Marc and Jean are taller than their father.*

Jean-Marc est plus grand que son frère.	*Jean-Marc is taller than his brother.*
Ce livre-ci est moins intéressant que celui-là.	*This book is less interesting than that one.*
Ma note à l'examen de mathématiques est plus mauvaise que la tienne.	*My grade on the math exam is worse than yours.*

2 Using meilleur (*better*) or pire (*worse*).
Note that meilleur can be spelled in one of four possible ways depending on the person(s) or thing(s) it describes: meilleur, meilleure, meilleurs, or meilleures.

Tes idées sont meilleures que les miennes.	*Your ideas are better than mine.*
La soif est pire que la faim.	*Thirst is worse than hunger.*

3 Using mieux (*better*) and moins bien (*less well*). Note that the difference between meilleur and mieux is that meilleur is an adjective, while mieux is an adverb.

Annelise parle mieux l'allemand que Bob.	*Annelise speaks German better than Bob.*
Je joue du piano moins bien que Jacques.	*I play the piano less well than Jacques.*
Les médecins sont mieux payés que les infirmiers.	*Doctors are better paid than nurses.*

Language practice 3

1 Complete the sentences with the correct comparative forms.

Example: Marie est *aussi grande* que son frère. (*as tall*)

a Harry est .... que son frère. (*less tall*)

b Nos cousins sont .... que nous. (*as tall*)

c Joyeux anniversaire, Marie ! Tu es .... qu'il y a un an ! (*taller*)

d Les grandes villes sont .... que la campagne. (*less calm*)

e La voiture de Karine est .... que celle d'Henri. (*bigger*)

f Le jogging est .... pour le corps que la natation. (*less healthy*)

g Je joue de la guitare, mais .... que toi. (*less well*)

h Noémie est .... que Georges. (*better paid*)

2 Complete the sentences to match the English translations.

a Je demande un .... emploi du temps.	*I'm asking for a better work schedule.*
b Tu aimes ces sacs ? J'en ai vu de	*You like these bags? I've seen better ones.*
c Tim joue bien, mais son frère joue	*Tim plays well, but his brother plays better.*
d Noémie chante bien ; Karine chante	*Noémie sings well; Karine sings less well.*
e Nous jouons .... aujourd'hui qu'hier.	*We're playing better today than yesterday.*
f Un match perdu est .... qu'un match nul.	*A lost match is worse than a draw.*

LANGUAGE BUILDER 4

Language discovery 4

12.10

Listen to the conversation again and repeat each line in the pauses.

Look at this excerpt from Conversation 2.

Oui, c'est la solution la plus logique.

Which of the following is the correct translation of la solution la plus logique ?

a the logical solution
b the more logical solution
c the most logical solution

Superlatives

When speakers of English state that someone or something is the *smallest* or *biggest*, the *best* or the *worst*, the *highest* or the *lowest* (using the ending *-est*), etc., they are awarding top or bottom place to one item from a list or group. This kind of expression is called a *superlative.*

Below are three kinds of superlatives used in French:

1 le plus (*the most*) and le moins (*the least*), used with an adjective.

Bill est le plus grand des trois fils de Sam.	*Bill is the tallest of Sam's three sons.*
Ses résultats sont les moins bons.	*His/her results are the poorest.*
Les plus jolies fleurs sont les roses.	*The prettiest flowers are roses.*

Note that the definite article agrees with the noun and the group or context for comparison is introduced by the preposition **de** (rather than **que**).

Cette piscine est la plus mauvaise de la ville.	*This swimming pool is the worst in town.*

2 Using le meilleur/la meilleure/les meilleurs/les meilleures (*the best*).

De nous trois, tu as le meilleur niveau.	*Of the three of us, you have the best level.*
Tes idées sont les meilleures.	*Your ideas are the best/the best ones.*

3 Using le pire/la pire/les pires (*the worst*).

Le deuil est le pire des souffrances.	*Bereavement is the worst kind of suffering.*

Notice that in this sentence, using the superlative is simply a matter of adding le, la, or les to the comparative adjective. So cette fleur est plus jolie (comparative) means *this flower is prettier*, and cette fleur est la plus jolie (superlative) means *this flower is (the) prettiest*.

Language practice 4

1 Give the comparative and superlative forms of the adjective, using plus or moins as indicated.

Example: Cette ville est jolie / *plus jolie* / *la plus jolie.* (*plus*)

a Ce livre est intéressant / .... / .... (*plus*)

b Cette fleur est belle / .... / .... (*moins*)

c Cette ville est animée / .... / .... (*moins*)

d Ce magasin est grand / .... / .... (*plus*)

2 Complete the French sentences with the comparative or superlative.

a Cette voiture est .... (*better*).

b Ces chaussures sont .... (*the best*).

c Cet ordinateur est .... (*the best*).

d Ces vêtements sont .... (*better*).

12.11

3 Listen to Conversation 2 again. Then explain to your friend what your own preference would be if you were asked to choose between living in the countryside or the city and what reasons would you give for your choice. Start with: Je préfère habiter....

SKILL BUILDER

1 Read the following passage. Then translate the passage into English paying particular attention to the verbs and pronouns you need to use.

Quand Charles et Jo étaient jeunes, ils aimaient recevoir de nombreuses cartes postales de leur oncle qui voyageait à travers le monde. Il leur envoyait de très belles cartes. Ils s'imaginaient des lieux magiques. L'année dernière, ils sont partis en vacances aux États-Unis, et ils ont pensé à leur oncle. Ils lui ont envoyé plusieurs cartes, pour le remercier et perpétuer la tradition.

2 Complete the sentences with a direct or indirect object pronoun as appropriate.

a Est-ce que tu peux .... prêter ton livre ?

b Non, je .... prête à Colin.

c Et Katie ? Quand est-ce que vous .... voyez ?

d Vous pouvez .... parler tout de suite ?

e Philippe .... parlera demain.

TEST YOURSELF

1 Complete the sentences below with the missing French comparatives and superlatives.

Example: Les vins de Loire sont de <u>bons</u> vins.

Comparative: Je trouve que les vins de Bourgogne sont *meilleurs* que les vins de Bordeaux.

Superlative: Pour moi, *le meilleur* vin est celui qu'on boit entre amis !

a Paris est une très <u>belle</u> ville.

Comparative: Je trouve que la ville de Rome est **1** .... que la ville de Paris.

Superlative: Ah non, je ne suis pas d'accord Paris est **2** .... ville du monde.

b Le train est un mode de transport très confortable.

Comparative: Je trouve que le train est **1** .... que la voiture.

Superlative: Ah oui, je suis d'accord, pour moi le train est **2** ....

c Le train est un mode de transport très écologique.

Comparative: Je pense que le vélo est un mode de transport **1** .... que le train.

Superlative: En vérité, le mode de transport **2** .... c'est la marche à pied !

2 Complete the text with the passé composé or the imparfait form of the given verbs.

Notre chien Loulou est espiègle. Hier, pendant que j' **a** .... (*écouter*) la radio, il **b** .... (*s'échapper*) du jardin. Vingt minutes plus tard il **c** .... (*revenir*) mine de rien, avec un autre chien, qui **d** .... (*être*) assez petit et très mignon. Heureusement ce nouvel ami **e** .... (*avoir*) un collier avec le numéro de téléphone de son maître. Mon mari **f** .... (*téléphoner*) immédiatement, et son maître **g** .... (*venir*) le chercher.

Remember to use **My review** and **My takeaway** to assess your progress and reflect on your learning experience.

13

In this lesson you will learn how to:

- Talk about the duration of past and ongoing events
- Form complex sentences
- Express wishes and desires
- Speak about possible future plans

Les études

My study plan

I plan to work with Unit 13

- ○ Every day
- ○ Twice a week
- ○ Other ___________

I plan to study for

- ○ 5–15 minutes
- ○ 15–30 minutes
- ○ 30–45+ minutes

My progress tracker

Day / Date	Listening	Speaking	Reading	Writing	Conversation
	○	○	○	○	○
	○	○	○	○	○
	○	○	○	○	○
	○	○	○	○	○
	○	○	○	○	○
	○	○	○	○	○
	○	○	○	○	○

My goals

What do you want to be able to do or say in French when you complete this unit?

		Done
1	....	○
2	....	○
3	....	○

My review

SELF CHECK

	I can ...
●	... talk about the duration of past and ongoing events.
●	... form complex sentences.
●	... express wishes and desires.
●	... speak about possible future plans.

CULTURE POINT 1

La formation professionnelle, les apprentissages *Professional training and apprenticeships*

Since 2019, all eligible French citizens have been able to draw on a CPF, or compte personnel de formation (*personal training account*). As of 2024, this scheme made available 5,000 euros per individual, to be spent on professional development. Via this route French citizens can obtain a range of certificates, documents, and diplômes (*qualifications*); these include un bilan de compétences (*summary of skills*) which can be used in future candidatures (*job applications*). In some parts of the world, apprentissages (*apprenticeships*) are seen as an increasingly attractive option for school-leavers. Let us take France as an example once again. In 2022, *Le Monde* published an article entitled Le succès fulgurant des apprentissages (*the lightning success of apprenticeships*). This article was inspired by a year-on-year rise in take-up of apprenticeships of 33%, mainly among les étudiants post-bac (*post-baccalaureate* students*). It quotes a young woman who completed her training to become ingénieure en bâtiment (*a building engineer*) thanks to un apprentissage. Léa comments that, if she had not been able to take this route, she would have been bloquée financièrement (*kept back for financial reasons*). Some apprentissages are incorporated within the educational pathway known as alternance (*apprenticeship degrees*). The journalist at *Le Monde* concludes that young people increasingly view such solutions as preferable to more traditional routes, such as university or business school.

* Le baccalauréat (or bac for short) is a qualification typically obtained by school-leavers in France. It is roughly equivalent to a high school graduation diploma in the US.

Visit the website. What is this institution? What is le compagnonnage?

VOCABULARY BUILDER 1

Look at the words and phrases and complete the missing English words and expressions. Then listen and try to imitate the pronunciation of the speakers.

LA FORMATION PROFESSIONNELLE	*TRAINING FOR A PROFESSION*
l'enseignement secondaire	*secondary education*
un baccalauréat, un bac	*baccalareate, school leaving certificate*
un baccalauréat professionnel	*professional baccalaureat*
un boulot (informal), un job	....
les bases du métier	*the basics of the job/profession*
un patron, une patronne	*boss*
postuler	*apply for a post/a job*
une responsabilité	....
EXPRESSIONS	***EXPRESSIONS***
choisir son parcours	*to choose one's path*
décider de suivre une formation	*decide to follow a course*
envisager son avenir	*envisage one's future*
préparer un dossier	*prepare an application*
être satisfait/satisfaite de son job	*to be satisfied with one's job*
Elle prend une année de césure.	*She's taking a year out/a gap year.*
C'est une expérience enrichissante.	*It's an enriching experience.*
Rachel fait des économies.	*Rachel is saving up.*
Je fais des études en génie civil.	*I am studying engineering.*
Il doit perfectionner son anglais.	*He has to improve his English.*
Elle suit une formation professionnelle.	*She is following a professional training course.*

Vocabulary practice 1

Complete the sentences with the correct words or phrases from Vocabulary builder 1.

a Alberto ne commence pas ses études universitaires tout de suite. Il prend ....

b Anne veut être ingénieure. Elle fait des études en ....

c Marc veut travailler aux États-Unis. Il va donc .... son anglais.

d Mo va suivre une formation à Paris. Parce que la vie y est chère, il fait des ....

e Beaucoup de gens trouvent qu'un apprentissage est une .... enrichissante.

Pronunciation practice 1

In English, the letter c can be soft or hard. For instance, camera begins with a hard c, while center begins with a soft c. The same applies in French. The c is soft when it is followed by an e or an i : un centre ; une place ; un cinéma ; ici. And c is hard when it is followed by a, o, or u: une carte ; un complot (*conspiracy*) ; une cuisine (*kitchen*).

However, if there is a cedilla attached to the c (ç), the c is soft: ça (*that*) ; un maçon (*mason*) ; déçu, déçue (*disappointed*).

13.02

Listen to the recording while reading the sentences. Note when the letter c is hard and when it is soft. Then listen again and repeat.

Cédric aime la cuisine des Caraïbes.	*Cedric likes Caribbean cuisine.*
Caroline exerce un métier difficile.	*Caroline does a difficult job.*
Céline passe son baccalauréat.	*Céline is taking her baccalaureate.*

CONVERSATION 1

Parcours scolaire et expérience professionnelle *Education and professional experience*

13.03

1 Here are a few words and expressions to help you understand the conversation.

le cacao	*cocoa*	grandir	*to grow up*
une coopérative	*cooperative*	poser une question	*to ask a question*
un confiseur	*(male) confectioner*	les yeux fermés	*without hesitation (literally: eyes closed)*
ONG	*NGO*		

13.04

2 Listen to the conversation without looking at the text. Then listen to the conversation again and read the text.

Charles has been invited to a local high school to talk to the students about his career path.

Prof. Je vous présente Charles, qui est, comme vous savez, apprenti chocolatier. Alors, Charles, est-ce que vous pouvez nous raconter votre parcours ?

Charles À la fin de mes études secondaires, je voulais faire une pause, pour voyager et pour réfléchir...

Prof. Une année de césure ?

Charles Oui. J'ai trouvé un petit boulot dans un restaurant. La cheffe de cuisine, que j'assistais, aimait préparer les desserts et elle m'a initié aux bases du métier... Puis j'ai travaillé dans une boulangerie pâtisserie, où j'ai découvert l'autonomie, les responsabilités, c'était super ! C'est une expérience que je n'oublierai pas !

Prof.	Et ensuite ?
Charles	J'ai fait des économies pendant six mois et je suis parti avec une ONG qui aide les producteurs de café et de cacao en Colombie. J'ai découvert la culture du cacao et j'ai perfectionné mon espagnol. C'était très enrichissant...
Prof.	Quelle belle expérience !
Charles	Oui ! À mon retour à Paris (il y a à peu près un an), j'ai décidé de faire une formation de confiseur chocolatier. Je suis cette formation depuis six mois déjà.
Prof.	Et pourquoi Bruxelles ?
Charles	Ben j'ai grandi à Paris et je voulais découvrir une autre ville, et Bruxelles, c'est la capitale du chocolat, non ?
Prof.	Ben oui ! Merci Charles, je sais que mes élèves ont beaucoup de questions à vous poser, qui veut commencer ? Oui, Julie ?
Une élève	Est-ce que tu es satisfait de ta formation ? Est-ce que tu la recommanderais ?
Charles	Oui, les yeux fermés, si vous envisagez de faire des études professionnelles, alors oui, allez-y !

3 Answer the questions.

a Why did Charles want to take a year off from education after high school?
b What two jobs did he do during that year?
c With what type of institution did Charles leave with when he went to Columbia?
d What decision did he make on returning to Paris?
e Is Charles entirely happy with the route he has followed into the workplace?

LANGUAGE BUILDER 1

Language discovery 1

In Conversation 1, Charles explains that before going to Colombia he saved up his money pendant six mois. He also explains that has been training to be a confectioner specialising in chocolate depuis six mois.

Complete Charles's sentences:

J'ai fait des économies .... six mois. Je suis cette formation .... six mois.

Which of the above actions is still going on?

Pendant, depuis, il y a *For, since, ago*

Look at the following statements:

(a) Louise a appris le piano pendant trois ans. *Louise learned piano for three years*;

(b) Laurent apprend le piano depuis trois ans *Laurent has been learning piano for three years*.

Notice that (a) uses pendant and (b) uses depuis, but both can be translated as *for*. So it is important to understand the difference.

Pendant is used for an activity that began in the past but is now over. For instance, when we read sentence (a), we naturally suppose that Louise is no longer learning the piano.

Depuis (*since, for*), by contrast, is used for an activity begun in the past but still ongoing at the time of speaking. So when we read sentence (b), we realize that, while Laurent began to learn piano three years ago, he continues to learn now.

Notice, too, that there is a difference between French and English when it comes to the tenses used with depuis/*for*. When depuis is used to talk about something that started in the past *but is still happening now*, it seems natural to speakers of French to use the present tense; this explains apprend in sentence (b). But English speakers use a special past tense (called the *past continuous*) to make the same kind of statement: that is why sentence (b) is translated using has been learning.

Another phrase you can use when referring to past events is il y a (*ago*), which goes before a stated length of time (not after, as in English): il y a trois ans (*three years ago*).

Laurent a appris le piano il y a trois ans. *Laurent learned piano three years ago.*

To translate a sentence such as *Maurice has been working in Milan for two years* into French, mentally add *and still does* to the end of it. This will remind you that because the action continues into the present (as shown by *and still does*) you should use depuis + present tense. Then you can be confident that the correct translation is: Maurice travaille à Milan depuis deux ans.

Language practice 1

1 Complete the sentences with pendant or depuis as appropriate. The first one has been done for you.

a Je suis une formation de professeur *depuis* deux ans.

b Et moi, j'ai suivi une formation de coiffeur .... deux ans.

c Mon copain apprend le japonais .... quelques mois.

d Mon cousin a travaillé comme chef de cuisine .... six mois.

e Louise travaille comme assistante d'anglais .... un an.

LANGUAGE BUILDER 2

Language discovery 2

Listen to the conversation again and repeat each line in the pauses.

When the teacher introduces Charles to his students, he says Je vous présente Charles, qui est, comme vous savez, apprenti chocolatier (*Let me introduce Charles, who is, as you know, an apprentice chocolatier*). Here, the teacher uses qui for *who*. When Charles talks about his experience in Paris, he uses this form of words: La cheffe de cuisine que j'assistais, et elle m'a initié aux bases du métier (the chef who I assisted, and she taught me the basics of the profession). Here, Charles uses que for *who*.

1 Can you figure out why two different words are used for *who*? If so, you will be able to complete this rule of thumb:

When choosing between qui and que in French, use .... for the subject of the verb and .... for the direct object of the verb.

2 Look at these two statements by Charles: c'est une expérience que je n'oublierai pas ; c'est une OGN qui aide les producteurs de cacao et de café. Based on these examples, does the rule concerning qui and que work for things as well as people?

Qui ou que ? *Who, whom, which, or that?*

Sentences in English can often be joined together to make longer sentences by using *who*, *whom*, *which*, or *that*. In French, qui and que can be used for the same purpose. A rule of thumb is that qui is used for the subject and que for the object of the nearest verb. Let's see how it works.

Sophie joue du piano.	*Sophie plays the piano.*
Sophie connaît Bob.	*Sophie knows Bob.*
Sophie, ... connaît bien Bob, joue du piano.	*Sophie, who knows Bob, plays the piano.*

To complete the last sentence, we need to ask whether Sophie is the subject or the object of the verb connaît. The answer is that she is the *subject* because she is the one who knows Bob (the object). Therefore, you use qui (because qui is always used for the subject): Sophie, qui connaît bien Bob, joue du piano.

Now let's go again, using the following three sentences:

Sophie joue du piano.	*Sophie plays the piano.*
Bob connaît Sophie.	*Bob knows Sophie.*
Sophie, ... Bob connaît, joue du piano.	*Sophie, who/whom Bob knows, plays the piano.*

So, should we use qui or que to combine the sentences? This time it is Bob, not Sophie, who is the subject of the verb, and Sophie is the object of connaît (she is the one *being known*). So now we have our answer: Sophie, que Bob connaît, joue du piano.

This rule applies to animals and things as well as people:

La chaise qui est là-bas est plus confortable.	*The chair that is over there is more comfortable.*
La chaise que je préfère est celle-là.	*The chair that I prefer is that one.*

Language practice 2

1 Complete the sentences with either qui or que, as appropriate.

a Le job .... j'ai actuellement est assez cool.

b La personne .... attend là-bas s'appelle Lorenzo.

c Est-ce que tu as lu le dernier roman d'Amélie Nothomb .... est paru l'année dernière ?

d La dame .... je viens de voir est artiste.

13.06

2 Now play the conversation again and play the professor's role. Speak in the pauses. Try not to refer to the text. The professor's role is shorter so when you are not speaking pay careful attention to what Charles is saying.

CULTURE POINT 2

Étudier à Montréal *Studying in Montreal*

Montréal is the second-most populous city in Canada, and the main city in le Québec (*Quebec province*), where a majority of people speak French as a first language. The name Montréal derives from Mont Royal (*Royal Hill*), an echo of a period stretching from the 16th to the 18th centuries, when francophone settlers gradually populated territories which they called la Nouvelle France (*New France*). The only city to have a larger francophone population is Paris. Montreal houses two English-language and two French-language universities. All undergraduate courses at the Université de Montréal are taught in French. Founded in 1878, it currently occupies eight campuses around the city. It strives to maximize sustainability and biodiversity, including on its main campus that covers some soixante-cinq hectares (*65 hectares*). The university is now home to a Centre étudiant des Premiers Peuples (*Student Center for First-Nation Peoples*), which offers a number of bourses pour personnes authochtones (*grants for people of Authochtone heritage*). Those wishing to study mainly in English can apply to McGill University, founded in 1885. McGill seeks to foster internationalism, for instance through its extensive programme d'échanges (*exchange program*) that welcomes international students from more than 150 countries. While they are perhaps the best-known names, the Universities of Montreal and McGill are only two of several substantial universities in this dynamic city.

Learn about universities in Quebec. Which universities do you know? Which ones are English-speaking and which ones are French-speaking universities?

VOCABULARY BUILDER 2

Look at the words and phrases and complete the missing English words and expressions. Then listen and try to imitate the pronunciation of the speakers.

UN CV	*CV (= CURRICULUM VITAE)*
des connaissances (fem.)	*knowledge*
un débouché	*job prospect*
déboucher sur	*to lead into*
élaborer	*to elaborate*
enrichir	*to enrich*
expliquer	*to explain*
postuler/candidater pour	*to apply for*
un professionnel/une professionnelle	....
un projet	....
EXPRESSIONS	***EXPRESSIONS***
Louise écrit une lettre de motivation.	*Louise is writing a cover letter.*
Léo candidate pour un poste intéressant.	*Léo is applying for an interesting position.*
Clémence a les connaissances requises.	*Clémence has the required knowledge.*
Ce cours me permet de m'épanouir.	*This course allows me to blossom.*

Vocabulary practice 2

Complete the sentences using words and phrases from the Vocabulary builder.

a Est-ce que tu as .... à ton avenir ?

b Ce poste m'intéresse. Je vais préparer un ....

c Ce poste m'intéresse. Je vais écrire une ....

d Paul a les connaissances .... pour ce job.

e Cette formation .... sur des jobs de toutes sortes.

Pronunciation practice 2

There are three kinds of liaison in French: required, forbidden, and optional. A liaison is forbidden in the following cases:

1 Before an aspirated h (you learned about this in an earlier unit): un hangar (do not pronounce the n of un), or des halles (do not pronounce the s of des).
2 After et (*and*). Je vais acheter un journal et un magazine (do not pronounce the t of et).
3 After a singular noun. Mon chat est mignon (do not pronounce the t of chat).

13.08

Look at the sentences below and note any forbidden liaisons. Then listen to the recording, and imitate the speaker's pronunciation.

On va visiter les Halles demain.

Louise et Albert sont chez moi. Clémence et Aline aussi.

Mon chat est mignon — ton chien aussi !

CONVERSATION 2

La lettre de motivation *The personal statement*

13.09

1 Here are a few words and expressions to help you understand the conversation.

les arts visuels et médiatiques	*visual arts and the media*	apporter	*to bring*
un échange d'un semestre	*a one-semester exchange*	approfondir ses connaissances	*to deepen one's knowledge*
comprendre	*to include*	le stage m'ouvrira sur...	*the internship will give me an experience of ...*
un stage	*internship*		

13.10

2 Listen to the conversation without looking at the text. Then listen to the conversation again and read the text.

Assia is applying to do an internship at the Université du Québec à Montréal. She consults Jo on the details of her application.

Jo Salut Assia, qu'est-ce que tu fais ?

Assia Je prépare mon dossier de candidature. Il y a un nouvel échange d'un semestre avec l'Université du Québec à Montréal. Si tout se passe bien, je pourrai y aller en janvier prochain. Et tu viendras me rendre visite, j'espère...

Jo Ce serait trop cool ! Mais ce n'est pas un stage ! Je croyais que tu cherchais un stage...

Assia Ben c'est un semestre d'échange à l'École des Arts visuels et médiatiques de l'UQAM, mais ce semestre comprend un stage...

Jo	Ah mais c'est génial ça !
Assia	Oui ! J'ai commencé à préparer mon portfolio et je suis en train d'écrire ma lettre de motivation. Tu peux m'aider ?
Jo	Bien sûr ! Montre-moi…
	Jo reads the letter.
Jo	C'est très bien. Tu as bien expliqué ton parcours jusqu'à aujourd'hui, ta formation, ta pratique de la photo et ton intérêt pour la ville de Montréal. Peut-être que tu pourrais donner plus de détails sur ce qui te motive dans ce projet.
Assia	Oui, tu as raison.
	Assia takes notes.
	« Cet échange me permettra d'approfondir mes connaissances théoriques, et le stage m'ouvrira sur le monde professionnel des médias. Ce semestre m'apportera de nouvelles compétences interculturelles. »
Jo	Oui ; il faudrait élaborer un peu, mais c'est ça ! Et après ?
Assia	« Après, j'aimerais travailler dans la communication… »
Jo	Oui, n'hésite pas à expliquer ton projet, et à donner des détails…

3 Answer the questions.

- **a** When is Assia planning to be in Canada?
- **b** Why is Jo surprised about Assia's plans?
- **c** Can you figure out what UQAM stands for?
- **d** What does Assia ask for help with?
- **e** What are Jo's main suggestions?

LANGUAGE BUILDER 3

Language discovery 3

Listen to the conversation again and repeat each line in the pauses.

Within Conversation 2, the following five verbs are used in the future tense: a) je pourrai ; b) tu viendras ; c) ce semestre m'apportera ; d) le stage m'ouvrira e) cet échange me permettra.

Which three future forms have regular stems (i.e., which three are based on the infinitive)? Which two are irregular?

Le futur (suite) *The future tense* (continued)

In Unit 10, you learned how to use the future tense of -er, -ir, and -re verbs. In each family of verbs, there are also some nonstandard patterns that you need to memorize. The verbs listed below have irregular future stems. These same stems are used in the conditional, as well.

Infinitive	Future stem	Future tense (je ; tu ; il/elle ; nous ; vous ; ils/elles)
aller	ir-	irai ; iras ; ira ; irons ; irez ; iront
appeler	appeller-	appellerai ; appelleras ; appellera ; appellerons ; appellerez ; appelleront
avoir	aur-	aurai ; auras ; aura ; aurons ; aurez ; auront
être	ser-	serai ; seras ; sera ; serons ; serez ; seront
jeter	jetter-	jetterai ; jetteras ; jettera ; jetterons ; jetterez ; jetteront
(se) lever*	lèver-	lèverai ; lèveras ; lèvera ; lèverons ; lèverez ; lèveront
pouvoir	pourr-	pourrai ; pourras ; pourra ; pourrons ; pourrez ; pourront
tenir	tiendr-	tiendrai ; tiendras ; tiendra ; tiendrons ; tiendrez ; tiendront
venir	viendr-	viendrai ; viendras ; viendra ; viendrons ; viendrez ; viendront
voir	verr-	verrai ; verras ; verra ; verrons ; verrez ; verront

* lever: *to lift up*; se lever: *to get up*

Language practice 3

1 Complete the sentences with the future form of the verb given.

a Nous ne *pourrons* pas arriver avant 11 heures. (*pouvoir*)
b Marise et Fatou .... voir leur grand-mère ce week-end. (*aller*)
c Yasmine .... tôt demain pour aller à la piscine. (*se lever*)
d Je .... le ballon plus loin cette fois ! (*jeter*)
e Tu .... manger chez nous, j'espère. (*venir*)
f Vous nous .... demain pour organiser notre sortie ? (*appeler*)
g On se .... après-demain, d'accord ? (*voir*)
h Avec cette formation, Jean-Marc .... beaucoup de débouchés. (*avoir*)
i Anne-Lise .... bientôt diplômée. (*être*)
j La présidente .... une conférence de presse. (*tenir*)

13.11

2 Now play the conversation again and play Jo's role. Speak in the pauses. Try not to refer to the text. If Jo were asking you these same questions, what might you answer about where and when you would like to study abroad?

LANGUAGE BUILDER 4

Language discovery 4

1 Listen to the conversation again and repeat each line in the pauses. Complete these phrases from the conversation:

a Ce .... trop cool !

b Peut-être que tu .... donner plus de détails.

c Oui ; il .... élaborer un peu.

2 What do you notice about these verbs? Which tense or tenses do they remind you of?

Le conditionnel présent *The present conditional*

Le conditionnel is used for eventualities rather than actual events. In other words, it is used to present an event as something that might and might not happen. Examples in English generally involve the words *would* or *could*, for instance *I would like to go* (j'aimerais y aller).

Je préférerais rester à la maison.	*I would prefer to stay at home.*
Je pourrais peut-être acheter les tickets sur place.	*I could perhaps buy the tickets on the spot.*

There are several conditional tenses in French, including the le conditionnel présent. To form that tense, take the future tense of the verb and replace the future ending with the following endings: -ais, -ais, -ait, -ions, -iez, -aient. Note that these are the same endings as used for the imparfait. Let's see how it works with pouvoir:

pouvoir (*future stem:* pourr-)

je pourrais	nous pourrions
tu pourrais	vous pourriez
il/elle/on pourrait	ils/elles pourraient

In sentences using le conditionnel, there is often also a verb in the imparfait, preceded by si (*if*). This is a common structure used in conversation.

Je pourrais t'accompagner si j'avais un ticket.	*I could go with you if I had a ticket.*
Si tu voulais, je viendrais avec toi.	*If you wanted, I would come with you.*

Language practice 4

1 Complete the sentences using the verb in brackets. Use either le conditionnel or l'imparfait.

Example: Si vous vouliez, nous *pourrions* nous réunir demain. (*pouvoir*)

a Si Monique avait une petite sœur, elle .... jouer avec elle. (*pouvoir*)
b Si Samuel .... là (*être*), il nous aiderait avec nos bagages.
c Si nous étions riches, nous .... au restaurant tous les jours. (*aller manger*)
d Si tu .... avant les autres (*arriver*), tu aurais le temps de mettre ton nouveau costume.

SKILL BUILDER

1 Complete the tables with le conditionnel.

aimer

j'aimerais	nous aimerions
a tu	**c** vous ....
b il/elle/on	**d** ils/elles ....

finir

e je	**g** nous ....
tu finirais	vous finiriez
f il/elle/on	**h** ils/elles ....

vendre

i je	**k** nous ....
j tu	**l** vous ....
il/elle/on vendrait	ils/elles vendraient

2 Tell a new friend two different things that you have been involved in for at least three years and then two other things you did at some point in the past for three years but are no longer involved with. You could start with: Je fais de l'équitation depuis trois ans....

3 What stage would you like to do if you could choose from any possibility? Tell your friend what your dream stage would be and what you would do once you had started. Start the conversation with: Si je pouvais, je voudrais faire un stage chez... .

TEST YOURSELF

1 Complete the story with the correct words or phrases from the word box.

pendant	perfectionner	il y a	région	baccalauréat
a décidé	Depuis un an	une année de césure		une carrière

a .... deux ans, Marie-Laure a eu son **b** .... et elle a décidé de prendre **c** .... Elle aime le paysage, donc **d** .... six mois elle a travaillé comme guide dans la **e** .... des Vosges. De là, elle **f** .... de poursuivre **g** .... dans le tourisme. Pour augmenter ses chances de réussite, elle a décidé de **h** .... son allemand et son italien. **i** .... elle est étudiante en langues modernes à l'université de Lausanne.

2 Complete the story using qui or que as appropriate.

Marie, **a** .... est ingénieure, travaille à Paris. Tous les jours elle prend un train **b** .... part d'Amiens à 7 h 21 et arrive à la gare du Nord vers 8 h 30. Normalement, Marie prend son petit déjeuner dans un café **c** .... elle aime bien, près de la gare. Jeanne, une collègue **d** .... Marie connaît depuis deux ans, la rejoint deux ou trois jours par semaine. Le reste de la semaine, Jeanne, **e** .... est comptable, travaille à domicile.

3 Complete the story with the correct words. Check against the translation for support.

Je fais des études en histoire de l'art et en muséographie, et mon rêve **a** .... de faire un stage au Musée du Louvre **b** .... un an. **c** .... avoir le temps de découvrir et de connaître tous les espaces du musée. **d** .... m'occuper de l'accueil des groupes scolaires et organiser les visites guidées, pour partager mon amour de l'art. Pour réaliser mon rêve, je **e** .... de mon mieux pour postuler au Louvre et j'espère qu'ils **f** .... mon potentiel.

I'm studying art history and museography, and my dream would be to do an internship at the Louvre Museum for a year. I would like to have the time to discover and get to know all the spaces of the museum. I would like to take care of welcoming school groups and organize guided tours, to share my love of art. To make my dream come true, I will do my best to apply to the Louvre, and I hope they will see my potential.

Remember to use **My review** and **My takeaway** to assess your progress and reflect on your learning experience.

Congratulations, you have now completed the second level of your studies! Put your skills to the test—take the A2 Assessment online at library.teachyourself.com and see how much you've learned.

14

In this lesson you will learn how to:

- » Talk about things that you are happy/sad about
- » Talk about possibilities and doubt
- » Choose from different ways of forming negatives
- » Express different moods

Des ennuis

My study plan

I plan to work with Unit 14

- ○ Every day
- ○ Twice a week
- ○ Other ___________

I plan to study for

- ○ 5–15 minutes
- ○ 15–30 minutes
- ○ 30–45+ minutes

My progress tracker

Day / Date	Listening	Speaking	Reading	Writing	Conversation
	○	○	○	○	○
	○	○	○	○	○
	○	○	○	○	○
	○	○	○	○	○
	○	○	○	○	○
	○	○	○	○	○
	○	○	○	○	○

My goals

What do you want to be able to do or say in French when you complete this unit?

		Done
1	....	○
2	....	○
3	....	○

My review

SELF CHECK

	I can ...
●	... express different feelings like happiness or surprise, doubt and delight, or necessity and certainty.
●	... express different moods, both the positive and negative.
●	... expand on the ways in which to phrase negative sentences.

CULTURE POINT 1

La tour Eiffel et ses ascenseurs *The Eiffel Tower and its elevators*

La tour Eiffel a été construite pour l'Exposition universelle de 1889, organisée sur le Champ de Mars, à Paris, pour célébrer le centenaire de la Révolution française de 1789. Édifiée (*built*) en un peu plus de deux ans par les équipes de Gustave Eiffel, celle qu'on appelle la Dame de fer (*the Iron Lady*) était à l'origine prévue pour être une installation temporaire qui devait être démontée (*should have been dismantled*) après vingt ans. Aujourd'hui, la tour Eiffel est l'emblème de Paris et est un des sites touristiques les plus visités au monde. Les ascenseurs originels, ouverts en 1889 et modernisés en 1899, étaient une prouesse (*a feat*) technique pour l'époque. Le mécanisme hydraulique, qui comprenait des pistons et des poulies (*pulleys*), était unique au monde. Deux ascenseurs historiques sont toujours en fonctionnement aujourd'hui, et la Société d'Exploitation de la Tour Eiffel a entrepris en 2008 de les rénover en respectant la technologie d'origine mais en rendant le système plus écologique. Les travaux de rénovation de l'ascenseur du pilier nord (*north pillar*) sont en cours, à la date de parution de ce livre (*at the time of this book's publication*). Avec la même consommation électrique, chacun des trois ascenseurs transportera jusqu'à 110 passagers, contre 92 aujourd'hui, à une vitesse de 2 mètres par seconde. Comme l'indique le site officiel du site, la modernité de la Tour doit rimer avec pérennité et durabilité (*the Tower's modernity must go hand in hand with longevity and durability*). On trouve des répliques de la tour Eiffel dans le monde entier, notamment à Las Vegas, à Blackpool, à Macao, à Hangzhou, et à Tokyo.

Check the website of la tour Eiffel. How many kilometers have the elevators covered?

VOCABULARY BUILDER 1

Look at the words and phrases and complete the missing English words and expressions. Then listen and try to imitate the pronunciation of the speakers.

LES ATTRACTIONS	*ATTRACTIONS*
un château	*castle, palace*
la fierté (nationale)	*(national) pride*
une icône	....
une merveille	*marvel, wonder*
un monument	....
nombreux/nombreuses (pl.)	*numerous, many*
un patrimoine	*heritage*
un son et lumière	*sound and light show*
un spectacle	*show*
un symbole	....
le tourisme	*tourism*
un touriste, une touriste	....

EXPRESSIONS	*EXPRESSIONS*
les Sept Merveilles du monde	*the Seven Wonders of the World*
Ils s'émerveillent de la tour.	*They marvel at the tower.*
les générations à venir	*future generations*
On a monté une exposition.	*An exhibition was staged.*
Ce musée attire de nombreux visiteurs.	*This museum attracts many visitors.*
le patrimoine français/belge	*French/Belgian heritage*

Vocabulary practice 1

Complete the sentences using words and phrases from the Vocabulary builder.

a La pyramide de Khéops et le Machu Picchu font partie des ....

b Il faut préserver le .... français pour les .... à venir.

c Les visiteurs s' .... de la Tour Eiffel.

d La ville de Paris va .... une exposition sur la photographie.

Pronunciation practice 1

You have already learned that the letter c can be hard or soft in French. The same applies to the letter g. In French, a soft g is pronounced like the letter g in *rouge*. A hard g is pronounced like the letter g in the English word *goat* or *goal*. Whenever g is followed by e or i, it is soft: un gilet (*waistcoat; vest*); le génie civil (*engineering*). And whenever it is followed by a, o, or u, it is hard: une gare (*station*); une gomme (*eraser*); un/une guide (*guide*).

14.02

Listen and repeat, noting where each letter g occurs and indicating whether it is hard (H) or soft (S).

Nos cousins germains nous rendent visite.	*Our first cousins are visiting us.*
Qui est notre guide aujourd'hui ? C'est Guillaume !	*Who's our guide today? It's Guillaume!*

CONVERSATION 1

L'ascenseur est en panne *The elevator is out of order*

14.03

1 Here are a few words and expressions to help you understand the conversation.

essoufflé, essoufflée	*out of breath*	une intervention en urgence	*emergency repair*
être désolé/désolée	*to be sorry*	bloqué, bloquée	*stuck*
C'est agaçant à la fin !	*It's getting annoying!*	un/une sénior	*senior citizen*
régler	*to fix*	durer	*to go on; to last*
s'inquiéter	*to worry*		

14.04

2 Listen to the conversation without looking at the text. Then listen to the conversation again and read the text.

Charles's fellow apprentice Andries has invited him to visit the apartment in Brussels which he shares with his sister Erna. Charles is delighted to go and see them.

Andries	Bonjour, Charles. Je te présente Erna, ma sœur.
Charles	Enchanté.
Erna	Enchantée.
Andries	Tu es essoufflé !
Charles	Un peu ! Je suis monté à pied. L'ascenseur est en panne...
Erna	Encore ! Mais c'est pas vrai ! Nous sommes désolés, Charles.
Charles	C'est pas grave...
Andries	Si, c'est grave ! L'entreprise de maintenance est déjà venue deux fois... C'est agaçant à la fin ! Il faut qu'on vienne régler ça au plus vite. Je m'inquiète pour Mme Cottin, qui ne peut pas monter et descendre à pied facilement.

Erna	Ça ne sert à rien de s'énerver, Andries ! Donne donc un verre d'eau à Charles. Je vous rejoins dans deux minutes.
	Erna calls the building maintenance campany.
Erna	Bonjour, je vous appelle pour vous signaler que l'ascenseur de notre immeuble est encore en panne.
Technicienne	Bonjour. Je suis désolée. Quelle est votre adresse ?
Erna	*Erna gives the address.*
Technicienne	Je vois que nous sommes venus la semaine dernière pour une réparation.
Erna	Oui, et il y a eu une intervention en urgence la semaine d'avant aussi. Une voisine bloquée dans l'ascenseur. C'est ennuyeux, ces problèmes à répétition !
Technicienne	Toujours le même problème avec la porte ?
Erna	Je ne sais pas, mais il faut que vous répariez cet ascenseur au plus vite. Notre voisine, qui est sénior, habite comme nous au cinquième étage et la situation ne peut plus durer. Les habitants de l'immeuble en ont vraiment assez. On n'arrive jamais à vous joindre.
Technicienne	Je vous comprends, c'est ennuyeux. Je vous envoie un technicien au plus vite.

3 Answer the questions.

a Why is Charles out of breath when he arrives at Andries and Erna's apartment?

b Who does Andries say he is worried about, and why?

c What does Erna ask her brother to do for Charles?

d When Erna calls the maintenance company, what does she say happened the week before last?

e How does Erna say the residents of the building feel about the situation?

LANGUAGE BUILDER 1

Language discovery 1

Erna says: on n'arrive jamais à vous joindre (*we never manage to contact you*). Based on what you already know about making negative sentences in French, can you identify how to say *never* in French?

La négation *Expressions of negation*

You have already learned that to say *not* in French normally requires not one word but two: ne + pas. Several other forms of negation also require two words in French. These include: ne + rien (*nothing/not anything*); ne + plus (*no longer/not anymore*); and ne + jamais (*never, not ever*). With these expressions, ne and rien/plus/jamais generally belong in the same place in the sentence as ne and pas. See below for examples:

Marc ne fait rien.	*Marc is doing nothing/Marc is not doing anything.*
Il ne sort plus.	*He no longer goes out./He does not go out any more.*
On ne te voit jamais !	*We never see you!/We don't ever see you!*

It is also important to note that (like *nothing* in English) rien can also be used as a subject pronoun. When this is the case, it precedes the verb, and ne, which is still required, occupies its usual place in the sentence:

Lisette lance : Rien ne me va !	*Lisette cries out: Nothing suits me!*
Rien ne m'inquiète.	*Nothing bothers me.*
Rien ne te dérange quand tu dors.	*Nothing bothers you when you are asleep.*

Language practice 1

1 Complete the sentences with a negative construction.

Example: Gabriel dit qu'on tourne une scène dans cette rue, mais je ne vois rien. (*nothing*)

a À une époque, je parlais bien l'italien, mais je .... le parle .... (*no longer*)

b On dit qu'on voit Douvres (*Dover*) depuis Calais, mais je .... vois .... (*nothing*)

c Ils disent que l'ascenseur a été réparé, mais ça .... marche .... (*never*)

d J'en ai vraiment assez ! .... marche dans cet immeuble ! (*nothing*)

2 Complete the sentences using le présent or le passé composé as appropriate:

Example: Tu n'a jamais vu *Jules et Jim* ? Mais c'est un film magnifique ! (voir/*never*)

a On dit qu'un acteur célèbre a visité notre ville hier, mais je ....! (voir/*nobody*)

b Il y a eu une lune rousse hier, mais à cause des nuages je .... (voir/*nothing*)

c .... comme prévu. (marcher/*nothing*)

d Nous .... lait. Tu peux passer au magasin ? (avoir/*no more*)

In spoken French, the word ne often disappears in negative constructions. For instance, someone might say C'est pas grave (*It's not serious*).

LANGUAGE BUILDER 2

Language discovery 2

Listen to the conversation again and repeat each line in the pauses.

Complete these sentences from the conversation:

Andries: ...Il faut qu'on .... régler ça au plus vite.

Ema: Je ne sais pas, mais il faut que vous .... cet ascenseur au plus vite.

Do you recognize these verbs? What is their basic/infinitive form?

Le subjonctif *The subjunctive*

If you start a sentence with Il faut que (*it's necessary that*) the verb that follows must be in le subjonctif (the subjunctive form). Le subjonctif is a special form that is sometimes required in French, including after expressions of necessity (il faut que, il est nécessaire que, etc.).

In the present tense, **le** subjonctif is formed by removing the -ent ending from the ils/elles present-tense form, then adding the following endings:

Endings for le subjonctif

je	-e	nous	-ions
tu	-es	vous	-iez
il/elle/on	-e	ils/elles	-ent

But you should be aware that some present subjonctifs have irregular stems. Faire, pouvoir, and savoir are among these; their subjunctive stems are fass-, puiss-, and sach-. For instance, Je regrette qu'il sache. (*I'm sorry he knows.*)

Let's compare the present-tense indicative and the subjunctive of aimer and finir.

aimer

indicatif (présent)		**subjonctif** (présent)	
j'aim-**e**	nous aim-**ons**	que j'aim-**e**	que nous aim-**ions**
tu aim-**es**	vous aim-**ez**	que tu aim-**es**	que vous aim-**iez**
il/elle/on aim-**e**	ils/elles aim-**ent**	qu'il/elle/on aim-**e**	qu'ils/elles aim-**ent**

finir

indicatif (présent)		**subjonctif** (présent)	
je fin-**is**	nous fin-**issons**	que je finiss-**e**	que nous finiss-**ions**
tu fin-**is**	vous fin-**issez**	que tu finiss-**es**	que vous finiss-**iez**
il/elle/on fin-**it**	ils/elles fin-**issent**	qu'il/elle/on finiss-**e**	qu'ils/elles finiss-**ent**

Other verbs have irregular stems that change in the nous and vous forms. These include:

(a) avoir (aie, aies, ait, ayons, ayez, aient);

(b) venir (vienne, viennes, vienne, venions, veniez, viennent);

(c) être (sois, sois, soit, soyons, soyez, soient).

Besides being used after expressions of necessity, le subjonctif is also often required after negative expressions, expressions of impossibility, possibility, or doubt, and expressions of positive or negative feelings. Here are some examples of phrases that take le subjonctif:

Il est impossible que je vienne.	*It's impossible for me to come.*
Je doute que Michel comprenne.	*I doubt that Michel understands.*
Je regrette que Léa ne puisse pas être là.	*I'm sorry that Léa can't be there.*

Language practice 2

1 Match the expressions that always require le subjonctif (a–d) with the descriptions given on the right (1–4).

a il est impossible que...	**1** ... is an expression of feeling
b sans que...	**2** ... is an expression of impossibility
c je suis content/contente que...	**3** ... is an expression of possibility or doubt
d il est possible que...	**4** ... is a negative expression

2 Complete the sentences with le subjonctif of the verbs indicated.

a Demain, il faut que nous .... à temps. (*arriver*)
b Il est regrettable que Jean .... absent. (*être*)
c Il est possible que vous .... le match. (*gagner*)
d Les enfants, ça m'énerve que vous .... aussi vite ! (*manger*)
e Je le savais sans qu'elle le .... (*dire*)
f Ça m'agace que l'ascenseur .... en panne. (*être*)
g Ça exaspère Mathilde que Ruth .... son anniversaire. (*oublier*)

14.06

3 Now play the conversation again and play Erna's role. Speak in the pauses. Try not to refer to the text.

CULTURE POINT 2

Daguerre et le daguerréotype *Daguerre and the daguerreotype*

Dans les années 1820 (*In the 1820s*), Nicéphore Niépce, inventeur de la photographie, expérimente l'utilisation du bitume de Judée (*bitumen of Judea*) pour fixer l'image sur une plaque de cuivre (*a sheet of copper*), placée dans une chambre noire (*camera obscura*). En 1829, il s'associe avec (*he partners with*) Louis Daguerre pour améliorer (*to improve*) son invention. Après la mort de Niépce, Daguerre poursuit les travaux et découvre qu'une plaque de cuivre recouverte d'argent (*silver-plated copper*) produit un bien meilleur résultat. Le jour de la découverte de son daguerréotype, Daguerre aurait dit « J'ai saisi la lumière, j'ai arrêté son vol ! » (*I have captured the light and arrested its flight*!). Grâce à son invention, Daguerre fait partie des 72 scientifiques, ingénieurs et mathématiciens français dont les noms sont inscrits (*whose names are engraved*) sur la tour Eiffel. En 1975, la cinéaste Agnès Varda réalise un documentaire (*makes a documentary*) intitulé *Daguerréotypes*. Habitante de la rue Daguerre, dans le quatorzième arrondissement de Paris, elle tourne son film (*she shoots her movie*) dans un rayon (*a radius*) de 50 mètres de sa maison, une limite imposée par la longueur du câble de la caméra. Dans son documentaire, elle interviewe les commerçants de la rue, et de temps en temps, ils s'immobilisent pour la caméra, comme aux débuts de la photographie. Agnès Varda explique que son film est un album de portraits de « Types et typesses » de la rue Daguerre, un hommage aux commerçants de sa rue, et à Louis Daguerre, pionnier de la photographie, dont les travaux ont permis plus tard, l'invention du cinéma.

Read this report on Varda's *Daguerréotypes*. What are the owners of the Chardon Bleu called?

VOCABULARY BUILDER 2

Look at the words and phrases and complete the missing English words and expressions. Then listen and try to imitate the pronunciation of the speakers.

COMMANDER	*ORDERING*
annuler	*to cancel*
contacter	....
confirmer	....
les consignes (fem. pl.)	*instructions*
un coup de fil	*phone call*
un courriel/un e-mail	*email*
une livraison	*delivery*
un livreur/une livreuse	*deliveryman/deliverywoman*
de la part de, de ma part	*on behalf of, from me*
une plainte	*complaint*
une référence	....
renseigner, se renseigner	*to inform, to get information*
des renseignements (masc. pl.)	*information*
un service	....

EXPRESSIONS	*EXPRESSIONS*
acheter sur Internet	*buy on the internet*
passer une commande	*to place an order*
Patientez s'il vous plaît.	*Please wait.*
Je vous passe Mme Lebrun.	*I'm putting you through to Mme Lebrun.*

Vocabulary practice 2

Fill in the gaps using words and phrases from Vocabulary builder 2.

a Il faut éviter d'acheter des livres .... (*One should avoid buying books on the internet.*)

b Je voudrais .... mon contrat. (*I would like to cancel my contract.*)

c Bonjour, je voudrais .... (*Hello, I would like to place an order.*)

d Vous pouvez .... M. Perez ? (*Can you put me through to Monsieur Perez?*)

e Est-ce que tu as reçu un .... de ma part. (*Have you received an email from me?*)

Pronunciation practice 2

When you listen to Conversation 2, pay particular attention to how each speaker's voice rises and falls. Do you notice a pattern?

CONVERSATION 2

La livraison *The delivery*

14.08

1 Here are a few words and expressions to help you understand the conversation.

personne n'est venu	*no one came*	renseigner	*to inform*
sans que je l'entende	*without me hearing him*	suprenant, suprenante	*surprising*

14.09

2 Listen to the conversation without looking at the text. Then listen to the conversation again and read the text.

Jo has been home waiting all day for a package that never arrived. She is sharing her feelings of frustration with Assia when she arrives for their get-together.

Assia	Alors, c'est arrivé ?
Jo	Non, j'ai attendu toute la journée et personne n'est venu. Il est impossible que le livreur soit passé sans que je l'entende.
Assia	Et ils n'ont pas téléphoné ?
Jo	Non ! Ni coup de fil, ni courriel, rien !
Assia	Ils exagèrent.
Jo	Oui, ça commence à m'agacer sérieusement !
Assia	C'est surprenant qu'ils ne t'informent pas.
Jo	Je les appelle...
	Jo calls the delivery agent.
Jo	Bonjour, je vous appelle au sujet d'un problème de livraison.
Opératrice	Oui, vous avez la référence ?
Jo	XRTJ 42 84 26 72
Opératrice	Mon ordinateur me dit que le livreur est passé aujourd'hui.
Jo	Ah non, impossible, je suis restée chez moi toute la journée et aucun livreur n'est venu.
Opératrice	Ah, je ne comprends pas, je me renseigne, patientez s'il vous plait...
	A little later ...
Opératrice	Je suis désolée, je n'arrive pas à contacter le service de livraison.
Jo	Écoutez, ça fait cinq jours que j'attends, ce n'est pas normal !
Opératrice	Oui, je comprends. Voilà ce que je vous propose. J'annule cette commande et je crée une nouvelle commande avec livraison urgente.

3 Answer the questions.

- **a** Why is Jo certain that she could not have missed the delivery person if they had come?
- **b** What communication, if any, has the company initiated?
- **c** What indication does the operator's computer give about the status of the delivery?
- **d** What five-word phrase does Jo use to express her annoyance to the operator?
- **e** What solution does the operator offer?

LANGUAGE BUILDER 3

Language discovery 3

1 Jo says: j'ai attendu toute la journée et personne n'est venu (*I waited all day and no one came*). What two French words together mean *no one*? And how are those two words positioned in relation to the verb? Are they placed (a) before the verb; (b) on either side of the verb; (c) after the verb?

2 Jo says: Ah non, impossible, je suis restée chez moi toute la journée et aucun livreur n'est venu. (*No, that's impossible, I stayed at home all day and no delivery man came*). In this sentence, what two words correspond to *no* in the English translation?

Personne et aucun avec ne *Nobody, any, anybody*

Earlier you saw that rien combined with ne, meaning *nothing*, can be used in two ways: as a subject (rien + ne), e.g., rien ne me va ! (*Nothing suits me!*); and as an object (ne + rien), e.g., Marc ne fait rien (*Marc is doing nothing*). The same is true of personne and ne, meaning *no one/nobody/not anyone*.

Je sonne à la porte, mais personne ne répond.	*I'm ringing the doorbell, but no one is answering.*
Je regarde, mais je ne vois personne.	*I'm looking, but I see no one/I do not see anyone.*

When personne + ne is used in le passé composé, the word order is as follows:

J'ai sonné à la porte, mais personne n'a répondu.	*I rang the doorbell, but no one answered.*
J'ai regardé, mais je n'ai vu personne.	*I looked, but I saw no one/I did not see anyone.*

When personne is used with le passé composé (and is the object), it belongs in a different place than pas/rien/plus/jamais. In fact, personne follows the past participle (je n'ai vu personne), while pas, rien, plus, and jamais precede the past participle. For example:

Il n'a rien fait.	*He did nothing.*
Je n'ai jamais été en Chine.	*I've never been to China.*
Nous n'avons plus adressé la parole à Roger.	*We no longer spoke with Roger.*

Finally, it is useful to learn how to say the equivalent in French of a statement such as *no question should remain unanswered*. Notice that in this sentence *no* precedes a noun (= *question*). One way to translate this into French would be: Aucune question ne devrait rester sans réponse (*no question should remain without an answer*). Here aucun/aucune is placed before a noun (question), and also agrees with that noun (aucune is feminine, while aucun is masculine). Notice, too, that ne follows aucun + noun.

Aucun journaliste n'était présent.	*No journalist was present.*
Il n'a remarqué aucune erreur.	*He did not notice any mistakes.*

Notice that aucun and aucune, combined with ne, are always singular. It might help to think of it as the equivalent of *not a single one* in English.

Language practice 3

1 Complete the sentences below by the negative expressions indicated.
Example: Ils sont déjà arrivés ? Mais je *ne* vois *personne* ! (*no one*)

a Tu sais où est Jean-Paul ? — Désolée, je .... en ai .... idée. (*no*)

b Tu me dis qu'ils sont là, mais je .... vois .... (*no one*)

c Louise voudrait qu'on remplace l'ascenseur, mais .... / .... est d'accord. (*no one*)

d .... lettre .... est arrivée aujourd'hui. (*no*)

2 Complete the sentences with the correct negative forms.

a Je .... ai .... visité le palais de Versailles. (*never*)

b Les gens .... font .... attention au patrimoine de la nation. (*no longer*)

c Le prix du pétrole a des hauts et des bas – pourquoi est-ce que les prix à la station-service .... baissent .... ? (*never*)

d Presque .... est venu au vernissage ? Ça m'étonne ! (*no one*)

LANGUAGE BUILDER 4

Language discovery 4

14.10

Listen to the conversation again and repeat each line in the pauses.

1 In which two of the following sentences from Conversation 2 is le subjonctif used? How many subjonctifs do those two sentences contain in total?

a Il est impossible que le livreur soit passé sans que je l'entende. (*said by Jo*)
b Mon ordinateur me dit que le livreur est passé aujourd'hui. (*said by the operator*)
c Oui, je suis désolée que nous n'ayons pas effectué cette livraison. (*said by the operator*)

2 Which of the following is the correct description of the verb form soit passé and why?

a subjonctif présent (= present subjunctive) **b** subjonctif passé (= past subjunctive)

Le subjonctif (suite) *The subjunctive* (continued)

So far all the subjonctifs you have learned have been present-tense ones. When you are referring to a past event and a subjonctif is required, you may need to use le subjonctif passé (*past subjunctive*). Look carefully at the following sentences: (a) Luc a appelé sa mère hier (*Luc called his mother yesterday*); (b) Je suis soulagé que Luc ait appelé sa mère hier (*I am relieved me that Luc called his mother yesterday*). Here, you can see to replace the past indicative form (= a appelé) by le subjonctif passé (= ait appelé), all you need to do is replace a (indicative) with ait (subjonctif). The past participle (appelé) remains unchanged. To see how this works in more detail, compare the tables below.

appeler (*perfect indicative*)

j'ai appelé	nous avons appelé
tu as appelé	vous avez appelé
il/elle/on a appelé	ils/elles ont appelé

appeler (*perfect subjunctive*)

que j'aie appelé	que nous ayons appelé
que tu aies appelé	que vous ayez appelé
qu'il/elle/on ait appelé	qu'ils/elles aient appelé

A similar rule applies if the verb takes être instead of avoir. Compare these two sentences: (a) Yves est passé hier (*Yves came by yesterday*); (b) Je suis ravi qu'Yves soit passé hier (*I am delighted that Yves came by yesterday*). Here, est (indicatif) has been replaced by soit (subjonctif), while the past participle (passé) remains unchanged.

Language practice 4

1 Replace the underlined verbs, using le subjonctif passé.

Example: Jean-Luc a manqué son bus. Je m'inquiète que Jean-Luc *ait manqué* son bus.

a Nous avons fini de manger. Ça t'énerve que nous .... de manger ?

b Tu as terminé tes devoirs. Je suis contente que tu .... tes devoirs.

c Marie a posté sa lettre. Tu dois être soulagé que Marie .... sa lettre.

d Vous avez obtenu votre bac. Nous sommes heureux que vous .... votre bac.

14.11

2 Listen to Conversation 2 again and play the part of Jo. You can repeat her lines or invent your own as long as they still fit with Assia's own lines. Pay particular attention to whether the stresses fall or rise when you are playing Jo's part.

SKILL BUILDER

1 Complete the negative sentences.

a L'ascenseur .... marche .... (*The elevator is not working.*)

b .... veut monter à pied. (*Nobody wants to go up the stairs.*)

c J'espère que cela .... se produira .... (*I hope this will never happen again.*)

d Mais, malheureusement je .... fais .... confiance aux personnes qui viennent réparer l'ascenseur. (*But unfortunately, I no longer trust the people who come to fix the elevator.*)

e Moi non plus, la dernière fois qu'ils sont venus ils .... ont .... fait. (*Me neither, the last time that they came they did not do anything.*)

2 State which of the underlined verbs are examples of le subjonctif and which are indicative.

a Les invités sont là. Il faut qu'on se presse. (*The guests are there. We must hurry up.*)

b Je suis sûr qu'ils sont devant la porte. (*I'm sure they're at the door.*)

c Je ne suis pas sûre qu'elle soit là. (*I'm not sure she's there.*)

d Nous doutons que Valérie arrive à temps. (*We doubt that Valérie will arrive in time.*)

e Il n'est pas certain que j'obtienne le poste. (*It's not certain that I'll get the job.*)

TEST YOURSELF

1 Complete the text with the correct verb form, choosing the present indicative or subjunctive, as appropriate.

Je suis désolé que l'ascenseur **a** .... (*être*) à nouveau en panne. Je sais que vous **b** n' .... pas (*être*) satisfaits et je vous comprends. Malheureusement, je doute fort que les techniciens **c** .... (*pouvoir*) venir le réparer aujourd'hui. Par ailleurs, je crains que les réparations vous **d** .... (*coûter*) cher. Je confirme que cet ascenseur **e** .... (*devoir*) être remplacé d'ici six mois à un an.

2 Write a sentence with the opposite meaning.

a Il arrive toujours à l'heure. Il ....

b Elle aime tout le monde. Elle ....

c Tout le monde la félicite pour sa victoire. ....

d Nous partons toujours en vacances au mois d'août. ....

Remember to use **My review** and **My takeaway** to assess your progress and reflect on your learning experience.

15

In this lesson you will learn how to:

- » Talk about things as they are or were happening
- » Give emphasis/distinguish between people and things by using certain pronouns
- » Use various pronouns in complex French sentences

La gastronomie

My study plan

I plan to work with Unit 15

○ Every day

○ Twice a week

○ Other ________

I plan to study for

○ 5–15 minutes

○ 15–30 minutes

○ 30–45+ minutes

My progress tracker

Day / Date	Listen	Speak	Read	Write	Converse
	○	○	○	○	○
	○	○	○	○	○
	○	○	○	○	○
	○	○	○	○	○
	○	○	○	○	○
	○	○	○	○	○
	○	○	○	○	○

My goals

What do you want to be able to do or say in French when you complete this unit?

Done

1 .... ○

2 .... ○

3 .... ○

My review

SELF CHECK

	I can ...
●	... Speak about simultaneous events.
●	... Ensure meaning of sentences is clear.
●	... Avoid repetition through the use of pronouns.

CULTURE POINT 1

Les guides gastronomiques *Gastronomy guides*

Le Guide Michelin a été inventé en 1900 par André et Édouard Michelin, fondateurs de la fabrique de pneumatiques du même nom. À sa création, le guide était gratuit et contenait des informations pratiques pour les automobilistes : cartes routières (*road maps*), adresses de restaurants et d'hôtels, mais aussi de garagistes ou de médecins. La première étoile « de bonne table » est apparue en 1926, et en 1933, les inspecteurs du Guide Michelin sont nés, responsables d'évaluer la qualité des établissements et d'attribuer les fameuses étoiles. Depuis, le Guide Michelin s'est agrandi (*has expanded*) et est devenu une référence mondiale, avec de bonnes adresses en Argentine, aux États-Unis, en Chine, en Turquie ou en Thaïlande. En 2020, le Guide Michelin a créé l'étoile verte, pour reconnaître l'engagement des établissements en matière de gastronomie éco-responsable (*environmentally friendly*). Il existe de nombreux autres guides gastronomiques tels que (*such as*) le Guide du Routard ou le Guide Gault et Millau. En 2010, le « repas gastronomique des Français » est inscrit sur la liste du patrimoine culturel immatériel de l'humanité de l'UNESCO. En 2019, est paru « 500 femmes qui font la différence dans les cuisines de France », qui répertorie (*which lists*) et met en valeur (*highlights*) le travail des femmes cheffes de France.

Lisez l'article suivant sur le site web de l'UNESCO. Quelles sont les caractéristiques du repas gastronomique des Français ?

VOCABULARY BUILDER 1

Look at the words and phrases and complete the missing English words and expressions. Then listen and try to imitate the pronunciation of the speakers.

LES HEUREUX HASARDS	*SERENDIPITY*
Il s'avère que...	*It turns out that ...*
chambouler	*to mess up*
la chance	*luck/good luck*
distraire	*to distract*
gâcher	*to spoil*
le hasard	*chance (= good or bad luck)*
inspirer, une inspiration	....
une invention	....
une rencontre	*chance encounter*
une trouvaille	*lucky find*
EXPRESSIONS	***EXPRESSIONS***
surprendre quelqu'un	*to surprise someone*
être tombé sur quelqu'un	*to have come across someone*
Il l'a fait exprès.	*He did it on purpose.*
Quelle surprise !	....
presser quelqu'un, se presser	*to hurry someone up, to hurry*
Luc est pressé, Sylvie est pressée.	*Luc is in a hurry, Sylvie is in a hurry.*
être chamboulé/chamboulée	*to be in a muddle*
l'attention (fem.), faire attention	*attention, to be careful/to watch out*
Tout est bien qui finit bien !	*All's well that ends well!*

Vocabulary practice 1

Complete the following sentences using words and phrases from the Vocabulary builder.

a Louise .... sur son ancienne collègue de bureau en faisant ses courses.

b Marc a tout gâché, mais il ne l'a pas ....

c Léa et Sophie vont être en retard. Il faut les ....

d Finalement, tout s'est bien passé ? Oui, on peut dire que tout est bien qui .... !

CONVERSATION 1

Heureux hasard *Serendipity*

15.02

1 Here are a few words and expressions to help you understand the conversation.

Comment ça ?	*How did that happen?*	un stand	*stall*
un mélange	*mixture*	partir en courant	*to run off*
un échantillon	*sample*	je m'en suis rendu compte	*I realized*

15.03

2 Listen to the conversation without looking at the text. Then listen to the conversation again and read the text.

Charles has just made a creative discovery and is excited to tell Eva all about it.

Eva	Salut Charles, tu as passé une bonne journée ?
Charles	Oui, excellente, j'ai inventé une nouvelle recette de chocolat !
Eva	Ah oui ? Comment ça ?
Charles	Bon, en fait, je ne l'ai pas fait exprès, ça s'est fait par hasard...
Eva	C'est bien toi, ça ! Raconte !
Charles	J'étais en train de préparer mon mélange d'épices quand la patronne est arrivée. Moi, je croyais qu'elle était au Salon du Chocolat.
Eva	Tu as dû être surpris !
Charles	Ben oui, je ne m'y attendais pas du tout. Elle m'a expliqué qu'elle avait oublié des échantillons pour le stand. Elle était très pressée, elle les a mis dans sa valise et elle est partie précipitamment.
Eva	Et ?
Charles	J'étais un peu chamboulé, et sans faire attention, j'ai mis de la coriandre dans mon chocolat. Je ne m'en suis pas rendu compte.
Eva	Tiens, c'est original.
Charles	Plus tard, j'ai goûté, et j'ai compris immédiatement que je n'avais pas suivi la recette.
Eva	Et alors, c'est bon ?
Charles	Ben oui, moi j'ai bien aimé, je le ferai goûter à la patronne après le salon.
Eva	Bravo Charles ! Ta première recette de chocolat ! Les gens vont adorer !

3 Answer the questions.

a Why is Charles pleased with how his day went?
b How did Charles's boss surprise him?
c What new ingredient did Charles put in his chocolate mix?
d Did he change the recipe on purpose?
e When will Charles ask his boss to taste the new recipe?

LANGUAGE BUILDER 1

Language discovery 1

When Charles is explaining how he accidentally created a new flavour of chocolate, he says: J'étais en train de préparer mon mélange d'épices quand la patronne est arrivée.

1 Given the context, can you figure out what this must mean, then translate the whole sentence into English?

2 Which of the following could correctly replace the phrase j'étais en train de préparer ? : (a) j'ai préparé ; (b) je préparais ; (c) je préparerai.

Être en train de faire... *To be in the process of ...*

As you saw in Conversation 1, we use the phrase être en train de + verb to express that someone is in the process of doing (something), that is, right now.

Il est en train de jouer du piano. *He is [in the process of] playing the piano.*

Notice the structure: *subject* (il) + *form of* être (est) + en train de + *infinitive* (jouer du piano). The same phrase can also be used with l'imparfait.

Léa était en train de regarder la télé. *Léa was watching TV.*

Language practice 1

Transform the following sentences by replacing the underlined verbs with être en train de.

Example: Pierre <u>écoutait</u> la radio quand son frère a téléphoné.
Pierre *était en train d'écouter la radio* quand son frère a téléphoné.

a <u>Nous regardions</u> un film d'Agnès Varda quand Manu est arrivé.
b Pardon ! <u>Vous mangez</u> ? Je ne voudrais pas interrompre votre repas (*interrupt your meal*).
c Qu'est-ce que <u>vous faisiez</u> quand je suis passé hier ?
d <u>Elles préparaient</u> le dîner lorsque leur amie a sonné à la porte.
e J'entends de la musique. Est-ce que <u>Pierre joue</u> du piano ?

LANGUAGE BUILDER 2

Language discovery 2

15.04

Listen to the conversation again and repeat each line in the pauses.

Charles says: Moi, je croyais qu'elle était au Salon du Chocolat. This could be translated adequately as: *I thought that she was at the Salon du Chocolat.* Notice that we do not need to translate the pronoun moi (*me*); even if Charles had not used it, we would know who is performing the action because he says je. This kind of pronoun, used to add emphasis, is known as a tonic pronoun.

1 Can you find another example where Charles uses moi to emphasize his own perspective?

2 Moi is the tonic pronoun that corresponds to je/me. Can you find a tonic pronoun that corresponds to tu/te? Who uses it?

Les pronoms toniques *Tonic pronouns*

The tonic pronouns in French are indicated in the table below:

Subject pronoun			Tonic pronoun			Subject pronoun		Tonic pronoun	
je			moi			nous		nous	
tu			toi			vous		vous	
il	elle	on	lui	elle	soi	ils	elles	eux	elles

Tonic pronouns have various uses.

1 They are used after prepositions (e.g. pour, contre).

C'est pour les garçons ? Oui, c'est pour eux. *Is this for the boys? Yes, it's for them.*

C'est pour les filles ? Oui, c'est pour elles. *Is this for the girls? Yes, it's for them.*

Tu joues contre qui ?—Contre lui. *Who are you playing against?—Against him.*

2 They are used for emphasis. For instance, it is possible to say:

Alors, Mme Richard, qu'est-ce que vous pensez, vous : oui ou non ? *So, Mme Richard, what do you think: yes or no?*

3 They can be used for effects of contrast and/or symmetry (a particular kind of emphasis):

Moi, je suis pour, mais lui, il est contre. *I am for, but he is against.*

4 They are used to head off or clear up confusions. For instance, since the indirect object pronoun lui can mean either *to him* or *to her*, it's sometimes necessary to add à + tonic pronoun to the end of an otherwise ambiguous statement.

Je lui ai donné le cadeau à elle. *I gave the present to her.*

Nous avons décidé de te donner une voiture à toi, mais pas à ton frère. *We decided to give you a car and to not give one to your brother.*

5 They can be used after cest:

Les gagnants, c'est nous !	*The winners are ... us!*
Le perdant, c'est lui.	*The loser is ... him.*

Language practice 2

1 Match the sentences with the tonic pronouns.

a Tu habites chez ton père ? Oui, j'habite chez ....
b Tu es d'accord avec Fatima ? Oui, je suis d'accord avec ....
c Vous partez en en vacances sans vos enfants ? Oui, nous patrons en vacances sans ....
d Tiens Emilio, ce cadeau est pour ....
e Bravo les filles, c'est .... qui avez gagné.
f Vous faites ce que vous voulez, mais ...., nous ne participerons pas.

1 vous
2 toi
3 elle
4 nous
5 eux
6 lui

2 Complete the sentences with a tonic pronoun.

a ...., je dis oui mais ...., tu dis non.
b Quelle surprise ! Vous êtes là, ... ?
c Voici Thomas et Benjamin. Tu as un livre pour ...., non ?
d Voici ton petit frère qui arrive. Tu veux partager avec .... ?
e Dans la vie, il faut toujours regarder devant ....

15.05

3 Listen to the recording of Conversation 1 again. This time in the pauses play the role of Eva—you can adapt what she says as long as it still makes sense within the overall conversation. Then imagine coming home at the end of the day and telling a friend about a positive accidental discovery you made at work.

CULTURE POINT 2

La presse francophone *The French-language press*

Il existe de très nombreux journaux en langue française. En France, pour les quotidiens nationaux (*national daily newspapers*), on peut citer *Le Monde* ou *Le Figaro* et pour les quotidiens régionaux (*regional daily newspapers*), *Ouest France*, *Le Parisien* ou *La Voix du Nord* par exemple. *L'Équipe* est le journal du sport, et *Les Échos*, celui de l'économie. Certains journaux sont accessibles uniquement en ligne, c'est le cas notamment de *Médiapart*, un quotidien d'actualité numérique (*digital daily newspaper*) créé en 2008, qui compte plus de 200 000 abonnés (*subscribers*).

L'offre de magazines hebdomadaires (*weekly*) et mensuels (*monthly*) est également très variée : *Paris Match*, *Elle*, *Le Point*, *Sciences et Avenir*, *Santé magazine*, *Ça m'intéresse* ou *Le Courrier international* sont certains des titres de la presse magazine française. Ailleurs (*Elsewhere*) dans le monde, on peut citer les titres suivants : *Le Soir* ou *La Libre Belgique* (Belgique), *Le Devoir* ou *Le Journal de Montréal* (Canada), *Le Temps* (Suisse), *El Watan* (Algérie), *Le Quotidien* (Sénégal), *L'Orient-Le Jour* (Liban), *Fraternité Matin* (Côte d'Ivoire) ou *Le Progrès Égyptien* (Égypte).

Il existe de multiples chaînes de radio et de télévision en langue française. La chaîne TV5monde, financée par la France, la Suisse, le Canada, le Québec et la Fédération Wallonie-Bruxelles, est un média unique qui relie les francophones sur les cinq continents. L'Union de la Presse francophone (UPF) regroupe les journalistes et les éditeurs de la presse écrite et audiovisuelle à travers le monde. Enfin, l'Agence France Presse, née en 1944 à la Libération de Paris, est une des grandes agences de presse (*news agencies*) internationales, dont la mission est de fournir (*to provide*) en permanence, partout dans le monde, une information fiable, vérifiée et immédiate (*reliable, verified, and immediate information*).

Visitez le site web de TV5monde et découvrez les ressources gratuites pour apprendre le français.

VOCABULARY BUILDER 2

Look at the words and phrases and provide the missing English words and expressions. Then listen and try to imitate the pronunciation of the speakers.

LES ACTUALITÉS (FEM. PL.)	***NEWS***
un article	....
un éditorial	....
un fait divers	*(short) news item*
un journal, des journaux	*newspaper, newspapers*
un journal en ligne	*online newspaper*
un/une journaliste	....
un hebdomadaire	*weekly (magazine)*
un quotidien	*daily paper*
un rédacteur/une rédactrice (en chef)	*editor(-in-chief)*
la rédaction	*editorial staff/office*
un titre, les gros titres	*headline, the headlines*

EXPRESSIONS	***EXPRESSIONS***
un article à la une	*front-page story*
faire la une	*make the front page*
faire les gros titres	*hit the headlines*
rédiger un article	*write an article*
Auparavant elle était journaliste.	*Previously she was a journalist.*

Vocabulary practice 2

Complete the text with words/expressions from the Vocabulary builder.

Florence Aubenas est **a** .... Elle écrit des **b** .... pour *Le Monde*. Auparavant, elle a travaillé pour *La Libération*, un **c** .... concurrent du *Monde*.

CONVERSATION 2

Qu'est-ce qu'on apporte ? *What shall we bring?*

15.07

1 Listen to the conversation without looking at the text. Then listen to the conversation again and read the text.

Assia and Jo are avowed foodies, so they are talking about the latest gastronomical festival ahead of going to meet friends for dinner.

Assia	Salut Jo, qu'est-ce que tu lis ?
Jo	Un reportage sur le Salon Omnivore au Touquet-Paris-Plage.
Assia	Ah oui, le festival de la gastronomie. Je croyais qu'il avait lieu à Paris.
Jo	Oui, moi aussi, c'est ce que je croyais. Pauline y est allée pour couvrir l'évènement.
Assia	Ah oui ? Qu'est-ce qu'elle a écrit ?
Jo	« Hier soir, les amateurs de gastronomie locale se sont régalés à la soirée de lancement d'Omnivore au Touquet-Paris-Plage. »
Assia	Intéressant, je peux lire ?
Jo	Oui, je termine l'article et je te le donne.
Assia	Au fait, tu as répondu à l'invitation d'Abou et François ?
Jo	Oui, oui, je leur ai envoyé un whatsapp ce matin, ils nous attendent chez eux vers 20 h 00.
Assia	Qu'est-ce qu'on leur apporte ?
Jo	Aïe, zut, je ne le leur ai pas demandé, apportons du fromage et du vin.
Assia	Oui, et un dessert ?
Jo	Oui, pourquoi pas ! C'est une bonne idée !

2 Answer the questions.

a Where is the Salon Omnivore taking place?
b Who has written an article about it?
c Who gets to read the article first—Jo or Assia?
d Who has invited Jo and Assia to their house, and what did they decide to bring?

LANGUAGE BUILDER 3

Language discovery 3

1 Halfway through the conversation, Jo says to Assia: je termine l'article et je te le donne.

What do te and le refer to?

2 A couple of lines later, Assia asks Jo what they are going to take to Abou and François's apartment, and Jo answers: Aïe, zut, je ne le leur ai pas demandé.

What do le and leur refer to?

Les pronoms doubles *Double pronouns*

You already know that object pronouns (e.g., me) can be *direct* or *indirect*. The pronouns me, te, se, le, la, nous, vous, les are used for direct objects, while me, te, se, lui, nous, vous, leur are used for indirect objects. You also learned that these pronouns are generally placed before the verb—not after the verb, as in English.

Marie vous connaît. — *Marie knows you.*

Chaque été, ma cousine m'envoie. une carte postale — *Every summer, my cousin sends me a postcard.*

But what if you wanted to say the equivalent of *My cousin sends it to me*? Clearly, you will need two pronouns: la and me. But does it matter which comes first? In fact, French speakers always use object pronouns in a set order. As they know that me always comes before la, they would say: Ma cousine me l'envoie. The table below sets out the order of all the traditional object pronouns, including y (*there/to it*) and en (*from it*).

Order of object pronouns in a standard French sentence

subject	me te se nous vous	le la les	lui leur	y	en	verb

Jean me le montre. — *Jean shows it/him to me.*

Marie la leur indique. — *Marie points it/her out to them.*

Ali nous la recommande. — *Ali recommends it/her to us.*

Richard lui en a donné trois. — *Richard gave three of them to her/him.*

Est-ce qu'il y a des fraises cette année ? Oui, il y en a beaucoup. — *Are there strawberries this year?—Yes, there are lots of them.*

Language practice 3

1 Translate the sentences below into French, paying close attention to the placement of the pronouns.

a Charles gave it to her. ....

b I am not surprised that he helps her. ....

c Eva spoke to him about it. ....

d Can you lend them to me? ....

2 Complete each answer by using the relevant pronouns.

Example: Assia veut nous montrer ses portraits ? Oui, elle veut *nous les* montrer.

a Charles indique la route à sa sœur ? Oui, il .... indique.

b Jo a recommandé ce restaurant à ses amis ? Oui, elle .... a recommandé.

c Eva a donné un bonbon à son cousin ? Oui, elle .... a donné trois.

d Est-ce qu'il nous reste des chocolats ? Oui, il .... reste.

e Est-ce qu'il y reste encore deux places pour la séance de 19 heures ?
Oui, il .... reste deux.

LANGUAGE BUILDER 4

Language discovery 4

15.08

Listen to the conversation again and repeat each line in the pauses.

At the end of Conversation 2, Assia asks whether Abou and François requested a dessert, and Jo answers: Je ne le leur ai pas demandé... (*I didn't ask them that* ...). Here, the placing of ne, me, en, and pas follows a specific rule governing word order in negative sentences.

Bearing this in mind, can you choose the correct phrase (a, b, or c) in order to complete the rule below?

In a negative sentence, object pronouns are placed: (a) after both ne and pas; (b) after ne but before pas; (c) before ne and pas.

L'agencement des phrases négatives *Word order in negative sentences*

You have learned that ne and pas generally go on either side of the verb. For instance, Jacques <u>n'aime pas</u> la musique classique. And you have also learned that when you use le passé composé, ne and pas go on either side of the *auxiliary* verb (avoir or être), for example elle <u>n'a pas</u> vu Jean-Marc (*she didn't see Jean-Marc*) or ils <u>ne sont pas</u> venus au concert (*they didn't go to the concert*).

Now it will be useful to learn where ne and pas are placed in relation to object pronouns. The rule is that, if there are any object pronouns in the sentence, they are placed between ne and the (auxiliary) verb, which is in turn followed by pas: see the table below.

Word order in negative sentences

subject	ne	me te se nous vous	le la les	lui leur	y	en	verb or auxiliary verb	pas	past participle

Je ne les connais pas très bien. — *I don't know them very well.*

Je ne vous l'ai pas donné. — *I did not give it to you.*

Il n'y est pas allé. — *He did not go there.*

Il n'y en a pas. — *There is none.*

Language practice 4

1 Complete the sentences.

a Je .... mes clés. (*I'm not giving my keys to him.*)

b Je .... mes clés. (*I did not give my keys to him.*)

c Elles .... la photo. (*They did not show the photo to them.*)

d Elles .... la photo. (*They are not showing the photo to them.*)

15.09

2 Now play the conversation again and play Assia's role. Speak in the pauses. Try not to refer to the text.

SKILL BUILDER

1 Complete the text using tonic pronouns.

a ...., je suis pour les produits bio, mais mon copain Marc n'est pas convaincu (*convinced*). Le réchauffement climatique m'inquiète, mais ça ne l'intéresse pas, **b** .... Et ses parents sont pareils (*the same*) ! Selon **c** ...., le réchauffement climatique n'existe pas. Mais **d** ...., je crois qu'il faut penser à l'avenir – je ne veux pas vivre dans un monde où c'est chacun pour **e** ....

2 Complete the text with the correct pronouns.

Charles veut devenir chocolatier, pour **a** .... arriver il doit compléter son apprentissage et achever son stage en tant qu'apprenti chocolatier en Belgique. Son chef **b** .... a rendu service en **c** .... demandant de créer des chocolats fantaisie pour Pâques. Charles a été très fier quand la chocolaterie **d** .... a vendu la plupart, c'est-à-dire tout sauf les deux que Charles avait mis de côté : un pour sa maman et l'autre pour Eva, qui **e** .... a encouragé tout au long de son stage à Bruxelles et **f** .... a présenté les grandes maisons de chocolat de Genève, lors de **g** .... visite à sa grand-mère.

TEST YOURSELF

1 Complete the narrative using the verbs indicated and the relevant pronouns

Charles et Eva sont en train de se parler en ligne quand ils **a** .... (recevoir) tous les deux un courriel **b** .... invitant à une soirée gastronomique pour marquer le premier anniversaire d'une de **c** .... pâtisseries préférées. Charles dit tout de suite « je veux **d** .... aller » et Eva, **e** .... aussi, dit qu'elle voudrait **f** .... aller.

L'invitation **g** .... demande de confirmer **h** .... présence à la soirée et de voter pour **i** .... pâtisserie préférée. La pâtisserie qui obtient le plus de votes sera servie lors de la soirée. Charles et Eva se mettent d'accord pour voter pour la même pâtisserie, un gâteau au chocolat, pour maximiser **j** .... chances. Maintenant, ils attendent avec impatience de connaître le résultat, mais même si **k** .... gâteau préféré n'est pas choisi, ils savent qu'ils vont se régaler car tous les desserts de cette pâtisserie sont délicieux.

2 Replace each occurrence of être en train de with a verb in the present or imparfait.
Example: Ils étaient en train de réfléchir à leur avenir. → *Ils réfléchissaient à leur avenir.*

a Tu étais en train de jouer du Mozart ? C'est beau ! Continue !

b Nous étions en train de faire un pique-nique quand la pluie a commencé (the rain started).

c Patrick et François sont en train de se parler. On les laisse tranquilles...

d Maman et papa sont en train de préparer le goûter des enfants.

Remember to use **My review** and **My takeaway** to assess your progress and reflect on your learning experience.

16

In this lesson you will learn how to:

» Explain cause and effect
» Use the passive voice
» Learn more about past participle agreements

Les festivals et le Québec

My study plan

I plan to work with Unit 16

○ Every day
○ Twice a week
○ Other ________

I plan to study for

○ 5–15 minutes
○ 15–30 minutes
○ 30–45+ minutes

My progress tracker

Day / Date	Listening	Speaking	Reading	Writing	Conversation
	○	○	○	○	○
	○	○	○	○	○
	○	○	○	○	○
	○	○	○	○	○
	○	○	○	○	○
	○	○	○	○	○
	○	○	○	○	○

My goals

What do you want to be able to do or say in French when you complete this unit?

		Done
1	....	○
2	....	○
3	....	○

My review

SELF CHECK

	I can ...
●	... explain the cause of something.
●	... use the passive voice.
●	... understand more about the past participle agreement.

CULTURE POINT 1

Les festivals *Festivals*

Les festivals permettent à une ville, à une région ou à un pays de développer le tourisme, en attirant un large public (***by attracting a large audience***), tout en soutenant (***while supporting***) la création artistique. Le plus vieux festival de France est Les Chorégies d'Orange, un rendez-vous de musique classique fondé en 1869 par le compositeur Hector Berlioz. Le plus grand festival de France est le festival interceltique de Lorient qui accueille jusqu'à 800 000 visiteurs chaque année (***which welcomes up to 800,000 visitors each year***) pour célébrer non seulement les musiques de Bretagne, d'Écosse, d'Irlande, du Pays de Galles, des Asturies et de la Galice, mais aussi d'Amérique du Nord. Parmi les festivals les plus célèbres (***Among the most famous festivals***), on peut citer le Festival de Cannes (cinéma), le Festival d'Avignon (théâtre), les Rencontres d'Arles (photo), le Festival des Jardins à Chaumont-sur-Loire, le Festival de la Bande Dessinée d'Angoulême, le Festival Chalon dans la rue, consacré aux arts de la rue, Montpelier Danse, ou Jazz in Marciac. Certains festivals se déclinent (***are replicated***) dans plusieurs pays ; c'est le cas des Francofolies, le festival des musiques francophones, avec les Francofolies de la Rochelle en France, de Spa en Belgique, de Montréal au Canada, de Bulgarie à Plovdiv, ou de Esch-sur-Alzette au Luxembourg. On peut citer d'autres grands festivals francophones comme le Festival d'Été de Québec, le Festival panafricain du Cinéma et de la Télévision de Ouagadougou (FESPACO), le Festival Gnaoua et Musiques du Monde à Essaouira, au Maroc, ou Montreux Jazz Festival qui se déroule (***that takes place***) chaque été pendant deux semaines sur les rives du Lac Léman, en Suisse.

Voici une vidéo du festival des Francofolies de Spa. Regardez la vidéo et dites pourquoi la narratrice aime ce festival.

VOCABULARY BUILDER 1

Look at the words and phrases and provide the missing English words and expressions. Then listen and try to imitate the pronunciation of the speakers.

À PROPOS D'UN FESTIVAL	*WHEN TALKING ABOUT A FESTIVAL*
une ambiance	*atmosphere*
une chanson	*song*
un groupe	*band*
la magie	*magic*
répéter, une répétition	*to rehearse, rehearsal*

LES GENRES DE MUSIQUE	*MUSICAL GENRES*
La musique...	
... classique	....
... acoustique	*acoustic music*
... folk	*folk music*
... orchestrale	*orchestral music*
... techno	....
... traditionnelle	*traditional music*
le blues	....
rock	....

EXPRESSIONS	*EXPRESSIONS*
Tu peux te libérer pour venir au concert ?	*Can you free time up to come to the concert?*
L'autre jour, j'ai rencontré Jean-Marc.	*The other day, I came across Jean-Marc.*
Ils se sont rencontrés au festival.	*They met each other at the festival. (by chance)*
Nous devons répéter pour être prêtes.	*We (fem.) must rehearse to be ready.*

Vocabulary practice 1

Complete the sentences with the words and phrases from Vocabulary builder 1.

a Je sais que tu aimes la musique ...., Debussy et Ravel en particulier, n'est-ce pas ?

b Ils aiment bien la musique ...., mais pas le style de danse en ligne qui va avec !

c Mes amis Pierre et Pauline .... au festival hier soir. Quelle coïncidence !

d Il faut .... beaucoup avant la représentation.

Pronunciation practice 1

16.02

Read the passage below and see whether you can spot where liaisons should be made. To help you, we have indicated how many liaisons there are. Then listen to the recording and see whether you got them all.

a J'aime beaucoup la musique folk [0].

b Mais les occasions où on peut en écouter ne sont pas fréquentes [2].

c Pour cette raison, je cherche sur Internet pour savoir où les festivals auront lieu [1].

d Il y en a normalement plusieurs au cours de l'été, dans ma région [1].

CONVERSATION 1

Les Francofolies de Spa *The Francofolies of Spa*

16.03

1 Here are a few words and expressions to understand the conversation.

J'attends une réponse.	*I'm waiting for an answer.*	découvrir	*to discover*
être de garde	*to be on duty*	formidable	*great*
Quel dommage !	*What a pity!*	à l'époque	*at the time*
grâce à elles	*thanks to them*		

16.04

2 Listen to the conversation without looking at the text. Then listen to the conversation again and read the text.

Eva et Charles go to a musical festival and they absolutely love the experience.

Eva Alors, tu as pris les places pour les Francofolies de Spa ?

Charles Ben non, j'attends la réponse de Nathalie et Mona !

Eva Ah, je ne t'ai pas dit, pardon, elles ne peuvent pas venir.

Charles Ah ! Et pourquoi ?

Eva Ben c'est à cause du travail de Mona, elle est de garde ce week-end-là.

Charles Et elles ne peuvent pas venir au concert du vendredi soir et retourner à Bruxelles après le concert ?

Eva C'est ce que je leur ai proposé, mais Nathalie ne peut pas se libérer le vendredi soir parce qu'elle a une répétition.

Charles Quel dommage, elles nous en ont tellement parlé de ce festival, c'est grâce à elles que je l'ai découvert. Bon, ben puisqu'elles ne peuvent pas venir, je prends nos places…

	After the festival, back in Brussels.
Eva	Ce qui m'a le plus frappée, c'est à quel point la programmation était variée.
Charles	Quel concert tu as préféré ?
Eva	Celui de Bigflo et Oli, ils étaient incroyables, et toi, qu'est-ce que tu en as pensé ?
Charles	Oui, formidable. J'ai beaucoup aimé Pomme aussi.
Eva	Oui, ce qui m'a le plus impressionnée, c'était l'ambiance, quelle émotion !
Charles	Oui, je suis d'accord avec toi, c'était magique !
Eva	Tu savais que les parents de Mona s'étaient rencontrés au festival ? Ça s'appelait le festival de la chanson francophone à l'époque.
Charles	Ah je comprends mieux pourquoi Mona y va chaque année !
Eva	Bon, presque chaque année !

3 Answer the questions.

a Why had Charles not yet booked the festival tickets?
b Why can't Nathalie go with them to the festival?
c What suggestion had Eva made to Nathalie?
d What struck Eva the most about the festival?
e Why is this such a special festival for Mona?

LANGUAGE BUILDER 1

Language discovery 1

In the conversation ce que appears once and ce qui appears twice—can you find these three occurrences in the text? Although they are different words in French, in English they can be translated by *what*.

Looking at the sentence structure can you guess why sometimes you need to say ce qui and other times ce que?

Ce qui ou ce que ? When to use ce qui and ce que

In Unit 13, you learned that the relative pronoun qui is used for the *subject* and que for the *object of the following verb*, and that qui/que always refer either to a *noun* or to the name of a person.

J'ai acheté le livre que tu voulais ; or Henri, qui vient ce soir, est un ami de Marc.

Sometimes, you may need to use a relative pronoun (qui or que) when there is no name/noun for it to refer back to. In these cases, you need to put in ce before qui or que to fill that gap.

Ce qui m'a le plus frappée, c'est à quel point la programmation était variée !

Translation: *What struck me most was how varied the program was!*

Literal translation: *That which struck me the most, that was how varied the program was!*

Ce qui m'a le plus impressionnée, c'était l'ambiance !

Translation: *What I was most impressed by was the atmosphere!*

Literal translation: *That which impressed me the most, it was the atmosphere!*

In brief, it is because relative pronouns need to refer back to something that ce is required in the examples above.

Language practice 1

1 In the sentences, identify the subject, verb, and object of the underlined clause.

Example: Luc accompagne sa mère ce soir, ce qui me ravit.

Subject: *ce qui* Verb: *ravit* Object: *me*

a Théo accompagne sa grand-mère ce soir, ce que je trouve sympa.

Subject: .... Verb: .... Object: ....

b Nous avons raté le train, ce que je regrette, évidemment.

Subject: .... Verb: .... Object: ....

c Nous avons raté le train, ce qui m'embête, évidemment.

Subject: .... Verb: .... Object: ....

2 Complete the sentences with ce qui or ce que/ce qu'.

a Tu as tout .... il faut pour le pique-nique ?

b Pas encore. .... manque, c'est le pain.

c .... me déroute, c'est que la consigne n'est pas écrite. Tout est en images !

d Tout est en images, ... je trouve déroutant.

LANGUAGE BUILDER 2

Language discovery 2

16.05

Listen to the conversation again and repeat each line in the pauses.

1 **Here is a variation on part of Conversation 1:** Pourquoi Nathalie ne peut pas se libérer vendredi soir ? — Parce qu'elle a une répétition. **Can you guess what a sentence starting with** parce que **expresses?**

2 **Here is another variation:** Nathalie et Mona ne peuvent pas venir au concert. C'est à cause du travail de Mona, elle est de garde ce week-end-là. — C'est dommage, c'est grâce à Nathalie et Mona que Charles a découvert le festival de Spa. **How would you translate** à cause de **and** grâce à **in English? Are they totally interchangeable or do they indicate a different type of reason for what has happened?**

La cause *Causation*

There are many words and expressions to indicate causation in French or indicate the reason which explains why something happened. A clause starting with parce que is the most common way of expressing causation:

Thomas n'est pas allé à l'école aujourd'hui parce qu'il était malade.	*Thomas did not go to school today because he was ill.*

À cause de and grâce à also express causation. Both can be translated by "because of" in English, but in French, they are used differently to explain the cause of what has happened.

- grâce à introduces a positive reason: Patricia a perdu son travail mais grâce à son expérience professionnelle et à son réseau, elle a trouvé rapidement un nouvel emploi. *Patricia lost her job but thanks to her professional experience and her network she quickly found a new job.*
- à cause de introduces a negative reason: Les transports sont perturbés aujourd'hui, à cause du mauvais temps. *Public transports are disrupted because of bad weather today.*

You will find that parce que is placed at the start of a full clause, but à cause de and grâce à are mainly used at the start of smaller groups of words that do not make up a full clause:

à cause de l'altitude / à cause de la tempête / à cause du vent / à cause des températures extrêmes / à cause de toi / à cause de vous.

grâce à toi / grâce à vous / grâce à l'aide de son professeur / grâce à mes parents / grâce à ses compétences / grâce à votre travail et à votre détermination.

Language practice 2

1 Complete the following sentences, choosing à cause de or grâce à as appropriate.

a .... ta recommandation, j'ai découvert une écrivaine intéressante.
b J'ai mal dormi .... bruit.
c .... Jean-Luc, je n'ai pas bien travaillé hier.
d J'ai passé une journée merveilleuse .... toi.

Rendre can be used with an adjective to express causation: je rends mon grand-père heureux (*I make my grandfather happy*).
Faire can also be used to express causation when it is combined with an infinitive: je fais ronronner mon chat quand je le caresse (*I make my cat purr when I stroke him*).

2 Complete the sentences using the verbs in the box—but read the tip box above first!

rendent	faites	fait	rend	rends

a Ce genre de musique me .... dormir.
b Trop de caféine .... Julie nerveuse.
c Mes collègues me .... heureuse quand ils sourient (*smile*).
d J'espère que je ne te .... pas triste avec mes histoires.
e Vous me .... rire avec votre histoire de fantôme (*ghost*) !

16.06

3 Now play the conversation again and play Eva's role. Speak in the pauses. Try not to refer to the text.

CULTURE POINT 2

Montréal *Montreal*

Avec ses 1,78 millions d'habitants, Montréal est la plus grande ville francophone d'Amérique, et la deuxième ville du Canada, après Toronto. Elle se situe (*is located*) au sud de la province du Québec, au bord du fleuve (*along the river*) Saint-Laurent. Son nom vient du navigateur français Jacques Cartier, qui l'a nommée Mont Royal, mais avant la colonisation française, l'île de Montréal était habitée par les autochtones de la nation Kanien'kehá:ka, les Mohawks. En mohawk, Montréal s'appelle Tiohtià:ke, qui signifie lieu où les nations et les fleuves s'unissent et se divisent (*place where the nations and the rivers join and divide*).

Montréal est une métropole multiculturelle qui attire (*that attracts*) des visiteurs du monde entier. Si vous visitez Montréal pour la première fois, commencez par l'emblématique parc du Mont-Royal, que les Montréalais appellent « la montagne » et montez jusqu'au sommet (*summit*) pour prendre un égoportrait (un selfie) depuis le belvédère de Kondiaronk. Ensuite, allez arpenter les rues (*roam the streets*) du Vieux-Montréal et du Vieux-Port pour mieux comprendre l'histoire de Montréal, et profitez-en (*take the opportunity*) pour visiter les nombreuses galeries d'art. Pour découvrir la gastronomie de Montréal, allez faire un tour au marché Jean-Talon, dans le quartier de la Petite-Italie ou allez manger un bagel ou un sandwich au smoked meat au Plateau, le quartier branché (*trendy*) de Montréal, connu pour (*known for*) ses maisons colorées et ses escaliers en spirale, mais aussi pour ses nuits animées. Pour vous déplacer, prenez le métro ou le bus. La ville de Montréal s'engage dans (*commits to*) la décarbonation des transports et électrise (*electrifies*) son parc de bus avec l'objectif d'atteindre (*of reaching*) zéro émission nette dans les transports en 2040 et une ville carboneutre d'ici à 2050 (*by 2050*). Et en allant prendre le métro vous découvrirez la ville souterraine (*underground*), un réseau piétonnier (*pedestrian network*) de 33 kilomètres qui relie (*links*) les stations de métro et les galeries commerciales. Bon séjour à Montréal !

Visitez le site web du bureau du tourisme de Montréal. Que pouvez-vous faire cette semaine ?

VOCABULARY BUILDER 2

Look at the words and phrases. Then listen and try to imitate the pronunciation of the speakers.

EXPRESSIONS QUÉBÉCOISES	*EXPRESSIONS FROM QUEBEC*
avoir la falle basse	*to be depressed*
se faire brasser le Canadien	*to be told off*
avoir les mains pleines de pouces	*to be all fingers and thumbs*
beurrer épais	*to exaggerate/lay it on thick*
échapper le balon	*to drop the ball/not be good enough*
être aux petits oiseaux	*to be on cloud nine*
la cerise sur le sundae	*the cherry on top of the cake*
tomber en amour	*to fall in love*

EXPRESSIONS	*EXPRESSIONS*
aménager/réaménager un espace	*furbish/refurbish a space*
faire dialoguer plusieurs cultures	*bring several cultures into dialogue*
fonder/inaugurer une galerie	*found/inaugurate a gallery*
organiser un défilé/une parade	*organise a procession/a parade*
dresser une liste	*draw up a list*

Quebec French, or québécois, differs at times from other varieties of the French language. In France, *fall in love* is tomber amoureux, and in Quebec, tomber en amour, which is closer to a translation from English. To reply to someone who says merci in France, you would say, je vous en prie, or de rien, while in Quebec, you would say bienvenue, a literal translation of the English *welcome*. Some aspects of the pronunciation also differ, but French speakers from Belgium, France, or Switzerland can understand québécois and vice versa.

Vocabulary practice 2

Match an expression from Quebec with a possible meaning in French:

1 Il a la falle basse.
2 Il a échappé le ballon qui lui était destiné.
3 Il est aux petits oiseaux.
4 la cerise sur le sundae.

a Il n'est pas à la hauteur.
b Il est déprimé.
c Le bouquet ; le comble
d Il est aux anges. (Il est heureux.)

Pronunciation practice 2

Listen to this recording of a French Canadian interview with a popular filmmaker and notice how the pronunciation and intonation differ from the recordings you have listened to before this unit.

CONVERSATION 2

À la découverte de Montréal *Discovering Montreal*

16.08

1 Here are a few words and expressions to help you understand the conversation.

Je me régale !	*I'm having an amazing time!*	plein de	*loads of, lots of*
		notamment	*namely, especially*
incroyable	*unbelievable*	l'art Autochtone	*First Nations art*
J'en ai entendu parler.	*I've heard about it.*	entièrement	*entirely*
des origines irlandaises	*Irish origins/roots*	bien sûr	*of course*

16.09

2 Listen to the conversation without looking at the text. Then listen to the conversation again and read the text.

Assia is talking online with Jo and telling her about how much she is enjoying getting to know Montreal, and Jo can't wait to go and meet up with her.

Assia Montréal est une ville formidable, je me régale ! Cette semaine, je suis allée au défilé de la Saint-Patrick ! C'était incroyable !

Jo Ah oui, ça me dit quelque chose ; j'ai lu un article sur la vie culturelle de Montréal qui parle justement de ce défilé.

Assia Tu savais que 12 % des Canadiens ont des origines irlandaises ? La parade de la Saint-Patrick de Montréal est une tradition qui remonte à 1824, et depuis 1928, l'événement est organisé par Les Sociétés irlandaises unies de Montréal. Les photos que j'en ai prises sont très belles ! Et les gens que j'ai rencontrés étaient très sympathiques !

Jo J'ai hâte de les voir.

Assia J'ai aussi découvert le musée des beaux-arts de Montréal qui a été fondé en 1860 et qui met en valeur les œuvres du patrimoine du Canada et du Québec, notamment l'art autochtone. On en parle peut-être dans l'article que tu as lu ?

Jo Ah oui, si je me souviens bien il est question d'une nouvelle galerie des « Arts du Tout-Monde. »

Assia C'est ça ! Elle a été inaugurée en 2019. Les espaces ont été entièrement réaménagés et font dialoguer des œuvres et des artistes du monde entier sur le thème du vivre ensemble. Ça m'a beaucoup plu !

Jo	Cool ! On pourra y aller ensemble quand je viendrai te voir ?
Assia	Bien sûr, je vais te préparer un programme de rêve ! Le week-end prochain, je vais à Québec. Je veux voir les œuvres de Jean Paul Lemieux et de Madeleine Des Rosiers. Il s'agit de deux artistes du siècle dernier que j'ai découverts récemment. Leurs portraits et leurs paysages me touchent beaucoup.
Jo	Ah tu sais, moi je préfère l'art abstrait. Tu es allée au Musée d'art contemporain de Montréal ?
Assia	Pas encore, mais c'est sur ma liste !

3 Answer the questions.

a What is the Montreal Museum of Fine Art especially famous for?
b Why is Assia going to go to Quebec?
c What museum has she not yet visited in Montreal?

LANGUAGE BUILDER 3

Language discovery 3

Assia says two things about the gallery: elle a été inaugurée en 2019 (*it was inaugurated/opened in 2019*), and les espaces ont été entièrement réaménagés (*the spaces were entirely refurbished*).

Why does the past participle inaugurée have a feminine singular ending, and why does the past participle réaménagés have a masculine plural one?

La voix passive *The passive voice*

Imagine a cat-and-mouse encounter that has the following outcome: le chat mange la souris (*the cat eats the mouse*). The structure here is *subject* (le chat) + *verb* (mange) + *object* (la souris). Another way of saying the same thing is: la souris est mangée par le chat (*the mouse is eaten by the cat*). In this second version, la souris is a subject that is having something done to it. This is an example of the *passive voice*. Whenever the passive is used in French, the past participle agrees with the *subject* (not the object) of the verb.

De nombreux touristes visitent la ville de Montréal chaque année
→ La ville de Montréal est visitée par de nombreux touristes chaque année.

La ministre inaugure la nouvelle station de métro
→ La nouvelle station de métro est inaugurée par la ministre.

The passive can be used across all the different tenses. For instance, ***the mouse was eaten by the cat*** = la souris a été mangée par le chat. Here, the tense used is le passé composé. To make a passive sentence in this tense, use être in le passé composé and add a past participle. As before, the past participle (mangée) agrees with the subject (la souris).

De nombreux touristes ont visité la ville de Montréal cette année
→ La ville de Montréal a été visitée par de nombreux touristes cette année.

La ministre a inauguré la nouvelle station de métro
→ La nouvelle station de métro a été inaugurée par la ministre.

To form the imperfect passive, use être in the imparfait (e.g. j'étais, tu étais) and add a past participle:

Souvent, dans notre immeuble, l'électricité était coupée. — *Often, in our building, the electricity was cut.*

Language practice 3

Change each active sentence below into a passive one.

Example: Une amie d'Assia a pris la photo qui a gagné le prix du festival.
→ *La photo qui a gagné le prix du festival a été prise par une amie d'Assia.*

a L'archéologue découvre un trésor de l'époque romaine.
Un trésor de l'époque romaine ....

b Les pompiers aident les victimes des inondations.
Les victimes des inondations ....

c Les journalistes ont interviewé la présidente.
La présidente ....

LANGUAGE BUILDER 4

Language discovery 4

16.10

Listen to the conversation again and repeat each line in the pauses.

1 Look at the following phrases from Conversation 2:

a les photos que j'en ai prises sont très belles (*the photos I took of it are beautiful*);

b les gens que j'ai rencontrés étaient très sympathiques (*the people I met were very nice*);

c On en parle dans l'article que tu as lu ? (*Did they talk about it in the article you read?*)

d Il s'agit de deux artistes du siècle dernier que j'ai découverts récemment (*They are two artists from last century whom I recently discovered*).

Can you allocate a gender (masc./fem.) and a number (sing./pl.) to each of the past participles used above? **a** prises ; **b** rencontrés ; **c** lu ; **d** découverts ?

2 Can you figure out why each of the four past participles above has an ending that is masculine/feminine and singular/plural? Complete the following rule of thumb by indicating whether a or b is correct or incorrect:

The past participle (PP) agrees with the direct object (DO) of the verb:

a when the DO comes *before* the PP.

b when the DO comes *after* the PP.

Concernant le participe passé *Concerning the past participle*

Here are two mutually related sentences:

a Paul a offert des fleurs à sa mère. — *Paul gave some flowers to his mother.*

b Les fleurs étaient belles. — *The flowers were beautiful.*

These could be combined as follows:

c Les fleurs que Paul a offertes à sa mère étaient belles. — *The flowers that Paul gave to his mother were beautiful.*

Notice that in sentence (c) above the feminine plural ending -es has been added to the past participle offert. This is because of the following agreement rule, which applies when you are using the perfect tense (with verbs conjugated with avoir).

The past participle (PP) agrees with the direct object (DO) of the verb when the DO comes before the PP.

In the examples the DO in sentence (a) was des fleurs, which came after the past participle offert (so there was no agreement). But in sentence (c), the DO les fleurs comes before the past participle. Therefore, offert must agree with the les fleurs and becomes offertes (feminine plural).

La pièce que j'ai lue était fascinante. *The play that I read was fascinating.*

The PP lue agrees with the DO la pièce because la pièce comes first.

Les gens que j'ai rencontrés étaient sympathiques. *The people I met were nice.*

The PP rencontrés agrees with the DO les gens because les gens comes first.

In the following sentence, the past participle vu agrees with the (preceding) direct object le film: Le film que j'ai vu était très bien (*The film that I saw was very good*). But we do not need to change the past participle vu to reflect this. It is only when the preceding direct object is feminine and/or plural that we need to change the spelling of the past participle.

Language practice 4

1 Using the relative pronoun que, combine the two short sentences into a longer one. Make any necessary agreements.

Example: J'ai mangé une glace. Elle était délicieuse. → *La glace que j'ai mangée était délicieuse.*

a J'ai acheté des fleurs. Elles étaient belles.
Les fleurs .... étaient belles.

b Nous avons trouvé du pain près de chez nous. Il était bon.
Le pain .... près de chez nous était bon.

c Tu as vu sa nouvelle maison. Elle est assez grande.
Sa nouvelle maison, ... , est assez grande.

d Vous avez choisi des lunettes. Elles sont chics.
Les lunettes .... sont chics.

16.11

2 Listen to Conversation 2 again and play the role of Assia (in the pauses) telling Jo what you have already done in Montreal. What would you have done that Assia did not do?

SKILL BUILDER

1 You have read a number of conversations in this book. Now it is your turn to write one. Read the context for the conversation and write what you think Assia and Jo would say.

Assia et Jo parlent de Montréal et de leurs projets. Jo a une liste de clubs de musique que son oncle lui a donnée lors d'un de ses précédents voyages au Canada. Assia, elle, voudrait visiter la Maison de la Photo de Québec, créée en 2019. Elle aimerait aussi voir les photos de Charles-Frédérick Ouellet, lauréat du prestigieux concours World Press Photo. Jo souhaite également accompagner Assia à ses cours car elle n'a jamais étudié à l'extérieur de la France et s'intéresse à connaître un système éducatif différent.

2 Complete the sentences using ce qui or ce que as appropriate.

a Vous avez gagné le premier prix, ... est formidable ! Bravo !

b Paul a raté le couscous, ... m'énerve !

c .... j'aime surtout, c'est la vie de campagne.

d .... m'attire dans ce projet, c'est son originalité.

e .... je regrette, c'est d'avoir envoyé le courriel sans le relire.

f .... nous ravit surtout dans ce film, c'est le décor.

g Nous avons fait .... nous avons pu pour vous.

h Nous avons fait .... était nécessaire.

3 Complete the short narrative with some of the expressions in the box. Not all expressions will be used.

grâce à	à cause de	fait
je sais	je ne sais pas	ce n'est pas possible

Selon les autres membres du chœur, je suis très organisé et toujours ponctuel. Ça me **a** .... rire car ce n'est pas du tout vrai. Hier soir, par exemple, j'ai oublié de mettre mon réveil. **b** .... cet oubli, je ne me suis pas réveillé ce matin. Heureusement, **c** .... mon amie Fatima, j'ai pu arriver à l'heure à la répétition. Très gentiment, elle m'a proposé de passer me prendre en voiture et de me déposer au théâtre. Ouf, je suis arrivé à 9 heures. Fatima est la meilleure des amies, **d** .... qu'on peut toujours compter sur elle.

4 In a and b below, combine the two sentences to make one longer one, paying attention to agreements.

Example: Elle m'a offert des roses pour mon anniversaire. J'aime ces roses.
→ *J'aime les roses qu'elle m'a offertes pour mon anniversaire.*

a J'aime les romans de Jules Verne. Il m'a offert des romans de Jules Verne à Noël.
J'aime les romans de Jules Verne ....

b Mes parents aiment en particulier la musique canadienne. Je leur ai offert la collection de Jean Leloup.
Mes parents aiment la collection de Jean Leloup ....

TEST YOURSELF

Choose the correct answer.

a Le festival interceltique de Lorient .... par la ministre de la culture. (*a inauguré/a été inauguré*)

b Le nouveau film de Jacques Audiard .... par les critiques et le public. (*a acclamé/a été acclamé*)

c La cathédrale Notre-Dame de Paris .... chaque année par des millions de visiteurs. (*a visité/est visitée*)

d .... la bourse Fulbright, Amina a pu étudier une année dans une université américaine. (*Grâce à/À cause de*)

e Nous n'avons pas pu assister au match de rugby .... la voiture était en panne. (*à cause de/parce que*)

f .... j'aime le plus dans les voyages, c'est la découverte de nouvelles cultures. (*Ce qui/Ce que*)

g .... me plait dans mon travail, c'est d'être en contact avec le public. (*Ce qui/Ce que*)

h La fête surprise que ses amis ont .... pour son anniversaire était très réussie. (*organisé/organisée*)

i Les boucles d'oreille que tu as .... à ta mère sont très originales. (*offert/offertes*)

Remember to use **My review** and **My takeaway** to assess your progress and reflect on your learning experience.

In this lesson you will learn how to:
- Relay what others have said
- Express the consequences of actions
- Make a hypothesis

Des réunions et des rencontres

My study plan

I plan to work with Unit 17
- ○ Every day
- ○ Twice a week
- ○ Other ________

I plan to study for
- ○ 5–15 minutes
- ○ 15–30 minutes
- ○ 30–45+ minutes

My progress tracker

Day / Date	Listening	Speaking	Reading	Writing	Conversation
	○	○	○	○	○
	○	○	○	○	○
	○	○	○	○	○
	○	○	○	○	○
	○	○	○	○	○
	○	○	○	○	○
	○	○	○	○	○

My goals

What do you want to be able to do or say in French when you complete this unit?

		Done
1	....	○
2	....	○
3	....	○

My review

SELF CHECK

	I can ...
●	... tell you what someone else has said.
●	... indicate that something will happen once something else has taken place.
●	... talk about things happening at the same time.

CULTURE POINT 1

L'immeuble *The apartment building*

De nombreux auteurs et cinéastes (*Numerous authors and filmmakers*) choisissent un immeuble comme décor pour leur histoire. Dans son roman ***La Vie mode d'emploi***, George Perec raconte la vie, entre 1875 et 1975, des habitants d'un immeuble. Situé au 11 rue Simon-Crybellier, une rue parisienne imaginaire, l'immeuble de dix étages de la cave jusqu'aux combles (*from cellar to attic*) est au centre d'une multitude d'histoires. Ce roman colossal, que Perec a mis dix années à écrire, est un immense puzzle que le lecteur doit reconstituer au fil des 99 chapitres qui le composent (*across the 99 chapters which form the book*). Cette œuvre publiée en 1978 est considérée comme le chef d'œuvre de George Perec et a inspiré de nombreux écrivains et artistes.

L'Élégance du hérisson, de Muriel Barbery, raconte l'histoire de Renée Michel, concierge d'un immeuble parisien, qui lit Marcel Proust et Léon Tolstoï en cachette (*in secret*), pour ne pas attirer l'attention des habitants de l'immeuble (qui la croient inculte). Ce roman paru en 2006 (*published in 2006*), a connu un grand succès en France et dans le monde, et a été adapté au cinéma par la réalisatrice Mona Achache.

Dans ***La Femme qui fuit***, Anaïs Barbeau-Lavalette raconte la vie de sa grand-mère, Suzanne Meloche, artiste et femme libre, qui rejette les valeurs traditionnelles de façon radicale, abandonne ses enfants, et consacre sa vie à la poésie et à la peinture. La partie centrale du roman se déroule (*takes place*) dans un immeuble de Montréal, à la fin des années 1940.

Enfin, dans un autre registre, mais toujours à Montréal, ***Paul en appartement***, de Michel Rabagliati, raconte l'installation de Paul et Lucie dans leur appartement du Plateau Mont-Royal. Paul est le personnage central d'une série (*of a series*) de bandes dessinées qui a reçu de nombreux prix littéraires. Cette série célèbre a été traduite dans de nombreuses langues.

Regardez la vidéo suivante. Qui sont les deux personnes que vous entendez ? Quelle est leur relation ?

VOCABULARY BUILDER 1

17.01

Look at the words and phrases and complete the missing English words and expressions. Then listen and try to imitate the pronunciation of the speakers.

LE VIVRE ENSEMBLE	*TOGETHERNESS*
un accord, être d'accord	*agreement, to agree*
un avis, donner son avis	*opinion, to give one's opinion*
une copropriété	*apartment building (with shared ownership)*
un syndic de copropriété	*residents' association*
une décision commune	*collective decision/group decision*
une discussion	....
un expert/une experte	....
une expertise initiale	*initial assessment (by an expert)*
une contre-expertise	*second opinion (by an expert)*
un président, une présidente	*chairperson*
une proposition	*proposal/suggestion*
une réunion	*meeting*
une société	....

EXPRESSIONS	*EXPRESSIONS*
Il faut prévoir des travaux.	*We must expect/plan for some building work.*
L'ambiance est assez tendue.	*The atmosphere is quite tense.*
Je te rappelle les termes du contrat.	*I remind you of the terms of the contract.*
Ça se complique !	*It's getting complicated!*
Nous sommes tous d'accord.	*We all agree.*
Tout se passe bien.	*Everything's going well.*

Vocabulary practice 1

a Lorsqu'un immeuble est vieux, il faut souvent .... des travaux.

b Est-ce que tout le monde est content ? Non, l'ambiance est assez ....

c Tout se passe sans problème ? Non, ça se .... !

d Est-ce que tout le monde est d' .... ? Sinon, on doit voter.

e Il faut .... les termes du contrat aux habitants de l'immeuble.

Pronunciation practice 1

17.02

Read through the phrases and try to figure out how to pronounce them. Then listen to the recording and imitate the pronunciation of the speaker.

le premier juin	le premier enfant	la première enfant
les premiers enfants	les premières enfants	
le dernier jour du mois	le dernier homme	la dernière femme
les derniers hommes	les dernières femmes	

CONVERSATION 1

Réunion du syndic de corpropriété *Meeting of the residents' association*

17.03

1 Here are a few words and expressions to help you understand the conversation.

une saga	*saga*	retarder	*delay*
un compte-rendu	*report*	au total	*in total*
remplacer	*replace*	rapidement	*quickly*
nécessaire	*necessary*	Aïe !	*Oh dear!*
durer	*to go on; to last*	parvenir à	*reach*

17.04

2 Listen to the conversation without looking at the text. Then listen to the conversation again and read the text.

Charles's new friends Andries and Erna have attended a residents' meeting to discuss the problem with the elevator in their apartment building. At the café, Charles and Eva ask the couple all about it.

Charles Alors cette réunion du syndic de copropriété, ça s'est bien passé ?

Erna Oh là là ! L'ambiance était tendue, et il y a eu des discussions animées.

Charles Ah bon ! Qu'est-ce qui s'est passé ?

Andries La saga de l'ascenseur continue... La présidente, Madame Dubois, a lu le compte-rendu de la dernière visite du technicien, qui recommande de remplacer l'ascenseur. Tu es au courant, Eva ?

Eva	Ah non, je ne savais pas, mais je ne suis pas surprise, il est constamment en panne, cet ascenseur !
Andries	Oui, mais notre voisine du deuxième, Madame van Eck, a répondu qu'elle préférait demander une contre-expertise à une autre société d'ascenseurs avant de prendre une décision.
Charles	Ah ! Ça se complique.
Erna	Oui ! Madame Willems a dit qu'elle était d'accord avec Madame van Eck, et qu'un deuxième avis d'expert était nécessaire. Mais ensuite, les Peeters, qui habitent au dernier étage, ont dit que la situation avait déjà trop duré et qu'un deuxième avis d'expert allait retarder les travaux. La présidente a rappelé que ces six derniers mois, l'ascenseur avait été en panne plus de 40 jours au total.
Eva	Et vous, qu'est-ce que vous avez dit ?
Andries	On a dit qu'on était d'accord avec la proposition initiale de remplacer l'ascenseur rapidement ; mais comme tous les membres de la copropriété n'étaient pas d'accord, il a été décidé de demander un deuxième avis. Et là, certains ont commencé à s'énerver et à la fin, on était tous tellement mécontents qu'on a décidé de mettre fin à la réunion. Madame Dubois convoquera une nouvelle réunion dans quelques semaines.
Charles	Aïe, aïe, aïe ! C'est difficile de parvenir à un accord.

3 Answer the questions.

a According to Erna, what was the atmosphere like at the residents' association meeting?

b What was the main subject reportedly discussed at the meeting?

c What recommendation was contained in the report read out by the president?

d On what point did the Peeters disagree with Mme van Eck and Mme Willems?

e Why did the meeting end?

LANGUAGE BUILDER 1

Language discovery 1

In Conversation 1, Andries tells Charles and Eva what other people said: Madame van Eck a répondu qu'elle préférait demander une contre-expertise *(Madame van Eck answered that she prefered to ask for a second opinion).*

Andries could have reported this opinion in a slightly different form by saying: Madame van Eck a répondu : « Je préfère demander une contre-expertise ». To put this in grammatical terms, we can say that Andries could have used direct speech, but instead he chose to use indirect speech to convey what Madame van Eck said at the meeting.

1 Can you spot the four remaining contributions to the meeting that are reported in indirect speech by Andries and Erna? These were made by:

- **a** Mme Willems
- **b** the Peeters
- **c** the chair of the meeting
- **d** Erna and Andries themselves

2 Can you figure out how the indirect speech is formed?

Le discours direct/indirect *Direct and indirect speech*

Let's examine these two sentences which convey the same information in different ways and focus on three key aspects of the transformations that occur when we use indirect speech instead of direct speech

Ma voisine dit : « l'ascenseur est encore en panne »

→ Ma voisine dit que l'ascenseur est encore en panne.

1 To relay what others say using the indirect speech, you need:

- a first clause: elle dit
- a conjunction, *to join the two clauses*: que
- a second clause: l'ascenseur est en panne.

2 When transforming direct speech to indirect speech, the subject of the second clause may change.

Ma voisine dit : « Je suis fatiguée de monter les escaliers »

→ Ma voisine dit qu'elle est fatiguée de monter les escaliers.

3 When relaying what someone said in the past tense, the tense of the second clause will change.

Hier, ma voisine a dit « Je suis fatiguée de monter les escaliers »

→ Ma voisine a dit qu'elle était fatiguée de monter les escaliers.

Language practice 1

1 Change the sentences from direct speech into indirect speech, using the present tense.

a Gabriel dit : « Si on veut acheter un ticket, c'est maintenant ou jamais. »
b Ma grand-mère nous dit toujours : « Il faut faire attention aux petits détails. »

2 Change the sentences from direct speech into indirect speech, using past tenses.

a La semaine dernière, tu m'as dit : « Tu dois voir le dernier film de Xavier Dolan. »
b Je les ai prévenus : « Vous allez manquer votre train ! »

3 Change the sentences from indirect speech into direct speech. Add s'il te plaît or s'il vous plaît if appropriate.

a Maman m'a rappelé que les bonbons étaient réservés aux enfants !
b Jean-Luc m'a prévenu qu'Erika ne mangeait pas de viande.
c Je dis à mes invités qu'ils peuvent garder leurs chaussures en entrant chez moi.
d Je leur ai demandé s'ils pouvaient apporter des baguettes pour le pique-nique.

LANGUAGE BUILDER 2

Language discovery 2

Listen to the conversation again and repeat each line in the pauses.

You have already learned to talk about causation in French, for instance by using parce que, à cause de, and grâce à. In Conversation 1, Andries recounts the end of the somewhat stormy meeting he had attended as follows: on était tellement mécontents qu'on a décidé de terminer la réunion (*people were so unhappy that they decided to end the meeting*).

How would you describe the purpose of the underlined section of that sentence—do you think it expresses a cause or a consequence?

Cause et conséquence *Cause and consequence*

You remember that the cause is the reason which explains why/how something happened: Thomas n'est pas allé à l'école aujourd'hui parce qu'il était malade. *(Thomas was sick and that explains why he did not go to school.)*

The consequence is the result or the effect of something which happened before, or of a previous situation: Thomas était malade, alors il est resté à la maison.

Amelia n'a pas encore son permis de conduire, donc elle ne peut utiliser la voiture de ses parents.

In those two sentences we have a cause followed by a consequence.

The table below contains some sample sentences, with translations of the conjunctions. In the final column, we have indicated which ones imply causation only, and which ones introduce an idea of consequence.

Elle avait 20 minutes de retard si bien qu'elle a raté son train	si bien que : *and so*	*consequence*
Puisque tu aimes ça, prends-en encore	puisque : *since*	*cause*
Il a fait du bruit en rentrant hier soir, alors il nous a réveillés.	alors : *therefore; so*	*consequence*
Comme les pommes étaient mûres, je les ai mangées.	comme : *as; since*	*cause*
Nous avons terminé la réunion en avance, et donc nous avons pu rentrer plus tôt à la maison	donc : *so*	*consequence*

Language practice 2

1 Fill in the gaps using the translation as a guide.

Example: Elle chante tellement fort qu'on l'entend dehors. *She is singing so loudly that she can be heard outside.*

a Nous marchons .... personne ne peut nous rattraper.
We are walking so quickly that no one can catch up with us.
b Il téléphone .... nous ne répondons plus.
He phones so often that we don't answer anymore.
c Il est .... il pleure de joie.
He is so happy that he is crying with joy.
d Elles boivent .... elles n'arrivent pas à dormir.
They drink so much coffee that they don't manage to fall asleep.

2 Choose the correct word to complete the sentences

a Elle donne des cours le soir donc/puisque elle n'est pas disponible pour sortir avec ses amis.
b Ils étaient fatigués parce qu'/alors ils sont allés se coucher
c Nous sommes tombés parce que/si bien que nous n'avons pas vu la déformation du trottoir
d Il a plu toute la journée comme/si bien que nous sommes trempés.

17.06

3 Now play the conversation again and play Andries's role. Speak in the pauses. Try not to refer to the text.

CULTURE POINT 2

Les langues officielles du Canada *Canada's official languages*

L'anglais et le français sont les langues officielles du Canada, mais les provinces canadiennes comme la Colombie-Britannique, le Manitoba ou le Québec n'ont qu'une seule (*have only one*) langue officielle, l'anglais ou le français. Au Québec c'est la Loi 101, ou la Charte de la langue française qui a fait du français la langue officielle (*which made French the official language*) en 1977. Les francophones qui vivent dans les provinces anglophones, comme les fransaskois (*francophones of Saskatchewan*) ou les franco-albertains (*the francophones of Alberta*), ont accès à l'éducation et à d'autres services en français. De même, les anglophones peuvent scolariser (*school*) leurs enfants en anglais au Québec. La province du Nouveau-Brunswick est bilingue français/anglais. Il y a plus de soixante-dix langues autochtones (*aboriginal languages*) au Canada, dont le cri, le mitchif, le mi'kmaq, ou l'inuktitut. Le parlement canadien a adopté en 2019 une nouvelle loi pour promouvoir (*to promote*) et préserver ces langues. Au Yukon, chacun a le droit d'employer le français, l'anglais, ou une langue autochtone du Yukon dans les débats de l'Assemblée législative. Les Territoires du Nord-Ouest ont onze langues officielles. La province de l'Ontario a voté une loi en vertu de laquelle (*by virtue of which*) les établissements scolaires autochtones peuvent décerner des diplômes. Le Collège Unama'ki offre des cours post-secondaires aux communautés micmaques de Nouvelle-Écosse depuis 1974. Enfin, pour terminer ce panorama linguistique du Canada, ajoutons que de nombreuses autres langues sont parlées au Canada. Selon le recensement de 2021 (*according to the census of 2021*), les plus parlées sont le mandarin, le panjabi, le cantonais, l'espagnol, l'arabe et le tagalog, mais on parle aussi des langues telles que (*such as*) le portugais, le polonais, le tamoul, le persan, l'ukrainien, ou encore le gaélique irlandais et le gaélique écossais.

Regardez ce document de Statistique Canada. Combien de personnes parlent mandarin ? Espagnol ? Arabe ?

VOCABULARY BUILDER 2

Look at the words and phrases and provide the missing English words and expressions. Then listen and try to imitate the pronunciation of the speakers.

LANGUE FRANÇAISE, LANGUE MONDIALE	***FRENCH, A GLOBAL LANGUAGE***
l'Académie française	*the French Academy*
l'Alliance française	....
un pays francophone	*francophone country*
un cours de langue	*language course*
s'exprimer/se perfectionner	*to express oneself/improve (in a language)*
le français classique/quotidien/soutenu	*classical/everyday/elevated French*
le franglais	....
un gallicisme	*Gallicism (= English corrupted by French)*
l'interférence linguistique	*linguistic interference*

EXPRESSIONS	***EXPRESSIONS***
parler sa langue maternelle	....
Nous sommes bilingues français/anglais.	....

Vocabulary practice 2

Complete the following sentences, using the Vocabulary builder.

a .... est un centre de la culture française et francophone.

b Le fait d'être .... français/anglais devient normal dans certaines provinces du Canada.

c Lorsque les francophones apprennent d'autres langues, ils n'évitent pas toujours les ....

d Lorsqu'on est bilingue, on peut être sujet aux interférences ....

Pronunciation practice 2

Diane Dufresne is a French Canadian singer whose québécois songs are instantly recognizable in Canada. Find and listen to her 'Hymne à la beauté du monde' ; you can find recordings as well as the lyrics online. After listening to the song, read the lyrics out loud and imitate the original intonation.

CONVERSATION 2

Projet de voyage *Travel plans*

1 Here are a few words and expressions to help you understand the conversation.

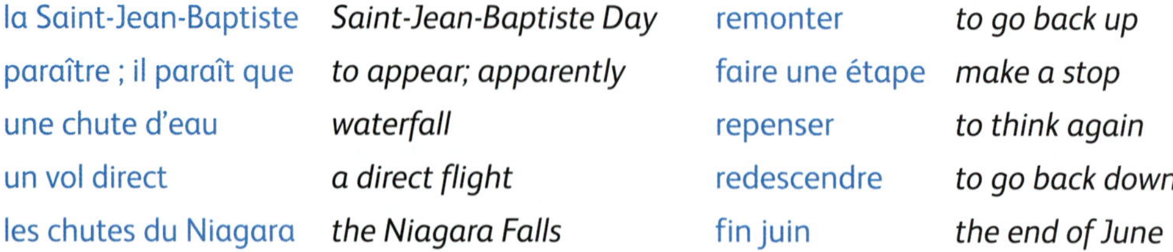

la Saint-Jean-Baptiste	*Saint-Jean-Baptiste Day*	remonter	*to go back up*
paraître ; il paraît que	*to appear; apparently*	faire une étape	*make a stop*
une chute d'eau	*waterfall*	repenser	*to think again*
un vol direct	*a direct flight*	redescendre	*to go back down*
les chutes du Niagara	*the Niagara Falls*	fin juin	*the end of June*

2 Listen to the conversation without looking at the text. Then listen to the conversation again and read the text.

Assia and Jo finalize their plans for Jo to come and visit Assia in Canada. Jo might just not be telling Assia everything about the trip.

Assia Alors, tu viens me voir quand ?

Jo Je pensais venir fin juin.

Assia Super ! Tu seras là pour la Saint-Jean-Baptiste, c'est la fête nationale du Québec. Il paraît qu'il y a des concerts partout en ville ; on m'a dit que c'était très sympa. On peut passer quelques jours à Montréal, aller faire un tour à Québec, et finir par Toronto, pour voir Ali et Marc.

Jo Ah oui ! Ça fait longtemps qu'on ne s'est pas vus ! Et si on commençait par Toronto ? J'ai vu qu'il y avait un vol direct depuis Paris.

Assia Ben oui, pourquoi pas. Si on a le temps, on pourra aller voir les chutes du Niagara, et en remontant vers Montréal, on pourra faire une étape à Ottawa.

Jo Excellente idée.

Assia Tu peux rester jusqu'au premier juillet ?

Jo Oui, oui, pourquoi, il se passe quoi le premier juillet ?

Assia C'est le jour de la fête nationale du Canada. En y repensant, il vaut mieux commencer par le Québec, et en redescendant à Toronto, on peut participer aux célébrations du premier juillet à Ottawa.

Jo OK, je vais chercher un vol Paris–Montréal avec un retour Toronto–Paris.

Assia Parfait ! Je commence à regarder les hébergements et les transports. On peut prendre le bus ou le train.

Jo Si c'est possible, je préfère le train.

Assia Oui, oui, je sais. Je regarde tout ça et je te dis.

3 Answer the questions.

- **a** Toward the end of which month is Jo intending to come and visit Assia?
- **b** In what province of Canada is Saint-Jean-Baptiste Day treated as a national festival?
- **c** In what Canadian city are Ali and Marc currently living?
- **d** Why does Jo suggest they start their tour in Toronto, rather than Montréal?
- **e** Having initially agreed with Jo's suggestion, why does Assia change her mind?
- **f** What two flight routes will Jo try to book?

LANGUAGE BUILDER 3

Language discovery 3

Read these sentences:

Ben oui, pourquoi pas. Si on a le temps, on pourra aller voir les chutes du Niagara et en remontant vers Montréal, on pourra faire une étape à Ottawa.

En y repensant, il vaut mieux commencer par le Québec, et en redescendant à Toronto, on peut participer aux célébrations du premier juillet à Ottawa.

a What do the three underlined verbs have in common?

b How would you translate them?

Le participe présent *The present participle*

Remontant, repensant, and descendant are referred to as participes présents in French. Le participe présent is the equivalent to an *-ing* verb ending in English, but its usage is much more limited than in English. To form le participe présent in French, you need to do the following:

1. take the nous form of the present tense;
2. remove -ons ;
3. add -ant.

Look at these examples, using donner, finir, and prendre respectively:

a (nous) donnons	**b** donn-	**c** donnant
a (nous) finissons	**b** finiss-	**c** finissant
a (nous) prenons	**b** pren-	**c** prenant

The present participle is often used following en to mean *as/while*, *upon* or *by doing something*:

Elle souriait en racontant l'histoire.	*She smiled while she was telling the story.*
Ils ont ri en entendant la chute de la blague.	*They laughed on hearing the punch line of the joke.*
En ajoutant du beurre, on rend la sauce onctueuse.	*By adding butter you make the sauce smooth.*

You can also reinforce the simultaneity of the actions by using tout:

Emilio préparait le repas <u>tout en parlant</u> au téléphone avec sa mère.

> There are only three verbs whose present participle cannot be obtained from the present-tense nous form in the usual way: avoir (ayant), être (étant), and savoir (sachant).
>
> L'avocate l'a défendu en sachant qu'il était coupable. (*The lawyer defended him while knowing that he was guilty.*)

Language practice 3

1 Below you will find a list of infinitives. Write out the present participle. In each passage, the first one has been done for you.

a aller :	en <u>allant</u>		**e** monter :	en ....
b rendre :	en		**f** écrire :	en ....
c réussir :	en		**g** dire :	en ....
d dormir :	en		**h** montrer :	en ....

2 Transform each sentence into one where you use en + the present participle of the underlined verb. The first one is an example.

a Il ne faut pas téléphoner quand on <u>conduit</u>. *Il ne faut pas téléphoner en conduisant.*

b Il ne faut pas parler quand on <u>mange</u>. ....

c Il ne faut pas courir quand on <u>descend</u> l'escalier. ....

d J'aime lire et <u>écouter</u> de la musique. ....

e Il mange et il <u>regarde</u> la télévision en même temps. ....

LANGUAGE BUILDER 4

Language discovery 4

17.10

Listen to the conversation again and repeat each line in the pauses.

When planning Jo's trip to Canada, Assia suggests: Si on a le temps, on pourra aller voir les chutes du Niagara (*If we have the time, we will be able to go to see Niagara Falls*). This is a conditional sentence, referring to a hypothetical situation. It has two clauses—one is the si-clause (equivalent to an *if*-clause in English); the other is the main clause.

Now complete the following rule of thumb by choosing between a and b:

In general, in conditional sentences the verb in the si-clause and the verb in the main clause are **a** in the same tense; **b** in different tenses.

La concordance des temps *Tenses that go together*

In French, as in English, certain tenses tend to be used together when they both occur in a conditional sentence. Notice the example sentences below, which start with a si-clause (*if*-clause):

a Si tu apportes les oranges = *event A; present tense,*
j'apporterai les pommes = *event B; future tense.*
(If *you bring the oranges, I'll bring the apples.*)

b Si tu apportais les oranges = *event A; imparfait,*
j'apporterais les pommes = *event B; conditional.*
(*If you brought the oranges, I would bring the apples.*)

Notice that **a** when the si-clause is in the present tense, the verb in the next clause is generally in the future tense. Here are two examples:

S'il fait beau demain, nous irons à la mer.

Si tu finis à l'heure vendredi, nous pourrons partir en week-end directement après le travail.

Meanwhile, when the si-clause is in l'imparfait, the verb in the next clause is generally in the conditional form:

S'il faisait beau demain, nous irions à la mer.

Si tu finissais à l'heure vendredi, nous pourrions partir en week-end après le travail.

Language practice 4

1 Make conditional sentences with the correct tense combinations.

Example: Toi tu apporteras des pommes et moi je ferai une tarte aux pommes.
→ Si tu apportes des pommes, moi je ferai une tarte aux pommes.

a Jacques arrivera lundi et il pourra m'aider à tout préparer. → Si Jacques ....

b Léa oubliera son cartable (*satchel*). Elle se fera gronder par la professeure.
→ Si Léa ....

c Je viendrai écouter ton concert, et toi tu viendras écouter le mien. → Si je ....

d Tout le monde y participera, et l'événement aura un grand succès.
→ Si tout le monde ....

2 Fill in the gaps in the two passages below. In each passage, the first one is done for you.

Moi je prévois de faire une surprise à Léo, qui passe son permis de conduire aujourd'hui. S'il a (*avoir*) son permis, je l' **a** .... (*emmener*) dans le restaurant près de chez lui, où il **b** .... (*pouvoir*) manger son plat préféré. Mais s'il **c** .... (*échouer*), je **d** l' .... (*inviter*) au restaurant quand même, parce qu'il **e** .... (*avoir*) besoin d'être consolé.

Moi je prévois de faire une surprise à Léo, qui passe son permis de conduire aujourd'hui. S'il avait (*avoir*) son permis, je **f** l' .... (*emmener*) dans le restaurant près de chez lui, où il **g** .... (*pouvoir*) manger son plat préféré. Mais s'il **h** .... (échouer), je **i** l' .... (*inviter*) au restaurant quand même, parce qu'il **j** .... (*avoir*) besoin d'être consolé.

17.11

3 Now play the conversation again and play Assia's role. Speak in the pauses. Try not to refer to the text.

SKILL BUILDER

1 Transform the sentences into reported speech, using the present tense throughout.

Example: Charles : « Cette pizza est délicieuse. » (*dire*)
→ *Charles dit que cette pizza est délicieuse.*

a **Eva :** « et ma flammekueche est excellente. » (*répondre*) → Eva ....

b **Jo :** « nous faisons une surprise à Assia. » (*expliquer*) → Jo ....

c **Assia :** « il fait très chaud à Montréal en été. » (*dire*) → Assia ....

d **Jo :** « j'apporte mes vêtements d'été. » (*signaler*) → Jo ....

2 In the passage below, find the terms that indicate causation/consequence. Indicate which ones express causation and which ones express consequence.

Charles et Jo sont arrivés à 20 heures au café des arts. Assia leur avait dit que c'était pour prendre un apéritif avec Paul et Abou si bien qu'ils ne se sont doutés de rien. Comme les invités étaient cachés derrière le bar, Charles et Jo n'ont rien vu en arrivant. Ils se sont assis en terrasse et ont commandé un verre. Tout à coup, tous les invités sont arrivés en criant « surprise ! ». Ensuite le gâteau est arrivé. L'ambiance était si festive que les passants se sont arrêtés et se sont mis à chanter joyeux anniversaire avec les amis de Charles et Jo. A 21 heures, le patron du café a demandé à tout le monde de rentrer dans le bar, à cause du bruit. À la fin de la fête, Charles et Jo ont dit merci à leurs hôtes – étant jumeaux, ils préfèrent toujours fêter leur anniversaire ensemble.

3 Combine the sentences to indicate that the actions are simultaneous.

a Je te téléphone. Je regarde la télé.

b Ils font leurs devoirs. Ils écoutent de la musique.

c Nous préparons le déjeuner. Nous chantons.

4 Make conditional sentences with the correct tense combinations

Example: Elle apportera des plantes et moi je ferai du jardinage.
→ *Si elle <u>apporte</u> des plantes, moi je ferai du jardinage.*

a Isabelle et Florence arriveront dimanche et elles pourront m'aider à tout préparer.
Si Isabelle et Florence ....

b Laurent oubliera sa valise (*suitcase*). Il se fera gronder par son père.
Si Laurent ....

c Nous viendrons voir ton show, et toi tu viendras écouter notre concert.
Si nous ....

d Sylvie et Marine participeront au spectacle. J'y assisterai.
Si Sylvie et Marine ....

TEST YOURSELF

Complete the sentences below:

a Si tu arrives en retard, nous .... (*ne pas pouvoir*) finir notre travail à temps.

b Je prends ma douche en .... (*chanter*) mes chansons préférées.

c J'ai composé ce poème en .... (*penser*) à toi.

d Si nous voulons avoir des places pour ce spectacle, nous .... (*devoir*) les acheter le plus tôt possible.

e Maman dit qu'elle .... (*ne pas être*) disponible le week-end prochain.

f Si tu .... (*gagner*) au loto, qu'est-ce tu ferais ?

g .... (*puisque/donc*) tu aimes l'Écosse, je propose d'aller écouter Annie Lennox à Glasgow.

h Je viens de finir le dernier roman de Marie Nimier et je l'ai beaucoup aimé. Je m'y attendais .... (*alors/parce que*) j'aime tous ses romans.

i Notre restaurant habituel était complet .... (*si bien que/puisque*) nous avons commandé un plat à emporter et avons mangé à la maison.

Remember to use **My review** and **My takeaway** to assess your progress and reflect on your learning experience.

18

In this lesson you will learn how to:

- Express an opinion in a variety of ways
- Talk about contrasting things/opinions
- Learn more about complex sentences

La démocratie

My study plan

I plan to work with Unit 18

- ○ Every day
- ○ Twice a week
- ○ Other ____________

I plan to study for

- ○ 5–15 minutes
- ○ 15–30 minutes
- ○ 30–45+ minutes

My progress tracker

Day / Date	Listening	Speaking	Reading	Writing	Conversation
	○	○	○	○	○
	○	○	○	○	○
	○	○	○	○	○
	○	○	○	○	○
	○	○	○	○	○
	○	○	○	○	○
	○	○	○	○	○

My goals

What do you want to be able to do or say in French when you complete this unit?

		Done
1	....	○
2	....	○
3	....	○

My review

SELF CHECK

	I can ...
●	... express an opinion.
●	... contrast between two things or people.
●	... use dont and ce dont with confidence.

CULTURE POINT 1

Systèmes politiques *Political frameworks*

Le Canada, la Belgique et le Luxembourg sont des monarchies constitutionnelles (*constitutional monarchies*). La Suisse et la France sont des républiques. Le Canada, la Belgique ou la Suisse sont des États fédéraux. Dans ces pays, les compétences sont partagées entre les institutions fédérales et des parlements et gouvernements locaux (*power is shared between federal institutions, local parliaments, and governments*). Le nom des parlements varie : en France, la chambre basse (*the lower house*) est l'Assemblée nationale, au Canada, c'est la Chambre des communes, et en Belgique la Chambre des représentants. La chambre haute (*The upper house*) s'appelle le plus souvent le Sénat. Les parlementaires (*The members of parliament*) s'appellent le plus souvent *les députées et députés*, et *les sénatrices et sénateurs*. En France, la Constitution du 4 octobre 1958 régit (*holds sway over*) le fonctionnement des institutions de la cinquième République. Le chef de l'État est le président de la République ; il est élu tous les cinq ans au suffrage universel direct. La France compte des régions, des départements, et environ 35 000 communes, à la tête desquelles se trouve un maire ou une maire, qui préside le conseil municipal (*chairs the municipal council*). La Belgique actuelle est composée de trois communautés linguistiques et culturelles : la Communauté flamande, la Communauté française et la Communauté germanophone. Les 581 communes belges sont gérées par des bourgmestres (*Belgian municipalities are managed by mayors*). La structure de la Suisse comporte trois niveaux : la Confédération, les cantons (*counties*) et les communes. Il y a 26 cantons, qui ont leur propre constitution, ainsi que leur propre gouvernement et parlement. La Suisse est une démocratie directe. Les Suisses et Suissesses élisent (*elect*) des représentant·e·s au parlement fédéral, cantonal et communal, comme dans toute démocratie représentative ; mais ils et elles prennent également part régulièrement (*take part regularly*) à des votes d'initiative populaire et à des référendums.

Quels sont les droits politiques des citoyennes et des citoyens suisses ?

VOCABULARY BUILDER 1

Look at the words and phrases and provide the missing English words and expressions. Then listen and try to imitate the pronunciation of the speakers.

PARTICIPER À LA VIE POLITIQUE	*JOINING IN POLITICAL LIFE*
voter	....
un vote, une voix	*vote (general), vote (of an individual voter)*
compter les voix	*to count the votes*
remporter une élection	*win an election*
se prononcer sur	*express a view about*
une question concrète/abstraite	*concrete/abstract question*
la démocratie directe	....
des élections (fem. pl.) fréquentes/rares	*frequent/rare elections*
un citoyen/une citoyenne	*male citizen/female citizen*
une initiative populaire	*(in Switzerland) proposal for a law made by private citizens*
un référendum	....
une loi fédérale	*federal law*
participer directement	*to participate directly*
des abstentionnistes (masc./fem. pl.)	*people who don't use their vote*
avoir du mal à comprendre	*to find it hard to understand*

EXPRESSIONS	*EXPRESSIONS*
tu as raison/tort	*you are right/wrong*
Les gens se sentent concernés.	*People feel involved/affected.*
à mon avis, selon moi, à mon sens	*in my opinion, as I see it, to my mind*
Le vote devrait être obligatoire.	*Voting should be compulsory.*
Chaque voix compte.	*Every vote counts.*
C'est imprudent/de la folie.	*It's unwise/madness.*
une bonne chose	*a good thing*
je ne suis pas sûr que (+ subj.)	*I'm not sure that*
faire de la pédagogie	*educate people*
rêver	*to dream*
tu rêves	*you're not being realistic (lit. you're dreaming)*

Vocabulary practice 1

Complete the sentences with the words and phrases from Vocabulary builder 1.

a Dans la démocratie ...., les référendums sont fréquents.

b Ce n'est pas toujours le parti qui gagne le plus de voix qui .... l'élection.

c J'ai .... à comprendre les gens qui ne votent pas.

d Aux États-Unis, il y a des lois .... et les lois au niveau de chaque État.

e Dans une élection, bien évidemment (obviously), chaque .... compte.

CONVERSATION 1

Le vote *The vote*

18.02

1 Here are a few words and expressions to help you understand the conversation.

du pain de mie	*sandwich loaf*
une eau potable propre	*clean drinking water*
une alimentation saine	*healthy food*
modifier	*modify*

18.03

2 Listen to the conversation without looking at the text. Then listen to the conversation again and read the text.

As a citizen of Switzerland, Eva has just voted in a referendum. Charles is intrigued by the voting system in Switzerland, and they discuss this.

Charles Alors, ça y est, tu as voté ?

Eva Oui, c'est fait ! Par contre j'ai oublié d'acheter le pain en rentrant.

Charles Ah ce n'est pas grave, il nous reste du pain de mie. C'était quoi le sujet de la votation ?

Eva Pour une eau potable propre et une alimentation saine.

Charles Et qu'est-ce que tu as voté ?

Eva J'ai voté pour. Je pense qu'il est important de limiter l'usage des pesticides.

Charles Je trouve que vous avez de la chance de pouvoir vous prononcer sur ces questions concrètes qui nous concernent tous.

Eva Oui, la Suisse est une démocratie directe, et on vote régulièrement sur des sujets proposés par les citoyennes et les citoyens suisses. On appelle ça des initiatives populaires. On peut même organiser des référendums pour modifier ou annuler une loi fédérale.

Charles	Je crois que c'est une bonne chose : ça permet à tous de participer directement à la vie politique.
Eva	Oui, mais il y a des gens qui ne se sentent pas concernés et qui ne votent pas.
Charles	C'est vrai, il y a toujours des abstentionnistes.
Eva	J'ai du mal à comprendre. À mon avis, le vote devrait être obligatoire, comme en Belgique.
Charles	Je ne suis pas sûr que ça incite vraiment les gens à aller voter. Selon moi, il faut faire de la pédagogie et expliquer l'importance du vote.
Eva	Je crois que tu rêves un peu ! Cependant je suis d'accord avec toi sur un point : il est essentiel d'aller voter et chaque voix compte.

3 Answer the questions.

a Is Eva for or against the unlimited use of pesticides?

b Does Charles have a positive or a negative view on how the Swiss engage in political decision-making?

c Do Eva and Charles agree on the need for voting to be made compulsory?

d Why does Eva think that Charles is "dreaming"?

e Do you think that Eva and Charles mainly agree or disagree on the importance of voting?

LANGUAGE BUILDER 1

Language discovery 1

1 In Conversation 1, when Charles asks which way she voted, Eva states she has voted in favor of the proposal, before explaining: Je pense qu'il est important de limiter l'usage des pesticides *(I think that it is important to limit the use of pesticides)*. **Notice that, if we removed the first three words from this sentence (Je pense que), Eva's opinion (that she does not support the unlimited use of pesticides) would emerge just as clearly. So what nuance of meaning is added by Je pense que? Decide which of the following statements is more accurate:**

a Je pense que suggests that Eva is aware of stating an opinion rather than a fact.

b Je pense que suggests that Eva thinks of her opinion as being random.

2 Besides je pense que, can you spot other phrases used to similar effect by Charles and/or Eva, just before they state an opinion?

Donner son opinion *Giving an opinion*

There are circumstances in which you might wish to indicate that you are stating an opinion, rather than a fact on which all agree. To do so at some point during a conversation can make the difference between sounding polite and not. In French, selon moi, à mon sens, and à mon avis are three slightly different ways of saying *in my opinion*.

If you wish to disagree politely, following the example of Charles in Conversation 1, you could say je ne suis pas sûr/sûre que ce système soit idéal (*I'm not sure that this system is ideal*). Effectively, you would be saying that the system you are discussing is far from ideal, or perhaps terrible! But the phrasing above would considerably soften the tone of your opinion.

If, on the other hand, you want to express strong opposition to what you are hearing, you can use a phrase such as il est inacceptable que (*it is unacceptable that*), followed by the subjunctive. Other useful phrases conveying mood or tone are tout à fait (*completely*) and pas du tout (*not at all*). One of the most interesting things about learning another language is learning how to state facts and opinions appropriately—and perhaps, therefore, more persuasively!

Language practice 1

1 Choose the most appropriate description of the tone of each sentence (use each description once). Then identify which words suggest a neutral tone, a polite tone and/or a strong tone.

a À mon avis, plus ça change, plus c'est la même chose. neutral / polite / strong

b Aux dernières élections, il y a eu un taux d'abstentionnisme élevé. neutral / polite / strong

c Je ne suis pas du tout d'accord avec ce que vous dites. neutral / polite / strong

2 Complete the sentences by choosing the option that gives a more moderate tone to the sentence.

a Ce que vous dites me surprend / m'exaspère.

b Il est impossible / difficile d'être d'accord avec M. Richard sur ce point.

c Votre argument ne me convainc pas tout à fait / du tout.

d Mes collègues ont tort / n'ont pas tout à fait raison.

e C'est de la folie ! / imprudent.

LANGUAGE BUILDER 2

Language discovery 2

18.04

Listen to the conversation again and repeat each line in the pauses.

At the beginning of Conversation 1, Charles asks whether Eva has already voted in the Swiss referendum, and Eva answers: Oui, c'est fait ! Par contre j'ai oublié d'acheter le pain en rentrant. Later, as they discuss different voting systems, Charles approves of the Swiss approach and Eva responds: Oui, mais il y a des gens qui ne se sentent pas concernés et qui ne votent pas. Finally, when Charles imagines the government persuading almost everyone to vote, Eva comments: Je crois que tu rêves un peu ! Cependant je suis d'accord avec toi sur un point : il est essentiel d'aller voter et chaque voix compte.

What do the underlined expressions have in common? Does the statement which they serve to introduce a) harmonize or b) contrast with the statement that comes before?

L'opposition *Opposing sides*

Often we link clauses together in such a way as to emphasize a contrast. Think about how you might join the following sentences together to form one longer sentence:

Victor a vingt-cinq ans. Axel a trente ans.

Obviously, you could simply write Victor a vingt-cinq ans et Axel en a trente. This is a simple statement of fact. However, if you wrote Victor a vingt-cinq ans mais Axel en a trente, you would be drawing a contrast between Victor's and Axel's ages. Perhaps in context you would go on to explain why you find the contrast significant, for instance by adding: donc Axel connaît mieux le monde du travail (*so Axel knows the world of work better*).

When drawing contrasts in this way, most speakers of English are unlikely to worry about using *but* again and again. However, each culture has its own linguistic sensibilities; and it so happens that, to avoid monotony, speakers of French treat mais as only one of many ways of pointing to a contrast. Here are some alternatives that they use quite frequently:

(mais) en revanche	*(but) on the other hand*	cependant	*yet; however*
(et) par contre	*on the other hand*	bien que	*although*
(et) pourtant	*and yet*	quoique	*although*

Note that bien que and quoique are always followed by the subjunctive. For example:

Je le ferai, bien que Pierre soit contre. *I will do it, although Pierre is against it.*

Variety is also desirable when it is a case of conveying a sense of continuity or comparison in French. So it is a good idea to learn the following expressions as alternatives to et:

également	*too, also*	ainsi que	*like, as*
aussi	*too, also*	tout comme	*just as*

Language practice 2

1 In each case, choose the option that conveys an idea of contrast.

a Thomas et Carlos adorent voyager, ... (*ainsi que / et pourtant*) ils aiment toujours rentrer chez eux.

b Ana and Pia se parlent en anglais .... (*bien qu' / comme*) elles apprennent cette langue depuis peu de temps.

c Renato habite à la campagne, ... (*et / et par contre*) Lola habite en ville.

2 Match a–c with 1–3 to form logical sentences.

a Renato adore habiter à la campagne ;	**1** ainsi qu'un roman.
b Comme vous,	**2** Lola également.
c Je lui ai acheté des fleurs	**3** je préfère les films policiers.

18.05

3 Now play the conversation again and play Eva's role. Speak in the pauses. Try not to refer to the text.

CULTURE POINT 2

La ville durable *Sustainable cities*

L'urbaniste franco-colombien Carlos Moreno, professeur à l'Université Paris 1 Panthéon Sorbonne, est un spécialiste de l'aménagement des villes (*urban planning*) et de la ville durable (*sustainable city*). En 2020, il a proposé la ville du quart d'heure, une ville dans laquelle les habitants peuvent satisfaire leurs besoins essentiels (*satisfy their essential needs*) en 15 minutes à pied ou à vélo : travailler, habiter, s'approvisionner (*get your supplies*), se soigner (*look after your health*), s'éduquer, avoir des loisirs (*have hobbies*). Les avantages de ce concept, selon Carlos Moreno, seront multiples : les habitants ne perdent plus de temps dans les transports et ont plus de temps pour leurs activités essentielles ; la pollution diminue ; les habitants nouent des contacts (*people make contacts*) et des relations entre eux. Cela se traduit par moins de stress, moins d'anonymat (*less anonymity*), moins d'inégalités donc, par une meilleure qualité de vie. C'est ce que Carlos Moreno et les membres de son équipe de recherche appellent la proximité heureuse.

La Ville de Paris, intéressée par ce concept, pense que c'est l'école qui doit être au centre du quartier, et a décidé en 2022, d'ouvrir au public, le week-end, les cours d'écoles et de collèges et de piétonniser les abords des écoles (*pedestrianize the school surroundings*). De nombreuses villes dans le monde développent des projets similaires : Barcelone, Bogota, Buenos Aires, Milan, Portland, Dublin, ou encore Melbourne qui a commencé à mettre en œuvre (*which started to implement*) un programme pilote de 20 minutes dans trois zones de la ville.

Regardez la vidéo suivante. Qu'est-ce que la ville du quart d'heure ?

VOCABULARY BUILDER 2

Look at the words and phrases and provide the missing English words and expressions. Then listen and try to imitate the pronunciation of the speakers.

LA VIE COMMUNAUTAIRE	*COMMUNITY LIFE*
de l'aide, une aide	*help (general, specific)*
une campagne	*campaign*
une pétition	....
un habitué/une habituée	*regular visitor*
un influenceur/une influenceuse	....
une campagne de sensibilisation	*awareness campaign*
en ligne	....
se réunir	*to meet*
une signature	....

EXPRESSIONS	*EXPRESSIONS*
C'est ce dont on a besoin.	*That's what we need.*
Nous sommes visibles.	*We have visibility.*
C'est ce que je me dis.	*That's what I tell myself.*
Ça avance ?	*Is there progress?*
les habitués du marché	*regular users of the market*
mettre en œuvre	*implement*
les besoins essentiels	*basic needs*
la proximité heureuse	*beneficial proximity*
l'aménagement des villes	*city planning/infrastructure*
se servir d'un outil de recherche	*to use a research tool*
On en est à 1 000 signatures.	*We've reached 1,000 signatures.*
Ça ne suffit pas.	*That's not enough.*
augmenter le total	*to increase the total*
Ça augmente.	*It's going up.*

Vocabulary practice 2

Match the expressions on the left with the sentences on the right that touch on the same subject.

a Nous sommes très visibles.
b C'est ce dont on a besoin.
c Je cherche en ligne.
d Le vivre ensemble nous importe.
e une pétition
f une signature
g un habitué
h une campagne de sensibilisation
i se réunir régulièrement

1 une personne qui fréquente souvent le même restaurant.
2 Il faudrait écrire votre nom en bas de la page.
3 Notre revendication a déjà 20 000 signatures.
4 Notre communauté est très soudée.
5 Je me sers de plusieurs outils de recherche sur Internet.
6 Cela nous aide beaucoup, n'est-ce pas ?
7 Notre marque est reconnue partout.
8 Nous nous retrouvons tous une fois par mois.
9 On va inciter les gens à y réfléchir.

CONVERSATION 2

La pétition *The petition*

18.07

1 Here are a few words and expressions to help you understand the conversation.

Je n'insiste pas.	*I won't say any more about it.*
distribuer des prospectus	*hand out leaflets*
efficace	*effective; efficient*
si	*yes it is*

18.08

2 Listen to the conversation a few times without looking at the text. Then listen again and read the text.

Jo has created a petition to defend the street market at the place Monge and she discusses her plans to gather signatures with Assia.

Assia Alors Jo, cette pétition, ça avance ?

Jo Non, pas vraiment, on en est à 9 000 signatures.

Assia C'est pas mal, mais c'est vrai que ça n'augmente pas très vite. Ce qu'il te faut, c'est organiser un événement pour attirer l'attention.

Jo Oui, je sais. Pauline m'a proposé son aide. On se réunit demain pour en parler.

Assia	Pauline ? C'est qui ?
Jo	Tu sais, c'est l'influenceuse dont je t'ai parlé.
Assia	Ah oui, c'est une excellente idée ! Ce dont vous avez besoin, c'est d'être visibles au marché !
Jo	Oui, c'est ce que je me dis, la campagne de sensibilisation en ligne ne suffit pas, il faut aller parler aux commerçants et aux habitués du marché.
Assia	Tu sais qui pourrait t'aider ? Émile !
Jo	Émile, c'est qui ?
Assia	Ben Émile, mon ancien voisin, le garçon dont tu étais amoureuse...
Jo	Ah lui ! Hors de question, je ne veux plus en entendre parler.
Assia	Bon, bon d'accord je n'insiste pas. Tu sais à quoi je pense ?
Jo	Non, dis-moi !
Assia	Tu pourrais aller distribuer des prospectus à la sortie de l'école !
Jo	Bof ! Je ne suis pas sûre que ce soit très efficace.
Assia	Ben si, moi je pense que c'est une bonne idée, les parents veulent une alimentation saine pour leurs enfants.
Jo	OK, on peut toujours essayer...

3 Answer the questions.

a Is Jo happy with the number of signatures which her petition has attracted so far?
b What is Assia's initial suggestion?
c Why has Jo arranged to meet someone called Pauline? What does Pauline do?
d Beside her initial suggestion, what does Assia think is needed?

LANGUAGE BUILDER 3

 **Language discovery 3**

In the conversation Assia remarks, ce dont vous avez besoin c'est d'être visibles au marché. A natural-sounding translation of this would be *what you need is to be visible in the market*. But if we wanted to translate it more literally, we could *say that of which you have need is to be visible at the market*. On the basis of this, can you figure out what single word in French corresponds to *of which* in English?

Dont *Of which, of whom ...*

Dont can be translated by *of which; of whom/whose; from which; from whom; about which; about whom*. Dont is a pronoun which replaces the following groups of words:

- de + quelque chose (de + something)
  Hier j'ai vu un très bon film. J'ai oublié le titre de ce film. →
  Hier j'ai vu un très bon film dont j'ai oublié le titre.

  Sur cette photo, tu peux voir ma chorale. Je fais partie de cette chorale. →
  Sur cette photo, tu peux voir la chorale dont je fais partie.
- de + quelqu'un (de + someone)
  La personne est boulangère, j'ai oublié le nom de cette boulangère. →
  La personne dont j'ai oublié le nom travaille comme boulangère.

  Voici la voisine. Je t'ai parlé de cette voisine. → Voici la voisine dont je t'ai parlé.

Because of this range of meanings, you will often see dont used with verbs that require de, such as: s'occuper de or se mêler de (*to get involved in*); avoir peur de (*to be afraid of*); parler de (*to speak about*).

Le livre dont je t'ai parlé a pour titre *Les Choses*.	*The book I spoke to you about is entitled Les Choses.*
Le dossier dont je m'occupe est très sensible.	*The case for which I'm responsible, is highly sensitive.*

Language practice 3

1 Complete the transformation of the following sentences, using dont.

a La vie politique ? Je ne me mêle pas de ça.
La vie politique, c'est une chose dont ....

b L'air propre ? On parle beaucoup de ce sujet.
L'air propre, c'est un sujet dont ....

c Le réchauffement climatique ? J'ai peur de ça.
Le réchauffement climatique, c'est une chose dont ....

d Net zéro, c'est un sujet fascinant. On en parle souvent.
Net zéro, c'est un sujet fascinant dont ....

LANGUAGE BUILDER 4

Language discovery 4

18.09

Listen to the conversation again and repeat each line in the pauses.

In Conversation 2, Assia says Ce dont vous avez besoin, c'est d'être visibles au marché ! This can be translated as follows: *What you need is to be visible in the market!* A more literal (and less natural-sounding) translation of the first clause (ce dont vous avez besoin) would be: *that of which you have need …*

Why is dont preceded by ce in Assia's sentence? Choose the correct option to complete the statement: (a) subject; (b) object; (c) antecedent.

When there is no noun or pronoun to serve as an ……………………, dont is preceded by ce.

Ce dont

In Unit 16, you learned how to use ce qui and ce que.

Ce qui manque, c'est le pain	(*What's missing is the bread*);
Tout est en images, ce que je trouve déroutant	(*Everything's in pictures, which I find confusing*).

You will probably remember that, in these examples, ce qui and ce que are required because there is no noun for qui/que to refer back to, so ce serves instead as the *antecedent*. A similar logic applies when dont is required in sentences where there is no noun for dont to refer back to.

Ce dont j'ai besoin, c'est un tournevis.	*What I need is a screwdriver.*
Les feux d'artifice font beaucoup de bruit, ce dont les chiens ont peur.	*Fireworks make a lot of noise, something which dogs are frightened of.*

Language practice 4

1 Complete the sentences using ce qui, ce que, or ce dont.

S'il te plaît, écris dans ta lettre pour le papa Noël :

tout **a** …………………… tu désires (*everything you want*) ;

tout **b** …………………… tu as besoin (*everything you need*) ;

tout **c** …………………… te plaît (*everything that you like/that appeals to you*).

Dis-moi :

d …………………… leur fait plaisir (*what they like/pleases them*) ;

e …………………… elles ont envie (*what they feel like*) ;

f …………………… elles n'aiment pas (*what they don't like*).

Est-ce que vous avez acheté :

g .... vous aviez besoin (*what you needed*) ?

h .... Lisette a demandé (*what Lisette asked for*) ?

i .... te semble approprié (*what seems appropriate to you*) ?

18.10 **2 Now play the conversation again and play Jo's role. Speak in the pauses. Try not to refer to the text.**

SKILL BUILDER

1 Compose sentences with bien que or tandis que/alors que by using the information in the table below.

	Système politique	Monnaie	Langues officielles
Belgique	monarchie consitutionnelle	euro	l'allemand, le français, le néerlandais
Canada	monarchie consitutionnelle	dollar canadien	l'anglais et le français
France	république	euro	le français
Suisse	république	franc suisse	l'allemand, le français, l'italien et le romanche

Example: *La Belgique et le Canada sont des monarchies constitutionnelles alors que la France et la Suisse sont des républiques.*

a Le Canada ....

b La France et la Belgique ....

c La Suisse et la Belgique ....

d La Belgique ....

2 Match a–c with 1–3 to form logical sentences:

a Muriel adore son nouveau poste,

b Comme ton père,

c Augustin lui a offert un cadeau,

1 ainsi que ses nouveaux collègues.

2 et moi également.

3 tu préfères la musique classique.

3 Complete the sentences with dont or ce dont.

a La pièce de théâtre .... tu m'as parlé m'a enthousiasmé.

b J'ai oublié l'histoire, mais .... je me souviens, c'est que l'actrice était fantastique.

c Par contre, les costumes, ... on m'avait beaucoup parlé, étaient anachroniques.

TEST YOURSELF

Imagine you are reading digital posts from two people who are debating whether the correct way to eat a British scone is to put the cream on first, then the jam, or vice versa. Fill in the gaps, using the translation as your guide.

Speaker A

Quand on mange un scone anglais, il faut mettre la crème Chantilly d'abord et la confiture après.

Speaker B

Ah non, je ne suis pas du tout d'accord ! **a** .... (*although*) vous soyez anglais, vous vous trompez. J'ai lu un article sur la Cornouailles sur Internet qui dit tout le contraire.

Speaker A

b .... (*even though*) vous basiez ce que vous dites sur un article de journal, j'ai du mal à vous croire.

Speaker B

Je ne sais pas **c** .... (*of what*) vous parlez.

Speaker A

Je n'accepte pas **d** .... (*what*) vous dites **e** .... (*although*) vous ayez fait des recherches sur Internet.

Speaker B

Vous citez des sources peu fiables, **f** .... (*which*) me rend méfiant.

Speaker A

g .... (*since*) vous ne me faites pas confiance, je n'ai plus rien à dire.

Speaker B

Je crois que nous nous répétons.... Peut-être devrions-nous terminer cette discussion et manger un scone !

Remember to use **My review** and **My takeaway** to assess your progress and reflect on your learning experience.

19

In this lesson you will learn how to:

- Give positive commands
- Give negative commands
- Talk about the distant past
- Talk about an imagined past

Nos origines

My study plan

I plan to work with Unit 19

○ Every day

○ Twice a week

○ Other ___________

I plan to study for

○ 5–15 minutes

○ 15–30 minutes

○ 30–45+ minutes

My progress tracker

Day / Date	Listening	Speaking	Reading	Writing	Conversation
	○	○	○	○	○
	○	○	○	○	○
	○	○	○	○	○
	○	○	○	○	○
	○	○	○	○	○
	○	○	○	○	○
	○	○	○	○	○

My goals

What do you want to be able to do or say in French when you complete this unit?

		Done
1	....	○
2	....	○
3	....	○

My review

SELF CHECK

	I can ...
●	... express a command.
●	... speak about the distant past.
●	... talk about a possible past.

CULTURE POINT 1

Le Pays basque *The Basque Country*

Le Pays basque (*País Vasco* en espagnol et *Euskal Herria* en basque) est une région transnationale située à l'ouest de la chaîne des Pyrénées, au bord du (*alongside the*) golfe de Gascogne. Une partie du Pays basque se trouve en France, l'autre en Espagne. La langue basque, parlée par plus de 750 000 personnes, soit environ (*that is to say approximately*) 28 % de la population, est une des langues les plus anciennes d'Europe. Antérieure aux langues indo-européennes (*prior to Indo-European languages*), son origine est toujours inconnue à ce jour. Le Pays basque est une destination touristique très prisée pour ses magnifiques plages, ses merveilleux paysages de montagne, sa gastronomie et ses traditions. Sur la côte, vous pouvez faire du surf, de la voile, ou bronzer à la plage dans les stations balnéaires (*beach resorts*) de Biarritz et de Saint-Jean-de-Luz, côté français, et de San Sebastian, côté espagnol. À Bilbao, découvrez le fameux Musée Guggenheim, dessiné par Frank Gehry. Pour les amateurs de randonnée, le chemin de Saint-Jacques-de-Compostelle passe par le village de Saint-Jean-Pied-de-Port, classé parmi les Plus Beaux Villages de France et situé au pied des Pyrénées. Dans les villages environnants (*the neighboring villages*), vous verrez peut-être une partie de pelote basque, le sport local. Vous pourrez aussi assister à un concert de chœur basque. Visitez Espelette, village basque typique avec ses maisons aux volets rouges, et capitale du fameux piment d'Espelette.

Chaque année en août, des millions de visiteurs vêtus de blanc et rouge se rendent aux célèbres fêtes de Bayonne. Enfin Bayonne est aussi la capitale historique du chocolat en France. C'est là qu'il est arrivé du Mexique, en passant par l'Espagne.

Visitez la page web suivante. Qu'aimeriez-vous visiter au Pays basque ?

VOCABULARY BUILDER 1

19.01

Look at the words and phrases and provide the missing English words and expressions. Then listen and try to imitate the pronunciation of the speakers.

LA CULTURE DU PAYS BASQUE	*THE CULTURE OF THE BASQUE COUNTRY*
un pays ; le Pays basque	*country, the Basque Country*
une côte, la Côte basque	*coast, the Basque coast*
impressionnant/impressionnante	*impressive*
intense	....
un interprète, une interprète	*interpreter*
participer à	....
passionnant/passionnante	*exciting*
une rencontre	*meeting; event*
sélectionner	....
soit	*in other words/namely*

EXPRESSIONS	*EXPRESSIONS*
côté espagnol/français	*on the Spanish/French side*
Laure travaille dans la communication.	*Laure works in communication.*
Nous communiquons en français entre nous.	*We communicate with each other in French.*
Il faudrait organiser une excursion.	*We should organise an excursion.*
soit 28 % de la population	*in other words, 28% of the population*
On est une vingtaine/une trentaine.	*There are about twenty/thirty of us.*
travailler en binôme	*to work in teams of two*

Vocabulary practice 1

Match the phrases on the left with the sentences on the right that express similar ideas.

a côté français, côté espagnol
b pouvoir communiquer sans interprète
c être une vingtaine
d travailler en binôme
e participer à une rencontre
f organiser une randonnée

1 Vous allez vous associer avec un partenaire.
2 Je vais assister à cet événement.
3 La France et l'Espagne partagent une frontière.
4 Nous sommes vingt personnes plus ou moins.
5 Tu prévois une promenade en groupe ?
6 Moi, je connais sa langue, et vice versa.

CONVERSATION 1

Les jeunes étoiles du chocolat *The young stars of chocolate making*

19.02

1 Here are a few words and expressions to help you understand the conversation.

une étoile montante	*rising star*
rassembler	*to bring together*
prendre des congés	*to take leave from work*
elle en profite pour...	*she's taking the opportunity to ...*
Je suis sur un petit nuage !	*I'm on cloud nine!*
Je vais me changer.	*I'm going to get changed.*
un artisan chocolatier ivoirien	*a master chocolatier from Ivory Coast*
chouette	*great; cool*

19.03

2 Listen to the conversation without looking at the text. Play it a few times and try to make out a few new words and phrases each time. Then listen to the conversation again and read the text.

Charles has been selected to participate in a convention of promising chocolate makers, organized by the Bayonne Chocolate Academy. Eva accompanies Charles to visit the region.

Eva	Alors, cette première journée ?
Charles	C'était incroyable ! Quelle chance j'ai eue d'être sélectionné pour participer à cette rencontre ! On est une trentaine, des quatre coins du monde. Les autres participants ont tous un profil impressionnant et tous sont hyper sympa. Je suis sur un petit nuage...
Eva	Génial ! Vous communiquez en quelle langue ?
Charles	Le programme est en français, et il y a des interprètes de et vers l'anglais, mais entre nous, on parle français, anglais, espagnol, portugais, arabe, c'est les Nations unies !
Eva	Qu'est-ce que vous avez fait aujourd'hui ?
Charles	Tu veux voir le programme ? Je vais me changer.
Eva	Oui, bonne idée, passe-le-moi s'il te plaît !
Charles	Prends-le, il est dans mon sac.
	Eva reads from the program.
Eva	Mot de bienvenue, présentation du programme et des participants, séance de dégustation, conférence d'Anne-Françoise Benoit... c'est qui ?

Charles	C'est une star du chocolat, une des premières femmes chocolatières à être reconnue dans un univers qui était encore entièrement masculin il n'y a pas si longtemps...
Eva	Heureusement que le monde change ! (*Eva continues reading.*)
Eva	Après-midi, atelier de création de chocolat en binôme. Ben dis donc, c'est intense !
Charles	C'était passionnant, j'ai travaillé avec Aminata. Je te la présenterai ce soir, elle est super sympa. Elle travaille à Abidjan, chez Axel Emmanuel Gbaou, le premier artisan chocolatier ivoirien. Elle veut se lancer elle aussi !
Eva	Cool !
Charles	Demain, on a des ateliers sur la création d'entreprise, la communication...
Eva	Et dimanche, excursion sur la Côte basque !
Charles	Tu sais, l'année prochaine, la rencontre a lieu à Oaxaca, au Mexique, la ville d'origine du chocolat. Ce serait chouette d'y aller ensemble !
Eva	Oh là là, ne m'embrouille pas s'il te plaît, une chose à la fois... N'oublie pas que la semaine prochaine on est à Montréal !

3 Answer the questions.

a Dans quelle langue le programme se déroule-t-il ?
b Vers quelle langue le programme est-il interprété ?
c Qui est Anne-Françoise Benoit ?
d Où travaille Aminata et quels sont ses projets ?
e Quel est le programme de la journée de dimanche ?
f Dans quelle ville et dans quel pays est-ce que le symposium des jeunes chocolatières et chocolatiers de l'année prochaine aura lieu ?

LANGUAGE BUILDER 1

Language discovery 1

When Charles asks Eva if she wants to read the program for the symposium he is attending, Eva replies: Oui, bonne idée, passe-le-moi s'il te plaît ! (*Yes, that's a good idea, pass it to me, please!*). As Charles needs to change, he suggests: Prends-le, il est dans mon sac (*Take it, it's in my bag*). Both Eva and Charles use an imperative form here: Eva when she says passe-le-moi and Charles when he responds with Prends-le. (If you want to review imperatives, see Unit 4.)

Can you figure out what the hyphens are used for here?

How to use the imperative with pronouns (part 1)

In Unit 4, you learned about the imperative. Here are three of the examples you were given: regarde; regardons; regardez. These and all other examples of the imperative in Unit 4 were based on -er verbs. You were asked to note that the tu-form imperative of such verbs (e.g., Regarde !) has no final -s (unlike the indicative form—tu regardes). Since then, you have added -ir and -re verbs to your skill set. So it is important to note that in the case of these verbs, the tu-form imperative is identical to the indicative. In other words, both end in -s (see the examples finis and prends in the table below). Remember that the **nous** and **vous** imperatives are the same as the present tense forms.

Infinitive	Tu-form imperative	Imperative
regarder	Regarde !	Look!
finir	Finis ton repas s'il te plaît !	Finish your meal, please!
prendre	Prends ton livre avec toi !	Take your book with you!

It is important to know how to combine imperatives with object pronouns, so that you can say (for instance) *give it to her* or *let's give them to him*. Note that the direct object comes first and that hyphens are used to link the verb with the two object pronouns, e.g., donne-le-moi (*give it to me*); donne-la-leur (*give it to them*); donne-les-nous (*give them to us*).

Imperative	Direct object pronoun	Indirect object pronoun
donne-*	le- (*it, masc.*) la- (*it, fem.*) les- (*them*)	moi (*to me*) lui (*to him/her*) nous (*to us*) leur (*to them*)

* Alternative imperatives would be donnez- (= *give*, vous form) or donnons- (= *let's give*).

Finally, if you only have one object pronoun, the word order and hyphenation will be as in the following examples: donne-le à Sophie (*give it to Sophie*); donne-lui le livre (*give him/her the book*); rends-la à ton frère (*give it back to your brother*); parlons-leur bientôt (*let's speak to them soon*).

It is possible to construct an imperative using en and a first-person or second-person singular object pronoun. In such cases, you should not use moi or toi but me (shortened to m'). For instance, if your friend asked whether you wanted some more pizza, you might answer Oui, donne-m'en encore un peu s'il te plaît.

Language practice 1

Imagine you are babysitting two sets of twins, Michel and Luc, and Sophie and Léa. Convert the elements given in parentheses into imperatives. Use object pronouns to replace the underlined words.

a Demander à Luc de rendre les jouets à Sophie (*rendre*) :
« Luc, ... , s'il te plaît. »

b Demander à Sophie et Léa de donner les crayons à Michel et Luc (*donner*) :
« Sophie et Léa, ... s'il vous plaît. »

c Dire aux enfants de se mettre à table (*se mettre*) :
Les enfants, ... à table !

d Dire aux enfants de se coucher tout de suite (*se coucher*) :
« Les enfants, ... tout de suite ! »

LANGUAGE BUILDER 2

Language discovery 2

19.04

Listen to the conversation again and repeat each line in the pauses.

Compare these two statements from Conversation 1 in which Eva uses the imperative:

Oui, passe-le-moi !

Oh là là, ne m'embrouille pas !

Where are the object pronouns in each statement? Why do you think the placement is different in each case?

The negative imperative and pronouns (part 2)

There are some differences between positive and negative imperatives. One is that not all the object pronouns used in negative imperatives are the same as for positive imperatives. See the following table:

ne	me te nous vous	le la les	lui leur	y	en	verb	pas plus jamais rien

Here are some negative imperatives which you can check against the table above so that you get used to the word-order rules:

Ne m'en parle pas !	*Don't speak to me about it!*
N'y pensons plus.	*Let's not think about it any more.*
Ne me les donne pas.	*Don't give them to me.*
Ne nous l'envoyez pas.	*Don't send it to us.*
Ne les lui envoyez pas.	*Don't send them to him/her.*
Ne nous en donnons pas la peine.	*Let's not give ourselves the trouble of doing it.*

Reading through these examples, you will see that there are no hyphens in negative imperatives. Also, you will notice that the word order is similar to the one you learned in Unit 4. The difference is just that there is no subject in (negative) imperatives, so ne always comes first.

Language practice 2

1 Convert the positive imperatives (underlined) into negative imperatives to complete the sentences. Once completed, the second sentence should convey the same message as the first.

Example: Crie moins fort. → *Ne crie pas* trop fort.

a Cours moins vite. → .... trop vite.
b Commencez plus tôt → .... aussi tard.
c Cette fois, travaillons en binôme. → Cette fois, ... de manière isolée.

19.05

2 Now play Conversation 1 again and play the role of Eva in the pauses provided. Pay particular attention to any commands she gives.

CULTURE POINT 2

Marseille

Marseille est la deuxième ville de France et le premier port du pays. Fondée en 600 avant notre ère (BCE) par des marchands grecs originaires de Phocée, d'où son surnom de cité phocéenne, Marseille est une ville cosmopolite ouverte sur le monde. Pour avoir une vue panoramique de la ville, montez à la Basilique Notre-Dame-de-la-Garde, qui veille sur les marins (*watches over the sailors*), les pêcheurs et toutes les Marseillaises et les Marseillais, qui la vénèrent (*who honor her*). Ensuite allez vous promener au Vieux-Port, un autre lieu symbolique de la ville, et faites un tour au marché aux poissons. À deux pas, découvrez le quartier populaire du Panier ; il s'agit du quartier mythique de Marseille, avec ses petites rues, ses façades colorées, ses artisans et ses cafés. Enfin, ne ratez pas le musée des Civilisations de l'Europe et de la Méditerranée, le MUCEM, dans le fort Saint-Jean. Ouvert en 2013 dans le cadre du (*in the framework of the*) programme de Marseille Capitale européenne de la culture, ce musée est mondialement connu pour son architecture et constitue un rendez-vous incontournable de votre visite à Marseille. Si vous aimez le sport, allez voir un match de l'Olympique de Marseille au stade Vélodrome. Les Marseillais·e·s adorent le football et vous feront partager leurs émotions. L'autre sport pour lequel on connaît Marseille, c'est la pétanque, inventée à La Ciotat, à quelques kilomètres, au début du vingtième siècle. À Marseille, prenez le bateau pour visiter l'île du château d'If, la prison du comte de Monte-Cristo, dans le célèbre roman d'Alexandre Dumas. Vous pouvez aussi aller passer la journée dans les Calanques, une magnifique côte rocheuse, à une demi-heure de la ville. Depuis Marseille, vous pouvez découvrir la Provence et la Côte d'Azur. Vous pouvez aussi prendre un ferry pour la Corse, ou pour l'Algérie. Un dernier conseil : tendez l'oreille (*prick up your ears*), vous entendrez les cigales (*cicadas*) ainsi que l'accent de la région, influencé par le provençal.

Combien de personnes ont visité Marseille Capitale européenne de la Culture en 2013 ?

VOCABULARY BUILDER 2

Look at the words and phrases and provide the missing English words and expressions. Then listen and try to imitate the pronunciation of the speakers.

MARSEILLE, CITÉ ANCIENNE	*THE ANCIENT CITY OF MARSEILLE*
l'architecture (fem.)	....
une basilique	*basilica*
une cigale	*cicada*
cosmopolite	*cosmopolitan*
une façade	*facade, front*
un marchand/une marchande	*merchant*
un marché aux poissons	*fish market*
un marin	*sailor*
une migration	....
panoramique	....
la pêche	*fishing*
un pêcheur	*fisherman*
rocheux, rocheuse	*rocky*
veiller, veiller sur	*to stay awake, to watch over*

EXPRESSIONS	*EXPRESSIONS*
une ville ouverte sur le monde	*a town open to the world*
C'est à deux pas d'ici.	*It's really close by.*
600 ans avant notre ère	*600 years Before Christ/Before Common Era*
Ils font partager leurs émotions.	*Their feelings are infectious.*
On va faire le tour du port.	*We'll walk around the port.*
La cité a été fondée il y a 2 600 ans.	*The city was founded 2,600 years ago.*
Nous allons tendre l'oreille.	*We'll listen carefully.* (Literally: *we'll stretch out our ear.)*

Vocabulary practice 2

Match the phrases on the left with the sentences on the right that express a similar idea.

a une ville ouverte sur le monde
b tout près
c une vue panoramique
d tendre l'oreille
e faire sentir

1 Depuis la basilique, on voit très loin dans toutes les directions.
2 Les Marseillaises font partager leurs émotions.
3 Marseille est une ville cosmopolite.
4 Le marché aux poissons est à deux pas d'ici.
5 Roger, écoute attentivement — tu entends les cigales ?

CONVERSATION 2

Origines *Origins*

19.07

1 Here are a few words and expressions to help you understand the conversation.

Je me lance dans un projet.	*I'm getting started on a project.*	se marier	*get married*
les arrière-grands-parents (masc.)	*great-grandparents*	à peine	*scarcely*
une tradition d'accueil des réfugiés	*tradition of welcoming refugees*	les retrouvailles (fem.)	*reunion*
On est plusieurs à être concernés.	*Several of us are affected by this.*	émouvant, émouvante	*moving*
travailler dans le bâtiment	*work in the building trade*	L'Algérie lui manquait.	*She missed Algeria.*

19.08

2 Listen to the conversation without looking at the text. Then listen to the conversation again and read the text.

Assia is doing some research on her Algerian origins. She talks to Jo about her project.

Jo Salut Assia, tu vas bien ?

Assia Oui, super, je me lance dans un projet sur mes origines.

Jo Ah oui !? Raconte !

Assia Pour notre projet de fin de semestre, on a choisi les migrations. Ici, il y a une longue tradition d'accueil des réfugiés, mais aussi de gens qui sont venus vivre au Canada pour tenter leur chance. On est plusieurs dans le groupe à être directement ou indirectement concernés.

Jo	Et donc, tu t'es dit que tu allais parler de tes grands-parents algériens, c'est ça ?
Assia	Oui ! C'est ça ! Leur histoire me touche beaucoup. Mon grand-père est parti en France pour travailler dans le bâtiment quand il avait 20 ans. Tu te rends compte, c'est très jeune ! Il venait d'une famille très pauvre, en Kabylie.
Jo	Et ta grand-mère ?
Assia	Il s'étaient mariés peu de temps avant son départ, elle avait 18 ans et elle venait elle aussi d'une famille très modeste. Mais elle n'est pas venue en France tout de suite.
Jo	Elle est restée à Tizi Ouzou toute seule ?
Assia	Oui, chez les parents de mon grand-père, mes arrière-grands-parents, qu'elle connaissait à peine. Tu imagines ?
Jo	Ça a dû être difficile !
Assia	Mon grand-père l'a fait venir en France rapidement, et l'année suivante, mon père est né. C'était l'époque de la guerre d'Algérie. Tout était difficile pour eux en France, et ils ne pouvaient pas rentrer au pays.
Jo	Et après la guerre ?
Assia	Ils n'avaient pas beaucoup d'argent et ils ont attendu longtemps avant de rentrer. Puis, au début des années 70, ils sont allés passer des vacances, en août, avec mon père et ma tante. Ça faisait presque 15 ans qu'ils n'avaient pas vu leurs familles.
Jo	Les retrouvailles ont dû être très émouvantes.
Assia	Oui j'imagine, j'ai demandé à mon père s'il y avait des photos de cet été-là.
Jo	Et tes grands-parents n'ont jamais voulu rentrer en Algérie ?
Assia	Mon grand-père aurait voulu faire construire une maison au village, pour les vacances, mais finalement ça ne s'est pas fait. Ma grand-mère ne l'a jamais dit, mais je crois que l'Algérie lui manquait et qu'elle aurait aimé rentrer.
Jo	Et comment tu vas raconter tout ça ?
Assia	Je ne sais pas encore très bien, je réfléchis...

3 Answer the questions.

- **a** D'où viennent les grands-parents d'Assia ?
- **b** Pourquoi c'était difficile pour eux de s'installer en France ?
- **c** Pendant combien d'années ils ne sont pas allés en Algérie et n'ont pas vu leurs familles ?
- **d** Comment la grand-mère d'Assia a vécu le fait de ne pas retourner en Algérie ?

LANGUAGE BUILDER 3

Language discovery 3

When telling the story of how her grandparents came to live in France, Assia says: Ils s'étaient mariés peu de temps avant son départ (*They had got married shortly before he left*). Later, she says: Ça faisait presque 15 ans qu'ils n'avaient pas vu leurs familles (*They had not seen their families for almost 15 years*).

Look at the verbs in these sentences. You will see that they are made up of avoir/être + past participle. On this basis, do they remind you of any other tense you have learned? Do you recognize which tense avoir and être are in?

Le plus-que-parfait *The pluperfect*

Since you have been using le passé composé, you may find it easy to add le plus-que-parfait to your skill set. This is the tense that corresponds to *had done* in English, for example *Since I had finished my work, I went home*. Here's le plus-que-parfait of faire:

faire (plus-que-parfait)

j'avais fait	nous avions fait
tu avais fait	vous aviez fait
il/elle avait fait	ils/elles avaient fait

As you can see, le plus-que-parfait is formed by taking l'imparfait of the auxiliary verb (here, avoir) and adding a past participle (here, fait). In the case of verbs such as aller or partir, which are formed with être, the past participle agrees with the subject; for instance, *Sophie had gone to the concert* becomes Sophie était allée au concert. See the table below for the entire pattern, including agreements:

aller (plus-que-parfait)

j'étais allé (*masc.*)	nous étions allés (*masc.*)
j'étais allée (*fem.*)	nous étions allées (*fem.*)
tu étais allé (*masc.*)	vous étiez allé/allée (*masc./fem. sing.*)
tu étais allée (*fem.*)	vous étiez allés/allées (*masc./fem. pl.*)
il était allé	ils étaient allés
elle était allée	elles étaient allées

Similarly, in most cases where reflexive verbs are used, the past participle agrees with the subject, for example Ils s'étaient réveillés tôt ce jour-là (*They had woken up early that day*). If you want to know an exception to this rule, you will find it in the grammar glossary.

For verbs conjugated with avoir, the agreement rules you learned for le passé composé also apply to le plus-que-parfait. For example: L'anné précédente j'avais donné une cravate à mon père, qui l'avait beaucoup aimée. (*The previous year, I had given a tie to my father, who had liked it a lot.*) Here, the past participle aimée has a feminine ending because it agrees with the preceding direct object l' (= la cravate).

Language practice 3

1 Complete the sentences using le passé composé followed by le plus-que-parfait.

Example: Hier, *j'ai visité* le fameux MUCEM. La veille, *j'avais visité* le Vieux-Port. (*visiter*)

a Hier, j .... mon cousin. La veille, j .... ma cousine. (*voir*)

b Hier, il .... à un concert. Avant-hier, il .... au cinéma. (*aller*)

c Mardi, Lou .... à 10 h du matin ; la veille, elle .... encore plus tard ! (*se lever*)

2 Replace le passé composé with le plus-que-parfait.

a Elles sont sorties assez tard. → Elles .... assez tard.

b Ils ont beaucoup aimé le film. → Ils .... le film.

c Elles se sont rencontrées à la basilique. → Elles .... à la basilique.

d Vous n'avez pas revu Aaron depuis ? → Vous .... Aaron depuis ?

LANGUAGE BUILDER 4

Language discovery 4

19.09

Listen to the conversation again and repeat each line in the pauses.

Now take a look a the following sentence from the conversation, paying attention to the underlined verb:

Ma grand-mère ne l'a jamais dit, mais je crois que l'Algérie lui manquait et qu'elle aurait aimé rentrer.

Like le passé composé and le plus-que-parfait, this tense is made up of avoir/être + past participle. But can you see what makes it different from them, and when it should be used? Check your answer against the explanation below.

How to use le conditionnel passé

Imagine someone is asked the question *What would you have done if you had known the truth?* and they answer: *I would have reacted differently.* The tense that is used in both the question and the answer is known as le conditionnel passé (*conditional perfect*). It is made by combining *would have* + a past participle (= *reacted*). The conditional perfect is used to talk about something that never happened, but could have happened at some point in the past; in the example above, *reacting differently* was something that could have happened but did not. To say *I would have reacted differently* in French, we could use J'aurais réagi différemment. So the verb aurais réagi is an example of le conditionnel passé. Here is a table showing the complete pattern:

réagir (conditionnel passé)

j'aurais réagi	nous aurions réagi
tu aurais réagi	vous auriez réagi
il/elle/on aurait réagi	ils/elles auraient réagi

So, to form le conditionnel passé take the relevant form of the auxiliary verb (in this case, avoir) and add the past participle (in this case, réagi). Here are some further examples, including a couple with verbs that take être:

Elle aurait chanté.	*She would have sung.*
Ils seraient partis.	*They would have left.*
Nous aurions aidé.	*We would have helped.*
Elles se seraient réveillées.	*They would have woken up.*

The above examples also serve to illustrate that the agreement rules for le conditionnel passé are the same as for le passé composé and le plus-que-parfait. For instance, because partir takes être, the past participle agrees with the subject in all three of the following phrases: ils sont partis (*they left*); ils étaient partis (*they had left*); ils seraient partis (*they would have left*).

Language practice 4

1 Using the top three rows as a guide, complete the table:

Infinitif	Passé composé	Plus-que-parfait	Conditionnel passé
chanter/*to sing*	j'ai chanté	j'avais chanté	j'aurais chanté
sortir/*to go out*	elle est sortie	elle était sortie	elle serait sortie
se lever/*to get up*	ils se sont levés	ils s'étaient levés	ils se seraient levés
finir/*to finish*	**a** j'	**b** j'	**c** j' ....
partir/*to leave*	**d** elle	**e** elle	**f** elle ....
se laver/*to wash**	**g** ils	**h** ils	**i** ils ....

*You can also translate se laver as *to wash oneself* if you want to emphasize that it is reflexive.

19.10

2 Listen to Conversation 2 again and this time play the part of Jo in the pauses provided—she is mainly asking short questions. When listening to Assia speak, pay close attention to the various uses of verb tenses.

SKILL BUILDER

1 Convert the following statements into imperatives, using the form indicated in brackets.

Example: Il ne faut pas marcher trop vite. (vous *form*) *Ne marchez pas trop vite !*

a Il ne faut pas courir dans les couloirs. (tu *form*) ....

b Il ne faut pas crier dans la rue. (nous *form*) ....

c Il ne faut pas commencer avant les autres. (vous *form*) ....

d Il ne faut pas faire la vaisselle. (tu *form*) ....

2 Convert the negative statements below into positive imperatives.

a Ne m'en parle pas ! .... !

b N'y pensons plus ! .... !

c Ne me les donne pas ! .... !

d Ne nous l'envoyez pas ! .... !

e Ne les lui envoyez pas ! .... !

3 Complete the sentences below with the verb indicated in the pluperfect.

a Si j' .... au loto, j'aurais fait le tour du monde. (*gagné*)

b Si tu .... au loto, tu aurais peut-être gagner. (*jouer*)

c Si nous .... notre chemin, nous serions arrivés plus vite. (*demander*)

d Si elle .... le droit, elle aurait aimé étudier l'histoire. (*choisir*)

4 Complete the sentences with le conditionnel passé.

a Si Marc et moi avions eu plus de temps, nous .... visiter le MUCEM. (*aimer*)

b Maintenant je me rends compte que j' .... commencer par le début. (*devoir*)

c Vous avez assez bien joué ce morceau. Mais vous .... ralentir un peu. (*pouvoir*)

TEST YOURSELF

Translate the following English sentences into French.

a Please give me your book! Do not give it to him!
b It is already 23:00. Let's go to bed.
c I told them "Please, hurry up!" as I didn't want to be late.
d We had not seen him for two years.
e They had loved the film very much.
f They had met at the cathedral.
g We should have reacted differently.
h If Marc and I had had more time, we would have visited the MUCEM.
i Now I realize that I should have started at the beginning of the story.
j You played this musical piece well, but you could have slowed down a little.

Remember to use **My review** and **My takeaway** to assess your progress and reflect on your learning experience.

20

In this lesson you will learn how to:

- » Talk about things that would have happened if other conditions had been met
- » Talk about the present, the future, and the past in relation to one another
- » Ask questions in various different formats
- » Express regret about past events

L'avenir

My study plan

I plan to work with Unit 20

- ○ Every day
- ○ Twice a week
- ○ Other ___________

I plan to study for

- ○ 5–15 minutes
- ○ 15–30 minutes
- ○ 30–45+ minutes

My progress tracker

Day / Date	Listening	Speaking	Reading	Writing	Conversation
	○	○	○	○	○
	○	○	○	○	○
	○	○	○	○	○
	○	○	○	○	○
	○	○	○	○	○
	○	○	○	○	○
	○	○	○	○	○

My goals

What do you want to be able to do or say in French when you complete this unit?

		Done
1	....	○
2	....	○
3	....	○

My review

SELF CHECK

	I can ...
●	... talk about things that could have happened in the distant past.
●	... ask questions in a variety of modes.
●	... ask questions using simple and complex inversions.
●	... master the use of conditional sentences.

CULTURE POINT 1

Prendre le temps de...

En octobre 2023, l'enquête (*the survey*) « et maintenant » organisée chaque année par ARTE, la chaîne de télévision (*TV channel*) franco-allemande, et France Culture, une des chaînes de Radio France, autour d'un thème de société, a porté sur le rapport au temps (*was about the relationship to time*) des Françaises et des Français. Dans cette enquête, la majorité des 30 000 participant·e·s a répondu que notre société allait trop vite. Pour ralentir (*to go slower*), les personnes interrogées choisissent de se mettre au vert (*go green*) (63 %), d'agir localement (41%), de se déconnecter des réseaux (40 %), de faire des puzzles, broder (*to embroider*) ou pêcher (*to go fishing*) (36 %), ou de traîner au lit (*sleep in*) (30 %). À la question de savoir s'il vaut mieux vivre 100 ans ou vivre à 100 à l'heure, 62 % des 26–34 ans répondent qu'ils préfèrent la longévité contre 28 % qui préfèrent l'intensité. Pour 61 % des enquêté·e·s, on s'accomplit (*we are fulfilled*) grâce au temps libre et non grâce au travail. Et en ce qui concerne (*concerning*) le temps libre justement, 37 % l'utilisent pour leur famille, 28 % pour soi, 13 % pour leurs amours, 12 % pour leurs amis, et 12 % pour leurs engagements (*commitments*). Mais à la question « si je pouvais, je consacrerais davantage mon temps libre à... » 26 % répondent : mes engagements. Et quant à ce que les participant·e·s aiment faire pendant leur temps libre : apprendre (26 %), les récits (18 %), sociabiliser (17 %) ou bricoler (*DIY*) (17 %). Enfin, à la question de savoir ce que les participant·e·s feraient s'ils ou elles avaient une année sabbatique, 48 % répondent des voyages, 19 % une passion, 11 % une reconversion (*career change*), 8 % une cause, 7 % mes proches (*my relatives*).

Et vous, qu'en pensez-vous ? Est-ce que le monde va trop vite ? Quelles sont vos priorités ? Est-ce que vous avez le temps de faire ce que vous souhaitez ? Si vous aviez du temps, qu'aimeriez-vous faire ? Répondez à l'enquête sur la page web suivante.

VOCABULARY BUILDER 1

Look at the words and phrases and provide the missing English words and expressions. Then listen and try to imitate the pronunciation of the speakers.

S'ACCOMPLIR, S'ÉPANOUIR	*FULFILMENT AND FLOURISHING*
s'accomplir	*to be fulfilled*
bricoler	*to do DIY*
déstresser	*to unwind*
se détendre	*to relax*
s'épanouir	*to flourish*
des loisirs (masc.)	*free time, hobby*
la longévité	....
un passe-temps	*pastime*
une passion	....
des proches (masc.)	*close relatives*
la qualité de la vie	....
ralentir	*to slow down*
une reconversion	*redeployment*
sociabiliser	*to socialize*

EXPRESSIONS	*EXPRESSIONS*
vivre à cent à l'heure	*to be always on the go*
consacrer davantage de temps à	*devote more time to*
Moi, j'aime broder et tricoter.	*I like to embroider and knit.*
Elle veut se déconnecter des réseaux.	*She wants to get off all the networks.*
Si tu avais une année sabbatique...	*If you had a sabbatical year ...*

Vocabulary practice 1

Match the phrases on the left with the sentences on the right that touch on the same subject.

1 aimer bricoler	**a** Elle va passer un mois à faire du jardinage.
2 prendre une année sabbatique	**b** Il va arrêter de vivre à cent à l'heure.
3 consacrer du temps à	**c** Je prends du plaisir à refaire ma déco.
4 se détendre	**d** Tu as un congé de douze mois ? Chic !
5 tricoter	**e** Je vais faire un pull pour grand-père.
6 ralentir	**f** Nous allons déstresser.

CONVERSATION 1

Surprise ! *Surprise!*

20.02

1 Here are a few words and expressions to help you understand the conversation.

Je n'en reviens pas !	*I can't get over it!*
se douter de quelque chose	*to guess something*
Je ne m'y attendais pas.	*I wasn't expecting that.*
le moins qu'on puisse dire	*to put it mildly/the least one can say*
un monde fou	*crazy numbers of people*
C'était l'enfer !	*It was hellish/a real nightmare!*
de justesse	*only just*
s'éclater	*to have a great time*

20.03

2 Listen to the conversation without looking at the text. Then listen to the conversation again and read the text.

Charles, Eva, Jo and Assia are in a bar at the airport. They talk about their projects.

Assia Quelle merveilleuse surprise, vraiment, je n'en reviens pas ! Je suis si heureuse !

Jo Tu ne t'en doutais pas un peu ?

Assia Je ne m'y attendais pas du tout.

Jo Tant mieux, la surprise est réussie !

Assia Vous avez fait bon voyage ?

Eva Le moins qu'on puisse dire, c'est que c'était chaotique. Notre train pour Paris a été annulé à la dernière minute, et il a fallu prendre un bus jusqu'à Bordeaux. Heureusement, ensuite, on a pu prendre le TGV sans problème. Mais à Paris-Charles-de-Gaulle, il y avait un monde fou au contrôle des passeports, c'était l'enfer ! On est arrivés à la porte d'embarquement de justesse !

Charles Oui, l'horreur ! Si on avait su, on aurait pris le vol direct de Toulouse à Montréal, mais évidemment, on ne pouvait pas prévoir que je serais sélectionné pour la rencontre des jeunes chocolatiers de Bayonne...

Eva Et on avait déjà acheté nos billets depuis Paris...

Jo Bon — l'important, c'est qu'on soit tous là, et vous allez voir, on va s'éclater !

Assia J'ai préparé un programme pour deux, mais je vais régler tout ça, vous allez voir !

A little later, at the party.

Assia Et quels sont vos projets ?

Charles	À partir de septembre, j'aurai fini mon stage et je chercherai du travail.
Assia	À Bruxelles ?
Charles	Oui, Eva et moi, on va habiter ensemble.
Jo	J'en étais sûre !!! Félicitations !
Eva	Merci ! Je crois que tu t'en doutais... Et toi Assia, quels sont tes projets ?
Assia	Je ne sais pas encore exactement, mais quand je serai rentrée à Paris, je voudrais continuer la recherche que j'ai commencée, sur mes origines...

3 Answer the questions.

- **a** Comment Assia réagit-elle quand elle voit Jo, Charles et Eva ?
- **b** Pourquoi est-ce qu'Eva dit que leur voyage à Montréal était chaotique ?
- **c** Quel autre itinéraire est-ce que Charles et Eva auraient pu choisir ?
- **d** Quelle est la grande nouvelle annoncée par Charles ?
- **e** Qu'est-ce qu'Assia fera à son retour en France ?
- **f** Qu'est-ce que les quatre amis ont fait lorsqu'ils se sont retrouvés à l'aéroport ? (voir l'image ci-dessous)

Jo, Charles, Eva et Assia se retrouvent à l'aéroport de Montréal.

LANGUAGE BUILDER 1

Language discovery 1

Reflecting on the various mishaps of his and Eva's journey from Europe to Canada, Charles concludes: Si on avait su, on aurait pris le vol direct de Toulouse à Montréal (*If we had known, we would have taken the direct flight from Toulouse to Montreal*). The tense which Charles uses in the si-clause (Si on avait su) is le plus-que-parfait, followed by le conditionnel passé (on aurait pris) which you learned about in Unit 19.

1 Complete the tables below.

passé composé	j'	ai	pris
plus-que-parfait	j'	**a**	pris
conditionnel passé	j'	**b**	pris
passé composé	il	est	venu
plus-que-parfait	il	**c**	....
conditionnel passé	il	**d**	venu

2 In earlier units you have already worked with si-clauses. Can you remember the combinations of verb tenses you have learned so far which can be used with si-clauses? What are they?

More about conditional sentences

In Unit 17, you learned about two combinations of tenses that are often used in conditional sentences. (Remember: these typically comprise a si-clause + a main clause.) Here are two fresh examples using those combinations:

Si tu veux, nous chanterons ensemble. — *If you want, we will sing together.*

Si tu voulais, nous chanterions ensemble. — *If you wanted, we would sing together.*

They are examples of the following rules:

a Si + présent, **main clause** futur.

b Si + imparfait, **main clause** conditionnel.

Now it is time to learn a third combination of tenses often used in conditional sentences:

Si tu avais voulu, nous aurions chanté ensemble. — *If you had wanted, we would have sung together.*

c si + plus-que-parfait, **main clause** conditionnel passé.

The rules governing the agreement of the past participle are the same as for the other perfect tenses you have learned (le passé composé and le plus-que-parfait). Here are some examples with comments, to serve as a reminder of those rules:

Léa m'a dit que si elle avait été aux retrouvailles, elle aurait aimé revoir ses amis de lycée.

Léa told me that if she had been at the reunion, she would have liked to see her schoolfriends.

Here, aimer takes avoir and there is no **preceding direct object (PDO)**; therefore aimé does not agree.

À propos de Léa : si tu l'avais vue, tu l'aurais prévenue ? (*agreement with PDO*)

Talking of Léa: if you had seen her, you would have informed her about it?

Prévenir takes avoir, and the **past participle (PP)** (prévenue) agrees with the PDO (l' = la).

Si tu avais invité Léa and Marie, elles seraient venues, je crois.

If you had invited Léa and Marie, they would have come, I think.

Because venir takes être, the PP (venues) agrees with the subject (elles).

Et si elles étaient venues, elles se seraient beaucoup amusées.

And if they had come, they would have had a lot of fun.

Because s'amuser is reflexive, the PP (amusées) agrees with the subject (elles).

Language practice 1

1 Complete the sentences using the verb indicated.

Example: Si j'avais su, j'*aurais évité* de voyager via Paris. (*éviter*)

- **a** Si tu avais été là, tu .... la connaissance de Patrick. (*faire*)
- **b** Si nous avions manqué notre train, nous .... l'avion aussi. (*manquer*)
- **c** Si vous aviez prévenu tes frères, ils .... tout de suite. (*venir*)
- **d** Si vous aviez prévenu tes sœurs, elles .... tout de suite. (*venir*)
- **e** Nous .... à ta fête d'anniversaire si nous avions été au courant. (*assister*)

LANGUAGE BUILDER 2

Language discovery 2

20.04

Listen to the conversation again and repeat each line in the pauses.

Towards the end of their evening together, Assia asks her friends: Et quels sont vos projets ? (*And what are your plans?*). Charles replies: À partir de septembre, j'aurai fini mon stage et je chercherai du travail (*From September I will have finished my internship and I will look for work*). The tense of finir which Charles uses here is called le futur antérieur.

Can you find another example of le futur antérieur in Conversation 1?

Le futur antérieur *The future perfect*

We use le futur antérieur to project ourselves into a perspective from which we look back at an event that has not yet happened. Here are some examples:

Nous aurons bientôt terminé notre projet	*We will soon have finished our project*
À deux heures, nous aurons passé trois heures à attendre notre avion	*At 2 p.m., we will have spent three hours waiting for our plane*
Dans cinq minutes Marc sera revenu	*In five minutes from now Marc will have come back*

As these examples show, to form le futur antérieur you need the future tense of avoir or être and the past participle of the verb in question (aurons terminé; aurons passé; sera revenu). The rules concerning agreement of the past participle are the same as for le passé composé, le plus-que-parfait, and le conditionnel passé.

Note that the conjunction *when* is never followed by the future in English: we say *I will pick you up when you arrive* (present tense), not *when you will arrive* (future). However, in French conjunctions such as quand and lorsque can be followed by the futur or the futur antérieur. For example:

Quand tu verras Léo la prochaine fois, dis-lui bonjour de ma part. (verras = *future tense*)
When you next see Leo, say hi to him from me. (*see* = *present tense*)

Quand ton avion aura atterri, téléphone-moi. (aura atterri = futur antérieur)
When your airplane has landed, telephone me. (*has landed* = passé composé)

Lorsqu'il sera redescendu, il nous parlera. (sera redescendu = futur antérieur)
When he has come back down, he will speak to us. (*has come back down* = passé composé)

Language practice 2

1 Complete the sentences using le futur antérieur.

a Quand il ...., tout sera plus clair. (*téléphoner*)
b Dans trois mois, il .... le projet. (*terminer*)
c Si tout se passe bien, nous .... le paquet avant le week-end. (*recevoir*)

2 In each case below, indicate why there is an agreement of the (underlined) past participle. Choose between: (1) the past participle agrees with the preceding direct object; (2) the past participle agrees with the subject.

a La répétition que nous avons entendue était très belle.
The performance we heard was very beautiful.
b Le commerçant lui avait vendu très cher les fleurs qu'il avait achetées.
The shopkeeper had sold him the flowers he'd bought at a very high price.
c Si elle avait su que c'était permis, Laure serait arrivée plus tôt.
If she had known it was allowed, Laure would have arrived earlier.
d Lorsque nous serons parties, nous allons te manquer !
When we've left, you're going to miss us!

20.05 **3 Listen to Conversation 2 and play the part of Assia.**

CULTURE POINT 2

Intelligence artificielle et éducation

La communauté éducative est en effervescence (*in turmoil*). L'accélération du développement de l'intelligence artificielle (IA) représente-t-elle une opportunité ou un danger ? Les tuteurs et chatbots virtuels vont-ils remplacer les enseignantes et les enseignants ? Pourra-t-on à l'avenir parler chacun dans sa langue maternelle, sans avoir à (*without having to*) apprendre une autre langue, grâce à l'interprétariat (*interpretation*) ou à la traduction automatique ? L'AI permet depuis quelque temps déjà (*for some time already*) de corriger l'orthographe (*spelling*) et la grammaire de textes écrits dans notre langue maternelle ou dans une langue que nous apprenons. Mais la nouveauté, c'est que l'IA peut désormais écrire des textes et produire des documents complexes. De même (*similarly*), l'IA est désormais capable de parler, et nous pouvons dialoguer avec des machines dans une autre langue. Alors, que penser de cette nouveauté ? Nombre de spécialistes de l'éducation sont optimistes et voient dans l'IA une innovation utile (*see AI as a useful innovation*) pour l'apprentissage des langues. L'IA permet par exemple de faire des exercices pour mémoriser le vocabulaire ou pour pratiquer sa prononciation. On peut aussi s'amuser à écrire un texte et le traduire dans notre langue maternelle. Mais attention, l'IA fait encore des erreurs, et il faut contrôler les traductions ou les textes écrits par la machine. Mais surtout l'IA ne remplace pas la communication avec une personne ! On peut donc s'entraîner et se perfectionner en faisant des exercices supplémentaires adaptés à ses besoins, mais pour vos discussions lors de votre prochain voyage en France, en Belgique ou au Canada, ou lors de votre rencontre avec des ami·e·s francophones, ce sera à vous de jouer (*it will be in your hands*), sans machine !

Lisez le blog suivant. Quels sont les avantages de l'IA ? À qui faut-il faire attention ?

VOCABULARY BUILDER 2

20.06

Read the words and phrases below. Then listen to the recording and imitate the pronunciation you hear. Fill in the gaps.

L'INTELLIGENCE ARTIFICIELLE/IA	*ARTIFICIAL INTELLIGENCE/AI*
un chatbot	....
contrôler	*to check*
corriger	*to correct*
désormais	*now/from now on*
un être humain	*human being*
mémoriser	....
une nouveauté	*novelty*
une opportunité	....
un optimiste, une optimiste	....
l'orthographe (fem.)	*spelling*
un/une spécialiste	....
une traduction	*translation*

EXPRESSIONS	*EXPRESSIONS*
depuis quelque temps déjà	*for some time now*
faciliter l'apprentissage des langues	*to facilitate language learning*
un texte écrit par une machine	*machine-generated text*
Un tuteur virtuel, c'est très utile.	*A virtual tutor is very useful.*
L'IA ne traduit pas toujours bien.	*AI does not always give a good translation.*
Seuls les êtres humains peuvent réfléchir.	*Only human beings can think.*
La traduction automatique s'améliore.	*Automatic translation is improving.*

Vocabulary practice 2

Match the phrases on the left with the sentences on the right that touch on the same ideas.

a un tuteur virtuel
b développer l'IA
c une opportunité
d un être humain

1 On améliore les systèmes qui imitent la pensée humaine.
2 Ces progrès ouvrent de nouveaux horizons.
3 On ne remplace pas une femme, un homme, un enfant.
4 Désormais les ordinateurs peuvent remplacer les professeurs.

CONVERSATION 2

À la nôtre ! *To us!*

20.07

1 Here are a few words and expressions to help you understand the conversation.

une lutte ; lutter	*battle; to fight/struggle*	des progrès (masc. pl.)	*progress*
une intervention	*intervention; contribution*	trinquer à quelque chose	*to toast something*
un chercheur, une chercheuse	*scientist; researcher*	l'amour (masc.)	*love*
les défis à relever	*the challenges to be met*	l'amitié (fem.)	*friendship*

20.08

2 Listen to the conversation without looking at the text. Then listen to the conversation again and read the text.

Charles, Eva, Jo and Assia are in a restaurant. They talk about the conference on climate change which they attended earlier.

Assia C'était très stimulant, cette conférence !

Charles Oui, j'étais content qu'il reste encore des places et que nous ayons pu vous accompagner. Les interventions étaient excellentes.

Eva Et les questions du public très justes.

Jo Oui, mais c'est dommage qu'on n'ait pas entendu les associations qui luttent pour la préservation de la planète.

Assia C'est vrai, mais c'était une conférence scientifique, avec des chercheuses et des chercheurs.

Charles Moi, j'ai apprécié qu'ils ne parlent pas uniquement des défis à relever, mais aussi des progrès accomplis.

Eva Oui, c'était encourageant.

Jo En êtes-vous bien sûrs ? Moi, j'ai entendu qu'il était urgent d'agir.

Assia Bon, on trinque à un monde meilleur ? Eva, que souhaites-tu ?

Eva Moi ? Que le monde soit plus juste !

Charles Et moi que notre planète soit préservée !

Assia Et pour nous, que désirons-nous ?

Jo De l'amour et de l'amitié !

Eva À l'amour, alors !

Tous Santé, à la nôtre.

3 Answer the questions.

- **a** Quel est le regret de Jo au sujet de la conférence sur le changement climatique ?
- **b** Qu'a pensé Charles de la conférence ?
- **c** À quoi est-ce qu'Assia propose de trinquer ?
- **d** Quels sont les souhaits d'Eva et de Charles ?
- **e** Et ceux de Jo et Eva ?

LANGUAGE BUILDER 3

Language discovery 3

While Charles and Eva express a view that the climate conference placed emphasis on progress to date, Jo asks: En êtes-vous bien sûrs ? (*Are you quite sure of that?*).

1 Can you identify the subject and the verb in this question? Choose the correct alternative in order to complete the following statement: In Jo's question, the verb (a) precedes (b) follows the subject.

Jo asks two further questions, as follows: Eva, que souhaites-tu ? Et pour nous, que désirons-nous ?

2 Of these further questions, which, if any, place the subject and the verb in the same relative position as En êtes-vous sûrs ? Choose from the following: (a) neither; (b) one only; (c) both.

Simple and complex inversions

You have learned to ask questions in three ways. First, you have simply placed a question mark at the end of a statement. For instance, to ask *Are you Monsieur Legrand?* you can say Vous êtes Monsieur Legrand ? Second, you have learned that, once you have added an interrogative word such as quoi, comment or où to the end of a request for information, you just need to add a question mark. Here are a couple of examples:

Tu t'appelles comment ?	*What are you called?*
Vous faites quoi ?	*What are you doing?*

A third way of asking a question is to begin with qu'est-ce que or est-ce que :

Est-ce que nous sommes arrivés ?	*Have we arrived?*
or Qu'est-ce que vous allez porter ?	*What are you going to wear?*

If you look carefully you will see that est-ce que literally means *is it that …?* and qu'est-ce que means *what is it that …?* And in each case, the subject (ce) comes after the verb (est). This shows that you can make a question in French by inverting the normal order of subject and verb, or putting the second element first:

Comment t'appelles-tu?	*What are you called?*

If you use inversion to ask a question, any subject pronoun you use must be linked to the verb by a hyphen:

Que fais-tu ?	*What are you doing?*
Comment vas-tu ?	*How are you?*

You will hear and read more complex inversions such as Où Pierre est-il encore allé se cacher ? (*Where has Pierre gone to hide himself again?*). Here you note that, although the subject is Pierre, the inversion requires us to add a pronoun (il) so as to be able to create an inversion between the verb and the pronoun. Some further examples:

Quand Paul part-il ?	*When is Paul leaving?*
Quand Emilia revient-elle ?	*When is Emilia returning?*

To ask *What is Léa doing?* you can use quoi: Léa fait quoi ? But if you use inversion to ask the same question, you should replace quoi by que: Que fait Léa? (*What is Léa doing?*)

You can also use qu'est-ce que to underline a fact rather than to ask a question, so, for example, Qu'est-ce qu'elle est intelligente ! (*How intelligent is she !*) is not a question about her level of intelligence, rather it is recognition that she is very intelligent. Some further examples: Qu'est-ce qu'ils sont doués ! (*How gifted are they!*); Qu'est-ce que les jumeaux sont malins ! (*How sly are the twins!*). These statements using qu'est-ce que can in themselves be abbreviated using inversion: Est-elle intelligente, cette fille !, which can simply be translated as a positive statement rather than as a question—*How intelligent is she!* or *She is just so intelligent!*

Language practice 3

1 Provide alternative forms of the questions below using est-ce que or qu'est-ce que.

Example: Karine et Camille vont où ? Où *est-ce que Karine et Camille vont* ?

a Vous partez quand ? Quand .... ?

b Tu fais comment pour réussir tes gâteaux ? Comment .... ?

c Les chaussures coûtent combien ? Combien .... ?

d Les enfants vont faire quoi demain ? Qu' .... ?

2 Provide alternative forms of the questions below. Do not use est-ce que or qu'est-ce que.

Example: Nous allons où maintenant ? Où *allons-nous maintenant* ?

a Vous faites quoi demain ? Que .... ?

b Vous vous appelez comment ? Comment .... ?

c Les autres sont où actuellement ? Où .... ?

d Elles sortent quand ? Quand .... ?

e Je dois faire quoi avant de partir ? Que. .... ?

LANGUAGE BUILDER 4

Language discovery 4

20.09

Listen to the conversation again and repeat each line in the pauses.

1 Charles uses the subjonctif twice in one sentence when he says: j'étais content qu'il reste des places et que nous ayons pu vous accompagner. What tense of the subjonctif is reste, and what tense is ayons pu?

2 Can you find two other sentences in the dialogue where the subjonctif is used?

Tenses of the subjonctif

You have already learned two tenses of the subjunctive (le subjonctif présent and le subjonctif passé), which are the only two that survive in modern spoken French. So the question arises: how to translate a sentence such as *Although he was feeling poorly, Marc went to the concert* into French? At first this will seem puzzling because, as you know, you would generally use the imparfait to translate *Marc was feeling poorly* (= Marc se sentait mal). But you also know that the subjunctive is required following quoique and bien que (both of which mean *although*). In fact, speakers of French use the *present* subjunctive in such cases, because in context they still understand it as referring to a past event. So this is the correct way to translate the sentence above: Bien qu'il se sente mal, Marc est allé au concert.

A similar solution exists for translating a sentence such as *Although he had felt poorly, he was already feeling better*: Bien qu'il se soit senti mal, il allait déjà mieux. Here, the idea otherwise conveyed by the plus-que-parfait, il s'était senti mal (*he had felt ill*) is conveyed by qu'il se soit senti mal, which is a passé du subjonctif. To see these possibilities side by side, see the table below, where we have used pleuvoir (*to rain*) as our example.

pleuvoir (*to rain*)

Indicative tense	Example	Subjunctive equivalent	Example
il pleut (présent)	Il pleut aujourd'hui. (*It's raining today.*)	qu'il pleuve (présent)	Je regrette qu'il pleuve aujourd'hui. (*I'm sorry it's raining today.*)
il a plu (passé composé)	Il a plu toute la journée. (*It rained the whole day.*)	qu'il ait plu (passé)	Je regrette qu'il ait plu toute la journée. (*I'm sorry it rained the whole day.*)
il pleuvait (imparfait)	Il pleuvait quand elle est arrivée. (*It was raining when she arrived*)	qu'il pleuve (présent)	Je regrettais qu'il pleuve quand elle est arrivée. (*I was sorry it was raining when she arrived.*)
il avait plu (plus-que-parfait)	Il avait plu la veille. (*It had rained the night before.*)	qu'il ait plu (passé)	Je regrettais qu'il ait plu la veille. (*I was sorry it had rained the day before*)

Language practice 4

1 Write modified versions of the sentences below, using either le subjonctif présent or le subjonctif passé.

a Mathilde n'a pas pu venir ce soir. Je regrette que ....

b Grand-mère peut venir demain soir. Papa est content que ....

c Vous réfléchissez profondément. Il faut que ....

d Ils ne nous ont pas répondu. Ça m'énerve qu' ....

20.10

2 Congratulations—this is your final speaking practice! First listen to Conversation 2 and play the role of Charles in the pauses. Then why not go and celebrate with friends, and discuss what you might all wish for and why?

SKILL BUILDER

1 Complete the translations of the following sentences.

a If you had been there, you would have met Patrick.
Si tu .... Patrick.

b If we had missed the train, we would have missed our flight.
Si nous .... notre vol.

c If you had invited your brothers, they would have come.
Si tu ....

d We would have come to your birthday party if we had known about it.
On ....

e If we had taken the 6 p.m. train we would have arrived home before dinner.
Si on ....

2 Use le subjonctif du passé to complete the sentences.

a Mon oncle, qui avait raté son vol, voulait partir en vacances.
Bien que mon oncle ....

b Benjamin est en retard. pourtant il était arrivé en courant.
Benjamin est en retard, bien qu' ....

c Nous avions finalement retrouvé nos valises, mais nous avons raté notre correspondance.
Bien que nous ....

3 Translate the sentences into French using a form of complex inversion.

Example: How does that young woman know that? *Comment cette jeune femme sait-elle cela ?*

a How does Anne-Marie read so much? ....

b Do the teachers know that they are receiving a prize? ....

c Are the children still in bed? ....

TEST YOURSELF

1 Complete the sentences using the correct form of le futur antérieur or le conditionnel.

a Paul nous manquera lorsqu'il .... (*partir*)

b Si j'avais su que le train aurait du retard, j' .... d'autres projets. (*faire*)

c Lorsque nous .... , nous pourrons partir. (*manger*)

d Si tu avais vraiment voulu trouver le bon chemin, tu .... sur un plan. (*chercher*)

2 Translate the sentences into French using a form of a complex inversion.

a How do Fatou and Assia know so much about gastronomy? ....

b Do the members of the public know that they are being filmed? ....

c Is my brother still at work? ....

3 Complete the sentences using the correct form of le subjonctif du passé.

a Eloi et Isabelle n'ont pas pu venir la semaine dernière. Nous regrettons qu'elles .... (*venir*)

b Jean et Paul ne m'ont pas répondu. Ça m'étonne qu'ils .... (*répondre*)

c Les grands-parents étaient arrivés tard dans la nuit. J'étais ravie qu'ils .... sains et saufs. (*arriver*)

d Marguerite est venue bien qu'elle .... souffrante. (*être*)

e Leila et Jasmine sont parties bien qu'elles n' .... pas .... (*finir*)

Remember to use **My review** and **My takeaway** to assess your progress and reflect on your learning experience.

Congratulations, you have now completed the final level of your studies! Put your skills to the test—take the B1 Assessment online at library.teachyourself.com and see how much you've learned.

Answer key

Pronouncing consonants in French

00.03

une puce soft, ici soft, ancre hard, cela soft, ça soft, culbuter hard

Days of the week and months of the year

1 a5 **b**4 **c**1 **d**3 **e**6 **f**2 dimanche ultimately comes from the Latin dies dominica (the Lord's day) **2 a**8 **b**4 **c**12 **d**2 **e**1 **f**6 **g**7 **h**5 **i**3 **j**11 **k**10 **l**9

Unit 1

VOCABULARY PRACTICE 1 **1** c **2** a **3** b **4** d

PRONUNCIATION PRACTICE 1 **1** bonjour; bonsoir; Garcia; Jo **2** Over to you ...

CONVERSATION 1 **2 a** Lausanne, Switzerland **b** Paris, France **c** Eva: English, French, Italian; Charles: English, French, Spanish **d** a neighbor **e** the fifth floor

LANGUAGE DISCOVERY 1 **1 a** tu **b** vous; **2 a** Tu **b** Tu **c** Vous; **3** Tu is informal, while vous (when used to address one person only) is formal. So young people generally use tu to address each other, even when they first meet. By contrast, vous should be used in all formal situations (e.g., meeting someone significantly older than you, or talking to your boss). Also, vous must always be used if you are addressing more than one person, because it is the only way to say *you* in the plural.

LANGUAGE PRACTICE 1 **1 a** F **b** INF **c** INF **d** F **e** INF **f** F **g** F **2 a** vous **b** tu **c** Vous **d** vous, vous **e** Tu

ACTIONS IN THE PRESENT **a** parles **b** parle **c** parlons **d** parlez

LANGUAGE DISCOVERY 2 **1** d **2** b **3** e **4** a **5** c

LANGUAGE PRACTICE 2 **a** habite **b** parles **c** habitons **d** parle **e** habites **f** parlons

VOCABULARY BUILDER 2 Mexican, Japanese, Turkish, Chinese

VOCABULARY PRACTICE 2 **1 a** anglaise *Rachel is English.* **b** chinois *Lian is Chinese.* **c** marocaine *Fatima is Moroccan.* **d** japonaise *Naomi is Japanese.* **2** chinois/chinoise – c; belge/belge – a; grec/grecque – **b**

PRONUNCIATION PRACTICE 2 Over to you ...

CONVERSATION 2 **3 a** a restaurant **b** Malian and French **c** a Canadian restaurant **d** writing a blog

LANGUAGE DISCOVERY 3 The masc. adjectives chinois and généreux are the same in the singular and the plural.

LES ADJECTIFS PLURIELS No -s is added to the plural in the case of chinois (masc. sing) or généreux (masc. sing). If a singular adjective ends in an -s or an -x, you do not add an -s to make it plural.

LANGUAGE PRACTICE 3 **1 a** ambitieuses **b** chinoises **c** indiens **d** généreuses **e** modestes **2 a** maliennes **b** canadiens **c** généreux **d** créatives

LANGUAGE DISCOVERY 4 I am happy. you are, we are

LANGUAGE PRACTICE 4 **a** est, est **b** est, est **c** suis **d** sommes **e** êtes **f** es **g** sont

SKILL BUILDER 1 (Sample answer): Sophie parle anglais et allemand. Elle habite à Berlin et elle est allemande. Elle aime la cuisine chinoise. **2 a** faux **b** faux **c** faux **d** faux **e** vrai

TEST YOURSELF 1 a tu **b** Bonjour **c** habite **d** habitent **e** parle **f** parlent **g** canadiens **h** américaines **i** suis, es **j** sont **2 a**2 **b**1 **c**4 **d**3 **e**6 **f**5 **3 a** est, habite **b** français, français, anglais, espagnol. Bruxelles **c** malienne **d** est, canadien, français **e** habite, parle, anglais

Unit 2

VOCABULARY BUILDER 1 architect, chef, journalist, start-up company

VOCABULARY PRACTICE 1 a hôpital **b** restaurant **c** école **2 a** avocat **b** cinéaste **c** professeure

PRONUNCIATION PRACTICE Over to you ...

CONVERSATION 1 Eva: photographe/suisse; Charles: apprenti chocolatier/française; Jeanette: architecte, néerlandaise; Bjorn: informaticien, danoise

LANGUAGE DISCOVERY 1 Eva uses un apprenti chocolatier prometteur, so she does not follow the rule (to drop un/une). The explanation is that when an adjective (e.g. prometteur) is added to a profession, un or une is also used.

PROFESSIONS + ADJECTIFS 1 a un apprenti chocolatier **b** architecte **c** un informaticien **2 a** inclusive **b** not inclusive **c** not inclusive

LANGUAGE PRACTICE 1 a Infirmière **b** avocate **c** vendeur **d** écrivain **e** boulanger

LANGUAGE DISCOVERY 2 do, make

THE VERB FAIRE There is no difference in pronunciation. Not counting the infinitive, faire is pronounced in four different ways.

LANGUAGE PRACTICE 2 1 a faites (make) **b** faisons (do) **c** font (do) **d** fait (make) **e** fais (do)

VOCABULARY BUILDER 2 Mum, Dad, parents, grandparents, cousin

VOCABULARY PRACTICE 2 a nièce **b** oncle **c** mari, parents **d** belle-sœur, beau-frère **e** mari, femme

CONVERSATION 2 2 a Jo's grandmother's 80th birthday **b** more than 60 **c** They are her aunts. **d** Yanis, 6 years old, cute **e** Over to you ...

LANGUAGE DISCOVERY 3 Ma and mon mean *my*; ma is feminine singular and mon is masculine singular.

LANGUAGE PRACTICE 3 a ta tante **b** son frère **c** sa sœur **d** notre grand-mère **e** votre cousin **f** leur belle-sœur

LANGUAGE DISCOVERY 4 Ma mère a deux sœurs. — J'ai douze cousins et cousines. — Tu as combien de cousins?

LANGUAGE PRACTICE 4 1 a avez **b** a, a **c** a **d** avons **e** ai, a **f** ont. There are possessives in **b**, **c**, and **e**, as follows: **b** Sa mère, son père **c** ton frère **e** mon petit frère. **2 a** l'anniversaire de la grand-mère de Jo **b** plus de 60 personnes **c** Catherine et Brigitte sont les tantes de Jo. **d** La personne la plus jeune sur la photo est Yanis. Il est mignon. Il a six ans.

SKILL BUILDER 1 a Bruxelles **b** a **c** est, a **d** habite, parle. **2 a**2 **b**1 **c**4 **d**3 **e**6 **f**5 **3 a**2 **b**4 **c**1 **d**5 **e**3 **f**7 **g**6 **4** Over to you.

TEST YOURSELF 1 a fais **b** ai **c** a, a **d** ma **e** mes **f** cinéaste **g** informaticien, médecin **h** journaliste, oncle

Unit 3

VOCABULARY BUILDER 1 cricket, tennis, rugby

VOCABULARY PRACTICE 1 **a**2 **b**4 **c**3 **d**1

PRONUNCIATION PRACTICE **1**b **2**b **3**b **4**a

CONVERSATION 1 **a** pétanque, weights, fencing, cycling and horseback riding **b** No. **c** Yes. **d** rock-climbing, horseback riding **e** cycling and horseback riding

LANGUAGE DISCOVERY 1 The opening question means *What do you feel like doing?*

LANGUAGE PRACTICE 1 **1** **a**4 **b**3 **c**1 **d**2 **2** **a** Est-ce que **b** Qu'est-ce qu' **c** Est-ce que **d** Qu'est-ce qu' **e** Qu'est-ce qu' **3** **a** Est-ce que Jean aime la voile ? **b** Est-ce que Béatrice et Marc aiment l'équitation ? **c** Est-ce que vous aimez faire du ski ? **d** Est-ce qu'ils aiment aller au restaurant le week-end ? **e** Est-ce que Leïla aime le golf ?

LANGUAGE DISCOVERY 2 *I like sailing* = J'aime la voile. – In the negative version, ne precedes and pas follows the verb (aime). – This is how a positive sentence becomes negative.

LANGUAGE PRACTICE 2 **1** **a** pas **b** n' **c** n', pas **d** ne, pas **2** **a** Elle va au cinéma. **b** Il mange au restaurant. **c** Isabelle aime la voile. **d** Béatrice et sa sœur aiment le football. **3** **a** Elle ne va pas au match de football. **b** Ils ne mangent pas au restaurant. **c** Milou ne travaille pas le week-end. **d** Ismaël n'habite pas à Lyon. **4** **a** Non, je n'aime pas jouer au cricket. **b** Non, elle n'est pas française. **c** Non, il n'habite pas à Marseille. **d** Non, ils ne travaillent pas le week-end.

VOCABULARY BUILDER 2 sitar, flute, saxophone, trumpet, triangle, xylophone, accordion, piano

VOCABULARY PRACTICE 2 **1**b **2**d **3**a **4**c

CONVERSATION 2 **2** **a** It is a special week when the museums open through the night. **b** The Comic Strip museum, the Musical Instruments museum, the Museum of fashion and lace. **c** trumpet (Charles), bagpipes and piano (Eva). **d** a mystery visit **e** They decide to visit the museum of fashion and the Comic Strip museum.

LANGUAGE DISCOVERY 3 le, la, la, les. Yes, there is a parallel; just as un is masc. sing. and une is fem. sing., so le is masc. sing. and la is fem. sing.

LANGUAGE PRACTICE 3 **1** **a** la **b** le **c** les **d** l' **2** la, le, un, des, des, les

LANGUAGE DISCOVERY 4 **a** de **b** du

LANGUAGE PRACTICE 4 **1** **a** du **b** au **c** de la **d** à la **e** à l' **f** de l' **g** des **h** aux

SKILL BUILDER **1** **a** the sports club **b** football, dancing, fencing, yoga, aikido, boxing **c** le football, le yoga, la danse, la boxe, l'escrime, l'aïkido **d** You need to send an e-mail to the address given. **2** Over to you ...

TEST YOURSELF **1** **a**1 **b**5 **c**3 **d**2 **e**4 **f**7 **g**6 **h**8 **2** **a** Qu'est-ce que, jouer au **b** un, le **c** Est-ce que, au basket, au basket **d** Est-ce que, du **e** à l', suis, j'ai, n', le, ne, pas, le, de la

Unit 4

VOCABULARY BUILDER 1 bank, park, post office, supermarket

VOCABULARY PRACTICE 1 **a** banque **b** livre **c** boucherie **d** fromage **e** boulangerie **f** bouquet (de fleurs)

PRONUNCIATION PRACTICE Over to you ...

CONVERSATION 1 3 a Yes. **b** delicatessen, fishmonger's, cheese shop, grocery **c** Yes. **d** a grocery **e** a park **f** a bookshop

LANGUAGE DISCOVERY 1 1 five **2** Il y **a** means *there is* or *there are*.

THERE IS, THERE ARE a une boulangerie (singular) **b** des banques (plural) **c** un parc (singular) **d** des salons de coiffure (plural)

LANGUAGE PRACTICE 1 1 a bibliothèque **b** supermarché **c** parcs **d** il y a, fleurs **2 a** Is there a bakery? **b** Are there two bakeries? **c** Is there a post office? **d** Are there two post offices?

LANGUAGE DISCOVERY 2 1 devant, après, derrière, avant **2 a** after **b** before **c** next to

GIVING DIRECTIONS d Les deux enfants sont devant la fontaine.

LANGUAGE PRACTICE 2 1 a derrière **b** à côté de **c** après **d** avant **2** Over to you ... **3 a** vrai **b** vrai **c** faux **4 a** à côté du **b** loin du **c** près de la

VOCABULARY BUILDER 2 square, mosque, synagogue

VOCABULARY PRACTICE 2 a piscine **b** passage piétons **c** arrêt

CONVERSATION 2 3 a Rue d'Angleterre **b** Rue Haute **c** nougat and marshmallow

LANGUAGE DISCOVERY 3 1 a The imperative **b** The subject **2 b, c**

LANGUAGE PRACTICE 3 1 a écoutez **b** arrêtons **c** reste **d** restons **2** a, e, f, h

LANGUAGE DISCOVERY 4 a du **b** de la – Du is used with masculine nouns and de la with feminine nouns (that begin with a consonant)

LANGUAGE PRACTICE 4 1 a eau **b** lait **c** chocolats **d** farine

SKILL BUILDER 1 a illustratrice – Aurélie Neyret is an illustrator. **b** livre – Today I must go to the library to find a book. **c** banque – I need some money – do you want to go to the bank with me? **d** épicier – We do our shopping at the grocer's. **e** voulons – We want to buy (some) bread before dinner. **f** loin – Is the bookshop far from your house? **g** vingt – There are twenty districts in Paris. **h** écoutons – Let's listen to (some) music tonight/this evening. **i** du, beurre, café – For breakfast I have (some) bread with (some) butter and a coffee. **2-3** Over to you ...

TEST YOURSELF a des banques, des librairies, des cinémas, des parcs et des supermarchés **b** il y a, librairie, boulangerie **c** à côté de la bibliothèque **d** allez au cinéma **e** est près, maison **f** Arrêtons de travailler **g** des, de l'

Unit 5

VOCABULARY BUILDER 1 pyjamas, toilet/W.C., shampoo

VOCABULARY PRACTICE 1 1c **2**a **3**d **4**e **5**b

PRONUNCIATION PRACTICE 1 The nous and vous forms of s'appeler only have one l (nous nous appelons, vous vous appelez), but all the other forms have a double l (e.g. je m'appelle). In the nous and vous forms the e is pronounced as in je; in the other forms it is pronounced as in architecte. As for se lever, the nous and vous forms have no accent over the e (nous nous levons, vous vous levez), but all the other forms contain è (e.g. je me lève). Where there is no accent over the e, it is pronounced as in je, but where there is a grave accent, it is pronounced as in mère.

CONVERSATION 1 2 a Eva sleeps in and Charles gets up early. **b** sport **c** lie in **d** Charles **e** to clean, sleep, read, speak with her parents, and have brunch with Charles

LANGUAGE DISCOVERY 1 **a** je me repose, je me réveille (x2), je me lève (x2), je me douche, je m'habille, je me maquille, je me couche, je m'endors = 10 in total **b** They use me before a consonant, m' before a vowel or (unaspirated) h. **c** These verbs are used when the speaker or speakers are doing something to themselves, e.g. dressing (oneself), showering (oneself), etc.

VERBES RÉFLÉCHIS (tu) te réveilles, (ils/elles) se réveillent

LANGUAGE PRACTICE 1 **1** **a**3 **b**1 **c**2 **d**5 **e**4

LANGUAGE DISCOVERY 2 No, it refers to something she is about to do – *I am going to do the cleaning.*

LANGUAGE PRACTICE 2 **1** **a** allons **b** manger **c** allez **d** va **e** manger **2** **a** va commencer **b** va partir **c** allons prendre **d** vont manger **e** allez faire **f** va se laver **g** vais aller

VOCABULARY BUILDER 2 scooter, motorcycle, tram

VOCABULARY PRACTICE 2 **a** déplacer **b** métro/le tramway/le train **c** orienter **d** transports **e** aimez

CONVERSATION 2 **3** **a** the Salon de la photo (Photography exhibition) **b** by metro **c** to avoid traffic **d** because the tram is nicer than the metro

LANGUAGE DISCOVERY 3 **1** The infinitive is prendre. It ends in -re, while parler and manger end in -er. **2** descend

LANGUAGE PRACTICE 3 **1** **a**4 **b**1 **c**2 **d**3

LANGUAGE DISCOVERY 4 **1** In French, there are three words for that: ce (masc. before a consonant), cet (masc. before a vowel) or cette (fem.). The choice depends on the spelling and gender of the noun that immediately follows. **2** Here, ce means *this*. All three words for saying *that* in French can also be used for saying *this*. Their common purpose is to highlight a particular thing.

LANGUAGE PRACTICE 4 **1** **a**4 **b**3 **c**2 **d**1

SKILL BUILDER **1** se coucher, s'endormir, se réveiller, se lever, se doucher, s'habiller **2** le matin – faire la grasse matinée, se lever, prendre le petit déjeuner; vers midi – bruncher, déjeuner; le soir – dîner, se coucher **3-4** Over to you ...

TEST YOURSELF **1** **a** me réveille **b** me lave **c** m'habille **d** me brosse **e** prends **f** vais attendre **g** descends **h** vais faire **i** prends **j** me couche **2** **a** vendez **b** attends **c** dépend **d** prenons **3** **a** ces **b** ce **c** cette **d** cet **e** ces

Unit 6

VOCABULARY BUILDER 1 anorak, coat, sandals, pullover, t-shirt

VOCABULARY PRACTICE 1 **a** des chaussettes **b** un manteau **c** des tennis **d** des chaussures **e** un pull **f** un tee-shirt

CONVERSATION 1 **3** **a** suit pants **b** grey **c** A pair of light grey striped trousers in wool and a pair of plain dark grey trousers in velvet — the second is more expensive. **d** He prefers the trousers in wool. **e** for the winter, some warm, red gloves in wool.

LANGUAGE DISCOVERY 1 There are 5 adjectives. They are placed after the noun they qualify, so rayé and gris are placed after un pantalon, and bleue, décontractée and légère after une chemise. A similar sentence is spoken by the salesperson: Voici deux modèles [...] en velours.

LANGUAGE BUILDER 1 - ADJECTIVES (CONTINUED) **Table:** **a** bleus **b** rouges **c** vertes **d** bleues **e** rouges

LANGUAGE PRACTICE 1 1 The correct answers are: **a** the same **b** different **c** the same. **2** (Sample answer) ... the feminine forms (blanche, blanches) are made by adding -he to the masculine forms (blanc, blancs). **3 a** bleus **b** blanches **c** gris **d** rouge **e** noirs

LANGUAGE DISCOVERY 2 Lequel refers to masc. sing. nouns, laquelle to fem. sing. nouns, lesquels to masc. plural nouns and lesquelles to fem. plural nouns.

LANGUAGE PRACTICE 2 1 a quel **b** quelles **c** quelle **d** quels **2 a** laquelle **b** lequel **c** lesquelles **d** lesquels

VOCABULARY BUILDER 2 presenter, sustainable/green, elegant, practical, unisex

VOCABULARY PRACTICE 2 a regarder **b** fête **c** sortir, rester **d** adore

CONVERSATION 2 3 a It can be worn for work or going out. **b** the dark green one **c** dark colors **d** it's an elegant unisex garment that is nice to wear. **e** lively colors (red, blue, yellow and green)

LANGUAGE DISCOVERY 3 1 veux, peux – These verb forms end in -x, unlike the other verbs presented so far. **2** Vouloir and pouvoir can be followed by an infinitive.

LANGUAGE PRACTICE 3 a peux – Can you buy some socks for me? **b** voulez – Which shirt do you want to buy? **c** peut – She can come tonight. **d** veulent – They want to go to the museum. **e** veux – I don't want to swim today. **f** pouvons – We can have a very quick lunch. **g** voulez – Do you want to take part in the photography session? **h** peut – What can we do to help you? **i** peux – Can you make (the) breakfast? **j** pouvons – We can wait until 10 o'clock.

LANGUAGE DISCOVERY 4 -là, -ci. Ce pull-là means *that pullover* (= the one farther away), ce pull-ci means *this pullover* (=the one close by). They are often used to contrast two items.

LANGUAGE PRACTICE 4 1 a3 **b**6 **c**2 **d**4 **e**1 **f**5 **2 a** celui-là **b** celle-là **c** celles-là **d** celui-là **e** ceux-là

SKILL BUILDER 1 Bleu is spelled in four ways – bleu (masc. sing.), bleue (fem. sing.), bleus (masc. plural) and bleues (fem. plural). Adjectives generally agree with the noun they qualify. **2** Over to you **3** Quel/over to you, Quels/over to you, Quel/over to you

TEST YOURSELF (Sample answers) **a** Lequel est-ce que tu aimes ? – J'aime celui-ci. **b** Lequel est-ce que tu portes – le rouge ou le vert ? – Le vert. **c** Vous chaussez du combien ? – Je chausse du 42. – Parfait. Je reviens. **d** Quel couleur préfères-tu ? Moi, je préfère les robes jaunes. **e** Est-ce qu'elle cherche une jupe courte ou longue ? – Plutôt longue, je crois. **f** Et vous avez une couleur préférée ? – Lui, il aime le vert, mais moi, je préfère le bleu marine. **g** Ils voudraient un t-shirt uni ou rayé ? – Rayé, en bleu et blanc. **h** Il a lieu à Dakar. Elles le regardent tous les ans. **i** Oui, car j'ai un entretien lundi. – C'est vrai qu'il faut être bien habillé pour un entretien. **j** Oui, surtout en laine. C'est bien pour l'hiver.

Unit 7

VOCABULARY BUILDER 1 biopic, comedy

VOCABULARY PRACTICE 1 1 a sous-titré, doublé **b** la billetterie **c** un billet, une place/un siège **d** le générique **2 a** Quand nous allons au cinéma en famille, nous regardons un dessin animé. **b** Elle aime les sièges dans ce cinéma. **c** Je préfère regarder le film en v.o.

CONVERSATION 1 3 a Saturday **b** They are all movies by women directors. **c** *Anatomie d'une chute* (*Anatomy of a Fall*) **d** Eva prefers the Dalida biopic, and Nathalie and Morna prefer comedies. **e** In front of the cinema at 7 p.m. on Saturday.

LANGUAGE DISCOVERY 1 a sortir **b** sortent **c** finit

LANGUAGE PRACTICE 1 **1 a** sors **b** choisissent **c** dormons **d** finit

LANGUAGE DISCOVERY 2 (Sample answer) Shall we meet in front of the cinema at 7 o'clock?

LANGUAGE PRACTICE 2 **1 a** On va **b** On aime **c** Nous allons **d** On préfère **e** Nous allons

VOCABULARY BUILDER 2 invitation, disc jockey, musician, pianist

VOCABULARY PRACTICE 2 **a**3 **b**4 **c**1 **d**2

CONVERSATION 2 **2 a** because she asks her to/she's busy **b** an invitation to the preview of the exhibition of young photographers. **c** 2 people **d** No **e** Go to the thrift store.

LANGUAGE DISCOVERY 3 The missing word is y, usually translated as *there* or *to it*.

LANGUAGE PRACTICE 3 **1 a** Nous y allons vers dix-huit heures. **b** Est-ce que vous y allez cette année ? **c** Jean-Pierre n'y va pas aujourd'hui. **d** Je n'y reste jamais après six heures du soir. **2 a** Jean- Jacques veut aller à la piscine demain. **b** Louise n'aime pas aller aux Catacombes. **c** Fatou préfère aller à l'école à pied. **d** Marie-Laure ne veut pas assister au match de rugby.

LANGUAGE DISCOVERY 4 **1 a** J'ai envie d'y aller. **b** J'ai envie de boire un café. **2** J'ai envie d'un café.

LANGUAGE PRACTICE 4 **1 a** Florence et Mo, vous avez envie d'aller au cinéma ? **b** Et Paul, tu as envie de venir avec nous ? **c** Il n'a pas envie de voir un film d'horreur. **d** Marie et Djamel ont envie d'aller au restaurant. **2 a** Est-ce que vous avez envie d'un thé ? **b** Nous n'avons pas envie d'un café. **c** Je n'ai pas envie d'un croissant.

SKILL BUILDER sortir, sortons, ai envie d', finis, vais venir, on, y, on, on, y, veux

TEST YOURSELF **1 a** sortir, partir **b** venir **c** finir **d** ouvrir **2 a** choisissons **b** sors **c** viens **d** dormez **3** sortons, partons, réfléchissons, finissons

Unit 8

VOCABULARY BUILDER 1 brasserie, pizzeria, aperitif, dessert, tiramisu

VOCABULARY PRACTICE 1 **a** server **b** customer **c** server **d** customer

PRONUNCIATION PRACTICE 1 s is pronounced like z in **c** and **d**.

CONVERSATION 1 **3 a** lunch **b** moules-frites **c** endive/chicory salad and croquettes **d** Just the dessert **e** No, because they ordered the same.

LANGUAGE DISCOVERY 1 **1** The server uses these different words because de la is used before a fem. noun beginning with a consonant, du before a masc. noun beginning with a consonant, and de l' before a masc./fem. noun beginning with a vowel (or unaspirated h). **2 c** de l'eau minérale

LANGUAGE PRACTICE 1 **1 a** de l'eau **b** une bouteille d'eau **c** du vin **d** un verre de vin **e** de la glace **f** deux boules de glace **g** des olives **h** un bol d'olives **i** glace **j** trois boules de glace

LANGUAGE DISCOVERY 2 All the expressions use the following structure: quantity + de + noun.

LANGUAGE PRACTICE 2 **1 a** Tu as trop de beurre. **b** Karine a assez de lait. **c** Karine a beaucoup de lait. **d** Nous avons un peu d'eau. **e** Mo a combien de pommes ?

VOCABULARY BUILDER 2 carrot, onion, tomato, papaya

VOCABULARY PRACTICE 2 (Sample answer) Pour le couscous, j'ai besoin d'oignons, de tomates, de carottes, de curcuma et de coriandre. Pour la salade aux fruits (over to you ...)

CONVERSATION 2 **3 a** cilantro, turmeric, gombos **b** 8 euros 80 centimes **c** zucchini **d** Jo **e** Over to you ...

LANGUAGE DISCOVERY 3 **1** **a** Vous en voulez combien ? **b** Vous en voulez combien ? **c** Tu en veux combien ? **2** de

LANGUAGE PRACTICE 3 **1** **a** Djamel et Marie en ont combien ? **b** Vous allez en acheter combien ? **c** Il y en a combien dans le quartier ? **2** **a** Il en boit beaucoup. **b** J'en ai un peu. **c** Nous en avons trop. **d** Vous en avez assez.

LANGUAGE DISCOVERY 4 Each verb in the recipe is in the infinitive, as an alternative to the imperative.

LANGUAGE PRACTICE 4 **1** **a** ajoute **b** Laisse **c** ajoute **d** fouette

SKILL BUILDER **1** **a** du pain **b** du poisson **c** du fromage **d** de la viande **e** des gâteaux **2** **a** How many baguettes would you like? – I would like three/three of them. **b** She eats three bananas every day? – Yes she eats a lot of them. **c** Do you have enough money? – Yes, we have enough. **d** I've too much work at the moment, and what about you? – Yes, I have too much also. **3** **a**2 **b**4 **c**6 **d**3 **e**5 **f**1 **4** f, c, e, d, b, g, a, h **5** (Sample answer) petit déjeuner: croissants, cereales, yaourt, cafe, jus d'orange; déjeuner: soupe de legumes, salade nicoise, charcuterie, fruits; goûter: the, brioche, tartines; dîner: quiche lorraine, bœuf bourgignon, crème caramel

TEST YOURSELF **a** des fraises **b** avons besoin **c** un peu de fromage **d** un kilo de pommes **e** trop **f** j'en ai assez **g** combien de fraises **h** une barquette **i** en a besoin **j** choisis

Unit 9

VOCABULARY BUILDER 1 dentist, ambulance, hospital, pharmacy/drugstore

VOCABULARY PRACTICE 1 **a** pharmacienne **b** médecin **c** des comprimés **d** toux **e** mal aux dents

CONVERSATION 1 **3** **a** twice a week, 10 kilometers **b** She asks whether his feet and legs hurt. **c** to avoid foods that are too fatty, salty or sweet **d** (before) to warm up, (during) not to overdo it **e** next weekend

LANGUAGE DISCOVERY 1 Eva would have asked: Tu n'a pas mal au bras ? or Est-ce que tu n'as pas mal au bras ?

LANGUAGE PRACTICE 1 **1** **a**2 **b**4 **c**1 **d**3 **2** **a**3 **b**5 **c**1 **d**4 **e**2

LANGUAGE DISCOVERY 2 **1** Il faut expresses what must happen. It is translated in various ways according to context, for instance *it is necessary, one must, one should, we must, or you must.* **2** Tu dois generally means you must.

LANGUAGE PRACTICE 2 **1** **a** On doit éviter de boire trop de café. **b** Nous devons arriver chez Marie avant 9 heures. **c** Vous devez travailler dur ce soir pour finir la présentation. **d** Tout le monde doit se réveiller plus tôt. **2** **a** Nous devons partir./Il faut partir. **b** Marie et Luc, vous devez travailler (dur) ce soir./Marie et Luc, il faut travailler (dur) ce soir. **c** Tu dois aller à l'école !/Il faut aller à l'école ! **d** On doit travailler dur/Il faut travailler dur.

VOCABULARY BUILDER 2 portrait, selfie, subject, mobile phone, to photoshop

VOCABULARY PRACTICE 2 **a** appareil photo **b** sujets **c** brillantes **d** photographe **e** photographie

CONVERSATION 2 **3** **a** Yes. **b** Abou **c** Natalia **d** Natalia **e** choosing which two photos are the best for the competition.

LANGUAGE DISCOVERY 3 **1** verts, courts – In the French, there is a definite article (les), while in the English, there is no article (we do not say he has the green eyes/the short hair). **2** The missing word is *adjective*.

LANGUAGE PRACTICE 3 **1** **a** bleu-gris **b** bruns **c** crème **d** châtains

LANGUAGE DISCOVERY 4 **1** magnifique, beau, beaux, beau, magnifique **2** These adjectives are placed before the noun.

LANGUAGE PRACTICE 4 **1** **a** une belle mer, une mer calme **b** un petit puzzle, un puzzle difficile **c** un bouquet cher, un joli bouquet **d** un jeune enfant, un enfant robuste **e** un homme fâché, un vieil homme **2** **a** grand **b** spacieuse **c** nouvel **d** électrique **e** vieille **f** jeune

SKILL BUILDER **1** (Sample answer) **a**3 **b**4 **c**1 **d**5 **e**2 **f**6 **2** (Sample translation) I must eat well, and we must both watch what we drink if we want to be on form for the match this weekend. Above all, we must sleep well so that we're not tired. **3** Over to you ...

TEST YOURSELF **a** as mal **b** marathon **c** j'ai mal **d** jambes **e** faut **f** dois **g** dois **h** au bras droit **i** fait mal **j** beau **k** brun **l** gros

Unit 10

VOCABULARY BUILDER 1 airport, itinerary, passport

VOCABULARY PRACTICE 1 **1** **a** 3 **b** 1 **c** 2 **2** **a** rendre visite **b** itinéraire **c** jusqu'à **d** vol **e** visiter **f** espérons

CONVERSATION 1 **3** **a** her parents **b** No. **c** by train, via Paris. **d** a cruise on Lake Geneva and a visit to CERN. **e** to Lausanne, by train

LANGUAGE DISCOVERY 1 **1** je vais voir, on va voir, ils vont t'adorer **2** infinitive

LANGUAGE PRACTICE 1 **1** **a** visiterons **b** passerons **c** partiront **d** arriveront **e** prendrons **2** **a** aimerez **b** donnerez **c** finira **d** sortirai **e** prendras

LANGUAGE DISCOVERY 2 **1** la semaine prochaine, le week-end prochain, l'année prochaine, le siècle prochain

LANGUAGE PRACTICE 2 **1** d, e, a, c, b **2** Over to you ...

VOCABULARY BUILDER 2 animal, animals, meow

VOCABULARY PRACTICE 2 **a**3 **b**4 **c**1 **d**2

PRONUNCIATION PRACTICE **a** yes **b** no **c** no **d** yes

CONVERSATION 2 **3** **a** in three weeks' time **b** in the Halles de Boulingrin, Reims, beginning at 3 p.m., Saturday **c** at a farm in the mountains around Reims. **d** There will be a trip to Reims, a gourmet lunch in town and then the return trip to Paris. **e** On her desk.

LANGUAGE DISCOVERY 3 il, le

LANGUAGE PRACTICE 3 **1** **a** me **b** te **c** le **d** la **e** nous **f** vous **g** les **h** les **2** **a** la **b** les **c** l' **d** l' **e** les

LANGUAGE DISCOVERY 4 The missing word is sur

LANGUAGE PRACTICE 4 **1** **a**2 **b**3 **c**1

SKILL BUILDER **1** Over to you ... **2** a Isabelle l'écoute. **b** Jean-Marc l'adore. **c** David, ne la taquine pas, s'il te plaît ! **d** Je l'aime beaucoup. **e** Je les aime moins. **3** a commencerons **b** prendrons **c** passerons **d** prendra **e** nous rendrons **f** servira **g** retournerons **4** ce week-end – le mois prochain – puis – la semaine d'après – à la fin de nos vacances

TEST YOURSELF **1** **a** planifient **b** aiment **c** achèteront **d** cultivera **e** élèvera **f** vendront **2** **a** le **b** la **c** la **d** l' **3** **a** sur **b** dessus **c** dedans **d** dans **e** sous **f** dessous

Unit 11

VOCABULARY BUILDER 1 adventure/misadventure, make/cancel a reservation, last week, They are adorable.

VOCABULARY PRACTICE 1 **a** réservation **b** rater **c** minutieusement, hics **d** retrouver

PRONUNCIATION PRACTICE 1 The following begin with an aspirated h : un hic, une haie, une halle, des hamacs, des hangars

CONVERSATION 1 **a** Le Lac Léman **b** elderflower and acacia honey **c** He brings up Jo's weekend in Reims.

LANGUAGE DISCOVERY 1 **a** none **b** each **c** each

LANGUAGE PRACTICE 1 **1** **a** voyagé **b** voyagé **c** avez **d** ont **e** fini **f** fini **g** avez **h** ont **2** **a** aimé **b** agi **c** prévenu **d** dormi **3** **a** Elle a ouvert la porte ? **b** Tu as passé trois semaines en Italie ? **c** Elles ont visité le musée d'art moderne ? **d** Ils ont fait le tour de la ville ? **e** Vous avez aimé ce film ? **4** **a** Non, elle n'a pas ouvert la porte. **b** Non, je n'ai pas passé trois semaines en Italie. **c** Non, elles n'ont pas visité le musée d'art moderne. **d** Non, ils n'ont pas fait le tour de la ville. **e** Non, je n'ai pas aimé ce film.

LANGUAGE DISCOVERY 2 puis (then), puis (then), ensuite (then)

LANGUAGE PRACTICE 2 **1** **a** il y a quatre mois **b** Il y a deux semaines **c** Le mois dernier **d** la semaine dernière **e** avant-hier **2** e, d, c, b, a

VOCABULARY BUILDER 2 specialty/speciality of the region, vine, (female) wine grower

VOCABULARY PRACTICE 2 **a** une spécialité **b** en bouteille **c** tente **d** vignobles, dégustations

CONVERSATION 2 **3** **a** just under one hour **b** a few kilometers from Reims **c** Jo lost her telephone. **d** They found it in her room at the farm. **e** They had to cancel their gourmet lunch (they found a little restaurant where they ate instead).

LANGUAGE DISCOVERY 3 **1** **a** as perdu **b** a perdu **c** avez perdu **d** ont perdu

LANGUAGE PRACTICE 3 **1** **a** avez vendu **b** ont rendu **c** a tendu **d** ai omis **e** a conduit **f** a mis **g** as pris **h** avons suivi **2** **a** avez fait **b** ai annulé **c** avez exploré **d** avons fait **e** ont visité

LANGUAGE DISCOVERY 4 **1** a = false, **b** = true **2** **b** (= the ones that follow être)

LANGUAGE PRACTICE 4 **1** a**2** b**1** c**6** d**5** e**3** f**4** **2** a entré – He entered/has entered the house. **b** montée – She went up/has gone up to the first floor. **c** arrivées – Coo-ee! It's Julie and Florence. We've arrived! **d** descendus – Jean and his brother went down/downstairs to open the door. **e** tombée – Marine, did you fall/have you fallen?

SKILL BUILDER **1** **a** avons réservé **b** a acheté **c** suis partie **d** sont partis **e** sommes retrouvés **f** est resté **g** avons visité **2** Over to you ...

TEST YOURSELF **1** **a** ont fait **b** sont allées **c** ont pris **d** sont arrivées **e** sont rentrées **f** est parti **g** est arrivé **h** ont passé **2** **a** me suis réveillé **b** me suis lavé **c** me suis habillé **d** ai pris **e** allé **f** nous sommes promenés

Unit 12

VOCABULARY BUILDER 1 mountain, postcard, to go on vacation

VOCABULARY PRACTICE 1 **a** VTT/vélo tout terrain **b** parapente **c** broutent **d** pentes **e** profiter de

CONVERSATION 1 a From Reims; it was Jo and Assia who went there, so perhaps they sent it. **b** Her grandparents, to the seaside or the mountains, in Switzerland, Italy, France and Austria. **c** They added to their stamp collection.
d Paul travelled for work (he wrote travel guides).

LANGUAGE DISCOVERY 1 j'étais, j'aimais, tu écrivais, on visitait, on achetait, on adorait

LANGUAGE PRACTICE 1 1 a ...j'adorais les films de Truffaut. **b** ... je parlais allemand couramment. **c** ...elle habitait en Italie. **d** ...ils arrivaient toujours en retard. **2 a** jouais **b** s'habillait **c** est arrivé **d** a vu **e** s'est réveillée, était

LANGUAGE DISCOVERY 2 Leur replaces à vos parents

LANGUAGE PRACTICE 2 1 a Tu lui as envoyé un cadeau. **b** Tu vas lui envoyer un cadeau. **c** Marie-Laure leur a déjà parlé. **d** Marc va leur écrire une lettre. **2 a** te **b** vous **c** lui **d** me **e** me/nous **f** leur

VOCABULARY BUILDER 2 live in the country/in town, ideal life, calm/quiet

VOCABULARY PRACTICE 2 a calme **b** de la place **c** pollué **d** cultiver **e** cadre de vie **f** sain **g** idéale

CONVERSATION 2 a The institut de sondage (Polling Institute) **b** According to Jo it is calmer, less polluted, people are less stressed, there's plenty of space and you can have your own garden and grow vegetables. **c** public transport and proximity to cinemas, museums and restaurants **d** a village with a market and some shops, a few restaurants and a cinema **e** She likes the hustle and bustle, and to watch people in the metro. **f** Jo thinks she has the soul of a photographer (so likes to observe people). **g** Assia thinks Jo likes local products, good eating and having leisure time. **h** individually

LANGUAGE DISCOVERY 3 To make comparisons in French, you can place plus or moins before an adjective.

LANGUAGE PRACTICE 3 1 a moins grand **b** aussi grands **c** plus grande **d** moins calmes **e** plus grande **f** moins sain **g** moins bien **h** mieux payée/mieux rémunérée **2 a** meilleur **b** meilleurs **c** mieux **d** moins bien **e** mieux **f** pire

LANGUAGE DISCOVERY 4 c

LANGUAGE PRACTICE 4 1 a plus intéressant/le plus intéressant **b** moins belle/la moins belle **c** moins animée/la moins animée **d** plus grand/le plus grand **2 a** meilleure **b** les meilleures **c** le meilleur **d** meilleurs

SKILL BUILDER 1 (Sample answer) When Charles and Jo were young, they liked to receive lots of postcards from their uncle who travelled all over the world. He used to send them beautiful cards. They imagined magic places. Last year, they went on holiday to the US. They thought about their uncle. They sent him several cards to thank him and carry on the tradition.
2 a me **b** le **c** la **d** leur **e** lui

TEST YOURSELF 1 a 1 plus belle **2** la plus belle **b 1** plus confortable **2** le plus confortable **c** plus écologique **f** le plus écologique **2 a** écoutais **b** s'est échappé **c** est revenue **d** était **e** avait **f** (lui) a téléphoné **g** est venu

Unit 13

VOCABULARY BUILDER 1 job, responsibility

VOCABULARY PRACTICE 1 a une année de césure **b** génie civil **c** perfectionner **d** économies **e** expérience

CONVERSATION 1 3 a to travel and to think **b** a job in a restaurant, a job in a bakery **c** an NGO **d** He decided to train to become a chocolatier **e** yes

LANGUAGE DISCOVERY 1 for

LANGUAGE PRACTICE 1 1 a depuis **b** pendant **c** depuis **d** pendant **e** depuis

LANGUAGE DISCOVERY 2 1 ... use qui for the subject of the verb and que for the direct object ... **2** Yes.

LANGUAGE PRACTICE 2 1 a que **b** qui **c** qui **d** que

VOCABULARY BUILDER 2 professional, project

VOCABULARY PRACTICE 2 a réfléchi **b** dossier de candidature **c** lettre de motivation **d** requises **e** débouche sur

CONVERSATION 2 3 a next January **b** She thought Assia wanted an internship, not a study term. **c** University of Quebec at Montreal/Université du Québec à Montréal **d** her covering letter **e** Assia should give more details on her motivation and talk about what she wants to do afterwards, and supply explanations and details.

LANGUAGE DISCOVERY 3 Apportera, ouvrira and permettra have regular stems; pourrai and viendras do not.

LANGUAGE PRACTICE 3 1 a pourrons **b** iront **c** se lèvera **d** jetterai **e** viendras **f** appellerez **g** verra **h** aura **i** sera **j** tiendra

LANGUAGE DISCOVERY 4 1 a serait **b** pourrais **c** faudrait **2** They are different from the tenses learned so far. They are like the imperfect, but the ending contains an r (serait, faudrait) or a double r (pourrais)

LANGUAGE PRACTICE 4 1 a pourrait **b** était **c** irions manger **d** arrivais

SKILL BUILDER 1 a aimerais **b** aimerait **c** aimeriez **d** aimeraient **e** finirais **f** finirait **g** finirions **h** finiraient **i** vendrais **j** vendrais **k** vendrions **l** vendriez **2** Over to you **3** Over to you

TEST YOURSELF 1 a Il y a **b** baccalauréat **c** une année de césure **d** pendant **e** région **f** a décidé **g** une carrière **h** perfectionner **i** Depuis un an **2 a** qui **b** qui **c** qu' **d** que **e** qui **3 a** serait **b** pendant **c** Je voudrais **d** Je voudrais **e** ferai **f** verront

Unit 14

VOCABULARY BUILDER 1 icon, monument, symbol, tourist

VOCABULARY PRACTICE 1 a Sept Merveilles du monde **b** patrimoine, générations **c** émerveillent **d** monter

CONVERSATION 1 3 a Because he has come up on foot (the elevator is broken). **b** Andries is worried about Mme Cottin because she can't easily walk up or down via the stairs. **c** to get him a glass of water **d** There was an emergency repair. **e** They have had enough.

LANGUAGE DISCOVERY 1 To say never, use ne + jamais.

LANGUAGE PRACTICE 1 1 a je ne le parle plus **b** je ne vois rien **c** ça ne marche jamais **d** rien ne marche dans cet immeuble **2 a** n'ai vu personne **b** n'ai rien vu **c** Rien ne marche **d** n'avons plus de

LANGUAGE DISCOVERY 2 The missing verbs are vienne and répariez. Their infinitive forms are venir and réparer.

LANGUAGE PRACTICE 2 **1 a**2 **b**4 **c**1 **d**3 **2 a** arrivions **b** soit **c** gagniez **d** mangiez **e** dise **f** soit **g** oublie

VOCABULARY BUILDER 2 to contact, to confirm, reference, service

VOCABULARY PRACTICE 2 **a** sur Internet **b** annuler **c** passer une commande **d** me passer **e** courriel/e-mail

CONVERSATION 2 **3 a** because she waited in all day **b** The company has not been in touch at all. **c** that the deliveryman called 'today' **d** ce n'est pas normal **e** to cancel the order and create a new one, with urgent delivery

LANGUAGE DISCOVERY 3 **1** Ne + personne = no one. Personne and ne are both placed before the verb here. **2** aucun + ne

LANGUAGE PRACTICE 3 **1 a** n' – aucune **b** ne – personne **c** personne – n' **d** Aucune – n' **2 a** n' – jamais **b** ne – plus **c** n' – jamais **d** personne – n'

LANGUAGE DISCOVERY 4 **1 a** and **c** **2** 3 times (soit passé, entende, ayons)

LANGUAGE PRACTICE 4 **a** ayons fini **b** aies terminé **c** ait posté **d** ayez obtenu

SKILL BUILDER **1 a** ne, pas **b** Personne, ne **c** ne, plus **d** ne plus **e** n', rien **2 a** ind/ind/subj **b** ind/ind **c** subj **d** ind/subj **e** ind/subj

TEST YOURSELF **1 a** soit **b** êtes **c** puissent **d** coûtent **e** doit/devra **2 a** Il n'arrive jamais à l'heure. **b** Elle n'aime personne. **c** Personne ne la félicite pour sa victoire. **d** Nous ne partons jamais en vacances au mois d'août.

Unit 15

VOCABULARY BUILDER 1 to inspire, inspiration, invention, What a surprise!

VOCABULARY PRACTICE 1 **a** tombe/est tombée **b** fait exprès **c** presser **d** finit bien

CONVERSATION 1 **3 a** He invented a new chocolate recipe. **b** His boss arrived while he was preparing his flavors, but he thought she was at the Salon du Chocolat. **c** cilantro **d** No, he was confused. **e** After the Salon has finished.

LANGUAGE DISCOVERY 1 **1** I was preparing my mixture of spices when the boss arrived. **2 b**

LANGUAGE PRACTICE 1 **a** Nous étions en train de regarder **b** Vous êtes en train de manger **c** vous étiez en train de faire **d** Elles étaient en train de préparer **e** Pierre est en train de jouer du piano

LANGUAGE DISCOVERY 2 **1** Ben oui, moi j'ai bien aimé **2** C'est bien toi (used by Eva)

LANGUAGE PRACTICE 2 **1 a**6 **b**3 **c**5 **d**2 **e**1 **f**4 **2 a** Moi, toi **b** vous **c** eux **d** lui **e** soi

VOCABULARY BUILDER 2 article, editorial, journalist

VOCABULARY PRACTICE 2 **a** journaliste **b** articles **c** journal

CONVERSATION 2 **2 a** Le Touquet-Paris-Plage **b** Pauline (Jo's influencer friend) **c** Jo **d** Abou and François ; cheese, wine and a dessert

LANGUAGE DISCOVERY 3 **1** te (*to you*) refers to Assia, and le (*it*) refers to the article. **2** Le (*it*) refers to the question that should have been asked (i.e. what they should bring); leur (*to them*) refers to Abou and François.

LANGUAGE PRACTICE 3 (Sample answers) **1 a** Charles le lui a donné à elle. **b** Je ne m'étonne pas qu'il l'aide. **c** Eva lui en a parlé, à lui. **d** Tu peux me les prêter ? **2 a** la lui **b** le leur **c** lui en **d** nous en **e** en

LANGUAGE DISCOVERY 4 b

LANGUAGE PRACTICE 4 1 a ne lui donne pas **b** ne lui ai pas donné **c** ne leur ont pas montré **d** ne leur montrent pas

SKILL BUILDER 1 a Moi **b** lui **c** eux **d** moi **e** soi **2 a** y **b** lui **c** lui **d** en **e** l' **f** lui **g** leur

TEST YOURSELF 1 a reçoivent **b** les **c** leurs **d** y **e** elle **f** y **g** leur **h** leur **i** leur **j** leurs **k** leur

Unit 16

VOCABULARY BUILDER 1 classical music, techno (music), blues

VOCABULARY PRACTICE 1 a classique **b** folk **c** se sont rencontrés **d** répéter

PRONUNCIATION PRACTICE a no liaisons **b** les_occasions, en_écouter **c** sur_Internet **d** en_a

CONVERSATION 1 3 a He was waiting to hear if Nathalie and Mona were coming. **b** Nathalie has a rehearsal on the Friday evening. **c** That Nathalie and Mona might go to the concert scheduled for Friday evening and return to Brussels afterwards. **d** She was struck by how varied the program was. **e** Her parents had met at the festival.

LANGUAGE DISCOVERY 1 C'est ce que je leur ai proposé – Ce qui m'a le plus frappée – ce qui m'a le plus impressionnée. Ce qui is used for the subject and ce que for the object of the verb.

LANGUAGE PRACTICE 1 1 a Subject: je, verb: trouve, object: ce que **b** Subject: je, verb: regrette, object: ce que c Subject: ce qui, verb: embête, object: m' **2 a** ce qu' **b** ce qui **c** Ce qui **d** ce que

LANGUAGE DISCOVERY 2 1 It expresses causation. **2** à cause de: because of, grâce à: thanks to – The first refers to something neutral or undesirable, the second to something good.

LANGUAGE PRACTICE 2 1 a Grâce à **b** à cause du **c** À cause de **d** grâce à **2 a** fait **b** rend **c** rendent **d** rends **e** faites

VOCABULARY PRACTICE 2 1 b **2** a **3** d **4** c

CONVERSATION 2 3 a First-nation art **b** She wants to see works by Jean Paul Lemieux and Madeleine Des Rosiers. **c** The Museum of Contemporary Art.

LANGUAGE DISCOVERY 3 Here, inaugurée agrees with the subject elle, and réaménagés agrees with the subject les espaces. Both are examples of the passive voice.

LANGUAGE PRACTICE 3 a est découvert par l'archéologue **b** sont aidées par les pompiers **c** a été interviewée par les journalistes

LANGUAGE DISCOVERY 4 1 a fem. plural **b** masc. plural **c** masc. sing. **d** masc. plural **2 a** is correct, **b** is incorrect.

LANGUAGE PRACTICE 4 1 a que j'ai achetées **b** que nous avons trouvé **c** que tu as vue **d** que vous avez choisies

SKILL BUILDER 1 Over to you ... **2 a** ce qui **b** ce qui **c** Ce que **d** Ce qui **e** Ce que **f** Ce qui **g** ce que **h** ce qui **3 a** fait **b** À cause de **c** grâce à **d** je sais **4 a** J'aime les romans de Jules Verne qu'il m'a offerts à Noël. **b** Mes parents aiment la collection de Jean Leloup que je leur ai offerte.

TEST YOURSELF a a été inauguré **b** a été acclamé **c** est visitée **d** grâce à **e** parce que **f** ce que **g** ce qui **h** organisée **i** offertes

Unit 17

VOCABULARY BUILDER 1 discussion, expert, society

VOCABULARY PRACTICE 1 a prévoir **b** tendue **c** complique **d** accord **e** rappeler

CONVERSATION 1 3 a It was tense. **b** the 'saga' of the (often broken) elevator **c** that the elevator should be replaced **d** Mme van Eck and Mme Willems wanted a second expert opinion, but the Peeters wanted to go ahead without one. **e** Everyone was annoyed/unhappy.

LANGUAGE DISCOVERY 1 1 Erna says 'Mme Willems a dit que…'; Erna says that the Peeters 'ont dit que…'; Erna says that 'La Présidente a rappelé que… Andries says 'On a dit que…' **2** To form indirect speech in French, the following pattern is generally followed: subject + verb of speech + *que* (= *that*) + reported words. Sometimes (as in English) tenses used in the reported words are changed.

LANGUAGE PRACTICE 1 1 a Gabriel dit que si on veut acheter un ticket, c'est maintenant ou jamais. **b** Ma grand-mère nous dit toujours qu'il faut faire attention aux petits détails.
2 a La semaine dernière, tu m'as dit que je devais voir le dernier film de Xavier Dolan. **b** Je les ai prévenus qu'ils allaient manquer leur train. **3 a** Maman m'a rappelé : « Les bonbons sont réservés aux enfants ! » **b** Jean-luc m'a prévenu : « Erika ne mange pas de viande. » **c** Je dis à mes invités : « Vous pouvez gardez vos chaussures en entrant chez moi. » **d** Je leur ai demandé : « Vous pouvez apporter des baguettes pour le pique-nique, s'il vous plaît ? »

LANGUAGE DISCOVERY 2 It expresses a consequence, because it is as a result of people being unhappy that they decided to end the meeting.

LANGUAGE PRACTICE 2 1 a si vite que **b** si souvent que **c** si heureux qu' **d** tant de café qu' **2 a** donc **b** alors **c** parce que **d** si bien que

VOCABULARY BUILDER 2 The French Alliance, a mixture of French and English, to speak one's mother tongue/first language, We are bilingual in French and English

VOCABULARY PRACTICE 2 a l'Alliance française **b** bilingue **c** gallicismes **d** linguistiques

CONVERSATION 2 3 a June **b** Quebec province **c** Toronto **d** She can get a direct flight from Paris to Toronto. **e** because on 1 July it's the national festival day of Canada, and by changing plans they can be in Ottowa on that day to join in. **f** a Paris-Montréal flight and a Toronto-Paris flight.

LANGUAGE DISCOVERY 3 a They all end in -ant, and they are all preceded by en. **b** (Sample answer) by coming back up towards Montreal – now I'm thinking about it again – by going back down to Toronto

LANGUAGE PRACTICE 3 1 a allant **b** rendant **c** réussissant **d** dormant **e** montant **f** écrivant **g** disant **h** montrant **2 a** Il ne faut pas téléphoner en conduisant. **b** Il ne faut pas parler en mangeant. **c** Il ne faut pas courir en descendant l'escalier. **d** J'aime lire en écoutant de la musique. **e** Il mange en regardant la télévision.

LANGUAGE DISCOVERY 4 b

LANGUAGE PRACTICE 4 1 a Si Jacques arrive lundi, il pourra m'aider à tout préparer. **b** Si Léa oublie son cartable, elle se fera gronder par la professeure. **c** Si je viens écouter ton concert, tu viendras écouter le mien. **d** Si tout le monde y participe, l'événement aura un grand succès. **2** (Sample answers) **a** emmènerai **b** pourra **c** échoue **d** inviterai **e** aura **f** emmènerais **g** pourrait **h** échouait **i** inviterais **j** aurait

SKILL BUILDER 1 (Sample answers) **a** Eva répond que sa flammenkueche est excellente. **b** Jo explique qu'ils vont faire une surprise à Assia. **c** Assia dit qu'il fait très chaud à Montréal en été. **d** Jo signale qu'elle apportera ses vêtements d'été. **2** pour (cause), si bien que (consequence), comme (cause), était si festive que (cause), à cause du (cause) **3 a** Je te téléphone (tout) en regardant la télé. **b** Ils font leurs devoirs (tout) en écoutant de la musique. **c** Nous préparons le déjeuner (tout) en chantant. **4 a** ...arrivent dimanche, elles pourront m'aider à tout préparer. **b** ...oublie sa valise, il se fera gronder par son père. **c** ...venons voir ton show, toi tu viendras écouter notre concert **d** ...participent au spectacle, j'y assisterai.

TEST YOURSELF **a** nous ne pourrons pas **b** chantant **c** pensant **d** devrons **e** ne sera pas/n'est pas **f** gagnais **g** Puisque **h** parce que **i** si bien que

Unit 18

VOCABULARY BUILDER 1 to vote, direct democracy, referendum

VOCABULARY PRACTICE 1 **a** directe **b** remporte **c** du mal **d** fédérales **e** voix

CONVERSATION 1 **3 a** against **b** positive **c** No (she is for, he is against).. **d** She thinks it's unrealistic to hope that educating people is a good enough alternative to compulsory voting. **e** Mainly agree.

LANGUAGE DISCOVERY 1 **1** Statement **a** is more accurate. **2** Je trouve que ; je crois que (x 2); À mon avis; selon moi

LANGUAGE PRACTICE 1 **1 a** polite **b** neutral **c** strong – à mon avis creates a polite tone, while pas du tout creates a strong tone. **2 a** me suprend **b** difficile **c** tout à fait **d** n'ont pas tout à fait raison **e** imprudent

LANGUAGE DISCOVERY 2 **b** (par contre, mais and cependant all serve to create a contrast between the two statements).

LANGUAGE PRACTICE 2 **1 a** et pourtant **b** bien qu' **c** et par contre **2 a**2 **b**3 **c**1

VOCABULARY BUILDER 2 petition, influencer, online, signature

VOCABULARY PRACTICE 2 **a**7 **b**6 **c**5 **d**4 **e**3 **f**2 **g**1 **h**9 **i**8

CONVERSATION 2 **3 a** No. **b** to organise an event to attract attention **c** Pauline is willing to help. She is an influencer. **d** Besides being visible at the market, to handout leaflets at the school gates.

LANGUAGE DISCOVERY 3 dont

LANGUAGE PRACTICE 3 **1 a** ...je ne me mêle pas. **b** ...on parle beaucoup. **c** ...j'ai peur. **d** ...on parle souvent.

LANGUAGE DISCOVERY 4 **c**

LANGUAGE PRACTICE 4 **1 a** ce que **b** ce dont **c** ce qui **d** ce qui **e** ce dont **f** ce qu' **g** ce dont **h** ce que **i** ce qui

SKILL BUILDER 1 Over to you ... **2 a**1 **b**3 **c**2 **3 a** dont **b** ce dont **c** dont

TEST YOURSELF **1** (Sample answer) **a** Bien que **b** bien que **c** ce dont **d** ce que **e** bien que **f** ce qui **g** Puisque

Unit 19

VOCABULARY BUILDER 1 intense, participate in/take part in, to select

VOCABULARY PRACTICE 1 **a**3 **b**6 **c**4 **d**1 **e**2 **f**5

CONVERSATION 1 **3** **a** French **b** English **c** a star of the chocolate world, one of the first women chocolatiers to become well known **d** Abidjan; she wants to launch her career in chocolate making **e** There is an excursion on the Basque coast. **f** at Oaxaca (Mexico)

LANGUAGE DISCOVERY 1 When there is only one object, a hyphen is used to join the verb to the object (Prends-le). Where there are two objects, a second hyphen is also used, to join the objects to each other (Passe-le-moi). Hyphens are used in positive, but not in negative imperatives.

LANGUAGE PRACTICE 1 **a** rends-les-lui **b** donnez-les-leur **c** mettez-vous **d** couchez-vous

LANGUAGE DISCOVERY 2 The object pronouns are le and moi in the first statement, and m' in the second one. The placement is different because different word-order rules apply to positive versus negative imperatives.

LANGUAGE PRACTICE 2 **1** **a** Ne cours pas **b** Ne commencez pas **c** ne travaillons pas

VOCABULARY BUILDER 2 architecture, migration, panoramic

VOCABULARY PRACTICE 2 **a**3 **b**4 **c**1 **d**5 **e**2

CONVERSATION 2 **3** **a** from Algeria **b** because the war between France and Algeria broke out shortly after the grandmother joined her husband in France **c** for almost 15 years **d** Assia thinks she missed Algeria and would have liked to go back.

LANGUAGE DISCOVERY 3 These verbs resemble the perfect tense, which is also made up of avoir/être + past participle. But here, avoir and être are in the imparfait (the imperfect tense).

LANGUAGE PRACTICE 3 **1** **a** ai vu, avais vu **b** est allé, était allé **c** s'est levée, s'était levée **2** **a** étaient sorties **b** avaient beaucoup aimé **c** s'étaient rencontrées **d** n'aviez pas vu

LANGUAGE DISCOVERY 4 This tense is different because it is made up of le conditionnel (the conditional tense) of avoir/être followed by le participe passé (the past participle) of the word for the action (aimer). This tense is used to talk about something that might have happened in the past, but did not.

LANGUAGE PRACTICE 4 **1** **a** ai fini **b** avais fini **c** aurais fini **d** est partie **e** était partie **f** serait partie **g** se sont lavés **h** s'étaient lavés **i** se seraient lavés

SKILL BUILDER **1** **a** Ne cours pas dans les couloirs ! **b** Ne crions pas dans la rue ! **c** Ne commencez pas avant les autres ! **d** Ne fais pas la vaisselle ! **2** **a** Parle-m'en ! **b** Pensons-y ! **c** Donne-les-moi ! **d** Envoyez-le-nous !/Envoyez-la-nous ! **e** Envoyez-les-lui ! **3** **a** avais gagné **b** avais joué **c** avions demandé **d** avait choisi **4** **a** aurions aimé **b** aurais dû **c** auriez pu

TEST YOURSELF (Sample answers) **a** Donne-moi ton livre s'il te plaît ! Ne le lui donne pas ! **b** Il est déjà 23 heures, couchons-nous. **c** Je leur ai dit « Dépêchez-vous s'il vous plaît », car je ne voulais pas arriver en retard. **d** Ça faisait deux ans qu'on ne l'avait pas vu. **e** Ils avaient adoré/beaucoup aimé le film. **f** Ils s'étaient rencontrés à la cathédrale. **g** Nous aurions dû réagir de façon différente. **h** Si Marc et moi avions eu plus de temps, nous aurions visité le MUCEM. **i** Maintenant je me rends compte que j'aurais dû commencer au début. **j** Vous avez très bien joué ce morceau de musique. Mais vous auriez pu ralentir un peu.

Unit 20

VOCABULARY BUILDER 1 longevity, passion, quality of life

VOCABULARY PRACTICE 1 **1**c **2**d **3**a **4**f **5**e **6**b

CONVERSATION 1 **3** **a** She seems to be very surprised. **b** because the train from Paris was cancelled and then there were crowds of people at passport control at Charles de Gaulle. **c** They could have taken the direct flight from Toulouse to Montreal. **d** He and Eva will live together. **e** She wants to carry on researching her family origins when she returns to Paris. **f** They took a selfie.

LANGUAGE DISCOVERY 1 **1** **a** avais **b** aurais **c** était venu **d** serait **2** si + present, main clause future, si + imperfect, main clause conditional, si + pluperfect, main clause conditional perfect

LANGUAGE PRACTICE 1 **1** **a** aurais fait **b** aurions manqué **c** seraient venus **d** seraient venues **e** aurions assisté

LANGUAGE DISCOVERY 2 Assia says quand je serai rentrée à Paris (see the end of the conversation).

LANGUAGE PRACTICE 2 **1** **a** aura téléphoné **b** aura terminé **c** aurons reçu **2** **a**1 **b**1 **c**2 **d**2

VOCABULARY BUILDER 2 chatbot, memorize, opportunity, optimist, specialist

VOCABULARY PRACTICE 2 **a**4 **b**1 **c**2 **d**3

CONVERSATION 2 **3** **a** that they did not hear from the groups that fight for the preservation of the planet **b** He liked that they did not only speak about challenges but also about progress so far. **c** to a better world **d** Eva wants a fairer world; Charles wants the planet to be preserved. **e** Jo wants love and friendship, and Eva mentions love.

LANGUAGE DISCOVERY 3 **1** a **2** c

LANGUAGE PRACTICE 3 **1** **a** est-ce que vous partez ? **b** est-ce que tu fais pour réussir tes gâteaux ? **c** est-ce que les chaussures coûtent ? **d** est-ce que les enfants vont faire demain ? **2** **a** faites-vous demain **b** vous appelez-vous **c** sont les autres actuellement **d** sortent-elles **e** dois-je

LANGUAGE DISCOVERY 4 **1** Reste is le subjonctif présent, and ayons pu is le subjonctif passé. **2** The other subjonctifs are: qu'on n'ait pas entendu, qu'ils ne parlent pas, que le monde soit plus juste and que notre planète soit préservé.

LANGUAGE PRACTICE 4 **1** **a** Mathilde n'ait pas pu venir ce soir. **b** grand-mère puisse venir demain soir. **c** vous réfléchissiez profondément **d** ils ne nous aient pas répondu

SKILL BUILDER **1** (Sample answers) **a** avais été là, tu aurais rencontré **b** avions manqué le train, nous aurions manqué **c** avais invité tes frères, ils seraient venus **d** serait venu à ta/votre fête d'anniversaire si on avait été au courant **e** avait pris le train de 18 heures, on serait rentrés avant le dîner **2** **a** ait raté sont vol, il voulait partir en vacances. **b** soit arrivé en courant. **c** ayons finalement retrouvé nos valises, nous avons raté notre correspondance. **3** **a** Comment Anne-Marie lit-elle tant ? **b** Les professeurs savent-ils qu'ils reçoivent un prix ? **c** Les enfants sont-ils encore au lit ?

TEST YOURSELF **1** **a** sera parti **b** aurais fait **c** aurons mangé **d** aurais cherché **2** (Sample answers) **a** Comment Fatou et Assia savent-elles tant de choses sur la gastronomie ? **b** Les membres du public savent-ils qu'on les filme ? **c** Mon frère est-il toujours au travail ? **3** **a** ne soient pas venues. **b** ne m'aient pas répondu. **c** soient arrivés **d** ait été **e** aient, fini

Index of grammatical topics

Notes